To the
Palace of Wisdom

STUDIES IN ORDER AND ENERGY
FROM DRYDEN TO BLAKE

By Martin Price

SOUTHERN ILLINOIS UNIVERSITY PRESS

Carbondale and Edwardsville

FEFFER & SIMONS, INC.

London and Amsterdam

TO

Maynard Mack and Harold Bloom

Preface

"The road of excess leads to the palace of wisdom." Blake's words remind us that all literature thrives on risk and over-statement, thrusts beyond the measured and judicious, and strains against order, if only to make us know what measure and order mean. This is a study of the way in which move-ments of ideas interact with literary form in Restoration and eighteenth century England, stressing the dialectical excess as much as the balance and moderation of the Augustans. If we can see the conflicts within Augustan literature, we are better prepared for the new directions poetry takes in the later eighteenth century.

Pascal's three orders—of flesh, mind, and charity—show how the traditional idea of universal Order begins to give way to the idea of men locked in self-enclosed and self-subsistent or-ders, seeming to use the same words but in fact unable to com-prehend each other's meaning. The masters of ironic satire exploit this division between orders to show the depth of man's folly. The comic writers, on the other hand, find new and un-expected connections between orders, fusing flesh and charity as forms of energy opposed to the rationalism of a false order of mind.

I have dealt selectively with a large body of literature, and I have tried to treat different kinds of writers more sympathet-ically than they in fact regarded or might have regarded each other. Nor have I hesitated to draw connections with recent writers where these seemed to illuminate the earlier works.

I am grateful to the John Simon Guggenheim Foundation and to Yale University for fellowship aid which made the writing of the book possible. I hope to supplement it in time with a study of relations of artistic and literary theory in the period. For discussions that have helped me greatly I am in-debted to Frank Brady, Dale S. Underwood, and Aubrey L. Williams. I owe special thanks to my kind and critical editor, Anne Freedgood, and I want to acknowledge the help of bursary aides, particularly Michael D. Clark and John T. Cullinan. Of my present colleagues, I shall cite only those whose names appear in the dedication; they gave encouragement when it was needed and gave it generously.

The notes are held to a minimum, but I have tried to specify particular sources from which I have drawn. I regret the omissions I have almost certainly made, and I would ask in turn the charitable recognition that not all resemblances need represent indebtedness.

Finally, there is the pleasant but hopeless task of recording how much this book owes to my wife.

MARTIN PRICE

Contents

Errata

Page 58, line 25: *For* in *read* is
Page 132, line 7: *For* moment *read* movement
Page 156, line 25: *For* second *read* fourth
Page 280, line 17: *For* Oh *read* On

I.

Ideas of Order: Introduction

1. The Fabric of Order

Order is one of those familiar words we despair of defining but cannot do without. It is not, of course, a word without meaning but a word with all too many overlapping meanings, and its power comes of the very range of meanings it can hold together. We speak of a moral order, of cosmic order, of political order; of orders in mathematics or architecture; of clerical or monastic orders; of logical order or the sensory order. The problem one has to face is not the obvious enough threat of semantic confusion. Rather, one must try to see how such a word rises from (and fosters in turn) the kind of analogical thinking that discovers common patterns in all kinds of experience. Traditionally, the idea of Order has been the belief in a single, universal design that shapes our world and accounts in rational terms for all that we find in it or in ourselves. Such a single Order has its elements, its local orders or patterns—the moral order of man or the cosmic order of the starry heavens—each with its own design. But they remain the elements of one large, coherent design, one universal Order. The local orders may be quite different in nature—organic or mechanical, aesthetic or obligatory, simple or complex. Whatever their differences each provides the assurance of living in a world that makes sense, of living within a system that has a unity such as might have been imposed by an intelligence like our own. The elements of that design, the local orders, can be arranged according to degree of complexity and formed into the great multiplex design we shall call Order.

One example of a local order that connects with other elements may show how the fabric of Order is woven together. Erwin Panofsky has traced the changing canons of human proportion in the arts—the relationships of scale according to which the human figure has been imagined (and perhaps even literally "seen") in different ages.[1] The diversity of human frames tended, in artistic representation, to be reduced to a few distinct types or classes. Tradition had handed down to the Renaissance artist two predominant types: the Vitruvian man, whose frame was the length of nine heads, and the pseudo-Varronic, with ten head-lengths. These canons were seen as "a visual realization of musical harmony; they were reduced to general arithmetical or geometrical principles . . . ; they were connected with the various classical gods, so that they seemed to be invested with an antiquarian and historical, as well as with a mythological and astrological, significance." The sheer complexity of this tissue of analogies points to the power of common ordering principles. But even more, Panofsky relates, these two types could be supplemented by an even shorter one (of seven or eight head-lengths) so as to give a triad of forms "which could be related . . . with specific gods, with the three styles of classical architecture"—the Doric man as opposed to the Ionic or Corinthian—"or with the categories of nobility, beauty, and grace."

As late as the beginning of the nineteenth century we can find these canons invoked and interpreted by Blake:

> It has been said to the Artist, "take the Apollo for the model of your beautiful Man, and the Hercules for your strong Man, and the Dancing Fawn for your Ugly Man."

For Blake, typically, the triad is absorbed into a fourfold unity, of which the three distinct types are the sundered parts:

> The Strong Man represents the human sublime, the Beautiful Man represents the human pathetic, which was in the wars of Eden divided into male and female. The Ugly Man represents the human reason. They were originally one man, who was fourfold; he was self-divided, and his real humanity slain on the stems of generation, and the form of the fourth was like the Son of God (*A Descriptive Catalogue*, 1809, in *The Complete Writings of William Blake*, ed. Geoffrey Keynes, London, 1957, pp. 578–79).

The full import of Blake's comments need not concern us now. It is enough to observe how the canons of proportion serve to suggest other twofold or threefold relationships. Each of these relationships has its own pattern: the three orders of Greek architecture derive from the different proportions of the temple columns, the contrast of Apollo and Hercules calls up contrasts of temperament as well as of physical form, etc. Yet the canons of proportion can recall any of these relationships by their simple resemblance of pattern. All three canons have in common the representation of man, all vary in one essential proportion which necessarily introduces variations of innumerable kinds. The sameness of the common human form gives emphasis to the varieties of scale and temperament; the differences are held together within a common species. We can see a similar relationship between the three orders of a common temple architecture or between the deities of the classical pantheon.

The idea of Order serves on a larger scale to bring together the diverse realms in which varieties of order are found. One can see this at work in a passage from Augustine's *The City of God:*

> The peace of the body then consists in the duly proportioned arrangement of its parts. The peace of the irrational soul is the harmonious repose of the appetites, and that of the rational soul the harmony of knowledge and action. The peace of body and soul is the well-ordered and harmonious life and health of the living creature. Peace between man and God is the well-ordered obedience of faith to eternal law. Peace between man and man is well-ordered concord. Domestic peace is the well-ordered concord between those of the family who rule and those who obey. Civil peace is a similar concord among the citizens. The peace of the celestial city is the perfectly ordered and harmonious enjoyment of God, and of one another in God. The peace of all things is the tranquillity of order (XIX, 13, trans. Marcus Dods).

Augustine's thought plays upon those common terms—and behind the terms upon the patterns of structure—that embrace all experience and relate each aspect of our lives to every other. The culmination of such an effort is the knowledge of God: those terms that describe and account for all our experience cannot but serve as well—in some fashion, at least—to name the attributes of God. Out of such a mode of thought come countless correspondences. They are startling in the way they overleap the seemingly dissimilar or incommensurate, but they are not, for Augustine, merely fanciful or trivial; they reveal a consistency of designedness in each part that points at last to the character of the Designer. The world of God's creation reveals the nature of its creator in ways that are too numerous and subtle to be readily grasped. Like a work of art it reveals in every element of its local texture the governing pattern of a meaning that, in turn, gives to every part a reason for being, a necessary place in the total design.

If we see the world held together by mathematical relationships which are also musical harmonies, as Augustine does, the music that is a principle of structure is also a devotional hymn of praise. We may see these analogies as commanding metaphors, but we must remember that they are avenues to knowledge of a solemn importance to those who study the rhetoric of the universe. If the rhetoric moves us today less with its persuasive cogency than with its formal richness and imaginative extravagance, we must be all the more careful to recognize these analogies as more than the metaphors of a secular modern poem.

The analogy between the ordering of the universe and the ordering of a work of art is probably as old as cosmological thought, and it persists in the subtlest of metaphysical systems. Aristotle can remark casually that "nature is not a series of episodes, like a bad tragedy" (*Metaphysics* XIV, 3; 984b). Again, in a biological work, "Absence of haphazard and conduciveness of everything to an end are to be found in Nature's works in the highest degree, and the resultant end of her generations and combinations is a form of the beautiful" (*On the Parts of Animals,* I, 5; 645a). Or again in the *Politics* (I, 5; 1245a), where he sees the relationship of ruler and ruled as fundamental in the order of the state, he finds this relationship in the very "constitution of the universe"; for "even in things which have no life there is a ruling principle, as in a musical mode."

The faith in nature as the handiwork of a divine artist survives well into the nineteenth century in the form of natural theology and the argument from design. The art the universe is seen to embody may vary from music to poetry to architecture; in later phases of thought the divine artist may become the divine engineer or mathematician, for it is the structural design above all that the analogy of art seeks to invoke. The more these structural qualities are abstracted from other symbols of value—from the hymn of praise that is music or from the temple of nature that the divine architecture creates as the scene of man's worship—the more the Designer is seen under the aspect of sheer craftsman rather than humane artist. From the time of Plato the divine has been associated with a comparatively abstract or formal beauty as well as with the fullness of concrete objects in which structural or formal principles are embodied, and the strain of Platonism in Christianity frequently moves toward an ecstasy of forms rather than adoration of the stubbornly particular incarnation.

We see a secularized version of this Platonism in eighteenth-century criticism, where it gives dignity to the formal and structural dimension of painting or landscape, awards grandeur to the general, and embodies the general in the simple forms of classical art—free as they are of undue particularity, common as they are to all the later cultures of modern Europe, dedicated as they seem to be to a celebration of the image of tempered or rational human dignity. If the images of Greek sculpture are those that might have seemed deceptively naturalistic or illusionistic to Plato, they have lost that danger through the centuries and in comparison with later works.

Implicit in the analogy of art is the idea of an artist who controls his work with rational clarity. The very task of embodying formal principles in concrete objects may introduce a note of conflict. Each principle may limit others, and the greater the number of principles, the less can any one be embodied with purity or strictness. Or again, the process of embodiment may be imagined as that of imposing principles upon resistant or recalcitrant material that will never yield completely to the design. The rational clarity of the artist's intention, therefore, is at best imperfectly realized, but the implicit design can be apprehended by our reason, as it abstracts from sense experience.

This rational design need not be a mechanistic one, as the analogy of a divine engineer implies. It can be an organic design such as the Stoics saw in the universe. Like man, the world has a soul and all the parts of the world are the parts of an organism; this not only accords with our image of ourselves as individuals, but, analogically, with our sense of ourselves as members of a society. Marcus Aurelius, for example, is not content with simply an empirically observed sequence of events or juxtaposition of things:

> In the series of things those which follow are always aptly fitted to those which have gone before; for this series is not like a mere enumeration of disjointed things, which has only a necessary sequence, but it is a rational connection: and as all existing things are arranged together harmoniously, so the things which come into existence exhibit no mere succession, but a certain wonderful relationship (*Meditations* IV, 45, trans. George Long).

The terms used here—fitted, rational, harmoniously, wonderful relationship—insist upon order as the embodiment of rational artistry. Mere succession or enumeration will not suffice; they do not account for events in terms of a rational design and therefore cannot reveal the full measure of unifying or ordering power that the world embodies. For order to be significant in the Stoic view, there must be enough diversity to make the unity telling, dramatic, worthy of reverence.

We are still, with different assumptions and another metaphysics, concerned about this tension between diversity and unity. Empirical science has established regularities in separate areas and constantly pushes toward some higher level of theory or law that will reduce separate areas to one. Yet this movement must always be restrained by the adequacy of evidence and the possibility of disproof: premature syntheses are prevented by stubborn diversities. Freud, in 1915, felt that it was only "for the present" that "our psychical topography has . . . nothing to do with anatomy." Again in 1920 he looked forward to the time when he might replace "psychological terms by physiological or chemical ones." That he did not, that others may, remain, respectively, fact and faith. "Without the belief in the inner harmony of our world," Einstein said, "there could be no science." And he put this in more traditional terms as well: "I cannot believe that God plays dice with the world."[2]

The push toward synthesis, toward the formulation of a unifying theory of all events, is not a belief from which matters of fact can be firmly deduced, and it is certainly a far vaguer principle of order than we find in the cosmologies of traditional religions. But it may remind us at least of the constant attraction of a vision that accepts the diversity of things and yet seeks the unfolding of a rational principle, or at least a law that is rationally apprehensible.

II. Order and Analogy

The extent to which the idea of Order (universal order) was taken for granted in Renaissance thought—and in the Christian-Classical traditions that fed it—has been amply shown in a series of studies by A. O. Lovejoy, E. M. W. Tillyard, Hiram Haydn, C. S. Lewis, and others.[3] There is no need here to study at length the great metaphor of the Chain of Being, as Lovejoy has done. One quotation will show the persistence of Augustine's vision of order into the sixteenth century: here is Sir Thomas Elyot's account in *The Governor* of the ordering of all things into degrees:

> Hath not God set degrees and estates in all his glorious works? First in his heavenly ministers, whom he hath constituted in divers degrees called hierarchies. Behold the four elements, whereof the body of man is compact, how they be set in their places called spheres, higher or lower according to the sovereignty of their natures. Behold also the order that God hath put generally in all his creatures, beginning at the most inferior or base and ascending upward. He made not only herbs to garnish the earth but also trees of a more eminent stature than herbs. Semblably in birds beasts and fishes some be good for the sustenance of man, some bear things profitable for sundry uses, other be apt to occupation and labour. Every kind of trees herbs birds beasts and fishes have a peculiar disposition appropered unto them by God their creator; so that in everything is order, and without order may be nothing stable or permanent. And it may not be called order except it do contain in it degrees, high and base, according to the merit or estimation of the thing that is ordered (From ch. I; cited by Tillyard, p. 9).

The idea of universal Order imposes unity in diversity by establishing hierarchies. The chain involves an ascent from least to greatest, and the value of each creature is established by its possession of those powers that bring nature to perfection: from the seemingly lifeless to the animate, from the vegetative to the sensitive, from the passionate or instinctive to the reasonable, from the deliberating reason to the intuitive—the ascent approaches the perfection of God. Yet the chain is more than a linear gradation of independent creatures; each creature is necessary to all others, for the chain subsists only so long as its links hold and the total order is preserved. If one link is broken the entire structure is altered or destroyed. Each kind, therefore, has its uniqueness and its special contribution, as do the members of a community founded on division of labor. The mechanical metaphor of the chain obviously does not suffice to suggest the full complexity of this organism that is the image of the world, with its limbs and circulatory system, its exalted head and sentient heart. But it can convey, as the image of the body cannot, an order that is stable, stratified, and divisible into parts.

The conflicts within this conception—the conflicts, one might say, of implicit metaphors that are loosely associated—have been made clear by historians. For the order to become sufficiently complex, another principle—the assumption of plenitude—must be invoked. This assumption—that God will wish to create all possible kinds of creatures—rules out a thin and limited order and accounts for the almost inevitable imperfections of a universal order. If they are not really imperfections of that order—if the powers of the divine artist may be deemed sufficient to meet any difficulty—they are at least imperfections of our awareness. We cannot read the divine work of art with sufficient skill; we can look for universal order, but our limitations reveal evils and defects that only God can sufficiently explain. Again, if all kinds of creatures may—or indeed, must—exist, there can be no clear boundaries between links in the chain, and the static hierarchy becomes a continuity with an infinity of members. When the idea of continuity is pushed far enough, it tends to undo the possibility of each creature having a clearly defined place and undermines the clarity of rational design. It demands, instead, a metaphor of creative energy pulsing through the whole organism.

These conflicts make clear the difficulties of analogical thinking that underlie the idea of Order. So long as the full consequences of a specific idea are not drawn out, the cluster of incompatible ideas can remain in equilibrium, each idea limiting the others, each conflict generating new metaphors that will present a picturable model and permit a compromise to be entertained.

The idea of limit is crucial to the idea of universal order; everything must find and keep its place if order is to be sustained. But participation in that universal order is conceived as an act of love as well as obedience. Each creature is attracted to a center but holds the place assigned it according to its nature, and the tension between reabsorption into unity and maintenance of diversity is caught in the intricate cosmic dance of the heavenly bodies. It is a formal and ceremonious movement, constantly varied and as constantly ordered; and Milton makes splendid use of it to present the nature of human order. Just as Satan in *Paradise Lost* is about to land on the sun and violate its light with his darkness, Milton presents the sun as the visible symbol of God in his ordered universe, both transcendent and immanent:

> . . . the great Luminary
> Aloof the vulgar Constellations thick,
> That from his Lordly eye keep distance due,

Dispenses Light from far; they as they move
Thir Starry dance in numbers that compute
Days, months, and years, towards his all-cheering Lamp
Turn swift their various motions, or are turn'd
By his Magnetic beam, that gently warms
The Universe, and to each inward part
With gentle penetration, though unseen,
Shoots invisible virtue even to the deep:
So wondrously was set his Station bright (III, 576–86).

The light is mysterious and remote, but it becomes in turn the ordering principle of time and the source of life (the "all-cheering Lamp"). Finally, it is associated with the warmth that penetrates, like grace, unseen and breeds precious gems within the earth or godlike powers within men.

We have had to set aside the metaphor of a chain of being in order to imagine the love that binds diversities together. The metaphors can be associated by seeing how each level of the chain exhibits comparable images of movement. The theme of love is diffused downward from the circles, "orb within orb," of angelic adoration or the "mystical dance" of heaven to the "starry sphere" which

Resembles nearest, mazes intricate,
Eccentric, intervolv'd, yet regular
Then most, when most irregular they seem (V, 622–24).

And we move downward to Paradise, where the choirs of birds

attune
The trembling leaves, while Universal Pan,
Knit with the Graces and the Hours in dance,
Led on th' Eternal Spring (IV, 265–68).

Each level of the chain reveals the dance-like motion of unity within diversity, of mutual dependence and individual distinctness. The dance depends upon the spontaneous self-limitation of each dancer within the large order, and we can see it in contrast to the mere maze, the "wand'ring mazes" of philosophy in which the fallen angels become lost, or the "intricacies" in which Adam becomes lost through vain speculation before Raphael sends him back to "the sweet of Life." The maze is what the mind creates for itself when it seeks "to rove / Uncheck'd." The check of self-limitation comes of devotion to what is given, "That which before us lies in daily life," the circuit of "Relations dear and all the Charities / Of Father, Son, and Brother" (VIII, 182–93; IV, 756–77).

III. Order and Orders

I have spoken of a single, multiplex Order that holds together the whole range of ideas or images of order of various kinds; it does this through the pattern of levels or degrees. At each level there is a different degree of awareness. What must be an animal's awareness of the world? If we accept the Cartesian view that animals are mechanisms, the question need not arise. But what of man? Is the ploughman's view of the world the same as the scholar's; the slave's the same as the monarch's; the Englishman's the same as the Spaniard's? We may assume that all creatures have different perspectives of a common reality (as Leibniz does, in allowing each monad its degree of perception of the universe), and we may assume that man, as man, tends to see things in one way—that there is a generic human view. But so long as the idea of degrees or levels is stressed, we must see even man in typically diverse forms.

Perhaps the most influential example of this is in Plato's Republic. Plato's ideal state is divided into distinct levels of citizens; each given its own measure and kind of education, in accordance with the powers of soul that are dominant at that level. Sir Ernest Barker shows the probable source of Plato's doctrine in the Pythagoreans, where the three classes of men—the lovers of Wisdom, the lovers of Honor, and the lovers of Gain—seem to correspond to three parts of the soul: Reason, Spirit, and Appetite. So it is in Plato's Republic. "The ruler must live by reason: therefore, Plato argues, he must abandon appetite, and he is accordingly brought under a communistic regime which prevents the play of appetite, and thus involves the paralysis of an integral element in human nature. Again, the farmer must live for the satisfaction of appetite; he must be regulated in that life by the external reason of the perfect guardian, and thus he suffers an atrophy of his rational life" (*Greek Political Theory: Plato and His Predecessors*, London, 1947, p. 199).

Each citizen becomes specialized, even as he remains a republic within himself: "Justice in the state," Socrates argues, "meant that each of the three orders in it was doing its own proper work. So we may henceforth bear in mind that each one of us likewise will be a just person, fulfilling his proper function, only if the several parts of our nature fulfil theirs"

(*The Republic of Plato,* trans. F. M. Cornford, London, 1941, pp. 139–40; 441c). There is a unity, a single tripartite order, within each man, and, analogously, within the state. Nevertheless each part of the soul tends to produce a pattern of life consistent with its nature—Spirit, for example, is fulfilled best in the military or administrative life of the guardians. In its degree of awareness the multitude may be said to inhabit a different world from that of the philosopher-king; at least, in its not-yet-ideal condition the multitude cannot philosophize and "is bound to disapprove of all who pursue wisdom" (p. 201; 493). These are parallel ways of life, each with its own regimen and its own end (within the larger end of the whole state, Justice). Like the clerical or monastic "orders," each class has its own rule of life and is distinguished from other orders designed for men of different nature or capacity. Some one significant characteristic—here, a condition of soul—demands an adjustment of all other elements of life in accordance with it and creates a unity within this suborder.

We can see a similar problem of classification in biological orders, or in the orders of architecture, or in those canons of proportion that Panofsky has traced. In so far as we stress the mutual dependence and ultimate harmony of these orders in one large, hierarchic Order, they create no disturbance to the traditional scheme. They may be stages within the large Order, through which one creature can move; or they may be fixed kinds, each of which is necessary to all the others. But when any of these orders is given self-sufficiency and set in opposition to the rest, its own internal coherence outweighs the coherence of the larger order.

The very pressure of opposition serves to impose coherence upon a world-view. Men are driven to seek ground and shelter for their differences, and it is not long before, as Hume found in English politics, "each of the factions has reared up a fabric" of speculation "in order to protect and cover that scheme of actions which it pursues" ("Of the Original Contract"). Or we may consider William Blake's comments on Lavater's *Aphorisms*. As he read the thirteenth, Blake underlined the last nine words and wrote in the margin, "All gold!" What Lavater had written was:

> Joy and grief decide character. What exalts prosperity? What embitters grief? What leaves us indifferent? What interests us? As the interest of *man, so his God—as his God, so he* (Keynes, p. 65).

We have now entered a second phase of the breakdown of the idea of universal Order. Men are not simply limited and partial in their vision; they confront each other with more than different perspectives of a common world. Each perspective has yielded a distinct world-picture, with its own kind of design, its own Order, and its own God. And the separate views have become autonomous, independent orders, each claiming exclusive truth.

This kind of opposition between rival world-views or orders goes back at least to the classical contrast between the orderly universe of Plato, Aristotle, and the Stoics and the universe of chance, the purposeless world evolving from a fortuitous concourse of atoms, of the Epicureans. This conflict was revived with the growth of Renaissance naturalism. In the seventeenth century the opposition of neo-Stoics and neo-Epicureans renewed the debate between virtue and pleasure as the ends of man, between reason and sense as his instruments of knowledge. Shaftesbury could see all philosophy summed up in this opposition, and Pascal before him played upon the mutual destructiveness of such systems by opposing Epictetus to the modern naturalist, Montaigne. "The evil of one," Pascal is reported to have said, "tends to neutralize that of the other." The Stoic Epictetus frees man of dependence upon external things but induces a pride in the self-sufficiency of reason. Montaigne destroys pride in reason and in moral self-righteousness but tempts man into skepticism and impiety. The opposition, Pascal asserts, shows that only Christian truth can reconcile what is sound in their contradictory views.

Yet it is Pascal who most tellingly states the situation of rival orders:

> There are three orders of things: the flesh, the spirit, and the will. The carnal are the rich and kings; they have the body as their object. Inquirers and scientists; they have the mind as their object. The wise; they have righteousness as their object. . . .
>
> The three lusts have made three sects; and the philosophers have done no other thing than follow one of the three lusts. . . .
>
> All the glory of greatness has no lustre for people who are in search of understanding. The greatness of clever men is invisible to kings, to the rich, to chiefs, and to all the worldly great. The greatness of wisdom, which is nothing if not of God, is invisible to the carnal-minded

and to the clever. These are three orders differing in kind . . . (460, 461, 793).[4]

Pascal divides men into three discontinuous orders. These could be, and in fact had been, presented as progressive stages of a gradual ascent. But Pascal stresses their discreteness and necessary rivalry. Each order is created by a "lust" (*concupiscence*), in its nature unlimited. What is more important, the order of wisdom is not that of the rulers. Far from being philosophers (although he dreams of the possibility in his letter to Queen Christina), Pascal's kings occupy the lowest of his orders—the order of the flesh.

One of the consequences of this opposition of orders is that each world view must find a way of accounting, in terms of its own ordering of experience, for the mistaken views of its opponents. Typically, the naturalistic neo-Epicurean view places great emphasis on the power of passions—fear, envy, pride—and on their infinitely subtle modes of rationalization. It may assert deliberate deception by priest or king in order to subdue the populace, but the real problem still to be faced is why people should be susceptible to deception, and here the naturalist produces a social psychology that constructs the whole pattern of orthodox belief from a few principles of rudimentary passion. Mockingly, the naturalist may acclaim the grandeur of the social edifice only to remind us of the baseness of the materials.

On the other hand, those who maintain the idea of universal Order can explain the naturalistic view as the contraction of man's godlike reason into a cunning that serves rather than controls his will. The naturalistic account of reality is simply the limited vision of fallen man, which can no longer comprehend the range of experience it knew before the fall. One of the great efforts to dramatize this fallen view was, of course, Milton's Satan; Satan could not persist in his pride without persuading himself that his world was ruled by sheer force, that his obduracy of resentment was the only response to an unjust and selfish punisher, that destruction itself was creative in a world where only force had value. From a Christian point of view, Satan's obduracy can be seen as a travesty of heroic endurance in faith. A passage like this from Kierkegaard's *The Sickness Unto Death* catches the Satanic demeanor as the "continuation of sin":

> Just because the demoniac is consistent in himself and in the consistency of evil, just for this cause he also has

a totality to lose. A single instant outside of his consistency, one single . . . imprudence, one single glance aside, one instant when the whole thing, or at least a part thereof, is seen and understood in a different way—and with that, he would never more be himself, he says. That is, he has given up the good in despair, it would not help him anyway, he says, but it might well disturb him, make it impossible for him ever again to acquire the full momentum of consistency, make him weak. Only in the continuation of sin he is himself, only in that does he live and have an impression of himself (Part Second, II, 1; trans. Walter Lowrie, pub. with *Fear and Trembling,* Anchor Edition, 1954).

This internalizing of order makes of each of the limited orders a peculiar pathologic state which, like paranoia, imposes its special vision upon all that confronts it. Men are locked up in private worlds, and the more order they achieve within them, the greater the disorder in the larger world of which they are members.

The internalizing of orders also produces debate and dialectic. The great exemplars of this kind of conflict are the Platonic dialogues, where the confrontation of Socrates with Callicles or with Thrasymachus is really a confrontation of different orders of experience which have a few key terms wherein they can meet. In Socrates' opponents there is a fundamental inconsistency. They avow a doctrine of unlimited amorality, which allows them to esteem only power; but there is a point at which they admit terms that make that doctrine untenable. Thrasymachus does so in the *Republic* in admitting that there is an art of living, that man has a peculiar virtue or function he alone can fulfill; in doing so, he gives primacy to the soul and to its end of measure or justice. Callicles in the *Gorgias* admits that some pleasures are better than others, and the acceptance of an explicit moral standard follows. In both cases these opponents attempt to account for all experience in terms that would make man a pleasure-seeking animal; their inability to create a consistent, self-contained, comprehensive order on those terms allows Socrates to invert their arguments and to assert his own, moral order, over theirs.

A Socratic paradox occurs, as Dorothea Krook has said, "in the overlapping area of . . . two worlds; and occurs with the greatest, the most explosive force (knowledge is virtue, for instance) at the points of intersection of the two worlds. And if one may imagine the world of appearances wholly superimposed upon the world of reality (the condition, one must suppose, of the dwellers in the deepest and darkest part of the cave), then the whole field becomes a field for paradox, and there is nothing, literally nothing, the master of dialectic can affirm that is not paradoxical." As Mrs. Krook suggests, the creator of a dialectic like Plato's begins with alternatives that are accepted as exhaustive, and the opponent "always *by definition* chooses the false alternative." The strategy of creating this pattern of dialectic leads us to the problems of ironic satire (*Three Traditions of Moral Thought,* Cambridge, 1959, pp. 323–34, 308).

IV. Order, Irony, and Satire

The period this book treats, from Pascal to Blake, is a great age of irony. Few periods have made such telling use of the dialogue: we see it in Dryden, Prior, Pope, Shaftesbury, Mandeville, Berkeley, Hume—to choose only the more striking figures. And no age has made more striking use of a fictitious narrator or speaker whose peculiar slant of vision is critical to an understanding of the whole work. Swift is the most conspicuous ironist of the age in his use of Lemuel Gulliver and the insouciant teller of *A Tale of a Tub.* But Pope's Socratic use of the Horatian or Juvenalian satirical speaker, Fielding's complex use of the self-conscious narrator, Sterne's Tristram Shandy, and Blake's dramatization in *Songs of Innocence and of Experience* of "the two contrary states of the human soul" are all instances of a literature that demands that we take account of a voice, of a point of view, of a state of the soul that may also imply a world view and a religion. "Without contraries is no progression," Blake wrote in his most overtly dialectical work, *The Marriage of Heaven and Hell.* "Contrary states" in that work exhibit precisely the opposition of orders that I have been trying to present:

> So the Angel said: "Thy phantasy has imposed upon me, & thou oughtest to be ashamed."
> I answer'd: "We impose on one another, & it is but lost time to converse with you whose works are only Analytics" (Keynes, p. 157).

Blake speaks of the "confident insolence sprouting from systematic reasoning" (157). We may reverse the sequence and see, as Hume does, that the choice of a system may arise from a taste for insolence. This has the value of reminding us of both sides of the transaction; if what a man believes determines his style, his style may also affect his beliefs. Hume speaks of the "sects which secretly form themselves in the literary world" and especially those that take different views of the dignity of human nature.

> Some exalt our species to the skies, and represent man as a kind of human demigod, who derives his origin from heaven, and retains evident marks of his lineage and descent. Others insist upon the blind sides of human nature, and can discover nothing, except vanity, in which man surpasses the other animals, whom he affects so much to despise. If an author possess the talent of rhetoric and declamation, he commonly takes part with the former: if his turn be towards irony and ridicule, he naturally throws himself into the other extreme ("Of the Dignity or Meanness of Human Nature").

A man may write satire because he is indignant, but he may also cultivate his indignation in order to write satire. The talent for irony and ridicule may rise from temperament, but the talent is fostered by a vision of man and the world that gives satire depth and resonance. The writer may simply "entertain" a view, but as he writes he acts upon that view, and the question of how sincerely or completely he holds it becomes an irrelevance for his readers, if not his biographer.

The prevalence of satire throughout the eighteenth century serves to force apart the orders that once were aligned in a universal Order and to set them in ironic opposition. The satirist is always demonstrating a failure. In comedy the wayward or absurd may, like the heart, have reasons of its own and elude all our judgments or demands. It will surprise us by the very frictionless ease with which it evades the responsibilities or choices we prepare for it, and it will make these choices seem less urgent than they did before. But satire insists upon failure, and the satirist must always assume a stance that allows his object to destroy itself (just as Socrates' opponents must always be made to choose the false alternative). The satirist may play the role of the naïve stranger dropped into a world whose motives he can only surmise from its outward gestures. He simplifies as he interprets, and his simplifications are unknowing judgments on all that he sees. Or the satirist may be the child whose simple candor evokes horrified repressive fear from his elders; all the child cannot see is the phantasy they try to impose upon him, as in Blake's *Songs of Experience*. Or the satirist may be a man of frank humor who finds, as Pope does in Walpole's England, that open laughter is no longer possible for the Great Man once he is imprisoned in schemes of wealth and power. In all of these cases the satiric speaker voices a discomforting failure to recognize invisible rationalizations and makes the demanding expectation that our actions precisely reflect our natures. If he listens long enough he will hear the sophistries of bad faith or the bellowing roar—Ionesco has given it the sound of a rhinoceros—of the herd released from bondage to individual responsibility and freedom.

The cultivated innocence of the satiric speaker expresses itself in deadly questions or in a kind of eloquent rage that sweeps away what has become tortured and deceptive.[5] This, if anything, is the typical "plot" of satire—a confrontation in which the satirist can engage his subjects in dialogue and pursue the dialectic of their exposure. He may pursue it actively by challenge or passively by eliciting from them their most abandoned folly. The dialectic will reveal that their pretended order is a chaos of inconsistency or that the elaborate attempt to sustain the appearance of one order can be fully and economically explained away in terms of another. What satire needs is the bold confrontation of two orders, one professed and the other ignored, each so closely parallel with the other that the transposition can be achieved at any point and carry all the rest with it.

Such confrontations involve an opposition of more than those outward images that create character and scene. "As the interest of man, so his God—as his God, so he." The satirist will settle for no less. He assumes that each man is consistent and reflective; from a man's actions one should be able to derive his system of beliefs. A failure of charity demands that we see a consistent mode of false worship, a mock church, a spurious liturgy; and Swift's *A Tale of a Tub* exposes the travesty religion becomes when its forms are used as a system of worldly power. Conversely, the failure to acknowledge the flesh gives us an image of would-be angels, who profess rigorous virtue and speak the language of self-sacrifice but who must satisfy their natural appetites in a form debased by its furtiveness. Mandeville shows us something of this in *The Fable of the Bees*, and Blake much more, in "The Sick Rose" and in the *Visions of the Daughters of Albion*.

The attempt to make one order a disguise for another yields a peculiarly nasty kind of disorder. It reveals its inconsistencies much as Spenser's Duessa does when she is stripped: instead of the richly bedecked, dazzling exaggeration of true beauty we suddenly find a loathsome hag with a filthy rump and a fox's tail, with none of the beauty of either woman or beast.

v. The Instance of Pascal

> The infinite distance between body and mind is a symbol of the infinitely more infinite distance between mind and charity; for charity is supernatural.
>
> All the glory of greatness has no lustre for people who are in search of understanding.
>
> The greatness of clever men is invisible to kings, to the rich, to chiefs, and to all the worldly great.
>
> The greatness of wisdom, which is nothing if not of God, is invisible to the carnal-minded and to the clever. These are three orders differing in kind.
>
> Great geniuses have their power, their glory, their greatness, their victory, their lustre, and have no need of worldly greatness, with which they are not in keeping. They are seen, not by the eye, but by the mind; this is sufficient.
>
> The saints have their power, their glory, their victory, their lustre, and need no worldly or intellectual greatness, with which they have no affinity; for these neither add anything to them, nor take away anything from them. They are seen of God and the angels, and not of the body, nor of the curious mind. God is enough for them. . . .
>
> All bodies together, and all minds together, and all their products, are not equal to the least feeling of charity. This is of an order infinitely more exalted.
>
> From all bodies together, we cannot obtain one little thought; this is impossible, and of another order. From all bodies and minds, we cannot produce a feeling of true charity; this is impossible, and of another and supernatural order (*Pensées*, 793).

This is Pascal's most extensive discussion of the three orders, and they are now ranked in a more traditional way as stages of ascent in a hierarchy. The highest is no longer an order of "will" but of "charity." The philosophers of "will" take pride in their wisdom: "it cannot be granted to a man that he has made himself more wise, and that he is wrong to be proud: for that is right." Their error lies in assuming that they have made themselves wise, for "God alone gives wisdom, and that is why *Qui gloriatur, in Domino glorietur*"

(460). The philosophers have failed to reach true charity: "They have known God, and have not desired solely that men should love Him, but that men should stop short at them!" (463). The order of charity is based upon a hatred of self-hood; it is a true ascent beyond the orders of the flesh and of the mind.

Yet, although Pascal distinguishes between the vertical ascending movement in Fragment 793 and the set of horizontal, coequal, and opposed worlds of Fragment 460, the two have important resemblances that are distinctive to Pascal's thought. Although the orders of flesh, mind, and charity grow more dignified and more inclusive in their awareness at each stage, they remain discontinuous. There is no gradation by which one moves easily from one to another, nor does one order prepare men for the next above it. Each man is locked in his own order until he has exhausted its possibilities; it is only by finding one order intolerable that he is finally disposed to go beyond it, and nothing he has come to believe in that order can serve him in his movement to the next.

This is an extreme way of stating what is implicit throughout Pascal. The double nature of man is his central theme. Man is at once great and wretched, reasonable and self-deceiving. He participates in two kinds of reality—one governed by his material nature, his passions, and his self-love; the other by his spiritual possibilities, his intuitions of the divine, and his love of God. All of his powers and actions have an ambiguity he can scarcely control; and their very greatness may serve to isolate him all the more from God. It is necessary, therefore, that man have those powers of awareness that can lead him to God, and at the same time that these powers bring him no satisfaction until they are turned to God.

Pascal becomes a vigilant critic of the misuse of these powers, and he makes unremittingly ironic distinctions between the elements that make up the double nature of man and his actions. "We make an idol of truth itself; for truth apart from charity is not God, but the image and idol, which we must neither love nor worship; and still less must we love or worship its opposite, namely, falsehood" (582). Man must accept his state of semi-darkness, in which God is neither fully revealed nor altogether hidden. "The knowledge of God without that of man's misery causes pride. The knowledge of man's misery without that of God causes despair" (527). "There must be feelings of humility, not from nature, but from penitence, not to rest in them but to go on to greatness. There must be feelings of greatness, not from merit, but from grace, and after having passed through humiliation" (525). Pascal sees all heresies as the reduction of this double truth to a single one: "unable to conceive the connection of two opposite truths, and believing that the admission of one involves the exclusion of the other, they adhere to the one, exclude the other, and think of us as opposed to them" (862). The great embodiment of the double truth is, of course, Jesus Christ; he "constitutes the middle course because in Him we find both God and our misery" (527).

No man of his age presented this paradox of man's plight with more thoroughness and intensity than Pascal. The sundering of an Order into orders, and man's necessary blindness to orders other than his own, which Montaigne found evidence for a relativistic view, Pascal interprets as evidence of man's fallen state. He rejoices at such evidence, because it constitutes a reason for man's coming to God. It shows man how intolerable independence from God is, and demands of him that he surrender the self-determination that is inevitable illusion.

The first of Pascal's orders, the order of the flesh, yields a secular world governed by egoism and controlled hatred, a world in which men are ruled by either their desire or their reverence for power. Power stimulates imagination, and imagination creates happiness. But this is imagination in the narrow sense of phantasy; and what it creates is a system of appearance and custom in which men find the stability of a shared dream. Such a world is hateful to the man who can see beyond it; but it is necessary, even providential, for the man who cannot. Man stumbles into a peaceful order, a system he neither earns nor understands. Any society is better than none; in the world of the carnal no society is more just than another, for the idea of justice has no meaning. The keeping of peace, any peace, is sufficient. This is the world of Hobbes's *Leviathan*.[6]

What is striking in the political thought of Pascal and Hobbes alike is the arbitrary and conventional nature of authority. Pascal recognizes man's need for society; it comes of pride, the desire for recognition or esteem, the fear of instability and social disorder. So in Hobbes the competitive quest for grandeur is the source at once of social life and of its disorder; there can be no peace in a world where by his nature each man must overcome every other lest he himself be overcome. Both men see the state as a necessary form of stability, and for Hobbes the undivided authority of a sovereign power is indispensable. Pascal sees the social order as the necessary subjection to power in a fallen world, and Hobbes sees the state as a necessary result of man's inherent selfishness.

Hobbes's *Leviathan* defends any state so long as it is sufficiently strong and stops short of denying its very justification, that is, does not arbitrarily demand of men their lives. Hobbes therefore can make such statements as, *"Honorable* is whatsoever possession, action, or quality, is an argument and sign of power."* All the traditional moral terms, once translatable into denominations of power only because the traditional view of Order assumed that power and virtue are harmonious, are now reduced to terms for simple power. It hardly matters who rules nor by what pretexts so long as the rule is stable.

It follows that the world of the flesh is a world of dress, of red robes and ermine, of cassocks and square caps. The role of Louis XIV, for example, was to become all the more an assertion of power, with the resources of art turned to the creation of effect, as that role lost its greater import. "Beneath the surface, even of Louis's ideas," writes a recent historian,[7] "a certain traditional notion of religious duty is still clearly discernible; but this is emptied of its true content by a new and purely psychological interpretation of the natural self of the ruler and his development—an interpretation which, even at this stage, appears to require scarcely any support from theological and ethical arguments." The surface becomes important, for it alone compels awe where the very nature of the inside becomes at best a problem and at worst an irrelevance. The ceremonious formalities of Louis's court create a dress so blindingly splendid and a management so exquisitely complicated as to exhaust any attention that might be paid to their limitations.

Custom and habit generate the illusion of legitimacy or justice in turn; the survival of power gives it authority and its antiquity seems to confer truth upon it. Pascal's dialectical sense of a double truth leads, finally, to a brilliant fragment on the attitudes toward illusion:

> *The reason of effects.* Degrees. The people honor persons of high birth. The semi-learned despise them, saying that birth is not a personal, but a chance superiority. The learned honor them, not for popular reasons, but for secret reasons. Devout persons, who have more zeal than knowledge, despise them, in spite of that consideration which makes them honored by the learned, because they

judge them by a new light which piety gives them. But
perfect Christians honor them by another and higher
light. So arise a succession of opinions for and against,
according to the light one has (337).

If the "dignity of man consists in thought," it is in man's
mind—in the second order—that we might expect to find his
true greatness. The superiority of thought to physical power is
clear enough: "By space the universe encompasses and swallows me up like an atom; by thought I comprehend the world."
The capacity for knowledge, so thoroughly muffled in the order of the flesh, gives man a kind of dominion over that which
outwardly rules him: "man knows that he is wretched . . .
but he is really great because he knows it." Still, as we have
seen, Pascal resists any Stoical deification of mind. The mind's
greatness lies in its ability to see through the impositions of the
world; but this penetration does not bring happiness, or even
equanimity. It is only the starting point for the upsetting process by which man knows himself a creature of God, for his
God is a hidden God who never quite reveals Himself as man
might wish.

The theme of the *deus absconditus* or hidden God is Pascal's
principal way of asserting the paradox of man's situation: "It
is incomprehensible that God should exist, and it is incomprehensible that He should not exist" (230). Every religious
choice must, from the point of view of the rational man, be a
wager. Later theologians may call it a leap, but Pascal insists
upon the power of self-interest which must still govern a man
who is not of the order of charity. Such a man must act by
calculation, even at the limits of the calculable. God might
have disclosed himself in nature, but he leaves men "in a
darkness from which they can escape only through Jesus
Christ" (242). Jesus "is a God truly hidden; . . . He will be
slighted; . . . none will think that it is He; . . . He will be a
stone of stumbling, upon which many will stumble, etc. Let
people then reproach us no longer for want of clearness, since
we make profession of it" (751).

The mysterious double nature of Jesus corresponds to the
doubleness of man and nature. For man as man, there is no
resolving this doubleness. He must always confront the paradox, "a thesis and antithesis *simultaneously* opposed and inseparable . . . for which there is no hope in this world of
solving the irreducibility."[8] As Lucien Goldmann sees Pascal's
thought, its tragic aspect lies in the fact that man *is* man to the
extent that he asserts the possibility of a synthesis, all the while

aware that this assertion itself cannot escape paradox, that the only certainty man can know as man is "an uncertain certainty, a postulate, a wager."

It is man's tragic plight to be placed inexorably in a mean between the extremes where alone he might find peace; this is "not equilibrium but permanent tension, unmoving movement" (Goldmann, p. 229), a tension that can be resolved for Pascal only in the transcendent and mysterious figure of Jesus Christ. Reason can find no certainties on which to rest except the wretchedness of man's condition. If it can discern the intolerable horror of the secular world view of the fleshly, it can only prepare the mind for an assent to more than it can itself understand. "We must know where to doubt, where to feel certain, where to submit. He who does not do so, understands not the force of reason. There are some who offend against these three rules, either by affirming everything as demonstrative, from want of knowing what demonstration is; or by doubting everything, from want of knowing where to submit; or by submitting in everything, from want of knowing where they must judge" (268).

The order of the mind, if it does not know where to submit, tends to become a rationalistic system, which deduces from its first principles all that the world contains or suggests. It claims utter command by thought over the pattern and purpose of human experience. But such command, Pascal shows, is illusory; the reason accepts first principles that fall short of the complexity of nature, and it builds upon them systems that flatter its powers. The infirmity of these systems becomes evident as we approach the limits of our understanding, the double infinity of the inconceivably vast and the infinitesimally small. In one perspective man is nothing, in the other all. "What will he do then but perceive the appearance of the middle of things, in an eternal despair of knowing either their beginning or their end. All things proceed from the Nothing, and are borne towards the Infinite. . . ." "Through failure to contemplate these Infinites, men have madly rushed into the examination of nature, as though they bore some proportion to her" (72). Faced with an incomprehensible infinity, man's reason boggles and resists; it defends itself with a fiction. "We represent some [premises] as ultimate for reason, in the same way as in regard to material objects we call that an indivisible point beyond which our senses can no longer perceive anything, although by its nature it is infinitely divisible" (72).

First principles, in so far as they are tenable at all, are given to reason, Pascal insists, not created by it. "We know truth, not only by the reason, but also by the heart, and it is in this last way that we know first principles; and reason, which has no part in it, tries in vain to impugn them." However much it may resent their source and question their authority, "reason must trust these intuitions of the heart, and must base on them every argument" (282). The possibilities of a rational universe are hopeless. We live, after all, and for good cause, less by the slow constructions of reason than by the "easier belief" of custom, which makes us believe "without violence, without art, without argument." Reason can scarcely take account of all that confronts it; it often "wanders, through want of having all its principles present. Feeling does not act thus; it acts in a moment, and it is always ready to act" (252).

The celebration of reason has usually been a celebration of human dignity. Man as rational animal is in command of his nature, both through the self-knowledge that gives him intellectual mastery and the self-government that gives him ethical control. In declaring the limits of reason to be the limits of God as well as man—in assuming that God cannot or will not act against reason—man asserts a continuity between the divine and the human, and constructs a universe that conforms to the powers of the human mind. The greater man's confidence in his rational power, the greater his sense of freedom: he can choose for himself, his choices have authority, and his use of choice is a proper fulfillment of his nature. For Pascal, however, man is neither so free as he dreams nor so wise as he trusts. He is always building, as Blake was to observe later, a mundane shell that shuts out the horror of the void and protects his world from foundering into chaos. But this same shell shuts him off from a knowledge of his full nature. In Blake the shell prevents man from realizing his capacities; it imposes upon him the tyranny of an inert, external nature. In Pascal a similar shell is created by the rationalism that lulls man with a dream of a world in which his mind is master.

Pascal's purpose is to place reason within a self that surrounds and undoes it. The self that acts with intuitive certainty is not anti-rational but irrational. It exists either below or above reason, a creature of custom and automatism on the one hand, of charity and grace on the other. The orders of flesh and charity have curious ways of meeting, and the most ambiguous term in Pascal is *coeur*. The ambiguity arises from the double object of the heart's love: self and God. Our "action is often determined, not by grounds which we could, or even by grounds which we *do* explicitly assign, but by a fundamental attraction to, or love of, either God or self as the case may be, which may not be actually present to the conscious mind at the moment."[9] The *coeur,* the *automate,* the force of love, the whole rationally groundless basis of behavior are frightening to the rational man and providentially beyond his control.

From this view of man's nature follow conclusions about his universe. His God is not simply the transparent rational Mind that he can know with confident love and easy assurance; nor is He to be sought in the design of nature, like the Pantocrator of Newton. God is at once knowable and unknown. Adequate knowledge of Him cannot be won by reasoning about nature; yet any knowledge that neglects the criticism of reason is likely to be superstition ("submitting to everything, from want of knowing where they must judge"). The universe is susceptible to scientific study (as Pascal, of all men, knew); yet its very mysteries throw us back upon the sense of how arbitrary and limited our scientific constructs are. We are left in desperate need of reason as a guard against self-deception and in desperate danger of the greatest self-deception of all, idolatry of reason.

If the orders of the flesh and the mind are rejected, the ultimate celebration Pascal allows the order of charity is somewhat chilling. First of all, it can be known only in its own terms, and Pascal's movement between will and heart, heart and charity, makes the difficulty of knowing it all the sharper. We can know what it is not, as in our knowledge of God, more confidently than what it is. Second, charity is "of an order infinitely more exalted" than the other two—but so exalted that it is totally divorced from the power of this world:

> The saints have their power, their glory, their victory, their lustre, and need no worldly or intellectual greatness, with which they have no affinity. . . . They are seen of God and the angels, and not of the body, nor of the curious mind. God is enough for them (793).

This radical separation between Christ and culture has its sublimity but also its destructiveness; it sets so abrupt a chasm between the orders as to imperil all aspiration. One must admire the power to draw distinctions, to insist upon the discontinuities of our experience and upon qualitative differences. Pascal forbids us those comfortable confusions that allow us to make easy substitutions: political action for personal honor, public service for private devotion, success for self-knowledge. And yet, does he? As soon as he must come to terms with the worldly power from which charity is set infinitely apart, he has lost the means of criticizing or governing it. To renounce the world, he must first submit to it, accede to its power, and accept that power as legitimate in its sphere.

If the world of power is a fallen world in which a hidden God bids man seek his private salvation, there is no principle of resistance. One cannot resist, one can only renounce. For resistance will itself seem further complicity in sin, further self-deception or pride. There is an almost inexorable logic by which the most radical rejection of the world becomes the most conservative submission to it. If all that is of value exists in another order, infinitely separated, which one cannot wed with lower orders, charity has achieved a purity that looks very much like irrelevance. Man can no longer take excessive pride in his reason, but can he trust his mind at all? Is nature merely a source of temptation and subsequent disillusion to the "curious mind?" Can man's moral virtues lead him somehow to spiritual vision, or do they inevitably produce pharisaism? Ronald Knox put the problem well:

> Pascal recognizes the classical proofs of God's existence and admits the force of them, but he dislikes them. You may almost say that if he had been in a position to do it he would have hushed them up. He *wanted* our fallen nature, left without grace, to be as weak and miserable as possible. . . . his picture of man's misery remained incomplete, lop-sided, if you could think of man unredeemed as possessing any sky-light, even, that gave on the supernatural (*Enthusiasm,* Oxford, 1950, p. 222).

The difficulties of Pascal's position arise in part from his rhetorical strategy; he takes much for granted and seeks to shock those men Shaftesbury was later to call "half-thinkers." Historians have observed that sentimentalism arose in England partly from the orthodox refutation of Hobbes's account of man as naturally predatory. Terms that had held together a composite view were split open by the very pressure of argument. So in Pascal we can see terms that have latent within them a celebration of the heart he did not intend, but could hardly control once the terms had been released. The reasons of the heart are invoked against the rationalist, but the heart can move from intuitive rightness to sympathetic artistry, even visionary wisdom.

At the very least Pascal's doctrine of the three orders is a brilliant rhetorical device for making us see false orders replacing true, disorder itself exhibiting a formal pattern that is a parody of what man might achieve or even thinks he has achieved. Yet the very dialectical brilliance produces paradoxes that men need to resolve, and the writers with whom we shall be concerned in this study sought to resolve them in ways that Pascal illuminates rather than anticipates. Some try to establish a continuity among all three orders; others reconcile two in order to overthrow the third. What gives Pascal a peculiar value for our purposes is the dramatic way in which he raises the question of orders and all but subverts the more traditional idea of Order.

II.

Dryden and Dialectic

I. The Verse Form

> He taught the gospel rather than the law,
> And forc'd himself to drive, but lov'd to draw:
> For fear but freezes minds; but love, like heat,
> Exhales the soul sublime, to seek her native seat.
>   To threats the stubborn sinner oft is hard,
> Wrap'd in his crimes, against the storm prepar'd;
> But when the milder beams of mercy play,
> He melts, and throws his cumbrous cloak away.
>   Lightnings and thunder (heav'n's artillery)
> As harbingers before th'Almighty fly:
> Those but proclaim his style, and disappear;
> The stiller sound succeeds, and God is there.

These lines from Dryden's "The Character of a Good Parson"
were written in 1699 and published in the *Fables*. The poem
is an expansion of Chaucer's portrait in the General Prologue
of the *Canterbury Tales*.

Dryden's poem of 140 lines (of which these are 30–41) is a
free adaptation of Chaucer, and uses the deposition of Richard
II three hundred years before as a parallel to the Revolution
of 1688. In the last lines of the poem the Good Parson becomes a fourteenth century counterpart of those non-juring
clergymen of Dryden's day who refused to swear loyalty to
William III. This topical cast is worth mentioning because it
gives point to Dryden's careful separation throughout of the
orders of clerical and secular authority. At times Dryden
sounds very much like Pascal in the force of this separation:

> His Savior came not with a gaudy show,
> Nor was his kingdom of the world below. . . .
> The crown he wore was of the pointed thorn;
> In purple he was crucified, not born (89–90, 94–95).

Even where Dryden admits the Church's need for "earthly

power," he makes a sharp distinction: "The prince may keep his pomp, the fisher must be plain" (101).

The lines quoted reveal the dialectical nature of Dryden's verse. The surface is acutely logical, and the logic is pushed beyond ordinary limits. The opposition within the first line is clear and extensive. The terms are large and resonant, and the resonance arises from the contrast of New Testament and Old, of good tidings as opposed to moral instruction, of the divine image of charity as against prohibition or dogma. These oppositions are caught up in the artful use of the verbs in the second line: *forc'd* and *lov'd*, *drive* and *draw*. The force must be turned by the Good Parson on himself; for him to *drive* at all requires a double coercion, a violation of his natural bent. And the contrast of *drive* and *draw* is heightened by the openness of the second vowel; the very set of jaw that is required to sound the words defines their difference through gesture.

> For fear but freezes minds; but love, like heat,
> Exhales the soul sublime, to seek her native seat.

The initial opposition is carried further, and the logic of that opposition is what governs these lines. We shift, as we might in Donne, from figure to figure within the logical opposition. The shift of figures is neither so bold nor so ostentatious as in Donne; no image is pursued so far as to build up an extended figure, nor does the shift turn upon the wrenching of a key term. But *draw* has given place to *exhale;* the soul is now not attracted to the good but released into vapor and the flight of its natural ascent. The love that warms it is an alembic; this is a release of the spirit from its bonds of selfhood. These lines are typical of a style that plays upon a tissue of metaphors without condensing them into firm images.

In the next four lines Dryden can move to the old fable of the traveler, the wind, and the sun. Its familiarity is useful in helping us to accept the shift, and it provides a secure basis for new metaphors. To see crimes as a cloak is a little allegory that summons up the conception I have already cited from Kierkegaard's treatment of the "continuation of sin" (p. 13); man becomes hardened by the prospect of cruelty and resists the God whom he sees as mere Punisher ("as his God, so he"). All this gives force to the phrase *cumbrous cloak;* the unnatural weight, both baffle and burden, drops away as readily as the soul arises in the lines above. The drama comes to a culmination in the last four lines of the passage, which draw upon I Kings 19:12, "And after the earthquake a fire; but the Lord was not in the fire: and after the fire a still small voice." The prophetic image of divine wrath becomes the outward show of force that serves simply to define the love within. The suddenness and simplicity of the last four words recall Longinus' praise of the simple boldness of the Bible—"and there was light."

This is admirable poetry by any standard. It achieves its end with less violence of paradox than the Metaphysicals and less fullness of image than the Romantics. It depends upon such conventional diction as *heaven's artillery* and *harbingers*. But their very conventionality is what Dryden wants to upset, as "what we commonly call *heaven's artillery*" becomes "what we commonly call *harbingers*." And the last line, with its suggestion of the still small voice, shows how insufficient are those terms in which we commonly speak of the divine presence. Again, this kind of poetry depends upon terms like *milder beams* or *melts* (in the seventh and eighth lines), terms general enough or metaphors so nearly dead as to accommodate at once the physical action and the moral influence. They are terms such as John Denham in "Cooper's Hill" used in that most influential of all heroic couplets, his lines on the Thames as an example to his soul:

> Tho' deep yet clear, tho' gentle yet not dull;
> Strong without rage, without o'erflowing full.

A poetry of this kind, based as it is on the dialectical play between terms, requires terms that are not too concrete. Concreteness demands a constellation of various attributes while the irony of dialectic requires a clarified opposition: its object must be split into aspects whose difference is telling. This difference can be made more telling by sound devices as well; not *coerce* and *attract,* but *drive* and *draw.* The closeness of the sound pattern heightens the acute difference that a few letters convey. Dryden carries to a new level of skill this art of sustaining sharp oppositions which in turn shape the words they absorb and govern their relationships. In the process, familiar words are awakened to new life, and we experience the wonder of seeing startling implications arise from the words we had come to trust as sound currency and use like worn coins.

In Dryden's earliest poetry, written in a late Metaphysical style, the images achieve an irrelevant concreteness and elude the logic, which is itself more vehemently paradoxical. Those notorious lines on Lord Hastings' smallpox illustrate this:

> Blisters with pride swell'd, which thro' 's flesh did sprout,
> Like rose-buds, stuck i' th' lily skin about.
> Each little pimple had a tear in it,
> To weep the fault its rising did commit:
> Who, rebel-like, with their own lord at strife,
> Thus made an insurrection 'gainst his life
> ("Upon the Death of Lord Hastings," 1649, ll. 57–62).

The second line has nothing to do with the argument at all, but the tracing of emblems of remorseful rebellion in the constitution of the pox has the excitement of logic tightened to the point of extravagance. Every detail, no matter how remote, is drawn into the pattern, and the very pursuit of the figure becomes a feat of tightrope balance. But there is also the tastelessness of a floridly false ingenuity. Such ingenuity can justify itself when its surprising disclosures have a miraculous aptness, when the tenuous argument leads to a conclusion that is confirmed on another level. Here the images exhibit the strain of effort but none of the brilliance of discovery.

The possibilities of Dryden's mature verse are more numerous than we commonly recognize today. Perhaps their fullest realization comes in that edged satiric style that mocks the blindness it describes:

> Ev'n what they cannot praise, they will not blame,
> But veil with some extenuating name.
> The sallow skin is for the swarthy put,
> And love can make a slattern of a slut
> (Lucretius IV, 143–46).

The feeble but ardent pursuit of euphemisms by lovers is beautifully rendered in the play on *sallow* and *swarthy* and the dubious magnification of *slattern* as opposed to *slut*. The ease of rationalization is caught in the verbal similarities; the thinness of it is caught in the almost inevitable collapse of *slattern* back into the *slut* it has tried to disguise.

The converse of this is the strong, magisterial tone in which the logic of the couplet serves to intensify the plain sense it asserts. In arguing against the fear of death, Dryden (in his version of Lucretius) must make clear that death is not an experience:

> So, when our mortal frame shall be disjoin'd,
> The lifeless lump uncoupled from the mind,
> From sense of grief and pain we shall be free;

> We shall not feel, because we shall not *be.*
> Tho' earth in seas, and seas in heav'n were lost,
> We should not move, we only should be tost
>   (Lucretius III, 9–14).

There is a niceness about the parallelisms in the last two couplets: the two negatives of *feel* and *be,* the negative *move* and the passive *tost.* The bold clarity of the last line is built up by the previous negatives and even more by the picture of all nature in turmoil, without sense or mind. There are prose virtues here, if we think of logic as a necessity of prose rhetoric; but they are realized in ways that achieve the density of meaning through heightened formal coherence that is perhaps our best definition of poetry.

I have chosen only those aspects of Dryden's verse that reveal the studied oppositions at the center of the dialectical process. These oppositions are often resolved in new harmonies, but in the process they discriminate between orders of experience that have been confused. The rhetorical forms of the couplet demand a degree of awareness from which the mind easily slides away. To this extent, one can understand Lytton Strachey's remark (in reply to Matthew Arnold) that Pope's criticism of life is "simply the heroic couplet itself." Those seemingly innocuous words that are as familiar and sustaining as bread and beer become structures in their own right, within which rival orders contend for assertion. This is a form that can treat the whole range of experience, and all it treats is submitted to the vigilance of the mind. The crucial theme in the dialectic of Dryden's poetry is the struggle for the mind by both flesh and spirit. The mind's stability and ordering power may fix the appetites in specious doctrine, or it may provide the spirit of man with a means of controlling his world. The record of that struggle is in those precise distinctions the couplet makes, refining them into nuances of sound and sense but also magnifying them through allusion and argument into mighty opposites.

II. The Heroic Plays

> Ev'n mighty monarchs oft are meanly born,
> And kings by birth, to lowest rank return;
> All subject to the pow'r of giddy chance,
> For fortune can depress, or can advance:

But true nobility is of the mind,
Not giv'n by chance, and not to chance resign'd
(Translation of Boccaccio's
Sigismonda and Guiscardo, 557–62).

The world of the heroic play is a world of chance.[1] Events
are never predictable. Victories are abruptly overturned;
power shifts between one faction and another; the populace
is swayed by the latest voice. For the central characters love
descends suddenly and irresistibly, and where it remains constant, its claims conflict with other loyalties, to parent or king;
it is likely at any moment to become half of an impossible
moral choice. Those who are indifferent to the claims of love
are driven by harsh compulsions of ambition; they fix their
desire upon an object that is always precarious. There is no
clear indication that their intention will succeed or their sacrifice be rewarded; no one can foresee how his life or even his
day will end.

In such a world the common specter is meaninglessness.
The gods are ineffectual; they do nothing to confirm the values
of men. To the lazy sensualist they seem gods at their ease,
untroubled by the "little emmets" below; to the fiery egotist
they seem criminal gods who have won their own power by
ruthlessness and condone cruelty in men. It remains, then, for
man to create his own meaning and his own values by self-
assertion. The traditional codes by which he lives have often
become a travesty of true Order: the Emperor who demands
reverence may be a debauched and guilt-ridden old man, as
in *Aureng-zebe*. In a world where the representatives of Order are too often self-centered, power-seeking men, the debased traditions seem more vicious than a state of nature.
Men manipulate, disregard, reject these traditions rather than
surrender their will, and they must do this whether they are
slaves of appetite or defenders of their own integrity.

In this world the hero stands out by the fullness and firmness
of his commitment. Only he can be fully tested, for he will not
bend to expediency and cannot live in a confusion of orders;
he must remain intransigently the lover, the patriot, whatever
he has chosen to be. He may have no basis for this choice
but will, the mere act of having chosen; the appeal to honor
or other sanctions is hard to maintain in a world of impossible
choices and of overriding chance. He may exult in his strength
of will; it is not the calm or serenity of the passionless Stoic
he will attain, but the posture of defiance and a passion of
self-fulfillment. The utmost self-assertion is achieved when ev-

ery reward is withheld from virtue, when the defiance must be carried to the point of furious battle or scornful self-sacrifice. This extreme becomes a spectacle of heroic obduracy, its gestures large and formal, its language preposterously orotund. Yet, even as it risks self-parody (and indeed courts it and accepts it in its defiance) it provides us with an image—stylized and purified—of a common situation most men will recognize and find true to the center of their own moral experience.

These works are an artful playing with postures that, in less pure form, are imposed upon all of us by skeptical minds or a precarious world. The playing—which allows us to see with comparative detachment what so often immerses us, to set at a distance by style what more often we face all about us as predicament—may both account for the extravagance of heroic drama and help to explain its appeal to a worldly and sophisticated audience. A comparably sophisticated audience today might expect a tragicomic extravagance that moves closer to the farcical; our present-day stage is filled with tragical farces—by Anouilh, Ionesco, Duerrenmatt, Genet, who accommodate the stylized gestures but confront them with the ludicrous. Ionesco professes to turn away from Molière because all of Molière's problems can be resolved. "There is no solution to the intolerable," Ionesco writes, "and only that which is intolerable is truly theatrical." He wants a "hard comedy, without finesse, excessive. No dramatic comedies either. But a return to the intolerable. Push everything to a state of paroxysm, there where the sources of tragedy lie. Create a theatre of violence: violently comic, violently dramatic. . . . Avoid psychology, or rather give it a metaphysical dimension."[2]

What Ionesco has pushed to the extreme of the farcically intolerable, the heroic play—at least in Dryden's hands—holds closer to traditional tragic form. But it is obvious, not simply from the tragicomic endings, but also from the argumentativeness of its heroes, the absurd effrontery of their heroism, the dance-like symmetries of their predicament, that the heroic play is trying for an experience different from the tragic. In making fate so obvious, oppressive, and busy an agent, Dryden prevents the action from moving inexorably to its central tragic reversal; instead, we are given a succession of reversals. The solution of any one problem only introduces the next. The fortuitous world makes these characters almost comically impotent. Only their intransigence gives them stability. These characters are not immovable, they are inextinguishable; and their movement, the constant reforming and redirection of their will and self, is the only form of constancy available to them. Dryden's heroic plays are closer to the comic than he himself ever admitted, or than most readers have been ready to see. But they also accommodate a near-tragic awareness of the instability of human assertion, even at its most splendid. As with Donne's lovers, of whom we are reminded so often, the heroic is carried to the point where its magnificence derives from its precariousness. Dryden's heroes are statements of the problematic nature of heroism, and as such they thrive on excess. They are themselves, as are so many of their speeches, conceived with the levity of brilliant overstatement, the dialectical excess of an extreme position.

Within the fortuitous world of the heroic play there are several attitudes taken toward experience, or, in Pascal's terms, several orders of experience. The naturalistic view, which is commonly taken by villains, has its coloring of Hobbesian thought and Machiavellian application. The naturalistic character seeks power for the sake of satisfying his desires or pursues it as an end in itself. Such a character may be the slave of a ruthless mistress who demands an act of treason before he can enjoy her; or it may be a cold, reptilian seductress like Lyndaraxa, whose only passion is for domination:

> Yes! I avow th' ambition of my soul,
> To be that one to live without control!
> And that's another happiness to me,
> To be so happy as but one can be
> (1 *Conquest of Granada,* II, 148–51).

Lyndaraxa is the quintessential Hobbesian woman: her life is a restless pursuit of power, and she can be content with nothing less than supremacy. In fact, Lyndaraxa is a grotesque heightening of what Hobbes saw in all men, and her death—like Nourmahal's in *Aureng-zebe*—is the final reduction of all her self-assertion to the phantasy of madness. Her disenchanted lover dies after giving her a fatal blow, and Lyndaraxa exclaims:

> Die for us both; I have not leisure now;
> A crown is come, and will not fate allow:
> And yet I feel something like death is near.
> My guards, my guards,—
> Let not that ugly skeleton appear!
> Sure Destiny mistakes; this death's not mine;

> She dotes, and meant to cut another line.
> Tell her I am a queen—but 'tis too late;
> Dying, I charge rebellion on my fate.
> Bow down, ye slaves:—   [To the Moors.]
> Bow quickly down, and your submission show.—
>   [They bow.]
> I'm pleased to taste an empire ere I go.
>   [Dies.]
> (2 CG, V, iv, 125–36.)

Dryden departs from Hobbes in showing Lyndaraxa's anxiety about fate, her need—in a delusive moment of triumph—to domineer over fate itself and to taste, if only for an instant, what her appetite has taken as its only object. There is a magnificent consistency in her nature, and Dryden can realize its frightening power. He does something even more outrageous at the close of *Aureng-zebe* with the death of Nourmahal, who rushes in feverish with the poison she has drunk:

> I burn, I more than burn; I am all fire.
> See how my mouth and nostrils flames expire!
> I'll not come near myself—
> Now I'm a burning lake, it rolls and flows;
> I'll rush, and pour it all upon my foes.

And as she sees her husband, the old Emperor:

> Pull, pull that reverend piece of timber near:
> Throw't on—'tis dry—'twill burn—
> Ha, ha! how my old husband crackles there!

It is all ludicrous, extravagant in the manner of Ovid; yet its tortured wit has a curious force in catching the explosion of a mind that can no longer contain the pressure of its will. These death scenes are the culmination, in each case, of the natural energy of passion. It breaks through the limits of reality into the regions of madness where it can still sustain itself.

The cases of Lyndaraxa and Nourmahal are only the extremes of the naturalistic view of life conceived according to Pascal's order of the flesh. Tellingly, in both *The Conquest of Granada* (1670) and *Aureng-zebe* (1675) the ruler is an old man who has outlived the active energy of conquest and declined into a debased sensuality. Of the Emperor in *Aureng-zebe* a courtier remarks:

> So he, who in his youth for glory strove,
> Would recompence his age with ease and love (II, i).

Still the Emperor, however sad his decline, is capable of total arrogance when he learns that a subject has been pursuing the woman he hopes to make his mistress:

> Did he, my slave, presume to look so high?
> That crawling insect, who from mud began,
> Warmed by my beams, and kindled into man?
> Durst he, who does but for my pleasure live,
> Intrench on love, my great prerogative (II, i).

The arrogance is painfully threadbare; the Emperor's image of the sun breeding life out of slime no longer carries the traditional force of the King as vice-regent of God. This Sun King is a petulant and impotent old man, and his despotic dream that all exists for his sole pleasure only confirms the barrenness of his self-assertion. As in Pascal's disenchanting view of the order of the flesh, power has ceased to have function except for the sake of failing pleasure; the impositions of the ruler are all imposition, without a trace of sanction or dedication.

Again, in lesser figures, we find the simple rule of appetite. Abdalla sees the futility of his love for Lyndaraxa, but he cannot resist:

> This enchanted place
> Like Circe's isle, is peopled with a race
> Of dogs and swine; yet though their fate I know,
> I look with pleasure, and am turning too
> (1 CG, III, 93–96).

The very clarity of utterance emphasizes the breakdown of rational control. It is, in this case, the language of the knowing victim, and it can parody the idiom of religion:

> Your love I will believe with hoodwink'd eyes—
> In faith, much merit in much blindness lies
> (2 CG, II, ii, 138–39).

Or, at the last:

> O that you still could cheat, and I believe!
> (2 CG, IV, ii, 121.)

Beside these naturalistic characters Dryden places another group. These are characters of principle as well as passion, figures who have the energy of the naturalistic characters without their limiting egoism. Almanzor bursts into *The Conquest of Granada* an invincible hero, a natural man. He has no known ancestry. He is free of the obligations imposed upon man in general by a social contract or upon particular men by their birth into an ordered society. He can say to the king, Boabdelin:

> Obey'd as sovereign by thy subjects be,
> But know that I alone am king of me.
> I am as free as nature first made man,
> Ere the base laws of servitude began,
> When wild in woods the noble savage ran
>   (1 CG, I, 205-9).

When Boabdelin hears this, his immediate response is that of a Hobbesian theorist; man in the state of nature is a wolf to man, and therefore the natural man who survives in society "should be hunted like a beast of prey" (212). But Almanzor's role as natural man implies a fuller conception of nature. He rejects Boabdelin's sovereignty, but he invokes the old Stoic law of nature as the rule of justice, the social dimension of universal Order. Almanzor's first words upon encountering the war of factions had been:

> I cannot stay to ask what cause is best;
> But this is so to me, because opprest (1 CG, I, 128-29).

So, now, he can reproach Boabdelin for failure to be a just king:

> I saw th' oppress'd, and thought it did belong
> To a king's office to redress the wrong;
> I brought that succor which thou ought'st to bring,
> And so, in nature, am thy subjects' king
>   (1 CG, I, 218-21).

Almanzor, then, is not the Hobbesian image of the natural man. He is not self-seeking; rather he is immediately moved to impose justice, as if by a natural instinct. He is a rebel against the existing social order, but he rebels in the cause of an authentic order. His rebelliousness is the necessary criticism of a mock-order, and his energy is the very pulse of life that should animate a true order:

> Vast is his courage, boundless is his mind,
> Rough as a storm, and humorous as wind:
> Honor's the only idol of his eyes (1 CG, I, 253-55).

He has the true authority of the "one great soul" who can command and order the restive populace; he is, in fact, the seventeenth-century superman.

Rough and wild, Almanzor provides a splendid contrast to the decadent Boabdelin, whose own legitimacy of rule is highly questionable in any case. But Almanzor is suspicious of all kings and believes none worthy of respect; he imputes to the Christian Ferdinand's true kindness and legitimacy of rule the same base, mercenary power-quest that he finds in Boabdelin and others. Like the satirist—whose name is derived from that rough beast, the satyr, in the folk etymology of the Renaissance—he is uncontrolled in his vehemence and indiscriminate in his suspicions. To that extent he resembles the naturalistic characters who explain away all legitimacy as the pretension of power; yet, unlike them, Almanzor holds to a principle of honor and legitimacy he finds embodied in no one but himself. He is not without a vision of a moral order, but he questions every actual claimant to that title. Nor does he rely upon any divine force beyond fallible men. When the Christian Duke of Arcos says of Ferdinand, "My king his hope from heaven's assistance draws," Almanzor mockingly replies, "The Moors have heaven, and me, to assist their cause." Almanzor is the loneliest character of all: he trusts no human order, he relies on no divine order, he creates his own.

Friendship—the personal, chosen relationship—outweighs in his mind all the impositions of sovereignty. He is a transparent man, without a mask:

> My heart's so plain,
> That men on every passing thought may look,
> Like fishes gliding in a crystal brook
> (1 CG, IV, i, 43–45).

He is also a man whose self-assertion is his only form of stability:

> The word, which I have giv'n, shall stand like fate
> (1 CG, III, 9).

He becomes, in fact, not only his own king but his own god. When he scorns Abdalla and withdraws his friendship, he professes to doom him:

> Like heav'n, I need but only to stand still,
> And, not concurring to thy life, I kill.

And godlike he commands fate:

> Thou know'st this place,
> And like a clock wound up, strik'st here for me;
> Now Chance, assert thy own inconstancy,
> And Fortune, fight that thou may'st Fortune be!
> (2 CG, III, i, 193–96.)

When Almanzor finds himself suddenly numbed by "the lethargy of love," he fights the chains of Almahide's beauty and struggles against her fettering of his will. When he finally accepts love, he accepts it heroically. Just as Nourmahal in her death throes cries, "I am all fire," so Almanzor embraces his love completely, "I am all o'er love, / Nay, I am love." This fury of identification is the heroic response, a full acceptance in contrast to the overpowering consumption by passion of Nourmahal. It is only the restraint of Almahide that prevents Almanzor from dismissing her vows to Boabdelin; her own integrity meets his and masters it with a rigorous observance of the scruples of honor. Yet, even as she restrains him, Almahide recognizes the value of his love. Until she knew Almanzor she "with a vulgar good [was] dully blest."

> 'Twas life becalmed, without a gentle breath;
> Though not too cold, yet motionless as death.
> A heavy quiet state; but love, all strife,
> All rapid, is the hurricane of life (1 CG, V, iii, 200–3).

"Rough as a storm, and humorous as wind," Almanzor becomes the animating power that awakens her to life, but it is a power she must govern for fear it destroy the life it creates:

> You, like some greedy cormorant, devour
> All my whole life can give you, in an hour
>   (1 CG, V, iii, 288–89).

She must impose upon both of them the sacrifice of their fulfillment for the sake of honor, the acceptance of a course that denies them every reward.

Throughout the play, we have, in contrast to Almahide's integrity, Lyndaraxa's artful teasing of her would-be lovers, alternately fanning their passion and dismissing them as their usefulness ebbs. She loves the king, whoever he happens finally to be. Almahide, in contrast, suffers the torture of conflict but sustains her self-command: "My heart's not mine but all my actions are." When Almanzor tempts Almahide most severely with a vision of ecstatic consummation, she can scorn his "mercenary" demands, "for whatever may be bought, is low." He has saved the husband she does not love; she loves him passionately; yet she is ready to stab herself rather than allow herself to surrender to him. When Almanzor, "half-converted," respects her virtue, she sets forth the discipline he must master: he must "mount above [his] wish, and lose it higher." When, for all her scruples, the Emperor falsely accuses them of adultery, Almahide once more asks Almanzor to save her husband's life and his kingdom. His exclamation as he accedes outdoes even Donne's canonized lovers in its brilliant ascent beyond this world:

> Listen, sweet heaven, and all ye blest above,
> Take rules of virtue from a mortal love!
> (2 CG, V, iii, 123–24.)

The natural man has become the courtly lover *par excellence,* capable of extravagant sacrifice just as he has been capable of heroic self-assertion. The self-assertion is still there, in Almanzor's defiance of heaven; this sacrifice of all hope of winning Almahide in order to save her husband's life is the highest pitch of refinement the world can achieve, and it is offered as a model rather than a tribute to heaven. But the play crowns this with the descent of Christian hope; Almahide's slave, a convert, teaches her mistress to transcend mere virtue:

> Virtue's no god, nor has she power divine:
> But He protects it, who did first enjoin.
> Trust then in Him; and from His grace implore
> Faith to believe what rightly we adore
> (2 CG, V, ii, 11–14).

At the close, Almanzor finds his better self in the Christian Ferdinand:

> Something so kingly, that my haughty mind
> Is drawn to yours, because 'tis of a kind
> (2 CG, V, iv, 155–56).

He turns out to be the son of Ferdinand's general, a foundling like Tom Jones, whose natural goodness now seems to have its source in his concealed origins. We may think of Dryden's words to the deists in *Religio Laici:* " 'Tis revelation what thou think'st discourse." The natural wisdom of which men boast is ultimately divine revelation in disguise; it is given to man, not created by him. Yet, for all the Christian wedlock of Almanzor and Almahide and their absorption into the court of Spain, the stress of the play has been upon the puzzling world that must be endured without revelation.

We are, consequently, left with unresolved questions. The natural man is capable of true greatness, and he can ascend to the highest level of neo-Stoic moral discipline. But is he truly natural, or does he seem natural only because he carries within

him a higher order of being? We see him from the first showing a sense of justice and a capacity for friendship; we find
him capable of more intense love than any other man. Is this
the order of the flesh outdoing the order of mind? Are free
and generous passions more to be trusted than those that,
sacrificed to principle, will subvert the principle and use it as a
disguise? Is the vigor of Almanzor the proper embodiment of
an order of charity in contrast to the crassly self-seeking or the
coldly righteous? These puzzles recur throughout the century
to follow. Clarissa Harlowe and Tom Jones, in their quite
different ways, are distinguished from their fellow creatures by
dangerously passionate natures and a capacity for goodness.
And the celebration in Shaftesbury of nature's varied order
gives an authenticity to wilds and deserts not to be found in
princely gardens.

Dryden's own treatment of the state of nature is always
marked by ambiguity. In his great political satire, *Absalom and
Achitophel,* he opens with that ironic picture of "pious times,
ere priestcraft did begin," times of liberty

> When nature prompted, and no law denied
> Promiscuous use of concubine and bride.

David, "Israel's monarch after Heaven's own heart," imparts
his "vigorous warmth" indiscriminately and scatters "his Maker's image through the land." Absalom's beauty and bravery
may be due to the "diviner lust" and "greater gust" with which
his father begot him. Again, in his version of the opening of
Juvenal's Sixth Satire, Dryden presents a mocking image of
"hard primitivism" and the chastity it produced:

> When in a narrow cave, their common shade,
> The sheep, the shepherds, and their gods were laid:
> When reeds, and leaves, and hides of beasts were spread
> By mountain huswifes for their homely bed,
> And mossy pillows rais'd, for the rude husband's
>   head . . .
> Those first unpolisht matrons, big and bold,
> Gave suck to infants of gigantic mold;
> Rough as their savage lords who rang'd the wood,
> And fat with acorns belch'd their windy food.
> For when the world was buxom, fresh, and young,
> Her sons were undebauch'd and therefore strong;
> And whether born in kindly beds of earth,
> Or struggling from the teeming oaks to birth,
> Or from what other atoms they begun,
> No sires they had, or, if a sire, the sun (3–7, 12–21).

And in his epistle *To Sir Godfrey Kneller* (1694) we find this passage written by poet to painter:

> Our arts are sisters, though not twins in birth;
> For hymns were sung in Eden's happy earth
> By the first pair, while Eve was yet a saint,
> Before she fell with pride, and learn'd to paint.
> Forgive th' allusion; 'twas not meant to bite,
> But satire will have room, wheree'er I write (89–94).

The last line recalls the play of Dryden's mind, the skeptical turning of the mind back upon itself which qualifies any unguarded statement and introduces a note of levity into an extreme position. The play upon the word *paint* is the very stuff of Augustan ambiguity. We see it again in that famous passage of Pope's *The Rape of the Lock,* where Belinda at her dressing table paints like the fallen Eve and "bids a purer blush arise" from her cheeks. We know that Belinda is applying rouge (unless she is striking her cheek with the back of her hairbrush), but, as Cleanth Brooks has said, she is not simply disguising nature. She is bringing it to its full realization; her cosmetic art is making the color more complete ("purer" in one sense), but it is also making it what Nature would have wished to achieve (*The Well Wrought Urn,* New York, 1947). Eve's painting, in Dryden's lines, is the bedizening of the fallen woman who can no longer enjoy naked innocence; but it is the beginning of art, which repairs the Fall and gives us, in Sir Philip Sidney's words, "a golden world."

A skeptical play of mind does not imply that Dryden seriously adopted naturalistic views or that he found a strict alliance between natural appetite and moral goodness, but rather, that he was capable of breaking down categories that were too pat. If Almanzor is nobler than all the Moorish court, this can be accounted for by the generosity of his large nature, or by his Christian origins and descent from a court that espoused heroic passion in the cause of piety. The architecture of *The Conquest of Granada* is designed to show, in the first play, the emergence of Almanzor into the moral rigor or neo-Stoic self-denial and then to include this, in the second play, within the Christian framework that transcends mere human virtue. Such lesser characters as Ozmyn and Benzayda play out comparable roles on a smaller scale; they do not have the fine excess of Almanzor, and their happy solution is more easily achieved. Closer to Almanzor's transfiguration is that of Morat, the villain of *Aureng-zebe,* whose fiery nature is finally absorbed at death into a moral order. The resolution Dryden provides cannot be underestimated, for it supplies a link with his major satires and religious poems. But the intensity with which he poses problems is equally important, and this can be seen throughout the heroic plays and tragedies. I will consider three of them here and defer *All for Love* to a later chapter.

In *The Indian Emperor* (1665) Cortez becomes a prototype of the troubled proconsul. He descends upon Mexico only to find it an earthly paradise, ruled by a benevolent rational monarch. Cortez falls in love with Montezuma's daughter; but the dignity and generosity of Montezuma are a rebuke to the conquistador who comes to despoil in the name of Pope and Emperor. Montezuma has his own cruel and superstitious rites, but Dryden makes these the blandly conventional ceremonies of an established church that serves a free-thinking monarch's power. Montezuma accepts a traditional Aztec faith, but the personal role he assumes is that of the rationalistic critic of the temporal claims of Christianity. Cortez offers little in reply. Pressed by his Aztec critics, he can only assert his honor and his need to carry out his imperial task, which he undertakes joylessly. When later in the play Montezuma is put to the rack by the Christian priest who wants the Aztec sacred ritual objects for their gold, Cortez is outraged at the priest's presumption and saddened by the curse of gold which, once it has entered Europe, will induce countless crimes of this sort.

In his fight against Cortez Montezuma's aggression arises only from his slavish devotion to his haughty empress; she disdains the claims of honor when they thwart her own appetites and assumes the typical naturalistic view of insatiate willfulness:

> For mean remorse no room the valiant finds,
> Repentance is the virtue of weak minds. . . .
> . . . daring courage makes ill actions good (III, i).

The closest that Montezuma himself can approach to this view is in his acceptance of greatness; in this he resembles Almanzor or Morat (in *Aureng-zebe*) as he addresses his gods:

> Great souls are sparks of your own heavenly pride:
> That lust of power we from your god-heads have,
> You're bound to please those appetites you gave (II, iv).

Montezuma accepts the fate of kings to the end: "Power is their life; when that expires, they die." But as an individual, Montezuma is the high-minded rationalist. Like the people of Voltaire's Eldorado in *Candide,* he mocks the mighty European emperor who "poorly begs" for the gold the Aztecs despise. He questions the Church that "nourishes debate, not preaches love," that confuses temporal power over new lands with spiritual power in men's souls, that subverts morality by setting a low price upon sin, and that threatens the undivided sovereignty of monarchs by its own temporal claims. Later, when he is suffering on the rack, Montezuma rejects the Christian priest's arrogant dogmatism; man cannot go beyond natural reason without risking the self-deceptions of pride. He cannot accept the authority of an "unerring head" of the Christian church:

> MONT. Man, and not err! What reason can you give.
> PRIEST. Renounce that carnal reason, and believe.
> MONT. The light of nature should I thus betray,
>   'Twere to wink hard, that I might see the day
>   (V, ii).

Montezuma's tolerant acceptance of a "middle way" between disbelief and dogmatism is met by the Christian priest's use of force and torture. In contrast to this conflict is the bond of honor that joins Montezuma and Cortez. If he must endure defeat, Montezuma generously exclaims, he will be happy to have a man like Cortez succeed him.

Both Cortez and Montezuma have a sense of the difficult and confusing plight of man. In despair Cortez can cry:

> We toss and turn about our feverish will,
> When all our ease must come from lying still:
> For all the happiness mankind can gain
> Is not in pleasure, but in rest from pain (IV, i).

Montezuma stabs himself when life has become intolerable; like Othello, he can reassert his original self in this one act: "He wants no subject, who can death command" (vii). Again we have the image of confused values and contradictions, of guilt and doubt; and meeting it is the assertion of self-command.

In *Tyrannic Love* (1669) Dryden created his first sketch of unruly greatness. Maximin is a "Thracian shepherd" become tyrant. He scorns his wife's high Antonine birth as well as her piety; where she sees divine Order acting in their son's death, Maximin sees only the spite and jealousy of gods threatened by human greatness.

As we first see Maximin, his restless valor seems the nobler for the slothful ease of Rome, which has chosen two "tame gowned princes" to rule. Maximin disdains a mixed state of checks and balances:

> Two equal pow'rs, two different ways will draw,
> While each may check, and give the other law.
> True, they secure propriety and peace;
> But are not fit an empire to increase.

Constitutional ideas are met by the force of conquest and the Hobbesian logic of absolute power; the concern with property ("propriety") is reduced to the caution of a "thrifty state" that would "rather lose a fight than over-buy."

Saint Catherine of Alexandria challenges the force of Maximin. She outdoes fifty Roman philosophers in a combat of reason, and although a captive she enters Maximin's presence with a "high air and mien" that show "the greatness of a queen." Maximin scornfully sets his philosopher-priest against her ("You gain by heaven," he tells him, "and, therefore, should dispute"), but the defense of Stoic virtue cannot withstand her ampler view. The Stoic virtues are accepted by the Christian but transformed and extended: "Yours but reach the action, ours the mind." When she converts his advocate, she arouses Maximin's love.

Catherine conquers the conqueror by her utter transcendence of his order; she scorns his gifts and promises, for she enjoys "the humble quiet of possessing naught." She rejects the view that sees the greatness of the gods in their indifference to the "little business of the world":

> This doctrine well befitted him who thought
> A casual world was from wild atoms wrought:
> But such an order in each chance we see
> (Chain'd to its cause, as that to its decree)
> That none can think a workmanship so rare
> Was built, or kept, without a workman's care (III, i).

This grand vision of Order is incidental to Catherine's assertion of an order of charity. But Maximin cannot begin to comprehend such transcendence:

> For what a greater happiness can be
> Than to be courted and be lov'd by me?

Catherine's scorn for his offer must take the only terms he can grasp, the language of power:

> Such pow'r in bonds true piety can have,
> That I command, and thou art but a slave.

The conflict between orders is given a masquelike presentation when a sorcerer calls up an "earthly fiend" to tempt Catherine. The fiend's power is overwhelmed by a guardian angel, before whom he can only bow:

> Thou, prince of day, from elements art free;
> And I all body when compared to thee. . . .
> Gross-heavy-fed, next man in ignorance and sin,
> And spotted all without, and dusky all within. . . .
> I reel, I stagger, and am drunk with light . . . (IV, i).

As Catherine's spiritual power is magnified, Maximin is revealed more and more as a maddened tyrant who thinks he is a god:

> I'll find that pow'r o'er wills, which heav'n ne'er found.
> Free-will's a cheat in any one but me;
> In all but kings, 'tis willing slavery;
> An unseen fate which forces the desire,
> The will of puppets danc'd upon a wire. . . .
> Mine is the business of your little fates . . . (IV, i).

Catherine is quick to point out the weakness and febrility of his self-assertion:

> Qualmish and loathing all you had before,
> Yet with a sickly appetite to more,
> As in a fev'rish dream you still drink on,
> And wonder why your thirst is never gone . . . (IV, i).

As Catherine converts others around him, the court becomes invulnerable to Maximin's power; his victims welcome death and martyrdom. His exasperation with his converted empress is eminently understandable: "Behead her, while she's in so good a mind." But the frustration of Maximin makes him the more assertive. "I love not for her sake but my own," he exclaims as he sends Catherine to death. "Our gods are gods 'cause they have power and will"; and so, "if this be sin, I do myself forgive." When his world crumbles, he defies the gods with magnificent bravura that recalls his disdain for mercantile Rome:

> Look to it, Gods, for you th' aggressors are.
> Keep you your rain and sunshine in your skies,

And I'll keep back my flame and sacrifice.
Your trade of heav'n shall soon be at a stand,
And all your goods lie dead upon your hand (V, i).

As his body gives way to death, his assertion persists:

I'll shake this carcass off, and be obey'd,
Reign an imperial ghost without its aid.

And his last words are the highest pitch of titanlike defiance:

I'll mount, and scatter all the Gods I hit.

Maximin looks back to Marlowe's Tamburlaine, and ahead to Camus's *Caligula*. Caligula is oppressed by the meaninglessness and absurdity of a world that has undone his rational and humane order. He seizes upon every whim of arbitrary power to create his own meaning by sheer fiat and to induce in others the same collapse of belief that he has undergone. He must absorb all control of his world into himself by one means or another, and he dies in the impossibility of his increasingly savage quest.

Maximin's plight does not have the same origins as Caligula's; he is no disenchanted man of reason, although he has lost a son to the jealous gods, as Caligula has lost a sister. It is his desire for Catherine as much as metaphysical anguish that leads him to commit his infamies. Nor does he become a sardonic teacher. Yet he does resist a force that seems meaningless to him, if not to us; he tries to impose meaning through force, to make the order of the flesh the order of his world even as something incomprehensible irrupts into it. *Tyrannic Love* is awkward in many ways, but its strength lies in Dryden's play of mind. He can entertain Maximin's own view of his situation sufficiently to make his plight far more compelling than Saint Catherine's. If Maximin's tyranny submits easily to moral diagnosis, his titanism still carries force and wins a sympathy it does not ask.

Don Sebastian (1689) is late enough in Dryden's career to show the survival of the heroic forms beyond the Revolution of 1688. The play has two heroes. The arrogance is given to Dorax, the Spanish renegade turned Moor; he is a man of disenchanted idealism whose speeches recall the Juvenalian satires Dryden was in the process of translating. The heroic will and mastery of fate are given to Don Sebastian and to Almeyda, whom he loves but at the last discovers to be his sister. There is, moreover (as in *Marriage à la Mode* and *The Spanish Friar*) a comic underplot concerned with profiteering and seduction: its motivation is consistently low, cunning, and fleshly.

The division of the heroic role allows Dryden to make Dorax a mordant railer: "all mankind," he says, "is cause enough for satire." He keeps looking for a true man, one that is "his maker's image" and he scorns the "glut" of the battle-field: "A hundred of 'em to a single soul."

The language of Dorax is echoed at moments by the Moorish despot, Muley-Moloch ("These are but garbage, not a sacrifice"); but the Moor's scorn is all complacent arrogance. He does not yearn, as Dorax does, to pay reverence to a true hero; nor does he know Dorax's bitterness at being dreadfully wronged by the one apparent hero he has known. Muley-Moloch can exclaim, "What's royalty, but power to please myself?" Don Sebastian (the true hero in whose motives Dorax is mistaken) takes a different view: "Kings, who are fathers, live but in their people." It becomes clear that Dorax, although he is a renegade and a rebel, is one only in the cause of righteousness. He can savagely attack the temporal ambitions of the Church, but he asserts a vision of Order and refuses to be drawn into treason:

> Why then, no bond is left on humankind!
> Distrusts, debates, immortal strifes ensue;
> Children may murder parents, wives their husbands;
> All must be rapine, wars, and desolation,
> When trust and gratitude no longer bind (II, i).

Dorax insists upon a distinction between rebellion and treacherous betrayal; and when his Christian faith revives within him, it too is called rebellion: "Down, thou rebelling Christian in my heart!"

Don Sebastian is a man who "seems ashamed / He's not all spirit," who can reject his captivity and fate:

> I beg no pity for this mould'ring clay;
> For, if you give it burial, there it takes
> Possession of your earth;
> If burnt and scatter'd in the air, the winds,
> That strow my dust, diffuse my royalty,
> And spread me o'er your clime; for when one atom
> Of mine shall light, know, there Sebastian reigns (I, i).

He cannot be conquered: "Souls know no conquerors." His love for Almeyda is as exalted as the Moorish Emperor's is

brutish, and Sebastian can look down upon the raging Emperor
with scorn from another order of awareness:

> Barbarian, thou canst part us but a moment!
> We shall be one again in thy despite.
> Life is but air,
> That yields a passage to the whistling sword,
> And closes when 'tis gone (III, i).

When the Emperor condemns Sebastian to death, Almeyda
also can rise to the sense of rebellious outrage we have seen
in Dorax. She turns upon the gods who have allowed the Emperor his power:

> O Pow'rs, if Kings be your peculiar care,
> Why plays this wretch with your prerogative?
> Now flash him dead, now crumble him to ashes,
> Or henceforth live confin'd in your own palace;
> And look not idly out upon a world
> That is no longer yours (III, i).

Her grandeur of spirit and rebellious defiance of unjust authority fuse the assertion of Sebastian and the moral indignation of Dorax. As Camus has pointed out, "The most elementary form of rebellion, paradoxically, expresses an aspiration
to order." The metaphysical rebel "blasphemes primarily in
the name of order, denouncing God as the father of death
and as the supreme outrage" (*The Rebel,* revised trans. Anthony Bower, Vintage Books, New York, 1956, pp. 23, 24).

Dryden reconciles rebel and hero in an impressive scene
between Dorax and Sebastian. Dorax has been envious and
unfair; Sebastian is just and kind. Their relationship is defined
by an undercurrent of references to Satan and God. Sebastian
knew

> as Heaven
> Foreknew, among the shining angel host,
> Who would stand firm, who fall (IV, iii).

When it turns out that the favorite Sebastian had preferred
—a man Dorax had taken to be an effeminate sycophant—
died in battle at Sebastian's side, all of Dorax's jealous reading
of events breaks down. Unlike Satan, he can recognize the
authentic goodness of his preferred rival and acknowledge his
superiority. In having become a vengeful renegade, in turning
from his life as Spanish and Christian Alonzo to the satirical
Dorax, he has "lost, like Lucifer, [his] name above." "Have
I," he asks, "been cursing heaven, while heaven blest me?"

Dryden has explored the pattern of rebellion and allowed for the power of Dorax's vision. Sebastian can attest to that in forgiving Dorax's vengefulness: "Thou meant'st to kill a tyrant, not a king." Dorax's outraged sense of justice has been born of error and confirmed by envy, but it has been a consistent vision with its own morality. If it buckles finally before true goodness, it does not lose its dignity. Satan reconciled is, up to a point, Satan justified; his rebellion has been against "the supreme outrage," and his pride proves less significant than his sense of justice. Dorax looks ahead, however dimly, to the romantic view of Satan, and it is the dialectical nature of Dryden's plays that allows him this force.

Once Dorax is reconciled, he thinks he has regained heaven:

> Joy is in every face, without a cloud;
> As, in the scene of opening paradise,
> The whole creation danc'd at their new being,
> Pleas'd to be what they were, pleas'd with each other
> (V, i).

It is a transitory joy, for Don Sebastian and Almeyda soon learn that their marriage is incestuous. Before he departs for his hermit's cell (as Almeyda for a convent) Sebastian voices the "impious" thoughts he must learn to subdue:

> one moment longer,
> And I should break through laws divine and human,
> And think them cobwebs spread for little man,
> Which all the bulky herd of nature breaks.
> The vigorous young world was ignorant
> Of these restrictions; 'tis decrepit now;
> Not more devout, but more decay'd, and cold (V, i).

We are close once more to the heroic primitivism of Almanzor.

Sebastian rejects these thoughts just as Almanzor eventually submits his to the discipline of the Christian court. Yet the assertions are memorable, and Sebastian's primitivism has had its support in Dorax's scourging satire of courts and priestcraft. The play imposes a moral order upon its events and looks to an order of the spirit in the religious exercise of its ill-fated hero and heroine; but it has given heroic feeling both strength and clarity of vision. The worlds of Dorax's satiric rage and of Sebastian's sinful love are worlds that have their own consistency and their own expression of the idea of justice. The vigor of their deep feelings and proud demands is a necessary part of the order Dryden creates, an order that risks anarchy and division so that it may include energy and greatness.

III. The Political Satires

The drama provides Dryden with a playground for conflicting ideas of heroism and of order. Such play can involve highly serious concerns, but it does not demand practical decision. Its dialectical freedom need not be too sharply resolved. In the political and religious poems, the process of ordering becomes more urgent; they are, in most cases, attempts to fix a judgment upon a specific occasion—the Monmouth-Shaftesbury movement in 1681 against the succession of James II, the protest of the Church of England against James's granting indulgence to Dissenters in 1687. In the process, Dryden magnifies and generalizes the occasion so that its specific issues become a local instance of the larger conflicts he has dramatized, but he tends to place more weight upon the one central conflict of the natural and the divine.

In both the political satires and the religious poems the dialectic moves between the spontaneous generation of order from below that is the rule of the multitude or of the private will and the descent of order from above that is divine right or true religious law. At stake in the conflict is the possibility of a mediating force that can reconcile the two and dissolve the paradoxes of a Pascalian view. That mediating force is the reason or the order of mind, and in these poems we see the rival powers struggling to win reason to their side.

The conversion that takes place in Almanzor becomes the central movement of *Absalom and Achitophel*.[3] Here David (Charles II) moves from the natural man to the sanctified ruler; in his movement, he leaves behind his son, Absalom, and he reveals the two possibilities open to the man of nature. David's generosity of spirit is disciplined by adversity. By the close of the poem, he has ascended to the role of a just and merciful monarch, while his son has fallen into the self-indulgence of rebellious outrage. Absalom (Monmouth, Charles's illegitimate son) is on his way to becoming a Lucifer; but he may still be reclaimed. He is, ironically, too good by nature to fall easily into conscious evil, and too naïvely proud to recognize how thoroughly he is being used as an instrument of that more Satanic figure, Achitophel (the first Earl of Shaftesbury).

The poem opens with a bold and skeptical view of the state of nature. I have already quoted from these lines above, but they must be considered more fully here:

> In pious times, ere priestcraft did begin,
> Before polygamy was made a sin;
> When man on many multiplied his kind,
> Ere one to one was cursedly confin'd;
> When nature prompted, and no law denied
> Promiscuous use of concubine and bride;
> Then Israel's monarch after Heaven's own heart,
> His vigorous warmth did variously impart
> To wives and slaves; and, wide as his command,
> Scatter'd his Maker's image thro' the land (1–10).

Dryden's attitude is hard to fix, and deliberately so. The first six lines call up the times of the patriarchs when Abraham could receive God in his presence, when the direct knowledge of God was not filtered through the self-interest and rituals of a clergy. They also call up the image of nature as the scene of the complete fulfillment of man's whole nature, a golden age without prohibitions and without guilt. To fall from such a world was indeed to be "cursedly confined," both in the traditional religious sense—in our fallen world, marriage is a sacramental institution administered by priestcraft—and in the "smart" naturalistic sense of losing the joys of polygamy. Both saint and rake might here agree; for if man was in a state of blessedness in being close to God, he was also in a state that looks to us like libertinism. David's "vigorous warmth" is an act of piety; he dispenses "his Maker's image" with the prodigality of the king distributing stamped coins or medals among a grateful populace. He serves God, he serves the interest of the crown, and he enjoys the pleasures of the rake.

All of this amusing *double-entendre* has its purpose in the poem. The image of pious and innocent times is not simply an ingenious way of releasing Charles from too harsh and moral a view of his adultery; it is a way of connecting (as we shall see again in Gay's Macheath or Fielding's Tom Jones) generosity of spirit with natural sexual energy. In contrast to David we have Achitophel, who can only "Punish a body which he could not please," and who produces

> That unfeather'd two-legg'd thing, a son;
> Got, while his soul did huddled notions try;
> And born a shapeless lump, like anarchy (170–72).

David is open, expansive, creative ("godlike"); Achitophel,

close, crooked, distracted with intrigue. Yet Dryden is not blinking the charge of promiscuity: David's freedom is also wantonness, and the libertine is likely to make a feeble king. At the outset, David and Absalom are counterparts:

> inspir'd by some diviner lust,
> His father got him with a greater gust . . .
> Whate'er he did, was done with so much ease,
> In him alone 'twas natural to please:
> His motions all accompanied with grace;
> And paradise was open'd in his face.
> With secret joy indulgent David view'd
> His youthful image in his son renew'd . . .
>   (19–20, 27–32).

But even though David remains indulgent, Absalom's energy boils over into murder; and his beauty, while it may be due to his father's "gust," is the instrument ambition can use to charm, perhaps to subvert. The son's excesses cheapen his father's vigor, and the defects of both men are spelled out in the unruliness of the people whom David should govern.

The next stage of Dryden's carefully arranged narrative, therefore, shows us the populace,

> God's pamper'd people, whom, debauched with ease,
> No king could govern, nor no God could please . . .
>   (47–48).

They are "Adam-wits," and one may think of the traditional view of Adam, that had lately been presented once more by Milton, as a man of all-encompassing intuitive wisdom. These are rather the "headstrong, moody, murm'ring race" about to fall or fallen: ignoble savages who

> led their wild desires to woods and caves,
> And thought that all but savages were slaves (55–56).

We have shifted from a state of nature as energetic self-fulfillment to a state of nature as restless self-assertion, whimsical arrogance, and competition. Dryden moves back in the Old Testament from David to the career of Moses and gives us a people who dream of the ultimate liberties of a republic (i.e., "State"):

> Now wonder'd why so long they had obey'd
> An idol monarch which their hands had made;
> Thought they might ruin him they could create,
> Or melt him to that golden calf, a State (63–66).

The obliviousness of this faction to the claims of "divine right" and the patriarchal authority of the king (recently asserted anew in Sir Robert Filmer's posthumous work, *Patriarcha*, 1680) prepares us for Absalom's disloyalty to his father and his God. The energies presented with calculated ambiguity at the opening of the poem have become frenetic and uncreative; the very claim by the headstrong Jews that they have created the monarch is a sign of their destructive self-engrossment. They are confident of their own powers to generate a social order; yet their very nature is the denial of order. What has seemed genial in David and more doubtful in Absalom is clearly debased in the rebellious subjects; if David's energy is to be reclaimed, it must be transformed and purged.

Dryden's satirical task, as it is Pope's in *The Dunciad*, is to make the populace and its leaders at once contemptible as individuals and awesome in the mass. We can despise the calculation of mercenary priests, but the turbulent passion they control in their less thoughtful adherents creates an image of terrifying power ready to be let loose. Dryden can reduce to luxurious greed the doctrine of transubstantiation:

Such sav'ry deities must needs be good,
As serv'd at once for worship and for food (120–21).

The power of such dogma over the multitude—"swallow'd in the mass, unchew'd and crude" (113)—fills out the threat of a barbarous energy all the more frightening for its mindless readiness to believe. Such a people is prey to rumors of plot and counterplot: the Jesuits can mingle with them and arouse sedition; the Whig opportunists can make of the Jesuits' activity a spectral Popish Plot. The anti-Catholic forces are born of the same folly and cunning as those they accuse; the state has become a maelstrom of "factions," whose common motive is the quest for power, disguised in slogans and pretenses.

Dryden is drawing upon the vision of Hell Milton had consummately defined a short time before in *Paradise Lost*. Milton made of the fallen angels a near-allegorical presentation of the sins of man—the deceitfulness of Beelzebub, the ignoble sloth and guile of Belial, the despairing rage of Moloch, the coarse materialization of the spirit of Mammon; and, of course, the pride of Satan, who at once heads and includes all these powers. Milton makes them formidable even as he denies them ultimate power. They assimilate the appearances of classical heroism and humanism (their obduracy, their foren-

sic skill, the splendor of their great temple). But the poem itself overthrows such power by measuring it against the power
to submit, against the self-conquest (which is a conquest of
just these hellish forces) within man, and against the final
heroism of Man-in-Christ. (The debates about whether Adam
or the Messiah is the hero of *Paradise Lost* make clear that it
is Man who is the hero in so far as he can become Christlike
and absorb the Messiah into himself.)

Dryden's world in *Absalom and Achitophel* is described in
metaphors that evoke the geography of Hell (at once internal
and external):

> For, as when raging fevers boil the blood,
> The standing lake soon floats into a flood
> And ev'ry hostile humor, which before
> Slept quiet in its channels, bubbles o'er;
> So several factions from this first ferment
> Work up to foam, and threat the government (136–41).

Their power to rebel is not due to the permissive will of God,
as in Milton's poem, but to the "fatal mercy" of David—the
besetting weakness we have already seen in his indulgence
of Absalom.

Milton's Satan is divided between Dryden's two titular figures. The dark side that we see in all its frustrate pride and
flailing desperation at the opening of the fourth book of *Paradise Lost* is embodied in Achitophel. The splendid Son of
Morning, the fallen Lucifer, still bright with angelic power,
but riddled with the self-deception and filial ingratitude that
pride exacts, is suggested in Absalom. Dryden is too much the
satirist to allow the baseness and the splendor their full tragic
mixture; he gives us the fury of Achitophel first and lets us
see it gain gradual control of the more virtuous Absalom. The
effect is less brilliantly ironic than Milton's, but no one has
ever wondered whether Absalom or Achitophel were the hero
of Dryden's poem. Dryden does not neglect the tragic element,
but he contains it within a satiric framework that limits its
scope.

This framework is, first of all, the heroic couplet. Never
before had the couplet done what it does in the portrait of
Achitophel:

> Sagacious, bold, and turbulent of wit;
> Restless, unfix'd in principles and place;
> In pow'r unpleas'd, impatient of disgrace:

> A fiery soul, which, working out its way,
> Fretted the pigmy body to decay,
> And o'er-inform'd the tenement of clay (152–58).

One can only point to the splendid descent of the vowels in the first line; the wonderful linking by sound of *wit* and *un-fix'd,* or of *in pow'r unpleas'd* with *principles and place;* the nice ambiguity of *impatient*—unable to endure, but also hurrying eagerly upon; or again of *working out its way,* with its suggestion of both the discipline of a Way and the headlong rush of escaping vapors. The triplet catches the energy of the soul; it is no longer the Aristotelian soul which is the ordering form of body and mind; it has become a travesty of the Christian soul which seeks to free itself from the prison of the flesh. The *pigmy body* plays upon the diminutive figure of the actual Shaftesbury and makes it a symbol of the human limits that all ambition defies and bursts. And the *fiery soul* calls up all at once, in ironic blend, the mystic's erotic adoration of the God with whom he would be one, the feverish human ambition of a man who defines himself in the act of breaking limits, and finally the damnation of the fallen angels, caught in the fires of Hell that are the outward form of their own restless pride. It is one of those passages that says concisely what only tiresome effort can unfold.

Again, the famous lines that follow play upon that favorite Augustan ambiguity—greatness seen in opposition to goodness, vehemence in opposition to calm, the unruly motion of the comet in contrast to the stable order of the planets:

> Great wits are sure to madness near allied,
> And thin partitions do their bounds divide;
> Else why should he, with wealth and honor blest,
> Refuse his age the needful hours of rest;
> Punish a body which he could not please;
> Bankrupt of life, yet prodigal of ease? (163–68.)

Here the opening lines of the poem begin to earn their full importance. David's "vigorous warmth" finds its concubines and brides and produces a handsome son, however treacherous he may become. But Achitophel's crippled, aging body can no longer contain his fire; his son is the mere casual by-product of those "huddled notions" that he now begets. Dryden looks ahead to the pattern Swift was to trace later in *A Tale of a Tub;* when the emperor's sexual passion is frustrated, the blocked semen shoots up as vapor into his brain and fathers dreams of conquest. The greatness of human ambition becomes a sordid displacement of natural vitality; the bankruptcy of "life" produces the passion of ambition, the replacement of external power for internal. David's sexuality, his possession of a body he can please, is a sign of comparative health, for all its profligacy.

Significantly, Achitophel's fury is possible only in a man of strictness and rigor. Like Shakespeare's Angelo in *Measure for Measure,* he has been a conscientious judge; like Angelo, he has given way completely once he has allowed himself to recognize his passion. But, unlike Angelo, Achitophel need not call those passions what they are; since they are political, they have innumerable disguises—most of all, the disguise of furthering "the people's will." Under the "patriot's all-atoning name," Achitophel can satisfy his personal ambition:

> So easy still it proves in factious times
> With public zeal to cancel private crimes (180–81).

Achitophel can righteously disdain to gather "golden fruit" but lend "the crowd his arm to shake the tree" (202–3). Defying his prince, he can, like Satan, hold up "the buckler of the people's cause"; and, like Satan, he can confirm rebellion in his followers with "jealousies and fears" of a fictitious tyrant. But what Achitophel still needs is a figurehead, a claimant whose own title will be weak enough to leave the monarchy dependent on the people's power. The pretense of a just claim for an illegitimate son in the disguise for the complete overthrow of monarchy, and the advocacy of the people's will against their true monarch is the disguise for Achitophel's own passion—destructive and ambitious, eager to undo and uncreate.

The temptation of Absalom is, as I have said, really the emergence of the other side of Milton's Satan. As Achitophel, serpentlike, "sheds his venom," the venom takes the form of impossible flattery. He offers Absalom a Messianic role, and his appeal involves a travesty of biblical prophecy: Absalom's birth has been signalized by a star of Bethlehem; he will become a "second Moses," the "dawning day" of the "sacred prophets' rage," or, in the words of Joel (2:28), the young men's visions, and the old men's dreams! "Thee, Savior, thee, the nation's vows confess." Achitophel stirs him with every temptation he knows, but finally with the one he himself values most: instead of the "barren praise" to be won by inglorious virtue, Absalom can have "solid power."

The process by which Achitophel calls forth the rebel in

Absalom splits the image of evil into its two aspects: primordial discontent, pride, and restlessness; corrupted virtue and
tarnished beauty. These are two aspects of Milton's Satan:
the second is shown to us at the outset of *Paradise Lost* but
gives way to the first. Here, by showing us the first working
upon the second in a process of overt and rapid temptation,
Dryden colors the tragic fall of Absalom with an element
of fatuity. In *Paradise Lost* Satan's original fall is left mysterious, and his temptation of others is given only in fragments of impressive eloquence. But Dryden collapses the process into a scene whose transparency and brevity make
Absalom an object of satire. Once he has become Achitophel's
instrument, Absalom is surrounded by a constellation of obvious fools and knaves. Like Milton's fallen angels, they represent the dimensions of the total evil that is embodied in the
threatened rebellion. But they approach the transparent mon-
strousness of the Seven Deadly Sins in Spenser's allegorical
House of Pride; for Absalom to accept their cause is proof of
a nature not only below good but below good sense.

Absalom's struggles in his temptation provide the first full
tribute to David's rectitude, both intrinsically as a man and
symbolically as a monarch:

> The faith's defender, and mankind's delight;
> Good, gracious, just, observant of the laws;
> And Heav'n by wonders has espous'd his cause. . . .
> Mild, easy, humble, studious of our good;
> Enclin'd to mercy, and averse from blood;
> If mildness ill with stubborn Israel suit,
> His crime is God's beloved attribute (318–20, 325–28).

Even more, Absalom accepts filial obligation. The people
might claim liberty if David were a tyrant (as he is not); but,
even then, "what was right in them were crime in me." But
Absalom cannot bear this much reality; as he feels his own
rebellion mount, he laments the power of "fate." He must be
freed at once of obligation and responsibility:

> Yet O that fate, propitiously enclin'd,
> Had rais'd my birth, or had debas'd my mind . . .
> I find, I find my mounting spirits bold . . .
> My soul disclaims the kindred of her earth;
> And, made for empire, whispers me within,
> Desire of greatness is a godlike sin
>   (363–64, 367, 370–72).

So another fiery soul frets its pigmy tenement of clay, and

the volatility of the rebellious spirit triumphs. At this point Absalom is close to the posture of Dryden's heroes in the plays; but his claim to that posture is belied by his passivity under Achitophel's influence and by the acknowledged obligation he rejects. And the following speech by Achitophel descends to a Machiavellian cunning that dismisses both the "divine right" of the monarch and the claims of the father:

> Nor let his love enchant your generous mind;
> 'Tis Nature's trick to propagate her kind.
> Our fond begetters, who would never die,
> Love but themselves in their posterity (423–26).

All of the naturalistic zest of the opening lines has now given way to a salacious cunning: from a generous and expansive freedom, it contracts to cheap calculation. Now "self-defense is Nature's eldest law" (458); we have moved from a robust primitivism to something darker and more cruel. In contrast, the natural generosity of David has now become sanctified as humility and mercy. The ambiguous natural "love" of the opening lines has split off into David's charity and Absalom's lust for power. The speaker of the poem invokes again the tragic view Absalom entertained as he fell, but it soon descends to a bitter irony. He may "lament" rather than "accuse," but Absalom is ready to "popularly prosecute the Plot" (490), a clear echo of his own earlier self-reproach:

> Why then should I, encouraging the bad,
> Turn rebel and run popularly mad? (334–36.)

It is necessary to dwell a moment longer on the matter of filial disobedience. Filmer's *Patriarcha* was a fantastic work in some ways, easily ridiculed by Locke in his *First Treatise of Civil Government,* but it raised serious questions about the nature of political authority. In tracing that authority back to the biblical patriarchs, Filmer made clear that society was not held together simply by the free consent of its members. "Society," as Peter Laslett puts it, "was not an intellectual construct at all, its members had not created it by taking thought, it was a given, natural phenomenon." If, as Filmer held, "authority could be exercised without consent, if in fact it was perpetually being so exercised, then there must be some other source of obligation. This other sort of obligation could only be by nature, not by choice, and observation showed that it was patriarchal."[4]

One may think in passing of how brilliantly Milton uses the

second half of the second book of *Paradise Lost*—once the "great consult" is completed and Satan departs from Hell—to uncover the weaknesses of Hell before he moves to Heaven. The fallen angels who remain behind, unconsoled by Satan's public speech, resort to fruitless diversions (all of man's great achievements—valor, art, philosophy, discovery—now become diversions, Pascal's *divertissements*) as they try to avoid recognition of their pain and their plight. Satan himself moves to an ironic recognition scene with his hideous offspring, Sin and Death, and his lofty angelic disdain must suffer the shock of accepting their ugliness as his own. Finally, he must form his league with Chaos itself, promising to return God's newly created cosmos to primal disorder; the sheer negation of Satan's role is exposed and finally fixed as he moves toward the lucid order of the created world.

In the same way, Dryden has gradually reduced all the pretensions of Achitophel and Absalom and, even more, reduced to nonsense their pseudo-rational appeals to the people. When he moves on to David's followers, the contrasts—as in Milton's Heaven and Hell—are strictly enforced. Beside the line that describes Shimei's cold cellars and hot brains we can place this rhetorical echo in the line on Barzillai: "Large was his wealth, but larger was his heart." Beside Achitophel's lumplike son we can place Barzillai's "fruitful issue." Beside Absalom's mounting rebellious spirits we can place the true ascent of Barzillai's son's, dead in battle:

> Now, free from earth, the disencumber'd soul
> Mounts up, and leaves behind the clouds and starry pole
> (850–51).

Beside the cunning and intrigue of men like Corah we can place the candor of those who practiced "the court" but "not the courtier's art," of men like Adriel, "True to his prince, but not a slave of state." These men are "frugal," not with their own wealth as in Shimei's miserliness, but with the royal funds that are needed to save the king from dependence. They warn David of his error and danger, but they see "their Maker in their master," too, as David finally speaks out.

Instead of an epic action, we have in the rest of the poem two telling contrasts: the opposed catalogues of Achitophel's supporters and David's; and the paired speeches—Absalom's demagogic address to the crowd and David's final speech from the royal throne. The action is internalized; all its potentialities are contained in the characters. The brilliant portraits

of the rebels are compounded of fierce impotence, mercenary
zeal, and hypocrisy. We move from the volatility of Zimri
("everything by starts, and nothing long") to the miserliness
of Shimei ("Cool was his kitchen, tho' his brains were hot"),
to the outrageous false witness of Corah ("The spirit caught
him up, the Lord knows where"), or, in Miltonic terms, from
Moloch to Mammon to Belial. And at last we move back to
Absalom, now "bowing popularly low"—mimicking Satan's
"foul descent" into "bestial slime" as he becomes serpentlike:

> Thus form'd by nature, furnish'd out with arts,
> He glides unfelt into their secret hearts (692–93).

All of Absalom's triviality is caught in the neat juxtaposition
of his rhetoric with a wry stage-direction: " 'Take then my
tears' (with that he wip'd his eyes)." The travesty of genuine feeling and virtue swells into a language of "names"
("That always cheat and always please") and into the gestures of a "pageant shew." The claims of the popular will are
expressed by men who are cynically making the people their
instruments; "And peace itself is war in masquerade." At this
point the voice of the speaker in the poem becomes most
explicitly didactic. The cool irony and the contemptuous invective are dropped; the fools must be made to see, to penetrate the masquerade they accept as reality. In seeking to dissolve the monarchy, they are destroying all law. In asserting
"might," they are bringing back the intolerable state of nature that Hobbes had presented—"nature's state, where all have
right to all" (794).

David's last speech, with its modest assertion of royal power
and its rejection of demagogic appeals, is the culmination of
the process of purgation we have seen his image undergo. He
speaks out of suffering, as father and king, reluctant in his
mercy to exercise his power; but he also sees the folly of Absalom, "gulled with a patriot's name,"

> The people's brave, the politician's tool;
> Never was patriot yet, but was a fool (867–68).

And he scornfully foresees the self-destructiveness of rebellion.
The poem closes with a Messianic vision, echoed from Virgil's
Fourth Eclogue, of a restored harmony: "And willing nations
knew their lawful lord." The satire rises to the full height of
prophecy.

The Medal (1682) is a simpler poem, as brilliant in its

language, but without the scale of allusion or the depth of characterization of *Absalom*. The tone is one of easier contempt, and the logic of the couplet is more consistently exploited to close in upon folly and cant. I want to consider two aspects of it that lead into the problems of the religious poems. One is the theme of relativism. In a world where the multitude (Plato's "great beast") rules, their power confers infallibility—it "sets the people in the papal chair" (87). Dryden creates the ultimate vertigo as the "arbitrary crowd." Swirling in unrest, it controls all political and religious sanctions, wrests Scripture at its will, and deposes God as well as king—

> God were not safe; his thunder could they shun,
> He should be forced to crown another son (216–17).

This is the clearest inversion of order, the counterpart of the heroic defiance of divinity by the heroes of the plays, but—as in the case of Absalom—a defiance without the authority of a greatness of spirit. Instead, it is a tyranny of louts and madmen released by Shaftesbury.

More interesting is the second theme: the kind of God Dryden gives to Shaftesbury. The satanic Achitophel is, in this poem, a rabid and salacious "pander," himself poxed by debauchery, infecting the nation until it has become mad. But Shaftesbury's cold egocentricity survives in the midst of his passions, and Dryden contrasts his selfish God with that of his insane Calvinistic followers:

> . . . thine (if thou hast any) must be one
> That lets the world and humankind alone;
> A jolly god, that passes hours too well
> To promise heav'n or threaten us with hell;
> That unconcern'd can at rebellion sit,
> And wink at crimes he did himself commit (277–82).

This looks ahead to Pope's Dulness, and her free-thinking followers' God,

> Wrapp'd up in self, a God without a thought,
> Regardless of our merit or default
> (*Dunciad*, IV, 485–86).

But it looks back as well to the corrupt sensuality of the Emperor in *Aureng-zebe:*

> Were I a god, the drunken globe should roll,
> The little emmets with the human soul

> Care for themselves, while at my ease I sat,
> And second causes did the work of fate;
> Or, if I would take care, that care should be
> For wit that scorned the world, and lived like me (III, i).

Here again we confront the meaningless world, a world drained of meaning by men for whom nothing has reality but their own pleasure.

IV. The Religious Poems

Dryden's *Religio Laici* (1682) is an attempt to achieve the Augustan balance that is one characteristic way of meeting Pascal's paradoxes. It is a position that accepts many of the painful truths Pascal reveals, and yet tries to create a rational order in the face of reason's limitations. What Dryden seeks to do is defend a religion that can make do without infallibility.[5] He goes about systematically disarming the Deist's trust in the absolute rightness of human reason, the Catholic's trust in the Church as infallible interpreter of revealed truth, and the Dissenter's trust in the infallibility of the individual conscience guided by Scripture. The central problem is the Bible itself: at once the voice of God, but an ambiguous and imperfectly recorded voice. The Bible becomes the word of a *deus absconditus;* we cannot do without it, we can never be wholly sure we live by it. But unlike Pascal, Dryden can make do with an imperfect solution and accept it without alternate revulsion from and surrender to the world. Dryden does not despair of the order of mind, and he need not as a result fluctuate between life in an order of charity and life in an order of the flesh. The mind creates no order of its own, in Dryden's view, but the mind can give shape to whatsoever of the order of charity can be made the world's concern.

The famous opening lines stress the precarious but valuable function of reason:

> Dim as the borrow'd beams of moons and stars
> To lonely, weary, wand'ring travelers
> Is Reason to the soul: and, as on high
> Those rolling fires discover but the sky,
> Not light us here; so Reason's glimmering ray
> Was lent, not to assure our doubtful way,
> But guide us upward to a better day.
> And as those nightly tapers disappear
> When day's bright lord ascends our hemisphere;

So pale grows Reason at Religion's sight;
So dies, and so dissolves in supernatural light.

As I read this passage, it insists no less than Pascal on the inadequacy of life as we know it simply by reason. We remain "lonely, weary, wand'ring travelers," without a clearly marked way; the only guidance we receive is the assurance of another order of existence which we know only when we transcend this darker world. But reason can lead us toward that transcendence.

Pope has a similar passage (expanded from Horace, Epistles I, vi):

This vault of air, this congregated ball,
Self-centered sun, and stars that rise and fall,
There are, my friend! whose philosophic eyes
Look through, and trust the Ruler with his skies,
To him commit the hour, the day, the year,
And view the dreadful All without a fear (5–10).

The transition is again between orders, between the experience of the "mighty maze" and the assurance that it is "not without a plan." In both, the union of reason and faith is celebrated, not the simple overthrow of reason. So, in Dryden, religion provides us with "supernatural light," but the tenor of the whole poem insists upon our seeing that such light is clear and certain only in those needful truths that men must be humble enough to accept as sufficient.

There have been those heroes of reason "whose lamp shone brighter"; but all their speculation ends, like that of Milton's fallen angels, "in wandering mazes lost." They fall, as in Pascal, between equally valid hypotheses: the Aristotelian unmoved mover and the Epicurean "noble work of chance." What has seemed for a moment a less doubtful way proves to be only "enchanted ground." So, too, both virtue and pleasure prove insufficient ends to govern man or content him; they are "leaky vessels which no bliss could keep." We return to the imagery of the opening lines, but with a difference. The heavenly bodies roll in majestic order—a "starry dance" about a "great luminary" (as we have seen in Milton). The "wiser madmen" who hope to create such an order in their lives by the power of reason achieve only futile revolutions:

Thus anxious thoughts in endless circles roll,
Without a center where to fix the soul:
In this wild maze their vain endeavors end.
How can the less the greater comprehend?

Or finite reason reach Infinity?
For what could fathom God were more than He
(36–41).

Dryden's "fathom" anticipates Pope's "presume not God to scan." In both cases the arrogance of the measuring reason is scorned and reduced; the difficult acceptance of a limited knowledge is imposed upon man, and out of the acceptance comes the possibility of hope.

The satire on presumption finds its contemporary target in the Deist, who "thinks he stands on firmer ground" (no doubtful way, no vanishing enchanted ground for him) and reasons his way to a vision of divine accountancy:

This general worship is to PRAISE and PRAY,
One part to borrow blessings, one to pay;
And when frail nature slides into offense,
The sacrifice for crimes is penitence (50–53).

The last line makes it all seem superbly easy, and the Deist goes further: since the good is not visibly rewarded or the evil punished on earth,

Our reason prompts us to a future state . . . (58).

To the extent that these are indeed "godlike notions," they hardly confirm the Deist's pride. What he takes to be his own strength and wit, the product of his own mind, is, in fact, "dropp'd from Heaven, and of a nobler kind." The couplet closes in upon him with its own elegant logic:

Hence all thy natural worship takes the source,
'Tis Revelation what thou think'st Discourse (70–71).

The nice weighting of syllables and dissonance of vowels in these last two nouns pivot on the wonderfully emphatic "think'st." Rarely has pride in discursive reason suffered so neat a sapping operation.

All the presumption of "fathom" is picked up again. Is the Deist naturally so much wiser than all the "giant wits" of antiquity (they were "wiser madmen" a few lines back)? The fundamental grossness of the Deist vision of reward and punishment is shown up by a material image of "sacrifice" such as the Greeks and Romans performed:

If sheep and oxen could atone for men,
Ah! at how cheap a rate the rich might sin! (89–90.)

As we look back from this to the Deist's proud deduction that "the sacrifice for crimes is penitence," we see the emptiness of those terms. Dryden plays upon the brute suffering of sheep and oxen:

> The guiltless victims groan'd for their offense,
> And cruelty and blood was penitence (87–88).

The irony has been elaborately woven: so far as the Deist talks sense, he *must* be prompted by God, for his incomprehension of what he says when he talks of penitence exposes his pride and folly. We are close by now to the tone of the voice speaking from the whirlwind to Job:

> Dar'st thou, poor worm, offend Infinity?
> And must the terms of peace be given by thee? (93–94.)

The accountancy figures give way. God may seem what man chooses to make Him, a powerless bookkeeper who compliantly tallies the price man sets on his own sins. But if He is a true God, man can never hope to set his own rates. To offend Infinity is to incur an incalculable debt:

> A mulct thy poverty could never pay
> Had not eternal wisdom found the way
> And with celestial wealth supplied thy store:
> His justice makes the fine, His mercy quits the score.
> See God descending in thy human frame;
> Th' offended suff'ring in th' offender's name . . .
> (103–8).

The Deist is confronted with the mystery of the Incarnation, and the metaphor shifts, as the Deist is left behind, from debt to sickness, from payment to cure. It is a beautiful demonstration of what reason cannot do and yet can discover: the very toppling of man's arrogance discloses the hope that is offered him. We may think of George Herbert's parabola of outrage in "The Collar"; its descent from loud protestation to quiet attention as a voice calls, "Child!"

The ironic overthrow of self-sufficient reason leads us to the "supernatural light" of the Bible which embodies, in a style "that speaks no less than God in every line," a rule of life defying the claims of natural appetite or interest. The doctrine itself becomes martyr-like in its surmounting of the world in an order of charity:

> Unfed by nature's soil, in which it grows:
> Cross to our interests, curbing sense and sin;
> Oppress'd without, and undermin'd within,

> It thrives thro' pain; its own tormentors tires;
> And with a stubborn patience still aspires (159–63).

Its transcendence of the world's values is seen in God's "boundless mercy"; for the order of charity defies the limits of rational accountability.

The status of the Bible has now become the central problem of the poem. It has been transmitted through fallible men, as Father Simon's *Critical History of the Old Testament* (1678; Eng. trans., 1682) has shown; it is enmeshed in "interest, Church, and gain." One cannot prove its validity by recourse to oral tradition, such as the Catholic Church has taken in its rule of faith; an "omniscient Church" if it existed would replace the Bible itself—proof in itself that it does not. One must somehow trust that "God would not leave mankind without a way," that the Scriptures must be "sufficient, clear, entire" in all necessary things. We have entered a realm of faith and probability; we can have no infallible authority. The oldest oral traditions may be comparatively the most trustworthy, but it is to the Bible itself that we must finally look for all we can hope to know:

> It speaks itself, and what it does contain,
> In all things needful to be known, is plain (368–69).

The bare simplicity of these terms is telling: the poem opened with a display of how little, after all, we need to know. The task of man is not to invent a way but to content himself with what is given.

In contrast to this humility, we are shown the sophisticated authority of the Church; and the mercantile figures are now flagrant. The Church locks up the Scripture and parcels it out at retail in a seller's market:

> As needy men take money, good or bad;
> God's word they had not, but the priest's they had.
> Yet, whate'er false conveyances they made,
> The lawyer still was certain to be paid.
> In those dark times they learn'd their knack so well,
> That by long use they grew infallible . . . (382–87).

This cool systematizing of avarice; the gradual sophistication of words until they have only effect, not meaning (as "infallible" here)—all this Dryden presents with an appreciative mock-gravity. And if the Catholic Church shows us the order of the flesh usurping charity through rational cunning, the

Reformation gives us the order of flesh in all of its naked brutality:

> The tender page with horny fists was gall'd
> And he was gifted most that loudest bawl'd. . . .
> While crowds unlearn'd, with rude devotion warm,
> About the sacred viands buzz and swarm,
> The fly-blown text creates a crawling brood;
> And turns to maggots what was meant for food
>   (404–5, 417–20).

We have, then, in both Catholic and Protestant, the anomalous situation of the order of charity hopelessly confounded with the order of flesh; the word of God descends only to be misused. Yet Dryden seeks a way to make this descent more than inevitable destruction or travesty; it is, after all, the reason—fallible as it is—that can sift truth from error. Father Simon's *Critical History of the Old Testament,* which exposed the false accretions and contradictions of the text, is the model of what each man's reason must perform:

> So nicely ponder'd, yet so strongly wrought,
> As nature's height and art's last hand requir'd:
> As much as man could compass, uninspir'd (245–47).

The reason's own powers are limited, but its "sifting care," when applied to religion, can free us of either a despair with the world or an arrogant desire "beyond our pow'r to know."

Bredvold tells us that the solution of the *Religio Laici* "merely substituted a judicious and learned individualism for the extravagant individualism of the Private Spirit" (*Intellectual Milieu,* p. 126). This seems to me an important substitution; "judicious and learned" are terms of weight. We may think of Swift's remark: "I am bound in all opinions to believe according to my own impartial reason; which I am bound to inform and improve, as far as my capacity and opportunities will permit" (*Thoughts on Religion*); or, again, in his sermon *On the Trinity,* "Every man is bound to follow the rules and directions of that measure of reason which God hath given him; and indeed he cannot do otherwise, if he will be sincere, or act like a man." Dryden has insisted in the poem on the need for one's own conviction:

> For my salvation must its doom receive,
> Not from what OTHERS but what *I* believe (303–4).

In a crucial passage, he dissents from Athanasius who has, like the Deist, tried to fathom the depths of God's mercy. He surrenders his "private Reason" only where he must, in those "points not clearly known" or "obscure," to the authority of his church and of public order. What seems to me important is the mediating role that Dryden gives to the order of mind; it does not, as it does in Pascal's paradoxes, necessarily harden into a self-subsistent rationalism (though it may in the Deist), and it makes possible a way of coming to terms at once and in the world with both charity and the flesh.

As the title of *Religio Laici* makes clear, the poem deals with the faith of an individual; its solution is the "precarious poise" (the phrase is Bredvold's) of the individual mind between authority and the private will, the poise of humble content with faith and probability as opposed to the rival forms of dogmatic infallibility. The ultimate authority is the Bible, and the final judge of its meaning is the individual mind, aware of deceptions from without and within, seeking to limit its appetite for more knowledge than is needful. The institution is accepted chiefly for its ensuring of "common quiet"; its traditions are respected but critically tested. The poem does not concern itself with the plight of the institution in the world; it does not directly enter that realm where religion and politics interfuse.

In *The Hind and the Panther* (1687) Dryden, now a Roman Catholic, departs from the position of the *Religio Laici* and shows its inadequacy as the principle of a Church. The Church, once it enters the world, must also enter into political existence, especially in a country that has both an established religion and a measure of toleration for rival sects. In the Panther Dryden gives us a brilliant account of an established church that has lost doctrinal stability through its tenets of compromise, and must depend more and more heavily upon political power to replace its dogmatic strength. In a sense the problem is like that suggested in *Absalom and Achitophel:* to the extent that David is a weak king who depends upon personal esteem and the gratification of the people's desire, his legitimacy of power falls into question. To depend upon the people is to encourage belief in their sovereign will; only when David reasserts his divine sanction and assumes a stance that befits it can he re-establish a rule of right. The Panther (the Church of England) is an institution in a false position, and the brilliant irony of the poem plays upon her embarrassment as she veers between high aspirations and feline cunning, between the professed order of charity and the actual order of fleshly power.

The Hind (the Roman Catholic Church in England) triumphs by the very freedom of her position; she has been dispossessed of her regal power, to become strong in the only power that she now aspires to wield—the power of spirit. Her only ambition is for toleration; that selflessness, like her immortality, is a sign that she is not simply of the world by being in it. Well before the Panther is introduced, we are shown the telling contrast of the milk-white Hind and the savage beasts that surround her. The dialectic of the poem requires a seeming digression in the presentation of those beasts. As the Baptist Boar and the rationalistic Fox (Arian and Socinian) are introduced—as disparate as Milton's Moloch and Belial— the fundamental distinction upon which the poem rests can be drawn. It is the nature of these beasts, and the reason for their savagery, that they cannot accept a transcendent truth. The Baptist Boar makes "grace" his ideological instrument of rebellion; Reynard's rationalistic race thrives on blasphemy:

> and nature's King through nature's optics viewed.
> Revers'd, they view'd him lessen'd to their eye,
> Nor in an infant could a God descry (57–59).

At this point Dryden introduces the moving account of his own career and faith. His own belief in a God who hides in a blaze of glory becomes the central motive of the passage. The "blaze of glory" and the "abyss of light" in which he now conceives God contrast with the "wand'ring fires" and "false lights" of his earlier skepticism. His simple acceptance sets a note of humility and freedom from passion:

> Good life be now my task: my doubts are done:
> (What more could fright my faith, than Three in One?)
> Can I believe eternal God could lie
> Disguis'd in mortal mold and infancy? . . .
> Can I my reason to my faith compel,
> And shall my sight, and touch, and taste rebel?
> (77–80, 84–85.)

The problem Dryden is facing is the conflict between faith and the senses, a conflict in which the control of reason is at stake. The Arian-Socinian Reynard, the prototype of all rejection of transcendent truth and perversion of God's will into man's, represents the alliance of reason and the sense (or, in Pascalian terms, of mind and flesh) against the divine. Dry-

den's faith has brought mind into subservience to the divine
(as indeed it was in the *Religio Laici*):

> Reason by sense no more can understand;
> The game is play'd into another hand (126–27).

Dryden is, most of all, rejecting the position of Anglican
rationalism, which held that God could demand no act of
faith that contradicted the evidence of the senses—a key issue
in the matter of Transubstantiation. But he is not rejecting
reason; instead, he is claiming it, in the old metaphor of just
rule and usurpation, for its rightful ruler (much as he calls
Absalom to his father-king and away from a false demagogic
alliance with the rebellious multitude). If the Anglican can
accept the mysteries of the Trinity and the Incarnation, there
is no sound reason for his failing to accept Transubstantiation.

> And if he can, why all this frantic pain
> To construe what his clearest words contain,
> And make a riddle what He made so plain? (138–40.)

Dryden has reverted to the bare and simple terms of *Religio
Laici*, although there has been a shift in the matters that it is
needful to know. We have moved from moral doctrines to
sacramental mysteries, but the appeal is still to a humble contentment with what is plain. The mercantile figures come
back, too, but now they become a version of Pascal's wager:

> Both knave and fool the merchant we may call,
> To pay great sums, and to compound the small:
> For who would break with Heav'n, and would not break
>   for all?
> Rest then, my soul, from endless anguish freed:
> Nor sciences thy guide, nor sense thy creed.
> Faith is the last ensurer of thy bliss;
> The bank above must fail before the venture miss
>   (143–49).

The image of the merchant-adventurer has been prepared
for earlier, when Dryden urges that we surrender our reason
to faith and venture from the shore (the shore of sense experience to which the timid cling), "And with a better guide a
better world explore." As in Pascal, the appeal is calculated
especially for the man of reason, and the mercantile figure
takes account of the self-interest that is the irreducible fact of
human nature. The order of charity will never reveal itself
adequately enough to persuade the sensualist or the rationalist;
yet upon the risk of trusting in its existence depend all the bliss

and repose that man most seeks. Dryden is playing upon the unstable nature of reason, divided between two alliances; in leaving sciences and sense behind, it need not cease to be reason.

This becomes clear when Dryden calls for the toleration of dissenters, both Protestant and Catholic. Tyranny is appropriate for beasts, but

> Man only of a softer mold is made,
> Not for his fellows' ruin, but their aid:
> Created kind, beneficent and free,
> The noble image of the Deity (247–50).

God distinguished man from beasts by unlocking

> the sacred treasures of his breast;
> And mercy mix'd with reason did impart,
> One to his head, the other to his heart:
> Reason to rule, but mercy to forgive:
> The first is law, the last prerogative (258–62).

As the Houyhnhnms reveal to us in their inspection of Gulliver, man is a weak and defenseless animal precisely because he does not need "horns of arbitrary might," claws to seize, or four feet to pursue. As in Pope's *Essay on Man,* it is from the "embrace he gives" that man's strength arises.

This is man in a state to which Christian charity can restore him. It is a state that *can* be recovered and that justifies the mercy of the "British lion"—James II's indulgence to Dissenters in 1687. Dryden is once more insisting upon a control of mind and flesh by charity, and setting it, as in *Absalom,* in dialectical contrast with a control of the outward forms (which are all that survive) of charity and mind by the cult of power (here, the repressiveness of an established church sustained by political power).

Having made the crucial distinctions, Dryden can return to the bestiality of the radical Protestants—the compound of Socinian Fox and Calvinist Wolf in the wild Dog—

> And some wild curs, who from their masters ran,
> Abhorring the supremacy of man,
> In woods and caves the rebel-race began (194–96).

Like Swift's Yahoos they are degenerate creatures, once domestic and now savage; like the multitude in *Absalom* they are natural energy perverted and debased ("And thought that all but savages were slaves"). They finally descend, like the dunces in Pope's great satire, to mere "matter, put in motion."

Dryden's object is to establish firmly the lowest common denominator of Protestant dissent before he introduces the Anglican Panther, for the instability of her power throws her into the company of the other beasts and allies her with them. Dryden prepares for the introduction of the Panther by a savage account of the Reformation in England; he shows the Church of England introduced, in Samuel Butler's phrase, "by our King Harry's codpiece":

> a lawless prince
> By luxury reform'd incontinence;
> By ruins, charity; by riots, abstinence.
> Confessions, fasts, and penance set aside;
> O, with what ease we follow such a guide,
> Where souls are starv'd, and senses gratified! (361–66.)

It is once more the reduction of professed spiritual claims to sense, of false charity to pampered flesh: "All would be happy at the cheapest rate" (375).

The crux of the poem is the ironic characterization of the Panther—"a creature of a double kind." She exhibits outward majesty of demeanor and "decent discipline," but the discipline turns out to be a grace of manner rather than of character. Beneath the shallow elegance and queenly condescension is a latent fierceness. She becomes a brilliant object of satire: a "mere mock queen" whose very gestures of authority betray her weakness. She must scamper to drink before the other beasts so as to sustain the appearance of being accorded priority; she becomes a bad actress who vainly tries to cover the disrespect her subjects show—

> Rul'd while she rules, and losing every hour
> Her wretched remnants of precarious pow'r (509–10).

The "lady of the spotted muff" keeps up appearances as best she can, but her fundamental lack of authority reveals itself in each protestation. Her straddling interpretation of the Eucharist (in the Twenty-eighth Article), resolute on compromise, ends in nonsense. She becomes, therefore, a failure in both the orders of charity and mind; in not knowing who she really is, she must be at once fierce and fearful. The Hind, in contrast, has the simplicity and assurance of one who does not need power, who trusts her own rightness and can afford to be charitable. When the Lion (James II) allows the Hind to drink at the stream, all the savage beasts are filled with awe at her beauty. Her beauty is inherently radiant ("As to be loved needs only to be seen"); it needs none of the desperate enhancement of dress or gesture that the Panther gives hers. The Hind's power clearly is of another order; it both terrifies and enrages the Panther.

The "lonely cell" of the Hind, a cottage with "plain fare," is opened hospitably to the Panther, a creature "so nicely bred, and so unused to fast." The pastoral reception of the great lady is a summons to candor of heart and mind that a worldly lady can never permit herself:

> A hearty welcome at a homely board
> Was freely hers; and to supply the rest,
> An honest meaning, and an open breast (1248–50).

The pastoral retreat ("a shed / With hoary moss and winding ivy spread") is like the simple home of Baucis and Philemon (Dryden was to translate Ovid's account of them later), associated in many paintings with the Supper at Emmaus, the counterpart of the improbable flesh into which God descends.[6] As the Hind says,

> . . . this poor abode
> Has oft receiv'd, and yet receives a god . . .
> This mean retreat did mighty Pan contain;
> Be emulous of him, and pomp disdain,
> And dare not to debase your soul to gain
> (1279–80, 1282–84).

The last line has the force of paradox, and the Panther's response is momentary awe. For a while the beast subsides (and, tellingly, in order to subside, she "pacified her tail, and lick'd her frothy jaws"). But the savagery of the Panther—who has learned to couple with the Calvinist Wolf—is always present. For all the Hind's "plain simplicity of love" and for all the promising communion of their feast, the Panther's malice reveals itself:

> Disdain, with gnawing envy, fell despite,
> And canker'd malice stood in open sight;
> Ambition, int'rest, pride without control,
> And jealousy, the jaundice of the soul;
> Revenge, the bloody minister of ill,
> With all the lean tormentors of the will (1364–69).

The "forc'd civilities," and "affected kindness" drop away under stress, and are resumed only out of policy. The Hind, in turn, is stirred by libel to indignation and satire, but disdains to score against the Panther's futile deceptions.

Dryden's treatment of the Panther is reminiscent of the satirical beast fable in Spenser's *Mother Hubbard's Tale,* and anticipates Swift's reduction in *A Tale of a Tub* of the ideology of institutions to the motives of shabby charlatans. The fullness of characterization that Dryden gives the Panther is a way of fixing the stance of the Anglican Church more vividly and precisely than any argument might permit and provides a matrix in which all the Anglican arguments can be placed. The inconsistencies of the beast fable—so delightfully travestied by Matthew Prior and Charles Montague in *The Hind and the Panther Transversed* (1687)—provide an opportunity (which more than justifies them) of waking sleeping metaphors whenever they can be used to greatest effect. We think of the Panther as a pretentious lady and as mock queen for the most part, but her "sharpen'd paws" are always there to remind us of her double nature. In the closing fable-within-a-fable told by the Hind, the graces of the Panther are stripped away; we have an image of the Anglicans as salacious Doves, "Voracious birds, that hotly bill and breed"—

> Like harpies, they could scent a plenteous board;
> Then to be sure they never fail'd their lord;
> The rest was form, and bare attendance paid;
> They drunk, and eat, and grudgingly obey'd.
> The more they fed, they raven'd still for more
>   (2254–58).

Here, in the final fable, the satire is transposed to a harsher mode, the events become more overtly savage, the invective more fiercely cutting; the Doves still preserve the name of "so mild a kind," but they no longer maintain the high style of the Panther's regality. The fable of the Doves has its own brilliance, but its bold reductive simplicity depends for its force on Dryden's careful management of the double image of the Panther for the length of the poem. It is the plausibility of the Panther he catches there, and she must make her claim to the order of charity with at least a well-sustained speciousness.

Only the central pattern of the debate between Hind and Panther need concern us here. It is a pattern of constancy opposed to instability: the Hind is free of the temptations of the world (although not of responsibilities to it), and the Panther is their captive. As a result, the Panther's arguments, by their nature, must be tortured justifications of expediency:

> Who can believe what varies every day,
> Now ever was, nor will be at a stay? (607–8.)

In such an argument the key term always "From solid substance dwindles to a sound." Protestant interpreters of Scripture

> have whirl'd
> The tortur'd text about the Christian world (690–91).

"Squadrons of text" are marshaled in the "battle-royal of beliefs." There is no "last appeal":

> The word is then depos'd, and in this view
> You rule the Scripture, not the Scripture you (757–58).

In contrast, the Catholic Church remains "one solid shining diamond, / Not sparkles shatter'd into sects like you," and when she must enter the world to defy heresy:

> She stoops from heav'n and meets 'em halfway down,
> And with paternal thunder vindicates her crown
> (1108–9).

This baroque image fixes the True Church beyond the world, free of its changes and temptations. Her catholicity is pictured as missionary zeal:

> From east to west triumphantly she rides,
> All shores are water'd by her wealthy tides.
> The gospel sound, diffus'd from pole to pole,
> Where winds can carry, and where waves can roll;
> The selfsame doctrine of the sacred page
> Convey'd to ev'ry clime, in ev'ry age (1122–27).

The English on the other hand send forth criminals and whores to colonize:

> Those are the manufactures we export;
> And these the *missioners* our zeal has made:
> For, with my country's pardon be it said,
> Religion is the least of all our trade (1136–39).

The contrast of zeal and trade is strong. It is a pitting of the Roman Church against the English state, and it carries out the pattern of a disinterested, persecuted devotion and a profitable monopoly. The next stage of descent would be the impious tradesmen of Holland who enter Japanese markets on humiliating terms (after the anti-Christian uprising of 1667–68) and "Sell all of Christian to the very name" (1146). So, too, the Hind can catch the toleration of the Latitudinarians (a toleration much like that of *Religio Laici*) in a striking image:

> Your sons of breadth at home are much like these;
> Their soft and yielding metals run with ease:
> They melt, and take the figure of the mold,
> But harden and preserve it best in gold (1481–84).

The hardened image of formalized interest is the more tellingly frozen for the seeming warmth of the "soft and yielding metals." The hardness of the gold is one reversal of Anglican pretensions; another is the resort to secular power when the Sword of Mercy fails:

> You lay that pointless clergy-weapon by,
> And to the laws, your sword of justice, fly (992–93).

All of these images catch the inconstancy of the Panther's Church: it exists in time and the world, it submits spirit to gain, it does not brave "martyrdom" but falls back upon secular power. The blindness of will that sustains this course must be expressed in abuse of mind as well, and the Panther's disingenuous defense of Henry VIII serves as an example of her debasement of terms:

> . . . conscience, conscience would not let him rest,
> I mean, not till possess'd of her he lov'd,
> And old, uncharming Catherine was removed (1501–3).

In *The Hind and the Panther* satire becomes a means of celebration; the Hind is glorified by the exposure of the Panther, and the satire confers upon her the dignity the Panther loses.

III.

Shaftesbury: Order and Liberty

i. The Triumph of Liberty

Anthony Ashley Cooper, the Third Earl of Shaftesbury (1671–1713), was the grandson of the Whig zealot who was Dryden's Achitophel, and in his grandfather's household he was the pupil of the man he called his "friend and foster-father," John Locke.[1] To his grandfather's Whig principles, if not to his zeal, he remained loyal throughout his life; to his teacher's empirical philosophy he became in time openly hostile.

> 'Twas Mr. Locke that struck at all fundamentals, threw all order and virtue out of the world, and made the very idea of these (which are the same as those of God) *un-natural,* and without foundation in our minds. *Innate* is a word he poorly plays upon; the right word, though less used, is *connatural.* For what has birth or progress of the foetus out of the womb to do in this case? The question is not about the time the *ideas* entered, or the moment that one body came out of the other, but whether the constitution of man be such that, being adult and grown up, at such or such a time, sooner or later (no matter when) the idea and sense of order, administration, and a God, will not infallibly, inevitably, necessarily spring up in him (Rand, 403).

This was written in 1709, when Locke, from whom he "ever concealed [his] differences as much as possible," had been dead almost five years. Shaftesbury pays tribute to Locke's writings on politics, economics, and education, and he attests to Locke's "sincerity as a most zealous Christian and believer." But he recognizes that Locke "had more faith, and was more learned in modern wonder-writers"—he is referring to Locke's use of travel accounts for anthropological evidence against the existence of innate ideas—"than in ancient philosophy."

For Locke, "neither right nor wrong, virtue nor vice, are any thing in themselves; nor is there any trace or idea of them naturally imprinted on human minds. Experience and our catechism teach us all!" (Rand, 404.)

Shaftesbury's great cause was the defense of the Platonic and Stoic vision of Order, and of those immutable ideas within man that come to awareness in experience but are anterior to it. Without the predisposition to recognize and to love order, we should never know it. These ideas are as much a part of our nature as the instincts of animals are a part of theirs. "Harmony is harmony *by nature,* let particular ears be ever so bad, or let men judge ever so ill of music. So is architecture and its beauty the same, and founded in nature, let men's fancy be ever so *Gothic.* . . . The same is the case of virtue and honesty" (Rand, 416–17).

It is the innateness of disposition rather than idea that Shaftesbury defends; he wishes to claim authority for the ideas once they arise. No one but "modern and barbarous schoolmen" would claim that "the very philosophical propositions about right and wrong were innate." The question Locke fails to face is "whether the passion or affection towards society was natural and came of itself, or was taught by art, and was the product of a lucky hit of some first man who inspired and delivered down the prejudice" (Rand, 415). Shaftesbury's concern for the "social hypothesis"—the natural sociability of man—is central to his system of belief. The "connatural ideas" within man correspond to the Order of which he is part. They confirm and are confirmed by it; they give man a ground for morality in his nature itself, free him of dependence upon the revealed will of an arbitrary God, and relieve him of the relativism that sees all law as the arbitrary invention of man. Man's nature is not so disorderly that it requires surrender to any force that will control it, as in Pascal and Hobbes. "Liberty and Freedom" are "the only way and means . . . which God and Nature has made necessary and essential to his manly dignity and character" (*Several Letters . . . to a Young Man at the University,* 2d ed., 1732, p. 7).

The "triumph of liberty," the allegorical engraving that Shaftesbury commissioned for *The Moralists,* he chose to have appear in all three volumes of the second edition of his comprehensive work, the *Characteristics of Men, Manners, Opinions, Times, etc.: "as that piece [The Moralists] and that very subject (moral and political) is the hinge and bottom of

all three and of the whole work itself, it will well become
every title-page, and may well stand three times over" (Rand,
449). The idea of liberty raises the first of the many dialectical problems Shaftesbury must face. "Tyranny," he writes,
"can never be exercised, but by one who is already a slave."
This is the view Milton's Abdiel had taken in his denunciation
of Satan:

> Unjustly thou deprav'st it with the name
> Of Servitude to serve whom God ordains,
> Or Nature; God and Nature bid the same,
> When he who rules is worthiest, and excels
> Those whom he governs. This is servitude,
> To serve th' unwise, or him who hath rebell'd
> Against his worthier, as thine now serve thee.
> Thyself not free, but to thyself enthrall'd . . .
> *(Paradise Lost, VI, 174–81).*

Milton's "Rational Liberty," as Michael puts it, "always with
right Reason dwells / Twinn'd, and from her hath no dividual
being" (XII, 81, 84–85). Shaftesbury's, too, is rational
liberty; it presupposes internal order and demands external freedom. Man is, by nature if not always in fact, a rational creature, and he must have the freedom to make a
rational assent to power. The man who desires to tyrannize is
a slave to his own passions; the man who assents to tyranny
distrusts his own reason.

The self-determination of rational assent presupposes the
continuity of a stable self which is neither a shifting configura-
tion of passions nor an externally imposed pattern of conventions. The former is subject to incessant variety of impulse,
the latter to changing fashions and winds of doctrine. Both
are ultimately the product of external accidents. Shaftesbury,
then, in marked contrast to Pascal, exalts the self and finds its
strength in the order of mind. Like Dryden, he recognizes the
struggle for control of the mind conducted by sense and soul:
"The good of life is either in the sensations of the body, or in
the motions and affections of the soul, or in the action of the
mind in thought and contemplation; or, if it be not in one of
these separately, it must be in some mixture of these, one with
another" (Rand, 57). In his philosophical notebooks he deals
with the conflict: the domination of soul and mind together
weaken sensual pleasures; and sensuality is in turn "the obstruction of this good which is in a mind."

Such is the opposition and fight of these two principles. Therefore, if the highest degree of this sort of good (viz., of a mind) be not attainable but by the loss of the other, then that other, as the meaner good, must be sacrificed to this greater; and the only true and real good is the enjoyment of a soul and mind freed from the incitements, commotions, and disorders of sense (Rand, 57–58).

The achievement of rational liberty is Shaftesbury's fundamental spiritual exercise, and his notebooks are a brilliant record of his dialogues with himself, nervous and passionate in the manner of his Stoic masters. At every point the seeming stability must be questioned. Is it mere externality? Is it devotion to something transitory? Is it dependent upon the fortunes of the world? The movement is always toward the essential:

> See in painting, see in architecture, where it is that beauty lies. Is it in every single stroke or stone, which unitedly compose the whole design? is it in any separate narrow part, or in the whole taken together? is it (suppose) in the foot-square of the building, or the inch-square of the painting? or is it not evident that if the eye were confined to this, the chief and sovereign beauty would be lost, whatever slender graces might appear in those imperfect fragments? Now consider and apply this. Consider painting and architecture itself, consider music and harmony, a voice, a face, to what does this refer? how stands it in the larger piece? how in the whole? what part is it? of what is this the image, reflection, shadow? where is the sovereign beauty? where the sovereign good? (Rand, 59.)

The movement continues until the inward order is found. Shaftesbury, so much the virtuoso and the amateur—the lover of art—can insist in soliloquy on the externality of all concrete objects. "Philosophical: a way of living, neatness, nature, husbandry, garden. . . . Off, off with these masks."

> Recover, resist, repel, strive, arm.—War! war! Or otherwise, what peace?
> The *to kalon* where?—Not there, if here.—Rival beauties. Antagonist ideas. Order against order; opposition. If this a *kosmos,* that a chaos, and vice versa.
> The idea of order here in these things. Why once admitted? why borne with? why endured? what order? and in what? [He cites Epictetus: "This body is only a finer mixture of clay."] For how long? and what then? Who the admirers? With whom in common? (Rand, 109.)

He reproaches himself for his failure to sustain the true idea of Self:

> Had it not been better to have been building this while after another manner? Better, sure, to have built a mind on this idea . . . clear, clean, sound, compact, and as a rock. There had been the arches! This the stone, iron, cement! This is the architecture that would have held and answered, been durable, practicable, accountable. This is safety, security: not that. These are proportions and numbers: not those (Rand, 110).

Perhaps the most personal statement of this internal warfare was written in 1703:

> Wilt thou venture again once more in thy life and try this experiment now? And with such impaired constitution, plain decline, and probably short remaining time?
> If such be the case, why admit this cheat and delusion? But thou hast admitted it. It crept on by degrees and under specious images of nature, virtue, public friends, and what not? Their rural-makers, recommendation of country life, agreeableness of a place, seat alterations, gardens, groves. Thus the villa, foreigners, envoys, court ladies, satisfaction of the great, imitation of the great in little. . . .
> Are these *propria?* are they thine? honestly thine? thy own very true and certain possessions properly belonging to thee and naturally thine? Call an imposthume so, a goitre, a polypus, or any worse excrescence (Rand, 126).

But even as Shaftesbury is berating his own weakness (and mocking himself for enjoying being introduced as "ce conte de Shaftesbury" to the Electress Sophia and the Queen of Prussia), even in these intense personal meditations, he is quoting and paraphrasing Horace ("if I have any honesty left," he wrote earlier to Locke [Rand, 306], "I owe it to your good friend and mine, old Horace"). So, too, he defines himself in the words of Epictetus, Marcus Aurelius, or Plato. Shaftesbury's mind is saturated in that philosophy he calls Socratic, civil, social, and theistic, the philosophy that maintained "that Nature had a meaning, and was herself, that is to say, in her wits, well governed and administered by one simple and perfect intelligence" (Rand, 359).

Shaftesbury's notebooks are remarkable for their unremitting effort to strip away illusion. The final test is the achievement of *prokopē* or improvement:

Ever remembering this, premising this, carrying this still along with thee, at all times—hereafter, now, this moment, in what thou art now doing, writing, exercising, studying; that it may be real studying, real exercise: not a cheat to abuse thyself, not a show, not fine thoughts to improve in conversation, not in the wretched pomp and *fucus* of meditations, even with self, much less for others, or with a thought towards others, as seeking a discharge, evacuation, vent (Rand, 239).

He must always resist the occasion when "for the sake of . . . other beauties, beauty itself, the *to kalon, to therion* is lost, out of sight, or faintly appearing." It is the "very real, true nature" he must seek, and what, according to that nature, is "truly graceful, proportionable, harmonious, and of the higher virtuoso kind; what can it be but virtue itself?" (Rand, 247–48). As for what Pascal calls the order of the flesh, Shaftesbury too draws the equation between the surrender to the senses and the worship of power. "The royal thing! —a body.—Majesty!—a body.—The impression it makes, the fear, wonder, admiration!—Body—body still. For what else but a vile servitude, a base homage and worship of this homebody is the occasion of such a prostitution to the body or bodies abroad?" (Rand, 149–50.)

I have quoted so extensively from Shaftesbury's letters and notebooks to remove the impression one still finds prevalent: that he was a shallow defender of gentlemanly virtues, who confused them with, and exalted them at the expense of, higher ends. Cardinal Newman, for example, speaks of Shaftesbury's doctrine as one "which makes virtue a mere point of good taste, and vice vulgar and ungentleman-like." It has, Newman says, "no better measure of right and wrong than that of visible beauty and tangible fitness. Conscience indeed inflicts an acute pang, but that pang, forsooth, is irrational, and to reverence it is an illiberal superstition. . . . To *seem* becomes to *be;* what looks fair will be good, what causes offense will be evil; virtue will be what pleases, vice what pains."[2]

Newman's account of Shaftesbury was not, of course, based on the notebooks, which were not published until 1900 and have been little regarded since then; but it is well to set his reductive account of Shaftesbury's views beside Shaftesbury's agonized search for precisely what was not visible or pleasing in any conventional sense of those words. When Shaftesbury speaks of the seemingly spontaneous moral judgment, arising almost instinctively, we must recall the painful effort by which, for Shaftesbury, virtue is attained and a true self created.

II. The Method of Dialogue

The self-dialogue of soliloquy is an exercise of spiritual discipline. The published dialogue is, for Shaftesbury as for Plato, a form of *therapeia*. Beneath the digressive, seemingly loose form of much of the *Characteristics* lies a deliberate policy. We have Shaftesbury's plan for the *Second Characters, or the Language of Forms,* the work on aesthetics he planned too late to complete. There he writes to himself:

> Nothing in the text but what shall be of easy, smooth, and polite reading, without seeming difficulty, or hard study; so that the better and gentler rank of painters and artists, the ladies, beaux, courtly gentlemen, and more refined sort of country and town wits and notable talkers may comprehend, or be persuaded that they comprehend, what is there written in the text (SC, 8).

We are caught by the phrase, "or be persuaded that they comprehend," and it recalls an earlier remark in the same plan: "Remember still, this the idea of the work, viz.: *Quasi.* The vehicle of other problems, i.e. the precepts, demonstrations, etc. of real ethics. But this hid: not to be said except darkly or pleasantly with raillery upon self; or some such indirect way as in Miscellany" (SC, 6). Shaftesbury describes his role: "What he discovers of form and method is indeed so accompanied with the random miscellaneous air, that it may pass for raillery rather than good earnest" (Ch II, 240). The secret dogmatism, or promotion of a moral philosophy, disguises itself by fetching the "natural idea from as familiar amusements as dress, equipage, the tiring-room, or toy-shop" (Ch II, 269). The "serious and downright philosophy" Shaftesbury "keeps still a mystery and dares not formally profess," not at least until he has prepared his readers for its acceptance. In *The Moralist,* he conceals his "strict imitation of the ancient poetic dialogue" (Ch II, 334, n. 1) by calling the work a "Rhapsody"; but he hopes that the esoteric design will become obvious to the reader who has mastered his meaning.

Shaftesbury admires the Socratic irony of Horace, and he

pays tribute to the dignity, humor, and pleasantry of the "Socratic genius" itself (Rand, 197). So, too, he finds the style of Jesus, in parable or repartee, "sharp, humorous, and witty"; "even his miracles themselves (especially the first he ever wrought) carry with them a certain festivity, alacrity, and good humor" (Ch II, 231). But the central motive of Socratic irony, whether Platonic or Stoic, Shaftesbury states most forcefully in his discussion of the dialogue:

> Remember that in the [use of appearances] one of the chief parts is the inversion, change, and transforming of the fancies or appearances, and the wresting of them from their own natural and vulgar sense into a meaning truly natural and free of all delusion and imposture (Rand, 168).

He cites examples of this "art" of "the inversion of the appearances":

> Quiet, ease, a sweet repose, happy retirement, tranquillity (not that which outward things establish; not that which must be owing to others; not a sea shore, not rocks, not woods or caves). To see, to feel things (not with the eye or by the touch, but in another manner). And as in Marcus or elsewhere (Rand, 171).

Shaftesbury sees this kind of rhetoric and wit as the very opposite of the buffoonery that turns everything to ridicule: "as that other glass crooks and distorts the objects, so this continually straightens and redresses what is amiss, and sets everything in its due light, so as to hinder all confusion" (Rand, 172). This art of "counter-discourse," of dialectical inversion and clarification, is, for Shaftesbury, the only art complete in itself; its aim is nothing less than man's discovery of his true end.

The Platonic dialectic is an ascending movement from opinion to true knowledge, but it is first of all an arrest of the soul. It halts the motion of *anatropē,* or inversion, the downward path men mistake for ascent; and it imposes *metastrophē,* or conversion. Plato is exercising what Socrates seeks, "an art of the speediest and most effective conversion of the soul, not an art of producing vision in it, but, on the assumption that it possesses vision but does not rightly direct it and does not look where it should, an art of bringing this about" (*Republic,* 518d). Plato finds a "loftier order of Being, or the imitation and awareness of it" surviving even in men "so habituated to their cavelike existence and so fettered to the senses and their insistent clamor that the cognition of superior reality, though implicit, is inhibited and suppressed."[3] These dim recollections Shaftesbury likens to the Stoic *prolēpseis* or preconceptions, which must be respected and educated, rather than dismissed. Common men may have "the right notion in general," but they may misdirect it: their love of order may lead them to endure a tyrant (as Pascal also noted, with less sense of outrage). They must learn "to apply these notions rightly, and to accommodate them to their proper subjects" (Rand, 29). It is this that Shaftesbury seeks to teach. For both Plato and Shaftesbury, the conversion that dialectic performs is, first, a redefinition of a critical term, a clarification of a misapplied notion; but, beyond that, it is a redirection of the soul, an awakening of the sense-bound man to the realm that his mind by its nature desires to inhabit. The therapy must be performed with good will (*eunoia*) or what Shaftesbury calls "good humor" and accepted in that spirit. Once defensiveness and egotism are thrown off, and the members of the dialogue join in free inquiry, dialectic can move forward. It is, as Robert E. Cushman puts it, "an irenic method through which men . . . become *self-convicted* of error and *self-convinced* of the truth" (p. 236). It is, moreover, a method that involves the whole man, both his intellect and his affections: "the whole scope of life is changed; aims, aversions, inclinings and declinings reversed, transferred; the whole thought, mind, purpose, will, different modelled new" (Rand, 24).

The *Characteristics* is, throughout, an exercise in such dialectic. The "raillery upon self," with its Socratic self-deprecation, appears notably in the final *Miscellaneous Reflections,* but it runs through the earlier treatises as well. Shaftesbury's dialectic, like Plato's, moves from the familiar to the philosophical. In both writers we rise from the unguarded statements of "half-thinkers" to the full assumptions implicit in them. "If philosophy be, as we take it, the study of happiness, must not everyone, in some manner or other, either skilfully or unskilfully philosophize?" (Ch II, 150.) Shaftesbury's method is to introduce a familiar attitude and to test its bases or latent implications. At the end of such a testing, Philocles can remark in *The Moralists:* "I have dwelt, it seems, all the while upon the surface, and enjoyed only a kind of slight superficial beauties, having never gone in search of beauty itself, but of what I fancied such. . . . I never troubled myself with examining what the subjects were, nor ever hesitated about their choice" (Ch II, 130). Or, again, in a more specific case: "though I once thought I had known friendship, and really counted myself a good friend during my whole life, yet I was now persuaded to believe myself no better than a learner" (Ch II, 40).

Shaftesbury's method is twofold. In the first place, he is appealing from the systems of his opponents (whether consciously formulated or simply enacted in their unthinking behavior) to the full experience of man. Here he is empirical and critical. If we are told that human nature is depraved, we must see whether we do not find honesty in ourselves and others. If we are told we can be led to God only by coercion or bribery, we must ask ourselves whether we can be led to the good by the appeal of its intrinsic merit or beauty. If we are told that God is to be appeased, we must recall our own testimony to his infinite goodness. At each point, a received attitude is confronted with our actual assertions and awareness, and we are forced to test dogma by experience. On the other hand, Shaftesbury starts from everyday experience and moves toward its philosophic assumptions. If I value a beautiful object, am I responding to its material content or to its form? If I have a sense of "inward numbers" that finds a reflection of itself in the outer world, do I not respond to a mind like my own which is ordering that world? Implicit in our sense of moral certainty or of the objectivity of taste is a belief in an absolute standard of order, and implicit in such a standard is trust in an ordering deity. The disclosure of these latent assumptions constitutes the pattern of ascent. "The admirers of beauty in the fair sex would laugh, perhaps, to hear of a moral part in their amours . . . they must allow still, there is a beauty of the mind, and such as is essential in the case." Again, in *The Moralists,* Palemon's melancholy proves to be disappointed love of a kind not at first envisaged, "but a nobler love than such as common beauties inspire"; and Philocles' discussion of love shows the same pattern of ascent as the speech of Diotima in Plato's *Symposium.*

We might restate Shaftesbury's method as the attempt, first, to free man's taste or good sense of the impositions of authority, convention, and false systems, and, second, to draw out of that taste or sense the "connatural" ideas, as Socrates draws out the latent recollections of those he questions. This twofold pattern exists within most of the treatises that make up the *Characteristics,* especially in the first two of the original volumes, where we move from the shorter treatises to the formal *Inquiry Concerning Virtue or Merit* and at last to the mythical "rhapsody" in which the dialogue of *The Moralists* culminates. Often the crucial term in both destruction and reconstruction is the same. The *Letter Concerning Enthusiasm* is a defense of skeptical freedom, of ridicule and raillery; these are the protection against, or the cure for, specious gravity and self-deception. They preserve our critical sense and encourage us to test doubtful claims by a free use of perspective. Humor becomes good humor, good humor becomes toleration, toleration becomes Christian charity. God Himself has a goodness we can recognize only in our "sweetest, kindest disposition." He does not want sycophants or parasites, beggars or bigots. Fanaticism is, therefore, a perversion of the enthusiasm that is divinely implanted, the Platonic *theia mania*.

In the second treatise, *Sensus Communis: An Essay on the Freedom of Wit and Humor,* raillery moves toward something like dialectic in the "free and familiar style" of dialogue. The importance of good humor or good will (the Platonic *eunoia*) leads to Shaftesbury's limiting his demand for liberty to "the liberty of the club." Proper raillery is not a contempt for common "preconceptions" but a freedom of wit among knowing men who are well disposed. The common preconceptions—the *sensus communis,* the common sentiment of our common nature, a "sense of partnership with human kind" —must be freed from Hobbes's dark version of human nature and the Calvinistic emphasis on human depravity. Man's "natural" social sentiments must be released from half-philosophers: "Men's first thoughts in this matter are generally better than their second: their natural notions better than those refined by study or consultation with casuists" (Ch I, 88). Shaftesbury's campaign against self-distrust is an appeal to those high implicit principles that exist, trivialized and wasted, in all our lives. Every man "courts a Venus of one kind or another" (Ch I, 92); Shaftesbury tries to turn him from the terrestrial to the celestial Venus by an increasingly "sober" defense of raillery that rises gradually to an appeal to man's inherent love of truth. Man will love true beauty once it is revealed to him. "For all beauty is truth," and it wins man to more than intellectual commitment.

In *Soliloquy, or Advice to an Author,* Shaftesbury moves on from the freed natural response to the discipline by which one becomes truly "natural." Each man has a demon or genius, a sage within himself, but most of his life is a flight from self-confrontation. Just as the poet creates a character, so each of us must create our own. The true artist, who discerns the proportions of goodness, is a "second Maker, a just Prometheus under Jove" (Ch I, 136). But most modern artists lack candor with themselves, seek easy success, and prostitute themselves, as other men lose themselves in *divertissements*. Poets need "the wisdom of the heart" as well as "exercise of the brain." Philosophy, so long as it is not dogmatic ("the most ingenious way of becoming foolish is by a system"), leads to the self-therapy and self-mastery that free the artist to create true works. To attain this freedom demands cultivation of "the sense of inward numbers," for the poet has a moral end which he can fulfill only as a morally free man. Shaftesbury has by now converted the lightness of humor into a deep moral enthusiasm, the freedom of ridicule into an intense search for moral reality, the process of artistry into a spiritual discipline. He has tried, as he puts it elsewhere, "to raise the masterly spirit of criticism" in his readers "and exalt them ever so little above the lazy, timorous, over-modest, or resigned state in which the generality of them remain" (Ch II, 313).

The Moralists begins with Philocles' lament for philosophy. It is "no longer active in the world" and has no place in polite conversation. Our refinement has become mere delicacy. Men are now too eager for grand hypotheses and "a little too cowardly to dare doubt." There seems to be no room left for a philosophy of true dialogue, "which goes upon no established hypotheses, nor presents us with any flattering scheme, talks only of probabilities, suspense of judgment, inquiry, search, and caution not to be imposed on or deceived" (Ch II, 9). Philocles regards the skeptical philosophy as "the prettiest, agreeablest roving exercise of the mind possible to be imagined" (Ch II, 18); but his skepticism is born of his reaction against the dogmatism of rationalists. It is an openness of mind such as Socrates promotes, freeing man of the stiffness of false opinions; and it is ready to respond to Theocles' enthusiasm and "reasonable ecstasy." Theocles' enthusiasm is not the fanaticism of zealots, but rather like "the pleasing transports" of the ancient poets. Significantly, when Philocles encounters Theocles he finds him reading Virgil rather than "some more mysterious book."

The movement of *The Moralists* is like that of the first three treatises: a gradual ascent from distrust of philosophy to a recognition that it need not be the enemy of liberty but is in fact its only source. Against Dryden's " 'Tis revelation what thou think'st discourse," we can set Theocles' words: " 'tis the province of philosophy alone to prove what revelation only supposes" (Ch II, 53–54). Theocles offers his skeptical friend "the divine hypothesis"; once admitted, it will "admit a total change in all your principles and opinions, yet would you still be the self-same Philocles, though better yet . . . than the present one" (Ch II, 101). The effect of the conversion is to give stability to the self. Theocles' rhapsodic view of the divine harmony and order of Nature finally moves Philocles to a new awareness:

> I shall no longer resist the passion growing in me for things of a natural kind, where neither art nor the conceit or caprice of man has spoiled their genuine order by breaking in upon that primitive state. Even the rude rocks, the mossy caverns, the irregular unwrought grottoes and broken falls of water, with all the horrid graces of the wilderness itself, as representing Nature more, will be the more engaging, and appear with a magnificence beyond the formal mockery of princely gardens (Ch II, 125).

But this passage, so often cited, is only a stage in Philocles' ascent. He chooses "obscure places to spell out that mysterious being, which to our weak eyes appears at best under a cloud." He has overcome cold indifference and become an impassioned lover who finds all the features of his mistress wonderful because they are hers. He is, therefore, as Theocles says, now "sure never to admire the representative beauty except for the sake of the original"; he is free, that is, of the senses and can find beauty even where they are affronted. (He is, in effect, a lover of the sublime as well as the beautiful.) He has risen beyond the taste of the vulgar and can respond to the "rustic" in architecture or to "dissonancies" in music, for he now seeks that beauty "which lies very absconded and deep" (Ch II, 130). He is prepared at last to find beauty in mind and reason, for "whatever is void of mind, is void and darkness to the mind's eye." Philocles has come to love the forming rather than the formed, the ordering power in the order. He is a lover of wisdom.

This sense of our common experience potentially existing on many levels, of the divine vision implicit in the familiar occasion, is, of course, common to most Platonic and Christian thought. Shaftesbury's originality lies, first of all, in his resolute pursuit of its paradoxical possibilities. The common gentleman, in his unwarped benevolence, shows a truer sense of God than the learned but uncharitable divine. We have a determined confrontation, not of a pastoral hero or a noble savage, but of a virtuoso or a refined and witty skeptic, with the "mercenary" men of God. It is one thing for the courtly lover to reveal that his mistress is really philosophy; it is another for a racy, scoffing wit to reveal that he himself is Socrates or Prometheus. Again, Shaftesbury's levels of experience differ from those of the traditional Platonic ladder in that they do not attain full transcendence at the close. Theocles is an enthusiast, but a rational enthusiast. Shaftesbury's God is not the pure idea of Plato or the ineffable One of Plotinus, a subject for mystical contemplation; he is, to borrow Blake's phrase, the Divine Humanity—man's goodness and artistry amplified to infinity. There is not, as a result, the peculiar "metaphysical" effect of the meeting of two realms in a moment of time that we find in much neo-Platonic allegory, but a continuity of movement from the partial good to perfect goodness. We move not from one kind of experience to another so much as from one degree of liberty to another; God is the stablest and worthiest object of our love, and accordingly He occasions the freest response.

The triumph of liberty is evident in Shaftesbury's literary method as well as in his system. The treatises begin with a "freedom" that the authoritarian calls impertinence (a defense of raillery, a scoffing at enthusiasm, an attack upon "magisterial" advice), and they gradually extend that freedom to man's right and need to examine all "received opinions." Man must be freed of what Blake calls "mind-forged manacles," and the method of free inquiry leads him to all he once thought to have gained from blind submission. Shaftesbury's religion, for example, denies that God is mysteriously transcendent yet preserves the experience of divine rapture and (rational) ecstasy. Shaftesbury's ethic denies man's radical evil yet restores the sense of moral triumph in the right ordering of the will. In general, Shaftesbury's system substitutes the discipline and reward of artistry for the moral warfare of orthodoxy, and the harmony and order of the mind's art for the promise of heavenly bliss. But these substitutions are accomplished only by raising to new dignity the ideas of artistry and of harmony. In both it is the triumph of the free and creative mind that is manifest; the work of art is more than an ingenious design and the world harmony more than a great machine.

This is the pattern of the *Characteristics,* and the levity of the work—at times a labored and tedious levity—stresses its tentative quality. It is a work that explores the possibility of giving back to man the potential dignity he had for Socrates, of establishing religion on man's free assent rather than upon his insecurity, of finding the surest evidence of religious conviction in the charitable temper. In a sense, Shaftesbury is substituting the regal Son for the tyrannical Father, as Blake was to do later. He artfully selects from religious experience its trust in God's goodness at the expense of its concern with God's justice, and he resolutely challenges the depressors of man's powers with our highest capacities for free benevolence.

Yet Shaftesbury, more than some of his disciples, is aware of his own "enthusiasm" and always ready to regard himself with irony. When he places his moralists in a natural setting, he is deliberately removing them from "the common affairs of life" to allow them a speculative freedom. His system is a speculative structure—with all its dangers—built upon and confirming what is phenomenologically given, our sense of an "eternal and immutable morality." It provides the interpretation of fact and value that every religious world view seeks to establish, and it may, as it did for Pope, serve ends quite different from Shaftesbury's. His specific applications are limited and polemical. But the system itself allows him to make clear the conflict between professed and true order, between the mock order of despotism or sensuality and the stable order of rational theism.

In this conflict the mock order claims the respect of the world and subverts true order in its name. Shaftesbury's intransigent rejection of this has a vigor that is not often allowed it. In reconciling liberty and order, in making liberty essential to a true order, Shaftesbury presents a critique of imposture in the broadest sense, and, in reviving a religious world view comparable with the orthodox Christian view, he makes plausible enough for serious consideration the question of whether the rest is not factitious, like the fopperies of the three brothers in Swift's *A Tale of a Tub*.

III. Art and Nature

Shaftesbury's aesthetic vision of cosmic order raises a number of problems, some of which we have already seen in Dryden and shall see again throughout the eighteenth century. Within the scale of worldly creation man occupies the highest place, for "a right mind and generous affection had more beauty and charm than all other symmetries in the world besides." But man is capable of error and perversion, and his works may be of a far lower order than God's immediate artistry in physical nature. Nature constantly provides a standard of "genuine order" by which man's works can be judged. But, in her vast economy, Nature may harmonize elements that in themselves are hardly admirable. The rainbow is, for Shaftesbury, one such case—"a nothing, a non-entity in virtuosoship" (SC, 113). Man, within his limited scope as an artist, can achieve more uniform order than nature, simply because the field within which he works is smaller and more readily subjected to design. We have then a superiority in Nature of total order, a potential superiority in man of limited order, and a meeting of the two in the highest level of order beneath God's own—man's conscious moral order.

Nature's economy may be seen in both small and vast segments, and where her design is not apparent it may be inferred from its presence elsewhere. The universal harmony depends upon variety, the existence of many things "terrible" or "contrary" to human desires but either "beauteous in themselves" (through a harmony of parts) or as elements of a grand and beautiful design. Shaftesbury frequently shifts between justifications; it is often hard to decide whether he commends the wilds of nature because they are absolutely free of men's inferior ordering, because they show intrinsic design, or because they make us aware of the power of Nature's order in encompassing even these unlikely elements. There is a touch of the paradoxical *credo quia impossibile* in Shaftesbury's regard for Nature's art. Theocles' rapture in *The Moralists* is induced by the way in which Nature's scope of order transcends man's comprehension. Her plan is beyond his powers of understanding but not contrary to his reason. The transcendence is quantitative rather than qualitative; it is too vast for him to know or even imagine, but he can trust its conformity with what he does know. This reflects Shaftesbury's faith in God's benevolent rationality, his assurance that God shows the same "good humor" toward man that Shaftesbury recommends between men.

It must be stressed that while the order that Shaftesbury finds in Nature may or may not exist in particular segments, it is certainly to be found in the whole—not at once, but with self-discipline and training on the part of the beholder. Just as in a painting or building we may be baffled by apparent incoherence, so we are in Nature, until we understand her art and learn how to look at her works.

The process is not one-sided. Nature's order may be perceptible in some degree to the untutored eye and encourage the self-discipline that makes more of it visible. What is more important for Shaftesbury's idea of liberty is that the perception of order in Nature is the act of a rationally ordered man. Nature does not compel terrified admiration by her power, any more than God does, although both may be revered for their infinite scope. Man's reverence is a free act of love, possible only while man has liberty from inner or outer compulsion. It is this theme of liberty that leaves Shaftesbury comparatively unresponsive to the heights and depths of natural forces as well as of human power. His religion has no place for mystery, for exultation or agonies, and he does not foreshadow theories of the sublime, like Burke's, that depend on fear. Nor is Shaftesbury concerned, as is Wordsworth, with the "ministry of fear." Man senses his own incompleteness, but he submits to law, not to will; to "the rule and government of the whole," not to mere power. So too, man's spiritual ordering is an individual concern, but its success makes him a social being; his end is in society. This is not to say that any actual society is the true end of man. The ideal social order is a rebuke to most that exist. But Shaftesbury's stress on ideal social unity and coherence is far from romantic solitude. For all of his praise of natural beauty, Shaftesbury warns against confusing spiritual discipline with a mere escape into nature. Tranquillity is to be sought, not in "romantic places, the rocks and seashores, wood, caverns, &c," but, as Marcus Aurelius tells us, in "the good ordering of the mind." Physical nature, although it may provide a theater for spiritual meditation or a temple for worship, must not overcome the liberty of the "inward eye" any more than worldly glory or wealth.

Natural phenomena are transitory; only their pattern is permanent. Man's mind also requires stability of pattern if it is to be free. Liberty of choice requires continuous identity. Here again Shaftesbury does not rule out egoistic motives; the self must be preserved, but it should not seek more than is necessary for preservation. The balance between selfish needs and benevolence is maintained by rational decision. Each man's rational self-government, Shaftesbury implies, will bring him to the point of becoming a co-operative member of a society. Society is ideally a constitution of constitutions, involving the possibility of rational assent at every point. It becomes therefore a higher kind of order than the natural harmony, whose order often exists in the whole rather than in each of the parts. Society, in short, reconciles liberty and order through rational assent. So Shaftesbury can speak of "that chief liberty, which is learnt by obedience and submission."

The characteristic note of Shaftesbury's doctrine is the stress on self-determination and voluntary submission. Shaftesbury is not so much concerned with distinguishing the faculties of man's mind as with stressing their interaction. He does not, like Francis Hutcheson later, seek to establish a new faculty, a moral sense inherently different from reason or the affections. His "moral sense" is a fusion of affection and reason, a directing of the affections to what, because it cannot be possessed, cannot be lost; a love not of the material but of what resides in matter as its informing principle. Such a love has its start in an object that is sensuously appealing, but it cannot remain at the level of sense. Fielding's treatment of love in *Tom Jones* (VI, i) is a telling parallel. Tom's rhapsodically ideal love for Sophia is clearly grounded in physical passion, but it is the element of benevolence that controls and characterizes all its manifestations and makes it more than the "voracious appetite" for "a certain quantity of delicate white human flesh."

There is a fusion in the intuitive act that allows Shaftesbury to call it by whatever name his context suggests—reason, affection, sense, taste. It may be heart instead of head if we recall the mind's susceptibility to false doctrine; or head more than heart if we consider the passions' attraction to sensual pleasures. It cannot be either alone, for if the discernment of a stable pattern and end to be sought is the task of reason, the response of love is the work of the feelings. Shaftesbury can therefore write "Trust your own heart whilst you keep it honest, and can lift it up to the God of *Truth,* as seeking that, and that only." Apparent reason may become fallible in the man of insufficient discipline who is an unconscious slave to passion or interest. "Wisdom is more from the *heart,* than from the *head. Feel* goodness, and you will see all things fair and good." Or again: "Fill your self with *Good;* and you will carry within you sufficient Answer to the *Bad,* and by a sort of instinct soon discern the one from the other" (*Several Letters,* pp. 24–25).

The beginnings of sentimentalism are apparent here, but

only the beginnings. Shaftesbury carefully distinguishes between the transitory impulse and the stable, disinterested love of the ordered object. The analogy of ethics and aesthetics may, we feel, do less than justice to either. Shaftesbury undervalues the sense of obligation, of the "ought" in ethics, and he restricts the beautiful to the presence of order, harmony, and unity in variety, for it is only in this way that he can emphasize the idea of liberty in moral choice—the absence of coercion, the stability of end, the escape from subjectivity. The disinterested love of beauty is itself evidence for more than egoism in man's nature; it provides the counterpart of the rational intuition in less momentous experience, the free assent to that which is good in itself. The aesthetic analogy supplies a kind of experience that suggests love as well as liberty. Whether the aesthetic experience be seen as right perception, right feeling, or rational approval, it is available only through discipline, through an ability to turn away from the glaring and transitory, through a resistance to the lower appeals that might distract us from penetrating multifariousness to the order that governs it.

Shaftesbury's conception of liberty is not a markedly romantic one. It is given a romantic turn only when the virtuous man is found not in the master of self-discipline but in the merely unworldly man. It is one thing to decry the influence of city and court; it is another to see virtue wherever such influences are absent. Order for Shaftesbury is rational control or the spontaneous movement of the disciplined heart. Once the heart is relieved of discipline and the double aspect of heart and mind gives way before the growing distrust of reason, the order becomes one of impulse, with spontaneity and freshness stressed at the expense of objectivity and stability. In Wordsworth, for example, the capacity for joy, for responding with strong feeling to Nature, often replaces any clear vision of an objective order in Nature; in fact, it is the joy that *creates* the order of Nature.

Order and liberty in Shaftesbury represent another aspect of the Augustan compromise. Shaftesbury differs from the greatest Augustans in his greater trust in man's natural goodness and his greater hatred of authority. In a sense, his optimism about man's capacities is, as R. L. Brett has suggested, one of the necessary elements of the satirical temper of the century.[4] In tragedy the forces of necessity are usually inscrutable; the tragic hero's lack of awareness may be culpable but not ridiculous. In satire, the norms transgressed are apparent to all, and the satiric victim is ridiculed for failing in what all men are capable of performing. Shaftesbury's theodicy leaves room for satire, as does Pope's. Man has the choice of rationally seeking his proper end or of being blindly converted to the ends of a Mind he ignores. He may be God's servant or merely the unthinking material of the divine architecture. For each man the choice involves his humanity. Shaftesbury's satire is turned upon the "half-thinkers," the slaves and despots, much as is Swift's and Pope's. In his burden that man must learn his own dignity and perceive his own freedom, he gives a Whiggish turn to a general Augustan theme.

IV. The Concrete Universal

Shaftesbury's theory of art seems to have developed out of his use of the analogy of aesthetic and ethical experience in the *Characteristics,* and, with the fragments that make up the *Second Characters,* it is the most complete and impressive theory recorded by an English writer of the age. Its interest does not lie simply in its typicality; however traditional many of his ideas are, Shaftesbury is an imposing theorist. Shaftesbury's theory of art is also interesting beyond its own province for its application of those large terms—order, proportion, harmony—in specific discussions of artistic practice. Like the notebooks, his writings on art give precision to terms whose meaning we might otherwise have lost or mistaken.

Shaftesbury is aware of art both as form and as imitation. In relating the two ideas, he is uncommonly fair to both. He is impatient with didactic art or the comparatively abstract art common to many religious climates. His zeal is strong in his attack upon the priestly hieroglyphic art of the Egyptians, which does little justice to the objects represented. This accords with his hatred of ecclesiastical tyranny, which again—like Blake later—he traces to Egypt. It is clear that for Shaftesbury the fullness of representation is in itself a symptom of liberty of thought. Humane ideas are fostered by "truly human forms," and divinity is to be represented by its continuity with man's best nature—after the "best, sweetest, and perfectest idea of humanity" (SC, 105). Tyranny destroys these forms and barbarizes men by its distorted image of humanity. A painting, like religion or the state, should not impose its total pattern at the expense of the part; rather, it should harmonize individual parts that intrinsically are imitations. This can be illustrated by Shaftesbury's elaborate plan for the painting of the Judgment of Hercules, where the hero is seen choosing between virtue and vice. In moral and historical painting Shaftesbury is clearly opposed to the kind of allegory that allows only such representation as is necessary for didactic purposes; he would have the meaning of the picture emerge from its formal and dramatic structure. Just as, in the matter of morals, Shaftesbury is unwilling to bypass free rational assent, so in the arts he is unwilling to stint full aesthetic perception. For him, undue formalism or didacticism denies the spectator the use of his powers of comprehension. (The didactic, moreover, is not the province of "the bard, the *vates,* the enthusiast.") Shaftesbury commends the structure whose meanings can be derived only from careful scrutiny of a representational design. Painting must avoid both the tyranny of hieroglyphic form and the tyranny of minute and meaningless particularity.

If Shaftesbury stresses the plenitude of parts in the painting, he stresses total design no less:

> The *characteristic* still, the truth, the historic is all in all . . . the thing *imitated,* the thing *specified* (reduced to its true form and species) is all in all, the whole delight, pleasure of the work, the secret charm of the spectacle. This accomplished and all is done. Instruction, moral description, truth (SC, 102).

Elsewhere he explains that without the "essential moral part" —"the note or character of nature . . . reason of the thing" (SC, 101)—there is "no history, no true form" (SC, 98). Everything in the picture should conspire to make this moral meaning emerge. Thus in the Judgment of Hercules, the fruitful moment must be carefully selected to reveal the nature of the choice in its full tension.

The "moral personages" of painting are shown in "air, gesture, attitude, action, motion"—all of which reveal the "affections" and their moral condition:

> What is it we see? A boy—therefore, sweet, pretty, innocent: But a cupid. A new case. A boy and beautiful boy, the most that is possible; but not innocent, not harmless, not wholly sweet, gentle, loving: but mischievous, treacherous, mocking, subtle. An urchin, half civil, demon, cruel, spiteful, proud, disdainful, tyrannical, capricious, imperious. Here a new story, a new lesson, an instruction, something learnt (SC, 98).

Again, in his account of animal painting, Shaftesbury gets at the moral unity he sees in all pictures:

> Is it a bull? See the same grum indifference, sullen security and ease, trust to his strength, the jealousy of his eye over his females on the approach of anything injurious to them, or any rivalship from his own kind.—Is it a bird? A tame one merely, and of the household kind? A cock? See his walk, his démarche, his carriage amongst his ladies; his generosity, even to the starving himself and neglect of his own sustenance! (SC, 101–2.)

The unity Shaftesbury commends in painting demands "a just imitation of nature," but "to some end and with some intent." The end of the painting cannot be sacrificed to the vividness of detail; colors, for example, must not be unmixed, for "the more pure the more ugly," "the more simple the more tawdry" (SC, 146, 144). Each part must be organically related to every other, both formally and (in historical painting) dramatically. Where hyperbole is used, as it must be in the heroic style, "the hyperbole must be *one,* only one, unique, simple" (SC, 157). The picture cannot sustain discordant exaggerations. The unity of the picture, by its coherence, imposes its own kind of truth—a "plastic" or "poetical" truth, which is of greater importance than the literal truth that is "historically true, poetically false" (SC, 137). What matters to Shaftesbury is the "inward truth" of the figures, their expressiveness of moral attitude, rather than outward conformity to conventional gestures.

In Annibale Carracci the "action [is] all theatrical." The picture is an "Imitation of an imitation; at second hand; not immediate, not original, from nature. Art by custom becomes a second model" (SC, 128). True "passion" or "soul" in painting is the "divine part and only Raphael's. Something which is above the modern turn and only antique species of grace. Above the dancing-master, above the actor and the stage" (SC, 151).

Unity prescribes a freedom from outward elaboration except in so far as such elaboration reveals inward character. This may lead in two directions: toward an emblematic art or toward an art at once representational and symbolic. In his own directions to painters, Shaftesbury stresses the "idea" to the point of suggesting a fairly thin allegory, but his own preferences in painters balance this suggestion. His regard for Raphael, Michelangelo, and Poussin points to an art with strong intellectual control but hardly thin representational value. The control is to be found in the ordering which makes the picture both a just representation (and therefore full in its meanings) and an organic unity (its meanings coherent and purposive).

Liberty demands of art a proper respect for the dignity of man; first, in its representation of him, second, in its appeal to his perception. Shaftesbury detests the "vile shrivelling passion of beggarly modern devotion," and the strength of his feeling can be seen in his attitude toward the image of Christ in religious art:

> Chief support of painting what?—Christ!—Wretched model. Barbarian. No form, no grace of shoulders, breast, no *démarche,* air, majesty, grandeur, a lean uncomely proportion and species, a mere Jew or Hebrew (originally an ugly scabby people) both shape and physique, with half beard peaked, not one or the other. Lank clinging hair, snivelling face, hypocritical canting countenance and at best melancholy, mad and enthusiastical in the common and lower way, not so well as even the Bacchanals and Bacchantes (SC, 120).

A note to this passage reads, "Here cite the poets, finest works of Apollo, Jove." It is to the classical gods that Shaftesbury looks for dignity and "good humor." Beside the passage on Christ, one may set this:

> all the true antique figures . . . have a deep, eager, severe ecstatic or enthusiastic air. . . . Stern and rigid the passion of the plain, prophetic, oraculous kind, fanatic and lymphatic. . . . Same passion by some of the modern painters in some of their saints.

One may think of Poussin's *Annunciation* (1657) in the National Gallery, London, and Sir Anthony Blunt's comparison of Poussin's Mary with Bernini's Saint Theresa:

> Bernini's figure is swathed in exciting, irregular, broken drapery; the head sinks to one side; the body is twisted into a strong contrapposto. Poussin's figure preserves a rigid symmetry, even to the pose of hands and feet; the drapery is clear-cut and without movement; the head is thrown back and not to one side; the nerves and muscles of head, arms, and hands are still under control. This is no swoon, but the intense expression of a conscious state of mind ("The *Annunciation* by Nicolas Poussin," *Bulletin de la Société Poussin,* Premier Cahier, 1947, p. 22).

Shaftesbury's moral attitudes cut him off from medieval and much Baroque art and suggest a limitation of the subject of painting to the intrinsically beautiful. In fairness, one must remember that for him the design is most important, the mere representation of classical serenity or severity is not enough. He can praise Michelangelo for "his muscling action and movements gigantic." "Other painters," he goes on, "too timorous and strict; sweet and natural; but unfit for any noble sally of genius, as Domenichino the judicious, correct, and Poussin" (SC, 154–55). It is not so much the ugly that he attacks as the degrading or slavish representation of man. The low or grotesque may have its function as a foil to the heroic ("So often Raphael himself; a cook, a pharisee, thyrsiter, amidst the other homerical forms"). If the low becomes the sole concern of the painter, as with the Dutch, it becomes degrading. His stress on the characteristic, the peculiar moral significance of the individual subject, however, makes clear that external beauty or ugliness is not Shaftesbury's primary concern.

In his treatment of nature, Shaftesbury again shows that the order he admires is not a thin one, a mere harmony of intrinsically beautiful parts. Nature's is a difficult beauty. To substitute simple regularity for it is an attempt to achieve order mechanically. The artist may come in time to imitate nature's "supreme order," but until he does, the natural is likely to be better than his artifice. With his achievement of discipline and a full vision of nature's order, man's "original first rude taste [is] corrected by rule, and reduced to a yet more simple and natural measure." Accordingly the "innocent child's eye" is better than the false taste of the adult; better "mere nature than half-way, elaborate, artful, merely critical judgment" (SC, 115–16).

Shaftesbury's use of "mere nature" is telling; it stresses again the value he places upon the discipline of the artist or the man of taste. Artistry or taste, like virtue, are not given but earned, and the contemplation of nature ensures that they will not be earned at too cheap a rate to be stable. The eye must be trained to look away from familiar sights. The natural is not to be sought empirically as the average case. No figure, Shaftesbury tells us, is "now extant in the world, which can be seen standing naturally upon the ground"; the "idea therefore must be taken from nature and drawn; instinct and what is innate; or from the ancient trunks and broken remains" (SC, 117). One cannot study the human body in such models as "naked porters" and "diseased courtesans." The rainbow is not worthy of imitation because it is a "mere miracle or prodigy (without *moral* or *doctrine*); a nothing, a juggle." When *"nature* herself paints (as sometimes in wantonness and as it were luxuriantly) she ought not to be imitated: not the picture, but *herself* only (her pure *self*) copied." The artist's task is to recover the tendency of nature, the idea, and to show its emergence from the actuality he paints.

Shaftesbury comes, finally, to a typical Renaissance reading of the Aristotelian discussion of poetic unity. If the imitative arts are more philosophical than history it is because they order experience so as to give us both pleasure in the emergence of form and wisdom in the moral significance of that form. Each element in the work has relevance to a total design, an end, which is at once formal and moral. To see man's coming to the awareness of necessity through recognition and reversal is to see a meaningful order in experience, concrete in its dramatic form and universal in its moral import. The pursuit of the "characteristic" is a search for individuality of form and complexity of moral insight. Like Dryden, Shaftesbury tries to hold together justness and liveliness, reasonableness and effectiveness. He finds, as Dryden does, a typical compromise in the probable. In art "historical truth must of necessity . . . give way to that which we call poetical, as being governed not so much by reality as by probability, or plausible appearance" (SC, 49). Therefore a "complete and perfect character is the greatest monster" in a poem, "and of all the poetic fictions not only the least engaging but the least moral and improving" (Ch II, 319–20, n.). The true poet must discover "Nature's propensity" and assign "to these high spirits their proper exorbitancy and inclination." The case of Ulysses is perhaps clearest:

> The passion of an Ulysses is toward that glory which is acquired by prudence, wisdom, and ability in affairs. 'Tis in favor of this character that we forgive him his subtle, crafty, and deceitful air; since the intriguing spirit, the over-reaching manner, and over-refinement of art and policy are as naturally incident to the experienced and thorough politician as sudden resentment, indiscreet and rash behavior to the often undesigning character of a war-like youth.

The poet is allowed every freedom in representing the "peculiar virtue and excellence of his hero. He may lie splendidly, raise wonder, and be as astonishing as he pleases." But he must also show the moral consequences of his hero's bold excess: "our passions, whilst in the strongest manner engaged and moved, are in the wholesomest and most effectual manner corrected and purged" (Ch II, 319, n.). The catharsis of tragedy provides that rational freedom for the spectator which is denied the tragic characters themselves. "They discern their own capacity, but not with force and recollection sufficient to redeem themselves and become their own. . . . And thus the highest spirits and most refractory wills contribute to the lowest servitude and most submissive state." As in the account of the Judgment of Hercules, the condition of moral tension is Shaftesbury's highest interest. This gives vitality to his conception of character and of moral instruction. Hercules, the urchin, the barnyard cock—each is a characteristic unity of varied moral qualities.

In his treatment of the arts we see once more Shaftesbury's concern with the triumph of liberty. The end of the work of art is our rational awareness of universals and our rational perception of proportion and harmony. Yet the fullness of Nature's individual creations is not stinted; the greater "their proper exorbitancy and inclination to exceed" in their peculiar characteristics, the richer the harmony. Shaftesbury cites, in a note, the *De Mundo* once attributed to Aristotle: "And perhaps Nature wants opposites too, and wants to make harmony out of them, not out of similars."

We find in Shaftesbury the dialectical movement so characteristic of his age. In his theory of art, as in his vision of nature, he is poised between plenitude and Order, between the characteristic seen as radically individual and distinctive and the characteristic seen as a peculiar harmony of universal principles. Nature's "genuine order" is a relief from the corruption or confinement of art, but the "natural" in man is the achievement of high artistry. Shaftesbury's "moral sense," like Pascal's *coeur,* shifts between spontaneous sentiment and obedience to objective law. These are not blunt inconsistencies and dull contradictions; they are the pulsation of a dialectical process that tries at once to do justice to the puzzles of experience and the inadequacy of our categories.

Seen from the point of view of the mock order of a servile world, nature expands into the freedom of "genuine order"; seen from the point of view of the sage or visionary, nature can be an obstruction, or at best the outward embodiment of "inward numbers," the product of a forming or plastic energy. Shaftesbury's apparent snobbery and excessive gentility have at their source an unremitting effort to connect the divine with the actual, to find God in man and nature, to make that right disposition, in which alone man can know God, an end in itself and an end that governs the least of our actions. He argues down the evidence for human depravity or traces it to self-distrust and the perversion of the natural; he selects from the attributes of God those rational and benevolent ones that man can grasp and imitate. He does this with the defiance (that becomes acutely tendentious in religion and politics) of a man seeking to uncover an important truth the world has conspired to conceal. But the defiance takes the form of therapy, a summoning up of the powers man has relinquished or guiltily suppressed.

IV.

Mandeville: Order as Art

Shaftesbury's work has come down to us coupled with Mandeville's. Both were considered dangerous freethinkers in their day, and they were attacked together by men like William Law. But their difference strikes us more sharply today. They seem a classic instance of the opposition of tender-minded and tough-minded, of the proponent of "not merely" and the defender of "nothing but."

Mandeville's great work, *The Fable of the Bees,* had its origin in a poem called *The Grumbling Hive, or Knaves Turned Honest* (1705). In the life of the bees Mandeville sketches a prosperous society, full of dishonesty but productive and flourishing ("every part was full of Vice, / Yet the whole mass a Paradise"). Once the society undergoes moral reform, it dwindles into a simple, wholesome stagnancy, where contentment has banished industry and "arts and crafts neglected lie." The moral Mandeville draws is a modest one:

> So Vice is beneficial found,
> When it's by Justice lopt and bound:
> Nay, where the people would be great,
> As necessary to the State,
> As hunger is to make 'em eat.

As Mandeville returned in later years to his fable and amplified it with extensive notes or "remarks," with essays, and finally with six dialogues, he tended to place less emphasis on the second line of his moral and more on the last three. The short poem grew into an attack upon the moralists and the defense of a naturalistic, even evolutionary, view of society.

1. Realism and Morality

I must plead guilty, and confess that the pleasure there is in imitating Nature in what shape soever is so bewitching, that it overrules the dictates of Art and often forces us to offend against our own judgment.[1]

These words can serve to introduce Mandeville's whole achievement, for his typical pose is that of realism and fidelity to nature. Nowhere does he use the pose more tellingly than in the dialogue where he opposes his philosophy to Shaftesbury's through a contrast of two paintings of the Nativity. One is by a Dutch realist, and shows a stable in minute detail—"hay and straw and cattle, and a rack as well as a manger." As one observer remarks, "nothing can be more like the head of an ox than that there." The other picture is the work of an Italian painter in the grand style. A colonnade has replaced the barn. "How skillfully is that ass removed, and how little you see of the ox; pray mind the obscurity they are both placed in. . . . Behold these pillars of the Corinthian order, how lofty they are, and what effect they have, what a noble space, what an area here is!" Mandeville takes delight in pitting against the Renaissance princeling the humble child, against Shaftesburian grandeur and decorum "the poor and abject state in which our Saviour chose to appear at his coming into the world." Shaftesbury's art represents "not nature, but agreeable nature, *la belle Nature;* . . . all things that are abject, low, pitiful and mean, are carefully to be avoided, and kept out of sight" (II, 33–34).

The choice of the Nativity makes the comparison all the more suggestive. Mandeville, his realism apart, insists upon God as unknowable, and he dismisses the arrogant attempts to see God as guarantor of worldly values. In severing the will of God from the mind of man, Mandeville leaves the exercise of virtue to that inspiration (really, an "election") by which alone man can devoutly follow the teachings of Scripture. All that can be expected of fallen man is a social order, neither so inherently good as to reflect a divine Order, nor vicious enough to seem a mere punishment for man's sinfulness. Since God's will is inscrutable, nothing that exists can be dismissed as worthless. The worth of the social order lies in making man's life tolerable or even happy, but this must never be confused with a genuine order that will make life good or blessed. In his power to entertain at once a severe moral judgment on the limitations of the social order and an intense absorption in its pleasures and beauty, Mandeville carries on the tradition of mixed genres in a typical Augustan way. He has much in common with such writers as Pope, Swift, Gay, and Fielding, who see both the triviality of a society that neglects its possibility of moral greatness and the charm, energy, and curious beauty of its oblivious activity.

The usual mock pastoral or "town eclogue" plays upon the way in which the city's noise and dirt, in all their ugliness, create a mock order that is the very denial of true pastoral. But in a teasing and mysterious way the mock order may turn out to seem an authentic order; and the ugly notes of the city produce their own kind of harmony. Mandeville forces this paradox into a rigorously articulated one, notably in the famous subtitle of *The Fable of the Bees,* "Private Vices, Public Benefits." As many have pointed out, Mandeville creates this paradox by playing upon terms. He designates as vice whatever motive has an ingredient of self-interest, no matter how small, or whatever action promotes personal satisfaction. Vice is the failure to maintain thoroughgoing, ascetic self-denial or rigorous adherence to those claims of our religion that are in utter opposition to the things of this world.

Pascal sees *le moi haïssable* threatening every profession of faith or selflessness. In a similar way, but more blandly and ironically, Mandeville insists upon naming as vice any action that can even theoretically be interpreted as promoting temporal happiness. It follows, of course, that "public benefits" must be the product of vice, especially if one construes as benefit any form of worldly success or prosperity.

Mandeville can see the thriving metropolis in its splendor and opulence, but he simultaneously sees it as the embodiment of all that the moral or religious man professes to abhor. This is the secular reversal of the Christian tradition of mixed genres—the tradition we see in Mandeville's Dutch nativity scene—the juxtaposition of a transcendent God with the humblest and meanest stable. Mandeville prizes the concrete diversity and rich disorder of actual life, and he insists that this world is the artistry of Providence, working, it is true, with such highly recalcitrant materials as ourselves. We have a clear choice of renouncing the world or accepting it despite our religion. God will bring order out of either choice, but the order He can make of our abstinence and self-denial is a far different one from the London we now enjoy. Do we want the innocuous idyl of a devout life, or are we content with the sumptuous "town eclogue" of an impious one?

Mandeville has two ways of explaining the rise of this great urban mock order. One of them is a parody of traditional theodicy (a form his argument frequently takes). Out of evil good is produced, but through natural causes. Providence manifests itself in the workings of our passions over a long period of time, and society emerges in a slow evolutionary process. So long as he wishes to rebuke man's pride in rational self-control, Mandeville sees all man's achievements as arising in this way from nature without man's knowledge or connivance. This is also the way of Pope in the *Essay on Man*: "Though man's a fool, yet God is wise."

But when Mandeville wants to show what man can accomplish for himself once he accepts and works with his fallen nature, he sees society as the creation of political cunning, and his realism becomes a means of celebrating the transforming power of man. Once he has stripped away the "moral virtues and other graces of a fair outside" and uncovered the "small trifling films and little pipes," he can show with delight "the wonderful power of political wisdom, by the help of which so beautiful a machine is raised from the most contemptible branches." All of the piety that might have been brought to showing the creation of a divine harmony from the unlikeliest materials Mandeville turns instead to showing the creation of a successful political order from the brutishness of man's nature.

One may recall the last part of *Gulliver's Travels*, where the distraught Gulliver reduces the glories of European culture to the complications of Yahoo bestiality. Mandeville turns this argument upside down. See, he says, what the Yahoo has made of himself! No dreary Houyhnhnm decorum for him—instead the bustle and splendor of a worldly London. Shaftesbury might have seen the highest art of man in his restraint of his animality and his attainment of disinterested benevolence. But Mandeville sees as authentic an art, and one more generally realized, in the creation of a complex society out of that very animality. Political order is a high art. Between "the vileness of the ingredients" and the wholesomeness of the "mixture" lies only the "wonderful power of political wisdom" (I, 6).

Mandeville's irony arises from his separation of morality from politics. Even more than Hobbes he can devote his attention to the intrinsic value of political order, for he has no desire to claim moral worth for it and no need to displace the common meanings of moral terms. The state emerges not from a social contract in which all men participate as equals, but from the ingenious manipulation by a few technicians of the frailty of others. Skillful politicians are the tamers of man; they teach him sociability by flattering him into self-sacrifice, that is, by offering him a more exquisite mental gratification than the senses can attain. The "moral virtues are the political offspring which flattery begot upon pride."

Like Hobbes, Mandeville must distinguish sharply between man in a state of nature and man in society. Far more than Hobbes, however, he can stress the art by which the politician creates order: "Sagacious moralists draw men like angels, in hopes that the pride at least of some will put 'em upon copying after the beautiful originals which they are represented to be" (I, 51–52). So long as the moralist—such a moralist as Shaftesbury—believes his noble vision, he is merely another dupe; the politician need only persuade others to live by it to the extent that they can. Shaftesbury is incapable of true art because he gives too much credit to nature: "[Two] systems cannot be more opposite than his Lordship's and mine," Mandeville remarks, with evident satisfaction. Shaftesbury's "notions . . . are generous and refined," a "high compliment to human-kind," capable of inspiring us with a high sense of the dignity of human nature. "What a pity it is that they are not true" (I, 324).

In these secularized doctrines we can see the old conflict of nature and grace. For Shaftesbury nature absorbs grace and becomes its clearest mediator. Just as the will of God is embodied in natural order, the grace given to man is found in his capacity for rational self-mastery (itself an imitation of God's art in nature). For Mandeville the separation between grace and nature is all but absolute: fallen man is irreparably selfish (with exceptions to be noted later) and nature without order. Instead of grace, man has art, and the order he creates is neither divine nor natural.

Yet this secular social order that is the achievement of man's art, while it may be all that is to be expected of man, is not all that man can imagine. Mandeville keeps alive throughout his work the image of an ascetic goodness, of a wholehearted sacrifice of one's passion to duty, of rigorous self-denial and rational adherence to the precepts of revelation. It is an image that serves to mock those like Shaftesbury who make comfortable compromises between virtue and happiness. Mandeville's stark and skeletal virtue is always "contrary to the impulse of nature," as goodness is to worldly happiness. Such virtue is an art higher than that of political craftsmen, but it defies practice save through God's unpredictable aid.

The distrust of nature provides a clear link between Mandeville and Pascal. Just as the fragmentation within man, the conflict of the three orders, is, for Pascal, a result of his fallen nature, the separation of the realms of nature and grace is its result in the outer world. To live in such a world, one must accept the order of a fallen nature, which is a rule of power, and yet always see it as evil. As Erich Auerbach has restated Pascal's view, "before God, nobody on earth suffers injustice, or to express it even more strikingly, . . . man can do wrong, but not suffer it; for, although the wrong you do your neighbor is truly wrong, the suffering neighbor, corrupted by original sin, suffers rightfully." Might "is right, but it is not good, it is evil; our world is evil, but it is right that it be so." Thus, Auerbach says, Pascal "got to the paradox of might as a pure evil, which one has to obey unconditionally, without any re-gard to possible benefit—but without devotion, or better, out of devotion to God."[2]

Pascal's severity, with its compound of Augustine and Machiavelli, eliminates one side of Mandeville's paradoxes. Mandeville invokes a moral rigorism like Pascal's, by whose standards man is incapable of goodness in the world. But Mandeville uses it not so much to teach resignation as to free man from an ill-conceived and hopeless task. Any effort to establish goodness through the satisfactions of the world is confused or hypocritical. What remains is to make the best of what is within man's power, to create a secular, utilitarian order. The selfishness of the politician who devises this order detracts not at all from its value, for its value lies in the ends it achieves. By being entirely divorced from morality, it achieves a new freedom and efficiency.

The political artist disdains moral judgment, and particu-larly judgment that claims divine sanction. God's will is above human understanding; and if God has created fallen man, who shall question (or worse, explain) His wisdom? Although men are "naturally selfish, unruly and headstrong creatures," they are not to be understood by simple moral categories:

> As most men are worse than they would seem to be, so again they are better, than from their actions, if we were acquainted with all, we would judge them to be; for, tho' the neglect of those duties, which interfere with their pas-sions, be almost general, yet it proceeds not, as some imagine, from want of faith, an aversion to religion, or an unwillingness to be good; but the insurmountable difficulty they meet with, in striving against nature, and conquer-ing their inclinations (*Free Thoughts,* p. 17).

Freedom from moral scruple and self-reproach releases man's best powers. He can create with sagacity and make the most of a corrupt world. He tolerates those who differ from him so long as they do not threaten his own happiness or make society impossible. Life becomes an exercise in prudence, its rewards the gratification of appetite or vanity. Those who are hobbled by moral guilt are in constant turmoil, aware of their own failures, moved to reform others no worse than themselves, tortured by the effort to reconcile the City of Man with their dubious vision of the City of God. Such men become dangerous, as the political and religious wars of the seventeenth century had shown: "Men may have extravagant notions, yet no criminal design, 'till human passion intervenes, and laying hold of the opportunity, turns that to wickedness and abomination, which was begun with the most innocent intention" (*Free Thoughts*, p. 184).

The desperation of these men, who conduct constant campaigns against Nature, is a primary source of social disorder. In their frustration, they generate superstition and cant, inevitably futile because "you can make no multitude believe contrary to what they feel, or what contradicts a passion inherent in their nature." Only "if you humour that passion, and allow it to be just, you may regulate it as you please" (*Honour*, p. 28).

Social order must abandon concern with motive and concentrate upon consequence. The wicked, from this utilitarian viewpoint, are simply those "who indulge their passions as they come uppermost, without regard to the good or hurt, which the gratification of their appetites may do to the society" (*Honour*, p. 196). The true political artists are those who "having studied human nature, have endeavoured to civilize men, and render them more tractable, either for the ease of governors and magistrates, or else for the temporal happiness of society in general."

The end of society is its own stability and peaceful subsistence. The best constitution is one that "provides against the worst contingencies" and "preserves itself firm and remains unshaken, though most men should prove knaves" (*Free Thoughts*, p. 297). Morality is of no concern except as the political artist may use its teachings as a means of social control. Presumably the man who is least affected or hampered by a worldly society will be most free to achieve a private morality; but he runs the risk of losing out to the aggression of others if he becomes too weak or too indifferent to social policy. One may dream of a world of men that have "frugality without avarice, and generosity without pride" (II, 260); but the very dream disarms us of the worldly wisdom by which we can survive in the world that exists.

We find a striking counterpart to Mandeville's "realism" in a writer who admired his candor—the Bernard Shaw of such a play as *Major Barbara*. "If man cannot look evil in the face without illusion," Shaw writes in his preface, "he will never know what it really is, or combat it effectually. . . . that is why the great scoundrels have been beneficent rulers whilst amiable and privately harmless monarchs have ruined their countries by trusting to the hocus-pocus of innocence and guilt, reward and punishment, virtuous indignation and pardon, instead of standing up to the facts without either malice or mercy." The priggish Stephen Undershaft feels sure he knows one thing, the difference between right and wrong; but Major Barbara can say, "There are neither good men nor scoundrels: there are just children of one Father; and the sooner they stop calling one another names, the better. . . . They're all just the same sort of sinner; and there's the same salvation ready for them all."

The Mandevillian politician in the play is Sir Andrew Undershaft, the munitions maker who will not refuse power because it may produce evil, or tolerate any pious defense of human poverty and abstinence. Barbara comes at last to see that there "is no wicked side: life is all one." She can accept Undershaft's money and feed fellow creatures with the bread it buys, "because there is no other bread." Asceticism is a refusal of life, and life cannot be refused by a religious person.

Shaw's heroes are dedicated to a religious purpose, however secular, temporal, and humanitarian the religion may be. Mandeville does not have the religious fervor of Shaw. He belongs to the age that secularized Puritan doctrine rather than to the age that reclaimed its zeal for a secular faith. He is concerned not so much with social liberty as with the abolition of the moral confusions that make politics a debilitating form of hypocrisy. He too is seeking unashamed acceptance of power for social ends, and he too sees the enemy in the man who wishes to enjoy both power and moral respectability. But Mandeville asserts no end for the people he frees; he is not the moralist Shaw is. His freedom must be complemented, as it was in time, by a specific utilitarian standard such as the greatest good of the greatest number. What makes Mandeville so stark and unsettling is his refusal to accommodate our need to make moral choices.

II. Man as Maker

The primary method of Mandeville's satire is one of genetic reduction. To show the source of an idea or an institution is not necessarily either to exalt or dismiss it. Shaftesbury, for example, is well aware of the natural origin of our experience of moral ideas, but he deems these ideas "connatural," absolutes our experience only brings us to recognize. Mandeville will have none of this; he is, if not completely relativistic, at least highly skeptical of an "eternal and immutable morality." If the ways of God are incomprehensible, we cannot have much assurance that any of our ideas have divine sanction. Their universality is a matter of empirical test.

Mandeville's program is to oppose origin to end, causation to purpose, passive prejudice to active choice. His causal explanations are extremely subtle; they are often sufficient, even if not necessary. All that we celebrate in ourselves can be accounted for in terms of what we would least wish to acknowledge. "The beginning of all things relating to human affairs was ever small and mean: man himself was made of a lump of earth. Why should we be ashamed of this?" (*Honour,* p. 131.) From one point of view Mandeville may be said to tease man with his shame; from another, he is emphasizing the neutrality of human motives, among which there is little to choose. Only disregard for motive will enable us to regard clearly the consequences of our acts.

Mandeville's paradoxes rest upon the familiar difficulties of conceiving human freedom. Our ethics are based upon an act of choice, and the idea of choice implies responsibility. The free man seems ultimately autonomous, and his action must be treated as if he could as readily have done one thing as another. Seen as the terminus of a causal sequence, however, our actions can never be construed as free in this manner. We can always find our behavior governed by passive responses to external forces. A Christian's behavior may be explained as a free acceptance of divine injunction, or as the inevitable result of education, as the satisfaction of trained passions or appetites. Man's reason, in this view, becomes the enactment on the conscious level of those uncontrollable irrational forces of which he remains comfortably unconscious.

This explanation of man's behavior is not merely a trick; as F. B. Kaye has shown, Mandeville has a long tradition behind him. The Epicureans stressed the blind causality that produced fortuitous order. Pascal, in discussing the order of the flesh, could emphasize the autonomy of the realm of physical causation; and Hobbes's method was, as Michael Oakeshott puts it, "to establish the artificial character of civil society by considering its generation." Hobbes's rationalism requires an explanation in terms of cause and effect. One can understand that which one can, at least in theory, produce. All that philosophy can give us is a knowledge of hypothetical efficient causes that account for the generation of things. This causal explanation is our stay against confusion in an essentially unknowable world, and its causal nature is the condition of its rationality. Mandeville is very close to Hobbes in this: he does not pretend to give the sole explanation of effects, but he presents a sufficient cause in terms of egoistic motives and passive susceptibility to flattery.

We can hold man's passivity in clearest focus by showing him acted upon by a designing mind. Yet at once we begin a regress: What motivates the designing mind? As Coleridge put it, "by what strange chance there happened to start up among this premier species of Ouran Outangs, yclept man, these *Wise Men.* . . . these law-givers, who so cleverly took advantage of this *Peacock* Instinct of Pride and Vanity" (II, 453, citing a MS note on a flyleaf of *The Fable of the Bees*). Pushed far enough, this regress would give us an entirely evolutionary view of society and reinstate the order of nature at the expense of art. Mandeville meets this difficulty by constantly distinguishing between man as puppet and man as artist. What elevates the artist above the condition of the puppet is his freedom from moral concerns, his complete absorption in the technique of statecraft.

The artist seeks to make no absolute choices; he is pragmatic and utilitarian. Mandeville admires his freedom from cant, but he does not seek, like Shaw, to identify this practical realism with moral superiority. (Shaw's Caesar in *Caesar and Cleopatra* is great because he knows that revenge is futile, but this expediency is one face of what can also be seen as moral nobility, and he can speak plausibly of the need to conquer the world or be crucified by it.) In Mandeville the artist's action does not claim more than expediency. The artist can work successfully with efficient causes. If Hobbes's philosophy establishes "true fictions" by reasoning, Mandeville's politician "proves" their truth in practice. Mandeville may attack the artist with great zeal, when he considers his work destructive to society, as he does that of the Roman Catholic Church; but on such occasions he is writing without paradox as a moralist. Moral criticism can be voiced so long as the context does not undermine all moral attitudes as artfully induced passions.

Mandeville's typical device is to dissolve the free and choosing self that Shaftesbury celebrates and give us instead a creature of prejudice, all of whose attitudes can be traced to his "self-liking" or vanity. Once we have abolished "connatural ideas" (the *pulchrum* and *honestum* of Shaftesbury) by which the reflective power measures all experience, we are left with a creature whose learned responses can be attributed only to pleasure and pain. No choices are pure; no judgments, free of interest. In his insistence upon the subrational order of man's conduct, Mandeville achieves a reductivism that meets Shaftesbury's simplification with its antithesis.

Hazlitt remarked that the "error of Mandeville, as well as of those opposed to him, is in concluding that man is a simple and not a compound being." This is an error only if we take Mandeville's ironic challenge in full seriousness; but Mandeville's *Fable,* like Swift's account of the Yahoos, is an ironic attempt to show how much of human complexity *can* be reduced to a few low principles of compulsion. The Yahoo cannot exist without the opposed simplification of the Houyhnhnm; so Mandeville's image of brutish man is meant to be set against the "refined notions" of a flattering moralist. When Mandeville departs from irony, as in the *Free Thoughts,* he becomes a moralist in his own style, a firm advocate of a middle way between extremes of ungovernable power—a proponent of a mixed state and a tolerant church establishment, and a loyal defender of the Whigs and Hanoverians. When, too, Mandeville comes in that work (as later in the second volume of the *Fable*) to consider the problem of human freedom, he can only point to the paradoxes that beset all our thought about it, among libertarians and determinists alike. The mystery is all that remains.

Hazlitt's remark, I think, misses one point: the simplification of Mandeville is an artful abstraction (and Mandeville, like Defoe, honors nothing so much as the power of "abstract" thinking) of one aspect of the whole complexity of human nature, set off against those descriptions that (in his eyes) are unwitting abstractions. His very abstractness, by its painful aptness in meeting all problems to be explained, forces us to see the abstractness of the view he opposes. The resultant of such abstractions is a complexity Mandeville can hardly be said to have missed seeing (any more than he missed seeing the Christ child in the lowly barn) and that became the preoccupation of the major moralists of the age—men like Pope, Swift, and Bishop Butler, who could see man with equanimity as a compound of self-love and self-transcendence.

Mandeville's model of society, like Hobbes's, is essentially a mechanical one, a field of blind forces creating a unity or harmony through the tension of their unplanned but inevitable relationships. The typical model of the moralist also employs some version of harmony, but the moralist's metaphor requires some suggestion of responsibility. It may be one of a drama, in which each actor must play his part; or a musical harmony, with some suggestion of a group performance; or of a body, with the moral personifications we find in the parable of the belly. Mandeville, by his radical distinction between reason (the way of self-denial) and passion, can render a mechanical analogy all the more plausible. But his very stress upon the orderliness of society allows him, at times, to create the fiction of an ingenious technician. The ultimate social order created as if by a technician stands in brilliant contrast to the state of nature.

The technician's art, as we have seen, is the secular counterpart of divine grace; all order grows out of his "artful management." So long as we see him succeeding in an heroic task we can regard society as a triumph of art. If we see the technician in the same aspect as other men, the whole process recedes into the blind work of nature. Seen in their evolutionary aspect, spontaneously shaping a world that is as delicately ordered as a work of art, the passions become a creative power. They are still seen by Mandeville as a mechanical or at most a chemical power rather than a biological one; the effect of the *Fable* is to reduce our pride in our natural goodness, not to awaken trust in our passions. Yet one has only to remove Mandeville's praise of the order of mind and to sanctify the natural passions in turn, and their constructive artistry becomes something to be cultivated or induced.

To the extent that he treats the natural evolution of man's social order, Mandeville is providing a ground not only for laissez-faire economics but for the celebration of the genius of individual passion and the organic growth of a "natural" society. He is contributing, in the largest sense, to the tendency to see man as a psychological phenomenon rather than as a moral agent, a tendency that will move increasingly into the study of man's perceptive processes and the bases of his knowledge.

But Mandeville will admit none of this; in his ironic view, the only heroes, apart from the inspired men of true virtue, are the artful managers. The dignity of Mandeville's technician arises from the fact that he is the only kind of man who can be seen as self-determined. This is because he is seen only under the aspect of his manipulation of others. The practicality of his aim requires him to throw off the vulgar ideas and received notions by which most men are governed. Because he is freed of the need to pursue moral ends at every turn, he can create a state that will harmonize competing interests by recognizing and using their nature. His goal is an "opulent, flourishing, and warlike state"; the freedom of appetite and satisfaction possible once man has divested himself of what Shaw calls the "seven deadly virtues."

This side of Mandeville anticipates the vitalists who are to follow, the enemies of cant who free man for mature self-realization. And like those vitalists—such as the early Blake—he emphasizes so fully the need to overcome moral restrictions upon the free intelligence that he allows the nature of the resultant order to be taken for granted. Blake attributes man's injustice more to his dedication to a moral code of punishment and reward than to any intrinsic selfishness; the "mature" man will not need or want to tyrannize over or repress others. Mandeville stresses the technical skill that social order demands, but is notably vague about any specific programs.

When Mandeville turns direct moralist, he can defend common values with vigor: "not only revealed as well as natural religion, but likewise humanity, reason, the interest of mankind, their peace and felicity, and almost everything in nature pleads for toleration"—and then the more familiar Mandeville adds—"except the national clergy in every country" (*Free Thoughts,* p. 215). When he defends William III, he belittles those who are "too severe critics on the actions of princes, and by bold conjectures, supply the gaps and hidden parts of history" (p. 328), surely the very counterparts of the Mandeville of the *Fable.* But Mandeville as moralist still builds upon a harsh realism. He seeks only to quiet the needless complaints against the existing order, and his method is not to deny their justice but their usefulness. Men should after all expect the court to be "a gaudy society of subordinate slavery, where each member has an object to envy, and none can subsist without the profoundest dissimulation" (p. 337). Men can achieve wisdom only "by daring to examine and look boldly into the face of things" (p. 335); they must learn to accept what cannot be otherwise and to see the advantages that arise out of nastiness. The "perpetual warfare" of the Court is a source of honesty; jealousy and rivalry produce "severe censors" who, from whatever motives, act as "safeguards to the liberty of the people" (pp. 341–42). The tone is very much that which Swift takes toward the shocked young "Platonick" lover who discovers the filth of his mistress's dressing room; man should

> bless his ravisht sight to see
> Such Order from Confusion Sprung,
> Such gaudy Tulips rais'd from Dung.

This attitude does not produce a positive program so much as a conservative distrust of repining and of reform. Like Burke, Mandeville can stress the value of custom as second nature, if not nature itself:

> When a schism has remained for several generations, has been examined, looked into, and the sovereign power, having found it to bring neither dishonor to God, nor detriment to the society, thinks fit to tolerate it in an authentic manner, then it becomes a lawful worship, which it is criminal to disturb (*Free Thoughts,* p. 226).

He has the typical conservative awareness of the complexity of the past, the unpredictability of planned reforms, and the elaborate interrelationship of structure that sustains a society. "As great lovers as men are of novelty, they look upon it as a weakness, and all have a great veneration for things not easily alterable, and such as are known to have been of great duration" (p. 119).

This conservatism replaces morality in Mandeville's politics; he is opposed to tyranny, but also to any extension of liberty that will disturb the balance of the state. He is not interested in elevating the poor to a state of fuller self-determination through charity schools. The poor man educated beyond his capacity to earn is simply a new malcontent, and, while the benefits to the man are doubtful, the damage to society is certain, in the loss of its cheap labor force. Mandeville abhors inhumanity, he tells us, "but to be compassionate to excess where reason forbids it, and the general interest of society requires steadiness of thought and resolution, is an unpardonable weakness." While Mandeville invokes all the conventional arguments for the greater happiness of the poor, he is most impressive in underlining the sentimentality of those who, for the sake of their own feelings, would save the poor from a condition in which they are comparatively content, and most striking in his observation on the "unreasonable vein of petty reverence for the poor, that runs through most multitudes . . . and arises from a mixture of pity, folly, and superstition" (I, 310–11). This free play of intelligence, chilling as it may be, catches the moralist in the intellectual confusions that warm humanitarianism sometimes induces.

Conservatism is the other side of Mandeville's mocking reductivism. If our institutions can be seen as the product of flattery and delusion, they can be shown as well to have an almost inestimable value. The conservative's awareness of social complexity reveals a toughness and stability in the social fabric that a moral view can seldom admit. Yet there is a painful limitation in all this. To be shown how well-ordered Hell can be does not reconcile us to it, and Mandeville's assurance that this is hardly the worst of all possible worlds does little to satisfy moral aspiration. The divorce between private and social morality is a difficult one to sustain; it is all but impossible to judge the success of a society without introducing some standard of justice or freedom. Without some implicit standard of liberty (even Hobbes's minimal standard, our need to be free from the threat of violent death), there is no way of preventing the individual from becoming entirely absorbed into the welfare of the state. Mandeville obviously accepts such a standard, as his non-ironic work makes clear, but he has no basis for invoking it except its obviousness. Mandeville, in short, takes his morality for granted while he proclaims his hard-headed technical realism, and he attributes to art—to the order of mind—the power and direction that can arise only from something more—perhaps charity—as well.

As a counterpoise to confused idealism this is shrewd and healthy. We can imagine Swift's own voice (say, at the close of *Gulliver's Travels*) in such words of Mandeville's as "what madness is it, that men should choose to be wretched, because they cannot be completely happy!" (*Free Thoughts*, p. 356.) But we can find in Swift, more than in Mandeville, the sense of man's natural capacity, even in his fallen condition. Mandeville's order of Art is essentially an ironic fiction, to be set against the divine Nature of such men as Shaftesbury. In its refusal to admit more than a controlling technical intelligence, it remains an artificial scheme—all the more brilliant, as I have tried to show, for its intense and consistent use of abstraction. Mandeville has subsumed all Order into the order of the flesh controlled by the order of mind. If God acts in this world, He acts through these orders. If man would attain the order of charity, he has only to make a clear choice, but at the expense of all that concerns the politician.

III. Causation and Style

Mandeville's literary achievement can be related to the more typical works of his age in two principal ways. As we have seen, his double system of values has much in common with the view embodied in mock-pastoral and mock-heroic forms. And his constant playing upon the paradox of man's freedom—the two aspects of all men's conduct, seen as morally responsible and actively willed on the one hand, and seen as mechanically ordered and either externally or subconsciously governed on the other—is one of the chief concerns of the principal novels of the century. These two forms of double vision and ambivalent judgment of man are not themselves unrelated. The heroic always posits a man in command of himself—and Dryden's heroic drama carries this as far as it can go —whereas the comic view tends to stress an order beyond man's intention. The fusion of the two produces a clash between conceptions of man; and, since each conception has its own typical forms, it produces a clash of styles as well.

Mandeville's work is built of the dialectical opposition of abstractions, and each abstraction generates its characteristic version of reality. The "fair outside" that man wears may be caught in his cantlike idiom about his virtues, in the moral vision that allures and thwarts him, or in the noble terms in which his social order can be imagined. The egoism within him can be caught in the incomparable pictures Mandeville creates of the energy of a bustling city, in the animal analogies he constantly invokes, in the mechanical patterns passionate actions create. In such a passage as the following one can see the conventional attributes of an all-but-idyllic order in the first part, the fashionable and sophisticated concerns ("a tolerable coat") in the next, and a mechanical figure in the last:

Let us examine then what things are requisite to aggrandize and enrich a nation. The first desirable blessings for any society of men are a fertile soil and a happy climate, a mild government, and more land than people. These things will render man easy, loving, honest, and sincere. In this condition they may be as virtuous as they can, without the least injury to the public, and consequently as happy as they please themselves. But they shall have no arts or sciences, or be quiet longer than their neighbors will let them; they must be poor, ignorant, and almost wholly destitute of what we call the comforts of life, and all the cardinal virtues together won't so much as procure a tolerable coat or a porridge-pot among them; for in this state of slothful ease and stupid innocence, as you need not fear great vices, so you must not expect any considerable virtues. Man never exerts himself but when he is roused by his desires: while they lie dormant, and there is nothing to raise them, his excellence and abilities will be forever undiscovered and the lumpish machine, without the influence of his passions, may be justly compared to a huge wind-mill without a breath of air (I, 183–84).

More explicit is the contrast of levels of style in a picture of the "choleric city captain":

His martial finery, as he marches along, inspires him with an unusual elevation of mind, by which endeavoring to forget his shop as well as himself, he looks up at the balconies with the fierceness of a Saracen conqueror (I, 131).

Mandeville makes the "elevation" literal, as the captain achieves a glorious obliviousness of the shops about him and of his own shopkeeperly self; and all of this is mechanically governed by the "finery."

The keynote of Mandeville's double view can best be caught in such a sentence as this: "To me it is a great pleasure, when I look on the affairs of human life, to behold into what various and often strangely opposite forms the hope of gain and thoughts of lucre shape men, according to the different employments they are of, and stations they are in." Mandeville's method works in two directions: from the manifold expression to the few determining principles (here "gain," but more generally egoistic satisfaction), and outward from the principles themselves into a plenitude of embodiments. Swift may suggest this plenitude in his incomparable lists of respectable perversions, but Mandeville elaborates the various expressions with all the affection of a natural theologian showing the design of God in his least creature. That Mandeville is deliberately inverting the argument from design becomes clear in his brilliant account of the lion:

> There is a real majesty stamped on every single lion. . . . When we look upon, and examine his massy talons, the size of them, and the labored firmness, with which they are fixed in, and fastened to that prodigious paw; his dreadful teeth, the strength of his jaws, and the width of his mouth equally terrible, the use of them is obvious; but when we consider, moreover, the make of his limbs, the toughness of his flesh and tendons, the solidity of his bones, beyond that of other animals, and the whole frame of him, together with his never-ceasing anger, speed, and agility; whilst in the desert he ranges king of beasts: when, I say, we consider all these things, it is stupidity not to see the design of nature, and with what amazing skill, the beautiful creature is contrived, for offensive war and conquest (II, 233–34).

When Milton's vision of Paradise is invoked—"Sporting the Lion ramp'd, and in his Paw / Dandl'd the Kid"—Mandeville's spokesman can reply in a memorable sentence, "The lion was not made to be always in Paradise." Mandeville's lion serves something of the function of Blake's tiger (see below, p. 400); he is a "beautiful creature" in his superb embodiment of energy; and his beauty, his fearful symmetry, is as authentic as the innocence of the lamb or the kid. God did not create such "prodigious strength of limbs and sinews" to "be quiet, and dandle a kid." The insight that sees both beauty and God's will in the destructive force of the lion grows out of analogical reasoning, but goes beyond the simple analogy into an aesthetic awareness.

On a comic level we can see the same vigor of detail and freshness of sense in the analysis of motive or the description of London manners. There is something of Chaucerian "nature" in the account of the peasant accosted by watermen:

> It is not unpleasant to see half a dozen people surround a man they never saw in their lives before, and two of them that can get the nearest, clapping each an arm over his neck, hug him in as loving and familiar a manner as if he was their brother newly come home from an East India voyage; a third lays hold of his hand, another of his sleeve, his coat, the buttons of it, or anything he can come at, while a fifth or sixth, who has scampered twice round him already without being able to get at him, plants himself directly before the man in hold, and within

three inches of his nose, contradicting his rivals with an open-mouthed cry, shows him a dreadful set of large teeth and a small remainder of chewed bread and cheese, which the countryman's arrival had hindered from being swallowed (I, 353).

Mandeville goes on to describe the peasant's incomparable pleasure as he moves along "very contentedly under a load of watermen, and with a smiling countenance [carries] seven or eight stone more than his own weight, to the water-side." And this picture of grotesque flattery and the bumbling pride that enjoys it also serves to characterize the actions of the greatest or most knowing men.

Mandeville's pleasure in illustrating his principles of pride and vanity is as great as Fielding's, and there is the same effect in his use of low buffoonery as in the novelist's use of a moral spectrum that distinguishes and relates the kinds of pride we can see in Blifil or Mrs. Western, in Partridge or Deborah Wilkins. In both authors there is a commanding simplicity of moral scheme and a fascination—we can see it again in Fielding's plea for the individuality of his innkeepers—with its range and variety of manifestation. The spectrum, moreover, provides vivid counterparts in low life for characters in high. Mandeville is fond of invoking the debasing analogy, drawn from low life or from familiar objects; he may be influenced in this by Hobbes, who is certainly a master of the method. ("And this is called Vain Glory; and is exemplified in the fable, by the fly sitting on the axletree, and saying to himself, what a dust do I make rise!") Mandeville's original fable of the grumbling hive, his parable of small beer, his account of the mixing of punch, his use of children's behavior to explain adult motives—all of these are means of seeing man simultaneously as he sees himself and as he might be regarded by a detached and amused Brobdingnagian king.

Perhaps the master image of *The Fable of the Bees* is that of London itself, whose "dirty streets are a necessary evil inseparable from [its] felicity." "If we would know the world, we must look into it," says Mandeville's spokesman, Cleomenes. "You take no delight in the occurrences of low life; but if we always remain among persons of quality and extend our enquiries no farther, the transactions there will not furnish us with a sufficient knowledge of everything that belongs to our nature." And Cleomenes sets up an "experimental situation" in which he contrasts an indolent with an active tradesman. They embody not only two different ways of life but two systems of value. From the industry of one Mandeville traces a Hobbesian pursuit of power: "his endeavors to advance his fortune *per fas & nefas* are always restless and have no bounds." From the timidity and sloth of the other Mandeville traces a moral view like Shaftesbury's: "he'll endeavor to cover over his frailty with the appearance of virtue; and what is altogether owing to his too easy temper and an excessive fondness for the calmness of his mind, he'll ascribe to his modesty and the great aversion he has to boasting." Thus, Cleomenes shows, the "natural temper will warp and model the very passions to its own bias" (II, 110–12). The orders of flesh and charity have now become the expressions of psychophysical temperaments (the traditional "humors"), and all professions of value have become the rationalizations of the necessities of one's nature. As Pascal said, "The three lusts have made three sects; and the philosophers have done no other thing than follow one of the three lusts." Mandeville excepts the order of the mind; there man makes conscious the demands of his nature, and there he chooses either to direct them into social order or, if he is pious, to restrain them as his faith directs.

The relation of Mandeville to the novelists' studies in moral consciousness can be seen more closely as we compare Mandeville and Defoe. In his first novel, Defoe created a character who still puzzles and troubles many readers; Robinson Crusoe seems to some an adventurer with a pretense of smug moralizing, to others an inept symbol of the Christian seeking his salvation in this world. The whole first part is shot through with seeming contradiction; yet the inconsistencies are so vivid and dramatically presented that they can hardly be dismissed as blunders. There is Crusoe plundering the sinking ship; after a pious declaration about the uselessness of wealth in his present situation, he quietly takes the bag of gold back to the island.

> . . . "O drug!" said I aloud, "what art thou good for? Thou art not worth to me, no, not the taking off of the ground . . . e'en remain where thou art and go to the bottom as a creature whose life is not worth saving;" however, upon second thoughts, I took it away. . . .

This sequence, like others throughout the first part of the book, shows the ambivalence of Crusoe's attitudes. All his life he has been torn between his father's advice (and his father's will) that he accept his proper station in life and de-

vote his energies to the decent endeavors of a devout tradesman, and his own inarticulate passion for self-realization.
Each adventure into which he is driven makes him regret his
choice; yet his choice as insistently asserts itself, almost unconsciously, beneath the level of open debate. Those who have
mocked the unimaginative conception of adventure miss the
point Defoe is making: Crusoe's career on the island becomes, increasingly, the counterpart of all he might have had
to do in the "middle station" of life which he rejected. Ian
Watt has put it very well in saying that Crusoe's island becomes "the utopia of the Protestant ethic."[3] There Crusoe's
sense of adventure is reconciled with the practicality and acquisitive skill of the manufacturer and merchant. But it is not
fair, I think, to deride the conception as mere grossness: the
"myth" of Crusoe has a double bearing—it exalts middle-class
endeavor by abstracting its creativity and practical value, but
it criticizes that endeavor by showing its innocence in isolation
in contrast to the competitive and destructive forms it may
take in society.

The heart of *Robinson Crusoe* is surely the dramatization
of the heroic technician, transforming nature by art. But Defoe
belongs to an earlier phase of the Puritan tradition than Mandeville; even as he celebrates the heroic individualism of
Crusoe, he reveals its cruelty (the selling of Xury in contrast
to the treatment of Friday) and egoism, and he explores its
possibility of redemption. Crusoe is in one aspect the amoral
technician of Mandeville's *Fable;* in another, he is the wayward
pilgrim finding his salvation in the difficult and often frustrating
task of survival. It is appropriate that he arrive at the island
with the good stock of "machinery," for it is his exploitation
of the materials of nature that is the center of attention. (A
more primitive level of achievement, however greater the ingenuity it might display, would lose the resemblance to the
commonplace labors of an English artisan that the book
stresses.) There are tasks for which Crusoe *is* poorly prepared, notably the making of pottery; but here, in the painful
effort and the small but solid success, Defoe achieves the most
fundamental dramatization of his industry. The forming of the
pot has been likened to the forming of a soul, and the analogy
can be accepted without overemphasis. The book relates
Crusoe's mastery of nature to his mastery of self; the outward
island and the inward jungle are, to some extent, counterparts,
yet at a level of symbolism that needs no insistence and is
more readily sensed than identified.[4]

The point of connection between Mandeville and the Defoe of *Robinson Crusoe* is the double view taken of man's will, which can be seen as rational self-mastery and mastery of nature, or as compulsive, subrational drive. In Crusoe the drive is finally reconciled with self-mastery. When he is tempted to overexploit nature, he is deterred by danger or frustrated by natural circumstances. He is guided by visions and voices that are never clearly distinguishable as either God's intercession or his own projections. Mandeville has freed his technician of the trouble, by making him undivided of mind and purely active *upon* nature. The rest of men, for Mandeville, still show a passive acceptance of powerful drives, elaborately rationalized and disguised, but none the less thoroughgoing. The third way, which Mandeville locks up in the gospels, is a way of conscious activity with moral aim. It is toward this third way that Crusoe moves, hesitantly, crookedly, but hopefully. Mandeville praises the doctrine of Christ, "which can only be learned from the New Testament, where" —his irony becomes telling—"it will ever remain in its purity and lustre" (*Honour,* p. 240). Whether Mandeville is simply amused by the irrelevancy to our lives of a divine vision or sincerely disturbed by it, he insists upon it in a way that makes all effort to bring the order of charity into relation to other orders seem quixotic. It must be either sainthood or folly, and Mandeville's world is not the home of saints. Defoe still looks for a connection between orders, although he is impressed by the conflicts and the deceptions. His technician, Crusoe, works toward a union of the order of mind and the order of charity; Mandeville's technician remains an ironic fiction, secure in the order of mind, operating with detached ingenuity in the order of flesh.

Mandeville, like Hobbes, stirs moralists to overstatement. Hobbes called forth from the orthodox early strains of sentimentalism as a defense of man's "relish" of goodness against the simple egoism that Hobbes postulated. So, in the case of Mandeville, as F. B. Kaye has noted, his orthodox critics move away from moral rigorism toward some recognition of the pleasures goodness affords. They must draw virtue and pleasure back together to make virtue relevant to this world, and the cool detachment of Mandeville's technician becomes an unnatural coldness.

Fielding's Blifil has been called a "sentimentalist's idea of a villain." To the extent that Blifil is all icy egocentricity, this is true; but in Blifil, as in Iago, the technical skill ("the slightest alteration of the single letter 's' ") is directed by strong and unconscious drives. The overtones of sadism (Blifil is anxious to marry Sophia *because* she detests him) are revealed sharply but without insistence; Fielding never risks the danger of allowing Blifil's peculiar energy to rival Tom's. Blifil is not allowed to become a Lovelace; the structure of *Tom Jones* depends upon a set of characters whose motives are never fully executed and therefore never become seriously threatening. Blifil's genius for manipulation has lost the freedom of Mandeville's technician. It is the product of compulsion, and it is doomed to failure.

Mandeville's technician, then, is a figure the age is not prepared to welcome, for he affronts moral sensibility. He becomes instead a Jonathan Wild, and the deviousness of Mandeville's analysis of motive is turned into that bold ironic formalism that is one of the best things in Fielding's style. We see anticipations of this in Mandeville himself. Here, for example, is Mandeville's account of the usefulness of eating houses, "the great schools for servants, where the dullest fellows may have their understandings improved; and get rid at once of their stupidity and their innocence":

> They are the academies for footmen, where public lectures are daily read on all sciences of low debauchery by the experienced professors of them, and students are instructed in above seven hundred illiberal arts, how to cheat, impose upon, and find out the blind side of their masters, with so much application, that in a few years they become graduates in iniquity (I, 304).

This ironic formalism is part of the mock-heroic game of the age. Mandeville uses it to catch the logic of the passions: the style defers to the rational motivation of the act, while it denies rationality to the actor. Mandeville is chiefly interested in those motives that go deeper than hypocrisy—those unrecognized and uncontrolled forms of self-love that are all the more powerful for their concealment. In showing the implicit logic of passion (it has an object and chooses the most efficient means of obtaining it), Mandeville is as resourceful and thorough as any writer of his age—a true heir of the tradition of La Rochefoucauld and Pascal. Nothing can make this order more striking than to present it as if it were the contrivance and social control of the artful politician. But the emphasis on rational artifice and control, upon order as art, has a fundamental ambiguity, for the power of art arises from its submission to the largely uncontrollable force of unconscious nature and its sensible recognition of its own limited function.

V.

Pope: Art and Morality

Pope is the greatest poet of his age, and, more than any other, the celebrant of Order. Like Shaftesbury, he constantly discriminates between authentic order and mock order. But, like Mandeville, he is willing to recognize the sordid origins in our nature from which splendor may arise. The crucial difference between Pope and Mandeville—the difference that brings Pope closer to Shaftesbury—is the one set forth by Pope's friend and editor, Warburton: "Rochefoucauld, Esprit, and their wordy disciple Mandeville had observed that self-love was the origin of all those virtues mankind most admire; and therefore foolishly supposed it was the end likewise." Pope sees a genuine transformation of self-love *into* social love, and he finds in that transformation a return to man's original nature, to his authentic self. I have chosen to deal first of all with Pope's *Essay on Man* (1733–34) and, particularly, with the third epistle, where Pope's relation to Shaftesbury and Mandeville is clearest. From that poem, I move backward to the earlier celebrations of order and forward to the Horatian satires, where the mock order is caught in its magnificence and horror.[1]

1. The Double Vision

In the third epistle of the *Essay on Man* Pope describes man's fall from a state of nature where the patriarch rules benevolently in the name of a universal Father whom all acknowledge and love. This ideal society gives way suddenly and mysteriously to the joint rule of Tyranny and Superstition, to the "enormous faith of many made for one" (III, 242). But this fallen condition (it is now a Hobbesian state of nature) is so intolerable that it drives man toward civil government. Man reaches what Blake was to call a "consolidation of error": the consequences of a false order become so starkly clear and painfully cruel that he must find an alternative.

> How shall he keep, what, sleeping or awake,
> A weaker may surprise, a stronger take?
> His safety must his liberty restrain:
> All join to guard what each desires to gain (275–78).

The last line is built of intense rhetorical oppositions: *all* against *each, join* against *desires, guard* against *gain.* In each opposition, the thrust of selfishness becomes transformed to the embrace of confederation. And Pope goes on:

> Forc'd into virtue thus by self-defence
> Ev'n kings learn'd justice and benevolence:
> Self-love forsook the path it first pursu'd,
> And found the private in the public good (279–82).

This is still calculation of advantage, but at least we have moved from blind appetite to seeming choice. It is not a truly free choice: men are forced into virtue, and virtue is still a mere form. One can see something close to Mandeville's evolutionary pattern: the result is more rational than the intention. The second line emphasizes an ironic situation in the spirit of Mandeville or Swift: kings are those most responsible for, and yet least compelled by, justice and benevolence. In the order of the flesh, as Pascal has told us, they are the masters of power. And even the final couplet sustains this ironic tone: man retreats from blind selfhood and suddenly finds not so much what he seeks but what he needs. We are moving from an order of flesh to an order of mind, from appetite to cognition; but the movement still seems more accidental than deliberate, more mechanical than rational. Expediency is not yet charity.

It is at this point that Pope separates himself from Mandeville:

> 'Twas then, the studious head or gen'rous mind,
> Follow'r of God, or friend of humankind,
> Poet or patriot, rose but to restore
> The faith and moral Nature gave before;
> Relum'd her ancient light, not kindl'd new;
> If not God's image, yet his shadow drew (283–88).

What comes to mind here is Shaftesbury's emphasis on connatural ideas; once man is forced into virtue, he discovers what in fact he knew all the time. Virtue is recalled, not invented (we may think of Plato's doctrine of recollection). God has placed these truths in nature and made them accessible to the human reason, but they must be constantly recovered anew. One might say that Pope is reconciling a keen Mandevillian sense of the origin of social order with the trust in human nature that Shaftesbury shows. The moment of transformation is all-important: it marks a new moment, from expediency to faith, from calculation to charity. "Self-love but serves the virtuous mind to wake" (IV, 363).

In this way Pope establishes a continuous movement between orders and yet preserves Pascal's sense of their discontinuity. The order of flesh is an unstable one which descends into intolerable anarchy, and its disorder stirs the mind to a rational expediency which is, at last, the occasion for recovering a vision of charity. In each stage there is continuity, but also novelty. Placed in the posture of co-operation, union, and social love, man finds something in his nature awakened to give meaning to his gestures, as man placed in the posture of prayer may be stirred to reverence. Pope is, perhaps, recalling the great scene at the close of the tenth book of *Paradise Lost,* where Eve's helpless prostration before Adam leads to the reawakening of their love for each other, and their love for each other, in its turn, leads them back, humble and suppliant, to God—whom they can now once more recognize to be Redeemer as well as harsh Judge. In Pope's poem, like Milton's, man recovers the image of God his despair has distorted and, in effect, destroyed.

The way of rational liberty must be forced upon men, but Pope does recognize sanction for it once it is attained, a sanction to be found in both nature and God. For Pope as for Pascal the "Kingdom of God is within us; the universal good is within us, is ourselves—and not ourselves." And Pope magnifies, throughout the *Essay on Man,* what is less than thought and what is more. The sure instinct of animals—"God in them"—serves as a standard by which to judge the failures of reason. And yet, once he has made clear the limits of reason, Pope can restore it to its place in a continuity that ascends from self-love to selflessness. Far more than Pascal, Pope stresses the continuity: man can move from a lower order to higher without casting off the world. The order of charity is not attained through an extinction of mind; it controls and extends the order of mind. Pope wrote to Swift in 1736 of his growth into philosophical maturity: "My understanding, indeed, such as it is, is extended rather than diminished: I see things more in the whole, more consistent, and more clearly deduced from, and related to, each other" (25 March 1736, *Correspondence*, IV, 5). Like Dryden, Pope is dramatizing the dialectical struggle for the mind, and he must give as much weight to Pascal's "is ourselves" as to "not ourselves."

The *Essay on Man* is, like all the work of Shaftesbury and Mandeville, an implicit dialogue, working between the extremes of selfhood and harmonious love. Man in his selfhood is insatiate, restless, soaringly ambitious, envious of all creatures both above and below his station. This pattern of selfhood is dramatized as the other voice in the *Essay,* the voice we hear only as the poet throws back its phrases, untwists its questions, shifts his own stance to meet its alternate self-pity and arrogance. It is difficult to characterize the interlocutor, for he is various and inconsistent, but some such sketch as the following may serve.

He is a man who, through uncritical use of his reason, sees the universe as a vast machine designed for his pleasure. Since his pleasures prove unstable, he adjudges the design imperfect: he is made too weak, he lacks the powers or pleasures of other creatures, he is not allowed sustained delight. This is a cosmic view that seeks to accommodate and stabilize man as center and end. Beyond man's vision—since his eyes are focussed on himself—is a quite different design with a quite different end, beautifully achieved: "Whatever is, is right."

Within his own mind, man places all value upon his reason —whether the ecstatic reason of the Neo-Platonists or the sober reason of the Stoic—and therefore upon his conscious control of his own actions. Here too he can complain either that his reason is not strong enough to master his universe or that the universe is inhospitable to his reason, for all his achievements crumble into conflict or vanity. Once more his desire for greater power is a blindness to an order he cannot discern. The complexity of human nature is such that reason is at most a director for the energy of passion, and its role can at most be the diversion of an irresistible ruling passion to a beneficent end. Since man is a creature of energy and appetite, he cannot be self-subsistent; he is inevitably incomplete. The quest of selfhood must always end in dissatisfaction; man can find happiness only in the surrender of self. What seems a chaos of passion that must be governed by reason is really a fluidity, a need for relatedness. In the authentic order of God's design the self-enclosing passion of pride will be dissolved in relationships, but the dissolution may come either through the growth of selfhood into a capacity for love or through the cracking and crumbling of its stubbornness into the rubble of which new structures are built.

Just as the interlocutor, the voice of selfhood, claims to be a creature of reason in a knowable universe, so in society he moves (as Hobbes had shown) toward tyranny. His will to use others, even God, as his instruments is fostered by a superstitious reverence for his own will. The creature of selfhood, like Blake's Urizen, is always seeking to build solid structures and always finding himself defeated by the reality of other selves and other wills. So, finally, in the search for happiness, we reach once more the futility of the quest for stability through insatiable acquisition of limited goods:

> Who ask, and reason thus, will scarce conceive
> God gives enough, while he has more to give:
> Immense that pow'r, immense were the demand;
> Say, at what part of nature will they stand? (IV, 163–66.)

The word *stand* is a key term throughout the *Essay*, for the selfhood—whatever its dreams of solidity—cannot stand, can never rest. But the design selfhood cannot perceive grants each creature a place, a point of repose within a vast movement—the repose won by maintaining relationships with others, of moving in a dancelike order, not the Stoical stability that is "fix'd as in a frost."

The voice of selfhood is one of the two voices of the *Essay;* the other is the complex one assumed by the poet which moves with remarkable tact from satire to comedy, from comedy to consolation.[2] At moments the poet's voice is the voice in the whirlwind, rebuking folly and presumption, affirming a universe beyond the imagination of selfish man. Again it is the voice of the satirist speaking out of an assurance in quiet rightness—the way is always obvious to man if he will see it. Most often, it is a superbly didactic voice, Socratic in its ironic detachment, offering the sharp and simple replies that may shock men out of the tortured questions, the whining self-pity, and the sophistry of selfhood. This therapeutic sharpness can be well conveyed in the couplet, whose logical rigor becomes the inevitability of inescapable truth, and makes error seem needless and willful:

> Who wickedly is wise, or madly brave,
> Is but the more a fool, the more a knave (IV, 231–32).

Obvious her goods, in no extreme they dwell;
Then needs but thinking right, and meaning well
    (IV, 31–32).

In lines like these the poet dramatizes the common sense
men can rarely sustain:

Vice is a monster of so frightful mien,
As, to be hated, needs but to be seen;
Yet, seen too oft, familiar with her face,
We first endure, then pity, then embrace (II, 217–20).

Like Milton's Sin "familiar grown," Vice pleases. The poet
must reawaken awareness and keep it sharp; he must, in
Blake's terms, "cleanse the windows of perception." The poem
becomes, therefore, not simply an essay about man's nature
but, like so many Socratic dialogues, the drama of man's refusal to accept his nature; less an exposition of a system of
belief than a dialectical and dramatic recovery of the traditional vision that opaque selfishness has obscured.

The stages of the dialogue are marked by the division into
four epistles. In the first two, as Maynard Mack has shown,
the emphasis is upon the destruction and clearing away of
illusions; in the last two, the movement of ascent becomes
dominant, particularly from the passage I have cited about the
creation of a true society. The final epistle closes in upon
individual moral choice, and ends with the recovery of the
vision—the order of charity—that alone makes man godlike.
Within the dialectical structure, the process of destruction becomes, beneath the surface, a means of redefinition and a
preparation for conversion, as it does in the Socratic dialogue.

In Dryden's *Religio Laici* the Deist proudly reasoned his
way to a view of God as divine bookkeeper and banker. This
proved to be the rationalistic distortion of revealed truth: behind the crass quantitative terms of the Deist lie the mysteries
of God's justice and mercy, and whatever truth the Deist attains is based upon the revelation he professes to do without.
So, here, in Pope's *Essay on Man,* the proud reasoner imagines
an elaborately mechanical universe. Such a universe accords
with Newtonian science (although Newton was by no means
a mere mechanist himself). But the mechanical model by
which man tries to think breaks down even as he creates it.
The complexity of the universe, like that of any elaborate field
structure, shades off into the mysteriousness of organism.

Pope (like Pascal) shows how the subtle interdependence
of parts overwhelms simple reasoning. The seemingly stable

viewpoint of selfhood and pride wavers into a disconcerting relativity:

> So Man, who here seems principal alone,
> Perhaps acts second to some sphere unknown,
> Touches some wheel, or verges to some goal;
> 'Tis but a part we see, and not a whole (I, 57–60).

The terms are at once mechanical and something more; the interdependence of the heavenly bodies moves toward a vision somewhat like Milton's "starry dance." And a term like *goal* suggests a purposiveness that silently includes the creature who ignores it.

Whereas the mind conceives clear-cut and separable orders, the universe teases us with boundaries that are too elusive to be defined:

> What thin partitions sense from thought divide:
> And middle natures, how they long to join,
> Yet never pass th' insuperable line! (I, 226–28.)

The universe may be built of "just gradation," in a hierarchical chain of being, but the subtleties of the design escape our limited categories. Each link in the chain is "for ever sep'rate, yet for ever near" its neighbor (I, 224). Pope is trying to hold together within Order both hierarchy and plenitude. The task of man throughout the *Essay* is to know his "point" in the hierarchy and to accept responsibility for maintaining it; it is also man's duty, as a corrective to any simple schematization, to sense the one life that circulates through all the seeming parts and binds them with love. In the first epistle, the difficulties this double vision creates are the means by which proud selfhood is shaken.

Man's pride is overthrown by the breakdown of those categories of thought that have supported it. The cosmic meaninglessness of which man complains only shows that he has looked for meaning in the wrong way. Man's expectation of stable bliss is bound to be disappointed so long as he conceives stability as simple duration in time and space. He must come to see "His time a moment, and a point his space" (I, 72). Only in this contraction from soaring presumption to humble minuteness lies the escape from time and space. Man is being prepared for a complete transcendence of the orders of flesh and mind. The serenity of the order of charity will become his when he reaches "The only point where human bliss stands still" (IV, 311), when the self is dispersed through all time and all space.

The contraction to a point is like the inward-turning spiral of a vortex; once man reaches the center, his mind can open out again into selfless love:

> Wide and more wide, th' o'erflowings of the mind
> Take ev'ry creature in, of ev'ry kind;
> Earth smiles around, with boundless bounty blest,
> And Heav'n beholds its image in his breast (IV, 369–72).

Man becomes the image of God, and Earth becomes Paradise. The universe ceases to be inert mechanism and becomes a living whole bound by the chain of love. Man's selfhood has dissolved into what Milton calls the "dear relations" of charity; as Pope puts it, man may "yet consider the *whole world* as his relations." We find Pope seeking, in his own way, what Blake was to consider his "great task" in *Jerusalem:*

> To open the Eternal Worlds, to open the immortal Eyes
> Of Man inwards into the Worlds of Thought, into Eternity
> Ever expanding in the Bosom of God, the Human Imagination.

Pope does not identify the Bosom of God with the Human Imagination, but in the *Essay* the power of man's imagination creates anew the image of God and the divine image of man.

The overthrow of pride and the limited reason of selfhood is the destructive task of the first epistle. The selfhood in the first epistle may be likened to Blake's figure, in *Milton,* of the Idiot Questioner,

> who is always questioning
> But never capable of answering, who sits with a sly grin
> Silent plotting when to question, like a thief in cave,
> Who publishes doubt and calls it knowledge, whose Science is Depair,
> Whose pretence to Knowledge is Envy, whose whole Science is
> To destroy the wisdom of the ages to gratify ravenous Envy
> That rages round him like a Wolf day & night without rest (41:12–18).

To such a figure Pope opposes the God who "lives through all life," the animate love that spends and renews itself in creation. All of the universe is instinct with the presence of divine love:

> Whose body Nature is, and God the soul;
> That, chang'd thro' all, and yet in all the same,
> Great in the earth, as in th' aethereal frame,
> Warms in the sun, refreshes in the breeze,
> Glows in the stars, and blossoms in the trees,
> Lives thro' all life, extends thro' all extent,
> Spreads undivided, operates unspent,
> Breathes in our soul, informs our mortal part,
> As full, as perfect, in a hair as heart,
> As full, as perfect, in vile Man that mourns,
> As the rapt Seraph that adores and burns;
> To him no high, no low, no great, no small,
> He fills, he bounds, connects, and equals all (I, 268–80).

The divine force becomes more and more overtly personified, until at the close the presence of God fills the space of the universe and orders it. The four verbs of the last line achieve a progression of meaningfulness; from *fills* and *bounds* we move to the implicit harmony of *connects;* and the final *equals* sums up most explicitly the point of the preceding lines, the equal value before God of all his works in his incommensurable transcendence of all. Pope's lines, with their constant play between stillness and movement (sun, breeze), distance and closeness (stars, trees), activity and abstract being (life, extent), unity and division, present God as both immanent and transcendent. The order of the universe is such that materials cannot be opposed to design. The indivisibility of substance finds its counterpart in an indivisible system. God is at once in the local movement and the patterned field, for each local movement both governs and is governed by all others. The order Pope creates is neither mechanical nor imposed; all mass, one might say, is transformed to energy.

The first epistle closes with an insistence on the bafflement selfhood creates for itself by the very categories of its thought. All the terms it invokes to lament its unhappiness can be converted into terms that define the Order it cannot see:

> All Nature is but Art, unknown to thee;
> All Chance, Direction, which thou canst not see;
> All Discord, Harmony not understood;
> All partial Evil, universal Good (I, 290–92).

It is in this sense that "Whatever is, is right"—not that each of us can find happiness, not that the world is without great suffering for many. The rightness lies in the artistry that harmonizes the needs of all creatures. Man acknowledges an ordering power (and the *Essay* starts from that assumption; it does not seek to prove the existence of God). But, too often, at any point where the Order runs contrary to his private interest, man accuses Order.

The tenor of Pope's optimism must be understood by setting it against the other voice in the *Essay*. The optimistic view might be restated simply as the claim that man's existence need not be an outrage if his expectations are trimmed to the recognition that he is not a favorite child of an indulgent parent. Optimism reminds us that since we must live in large part through others, we find our real identity (whether we wish to or not) as much in membership as in uniqueness. The *Essay on Man* is a work that recalls us to what we know, and demands of us the maturity from which we regress into infantile complaint and egocentric hope. If it claims an essential goodness for the universe, it does not claim that man will find that goodness in his individual existence—only that he can hope to create a limited happiness so long as he can learn to make do with that.

The second epistle submits the experience of self to the same reinterpretation that the conception of the universe has undergone in the first epistle. The distinctions men have drawn, in the pride of a partial view, must now be surrendered: Grace and Virtue, Reason and Sense must be reconciled, just as the seeming "parts" of the universe have been made to merge in unity. Mandeville's Calvinistic opposition of Grace and Nature and Shaftesbury's neo-Stoic opposition of Reason and Sense are both, for Pope, sources of confusion or pride, possibly of despair. The interdependence of all man's faculties must be recognized; only "subtle Schoolmen teach these friends to fight" (II, 81).

The only stability for which man can hope is that of order within movement, a "balance" of "well-accorded strife" (II, 120–21). The dynamism of the mind arises from its ruling passion, which (like Mandeville's "predominating passion") may take subtle and devious forms of expression, but must have expression. Pope's reason is no sedate ruler but a "weak queen" whose power is likely to be usurped by a "favorite" passion. Reason is not strong enough to suppress, only to direct. Thus any attempt to separate reason from the passions as an independent and magisterial faculty breaks down. Since reason cannot originate, and the ruling passion cannot be buried, the two must work together if reason is to work at all. As a result, we cannot entertain the illusion of acting by absolute standards of rational virtue; we cannot achieve the purity of motive that Shaftesbury seeks and Mandeville, in his rigoristic account of virtue, at least pretends to demand. "Virtuous and vicious ev'ry man must be" (II, 231). Our actions must be given value not simply on the score of their source but of their end; without a rigoristic test of motives, we cannot escape the pragmatic test of consequences.

But, while Pope undermines rigoristic standards of virtue, he does not simply yield, as Mandeville does in his other aspect, to utilitarianism. He would be more consistent if he did, but he is interested in something more than consistency. He wants to make as much sense as he can of the puzzles and contradictions of human nature, and in so doing to escape the kind of simplification that creates systems. We have already seen how selfish motives can, in society, be transformed to social; the same is true of the individual motive:

> Lust, through some certain strainers well refin'd,
> Is gentle love, and charms all womankind . . .
> Nor Virtue, male or female, can we name,
> But what will grow on Pride, or grew on Shame
> (II, 189–90, 193–94).

By using the metaphor of the scion and the stock Pope can once more do justice to both continuity and discontinuity. The scion is not of the same source as the stock, although they become one organism. Pope is keeping alive, as Dryden had, the idea of the divine descent of virtue, even though it can live on earth only when mixed with the energies of self-love and passion. Unlike Mandeville, Pope does not identify virtue and vice or make the difference between them merely social usefuless. It is hard, in the mixture that is human nature, to determine "Where ends the Virtue, or begins the Vice" (II, 210). But Pope has only scorn for those fools

> who from hence into the notion fall,
> That Vice or Virtue there is none at all.
> If white and black blend, soften, and unite
> A thousand ways, is there no black or white?
> Ask your own heart, and nothing is so plain;
> 'Tis to mistake them, costs the time and pain
> (II, 211–16).

We are back once more to the connatural ideas of Shaftesbury. Pope wants to give back the sense of moral discrimination and moral certainty, even while he denies that we can elect the right with pure, disinterested self-mastery. The choice allowed man is a limited one, but, as these lines show, it is a real choice. To the extent that man is awake to his moral existence, his sense of his limitations does not preclude his making meaningful choices. But all men are ruled to some degree by their passions, and it is the nature of the passions to create a mock order in which man seeks toys and distinctions that replace true ends. Some of man is (or some men are) capable of authentic moral existence; most are comforted by *divertissements*—"In Folly's cup still, laughs the bubble joy" (II, 288). The poem offers a double consolation appropriate to the double nature of man: man is neither sublimely free nor totally helpless; he can live by the right if he chooses, at least to a sufficient degree, or if he fails, he can at least enjoy the insensibility that shields him from a full sense of his failure. We heroically resist Circe, or we become absorbed in the pleasures of bestiality. The second consolation is ironic enough to seem a curse; it is overthrown at the close of the poem by the vision of truly substantial joy that man earns through the choice of virtue.

In the third epistle Pope shows man's double nature in society, where the recovery of a true social order brings "Th' according music of a well-mix'd state" (III, 294). Throughout the epistle man's sociability is emphasized: "The strength he gains is from th' embrace he gives" (III, 312). The embrace with which the epistle concludes is one of mutual dependence and social love, but it grows out of the "fierce embrace" of passionate love:

> Each loves itself, but not itself alone,
> Each sex desires alike, till two are one.
> Nor ends the pleasure with the fierce embrace;
> They love themselves, a third time, in their race
>   (III, 121–24).

The peculiar force of the *Essay* comes of its constant conversion of terms: out of the dependence that passion creates comes the source of a new subsistence of each in all. The process of sublimation and transformation is constant; a limitation in the order of flesh or of mind becomes a turning point for the conversion to the order of charity. In that way, Pope's poem has, when one looks at it closely, more the effect of Metaphysical wit than versified argument; it is dialectical rather than didactic.

What remains in the fourth epistle is to redirect the search
for happiness, to turn it from external to internal, from acquisition to creation. This final movement of the poem is the
most sharply hortatory. Man must be made to relinquish what
by now he cannot help but see is error, and Pope assumes a
tone of contempt much like that of Socrates for the self-in-
flicted misery of sordid greatness (the greatness espoused by
Callicles in the *Gorgias* or Thrasymachus in the *Republic*).
Once more Pope holds together alternative views. He sets no
rigorous distinction between the categorical demands of moral
obligation and the rewards of moral self-approval. "The soul's
calm sunshine, and the heartfelt joy" (IV, 168) are the
"prize" of virtue, and the "calm" balances the "heartfelt" as
moral rectitude might be said to balance happiness. This is
something of a muddle; it suggests that obligation is by its
nature absolute—that the right cannot be withstood by anyone
who claims to be a man—and yet it offers rewards of joy to
those who accept the obligation. But, cf course, man is a
muddle, and so are his motives; and each kind of motive
requires its own appeal. The order of charity is an absolute
claim; but man, so little a creature of absolutes, may be assured that his full nature will be accommodated by Order.

The movement from external to internal completes the
movement we have seen throughout the *Essay:* from the time-
bound and spatial to the transcendent, from the compulsion
of passion to the choice of goodness, from the complaints of
selfhood to the self-surrender of love. Like Milton's Adam
and Eve, who must be weaned from the memory of a physical
Paradise to the creation of a "Paradise within thee, happier
far," man must learn that all materials and occasions can serve
his will:

> Fix'd to no spot is happiness sincere,
> 'Tis no where to be found, or ev'ry where (IV, 14–15).

The demands of maturity become inescapable:

> The boy and man an individual makes,
> Yet sigh'st thou now for apples and for cakes?
> Go, like the Indian, in another life
> Expect thy dog, thy bottle, and thy wife:
> As well as dream such trifles are assign'd,
> As toys and empires, for a god-like mind (IV, 175–80).

At the close of the poem, the interlocutor can be addressed
as a responsible moral agent, a man whose life is one of con-

stant choices, who is capable at last of living in the order of charity.

The central contradictions of Pope's *Essay* lie in the conflict between an aesthetic vision and a moral one. The aesthetic vision of Order sees all absorbed in the complex harmony of the divine work of art. Such an Order cannot be undone by man; every violation will at once be contained. The Order will re-form and, with the slightest alteration, make of that violation an element of its design. The individual is ultimately powerless, and, consequently ultimately irresponsible. Whatever he does will be used for the best. The moral vision on the other hand insists upon the inescapable claims of virtue. It rises to intense satire upon the false goal and to scorn for the abnegation of choice. The aesthetic vision is essentially a comic pattern in which man stumbles into a greater success than he can plan; the moral vision is largely a satiric pattern in which the failure of man is shown to be contemptibly foolish.

Pope cannot resolve these contradictions, but he can prevent them from simply cancelling each other out. While the large Order is undisturbed by the act of violation, the immediate cost in pain to others is clear:

> There, in the rich, the honour'd, fam'd and great,
> See the false scale of happiness complete!
> In hearts of kings, or arms of queens who lay,
> How happy! those to ruin, these betray.
> Mark by what wretched steps their glory grows,
> From dirt and sea-weed as proud Venice rose;
> In each how guilt and greatness equal ran,
> And all that rais'd the hero, sunk the man.
> Now Europe's laurels on their brows behold,
> But stain'd with blood, or ill exchang'd for gold;
> Then see them broke with toils, or sunk in ease,
> Or infamous for plunder'd provinces.
> Oh wealth ill-fated! which no act of fame
> E'er taught to shine, or sanctify'd from shame!
> (IV, 287–300.)

The *Essay on Man* is a poem about man in this world. While man may come at last to seek "What nothing earthly gives, or can destroy" (IV, 167), he seeks it by involving himself in the world:

> Happier as kinder, in whate'er degree,
> And height of Bliss but height of Charity (IV, 359–60).

II. The Problem of Scale: The Game of Art

> All play moves and has its being within a play-ground marked off beforehand either materially or ideally, deliberately or as a matter of course. . . . All are temporary worlds within the ordinary world, dedicated to the performance of an act apart.
>
> Inside the play-ground an absolute and peculiar order reigns. Here we come across another, very positive feature of play: it creates order, *is* order. Into an imperfect world and into the confusion of life it brings a temporary, a limited perfection. Play demands order absolute and supreme (*Homo Ludens: A Study of the Play Element in Culture,* Boston, 1955, p. 10).

In these observations of J. Huizinga lies a problem we encounter in the early poems of Pope: the problem of scale. Scale is one of those conventions that are rooted in our deepest feeling and built into the artistic forms that shape our images of value. Smallness may be associated with pettiness in the insect, innocence in the child, intensity or grace, or with any combination of these, as we see in the shifting impressions Gulliver has of Lilliput. And the poet may work within one set of associations or play back and forth between several.

The interplay of associations of scale is a primary technique of the mock-heroic, but it has other uses as well, and no poet shows more sensitivity to its possibilities than Pope. One of the uses arises from the nature of a work of art, especially the painting, which is at once smaller in scale and more finely organized than the object it represents. This implicit association between reduction in scale and fineness of organization operates throughout Pope's description of nature. Pope tends to see landscape as the design of a divine painter. This produces that tension we always feel in seeing a framed landscape: the sense of receding space played off against the flat design and the formal limits of the composition. We are aware of two scales—of depth and flatness, the scene that is represented and the work that is made. The preoccupation of the age with the relation of poetry to painting reinforces this double awareness, and it becomes most evident in the pastoral poem, where the formality of a golden age and the innocuousness of its actions contribute to the sense of reduced scale. Blake was to claim the pastoral world for the child more successfully than anyone before him, but Ambrose Philips' work shows that there was in Pope's day an interest in both "rustic" pastoral and "infantile" verse (the latter won Philips the name of Namby-Pamby). These two distortions of true poetic art (as Pope saw them) led Philips into bathos; they stand as rough border areas that define the character of the garden they surround.

Pope's early pastorals deliberately seek a high degree of formalization. They impose a classical form upon a native landscape; they attempt a full circle of seasons, of times of day, of kinds of landscape, of the ages of man, and of his typical passions.[3] This organization is apparent in "Spring," where Pope presents the familiar contest of shepherds about the superiority of their mistresses. Within the symmetrical dialogue is the symmetry of a wager, so far conventional enough. When we look at the stakes, the lamb that sees his "dancing shade in the fountain pool" is matched by an ivy bowl that bears representations of the four seasons and of the zodiac. The lamb calls our attention to the mirror of art; the bowl, to the pastorals themselves as man-made images of nature.

These are poems whose artifice is insistent. Their picture of "the tranquillity of a country life" is made ideally inclusive of seasons and feelings and yet ideally simple, in "exposing the best side only of a shepherd's life, and in concealing its miseries" (Pope, *A Discourse on Pastoral Poetry*). The shepherds and their actions are reduced to a toylike charm, where the mechanism that propels the figures (as they emerge from a clock or perform a country dance on a music-box lid) is the chief source of wonder. How lifelike and yet how beautifully free from the complexity of life! The passions of the love-sick shepherds are pure and intense, but they are also conventional and orderly. But if the figures are conspicuously the product of artifice, they remind us nevertheless that other passions, less ordered and more immediate, may seem like this in a large enough perspective. In the spontaneous harmony of a golden age, all nature, and man within it, dances in concert. We can look beyond this to a denser order, in Pope's *Essay on Man,* where the movements are more wayward and violent and the measures more complex but where the dance and the harmony include the least gesture.

In the pastorals, man and nature, order and spontaneity, are one. A desolate lover can command the death of "every flower." Another can protest the bitter contrast between the harvest yield and his own frustration; such discord should not be. If "sultry Sirius burns" without, it is shocking that "eternal winter reigns" within the breast. When Daphne dies,

> Now hung with pearl the dropping trees appear,
> Their faded honors scatter'd on her bier (*Winter,* 31–32).

The winter landscape becomes a company of mourners; the trees hold glittering ice that melts into tears, and the leaves that were once their crowning "honors" ("the honors of their head" would be a typical poetic periphrasis for "hair") are cast ceremoniously upon the dead. The fixing of emotion in conventions, the turning of artlessness into unconscious elegance, the very play between art and nature that runs throughout serves to make this world self-contained and limited and yet a paradigm for a greater one. Its scale is like that of a stage, its actors become dancers seen from a distance.

In general, one can distinguish between two tendencies in pastoral. The first is to recreate a golden age in which all art is nature and all nature art, where every lament is an elegy, every scene a painting, every feeling a lyric. Emotions as well as actions are tender and harmless; if grief enters, it composes into song. Often, as in the resolution of the singing match or the lament for Daphne, a "comic" resolution is found. Neither shepherd can lose the match, and Daphne cannot really die but will be translated by metamorphosis to a new life ("our Goddess, and our grief no more!"). Such pastorals impose upon reality our recollection of a lost innocence.

In the second kind of pastoral the picture of innocence is less pure. Here innocence is threatened; it must survive real attacks and encounter real despair; this is a world of true and false shepherds, of disillusioned and recovered innocence. It is the world of *The Shepherd's Calendar* and *Lycidas,* where sublimity is possible because the pastoral scene has become a metaphor for spiritual integrity, for the "organized innocence" that is earned through test and doubt. The first kind of pastoral, which Pope writes in his early suite, so consistently stresses the fusion of art and nature, so precisely manipulates nature into the most artificial yet appropriate forms, that it cannot risk the range of experience sublimity demands. It is a picture of life without consequences, where the swan's death is all song, and the world of moral choices is reduced to a theater of miraculous interventions. This kind of pastoral suggests at every turn a scale that is less than the plenitude of a full and various reality.

In Pope's comparison of Homer and Virgil (in his Preface

to the *Iliad*) we find a number of figures that govern his thought about art and nature. The pastorals may be said to present "an uniform and bounded walk of Art" which suggests but hardly encompasses "the vast and various extent of Nature." Art "can only reduce the beauties" of Nature "into a more obvious figure, which the common eye may better take in, and [it] is therefore more entertained with them." The common eye, as Shaftesbury made clear, is an untrained eye, more easily impressed with the confusing richness of the "wild paradise" than with its implicit order, just as the common heart in the *Essay on Man* is more readily moved to see the waste and frustration of its life than the demand of moral choice. The "ordered garden" of the pastorals is a redeemed image of Nature, redeemed from the common eye's error, not Nature's own: the scale of Nature's art is too vast for comprehension and the order of Providence often too complex for merely rational conviction. This Art, then, is a straitening of Nature's true but invisible order, a reduction to smaller scale and greater clarity of what we cannot readily perceive in the macrocosm. The reduction in scale and the emphasis upon artistic order at the expense of profusion and wildness produce diminished intensity: Virgil's poetic fire is "discerned through a glass, reflected from Homer, more shining than fierce, but everywhere equal and constant." But if one kind of intensity is lost—the energy of the unencompassable particular—another intensity is recovered: the elegance of what can be called an "internal sublime," a suggestion of infinity in complex structure rather than in the overleaping of conventional form. Hegel suggests this kind of infinity when he describes classical art as having the self-limitation and boundlessness of a sphere.

In *Windsor Forest* Pope attempts the more complex pastoral.[4] Here the landscape is at once actual and ideal, English and Arcadian. It recalls the disasters of the past and looks to hope for the future, and it constantly suggests an ideal order, a *concordia discors,* such as Denham found in the Thames: "Strong without rage, without o'er-flowing full"—at once bountiful and regal, orderly and tranquil. As in Denham's poem, so in Pope's the discord from which order is born is symbolized in the chase. Denham's wounded stag is likened in turn to a declining statesman, a prince of the soil, a bold knight-errant; an assaulted ship, a dying hero or king. Within the "more innocent, and happy chase" are reconciled the savagery of human war and the innocence of harmonious peace, where all cruelty is sport and all victims, however noble, less than human.

More famous than Denham's stag is Pope's pheasant in *Windsor Forest:*

> See! from the brake the whirring pheasant springs,
> And mounts exulting on triumphant wings:
> Short is his joy! he feels the fiery wound,
> Flutters in blood, and panting beats the ground.
> Ah! what avail his glossy, varying dyes,
> His purple crest, and scarlet-circled eyes,
> The vivid green his shining plumes unfold,
> His painted wings, and breast that flames with gold?
>   (111–18.)

These lines, which Wordsworth praised (or at least exempted from censure) for their freshness and fidelity to nature, have been called "a moral *exemplum,* less about the beauty of pheasants than the transience of all beauty."[5] They achieve this generality through their account of the fall of a great and regal figure; just before these lines, Pope has compared the hunters' quarry to a besieged capital, a "thoughtless town, with ease and plenty blest." Again, a few lines below, the breeds of fish are seen in scaly brilliance which is also royal dress:

> Our plenteous streams a various race supply;
> The bright-ey'd perch with fins of Tyrian dye,
> The silver eel, in shining volumes roll'd,
> The yellow carp, in scales bedrop'd with gold,
> Swift trouts, diversify'd with crimson stains,
> And pikes, the tyrants of the watry plains (141–46).

The dying pheasant involves all the splendors of the heroic, the opulence that we associate with greatness of spirit and power. The "sylvan war" of Windsor Forest—the chase, the angling, the pursuit by Pan of Lodona—is the muted and idyllic counterpart of the destructive heroism of actual combat. Again, the scale contains and composes them.

The opening section of *Windsor Forest* is governed by the pastoral theme of an ideal order that excludes nothing and embraces all in a single harmony. Its typical resolution is one of suspended consequences:

> Here waving groves a chequer'd scene display,
> And part admit, and part exclude the day.
> As some coy nymph her lover's warm address
> Nor quite indulges, nor can quite repress (17–20).

We may wish to recall Keats' "Bold lover, never, never canst thou kiss, / Though winning near the goal" ("Ode on a Grecian Urn") or again, "their lips touch'd not, but had not bade adieu" ("Ode to Psyche"). Pope's little simile is not so resonant, but he has created his suspended lovers, his "equilibrists," whose innocence is neither denial nor consummation. They are neither the "Grand Parents" who founded Milton's "wedded love" nor the doomed innocents of Byron's "ambrosial sin"; yet in their way they embody the harmony that holds division within its frame without reducing it to unity. And this coy nymph foreshadows the nymph Lodona who is pursued by Pan and whose innocence is preserved by divine metamorphosis—"melting as in tears she lay, / In a soft silver stream dissolv'd away" (203–4). Violence is deflected, consummation suspended, action transmuted to art; and Lodona becomes the typical pastoral image of art, the reflecting water in which the world is framed:

> In the clear azure gleam the flocks are seen,
> And floating forests paint the waves with green (215–16).

We may be reminded in reading *Windsor Forest* of the *hortus conclusus:* the walled garden, beautifully fertile, in which repose the Mother and Child, an assemblage of saints, and a gathering of mild beasts. In one corner of the foreground and in much smaller scale, lies defeated, on his back, the inevitable serpent—always present but now innocuous.[6] So in Pope's garden of "peace and plenty" is the memory of desert—a desert of tyranny and blasphemy, which has at last given way to the "peaceful cottage" and "yellow harvests," to "home-felt quiet." At the close of the poem the Nimrod figure, the tyrant, destroyer, and conqueror, is elevated to the allegorical force of Discord and imprisoned in Hell by Anna —the Queen who has brought the end of war with the Peace of Utrecht.

The poem opens out from its pastoral landscape of art first into a pastoral vision where the energies of life are tamed into artistry, and finally into a messianic vision of a redeemed world with London as its New Jerusalem. The trees of Windsor Forest become the materials of a new art of commerce; the oaks transformed into the navies of trade carry England to the world, the world to England. Again the note of unity in variety is maintained: "feather'd people," "naked youths and painted chiefs" come to England to "admire"; but the freed Indians "in their native groves / Reap their own fruits, and

woo their sable loves" (409–10). Peace brings all the world
to a harmony that grants to each people its own glory and its
own greatness: "And other Mexicos be roof'd with gold"
(412). The scale of the poem has shifted from the artful
composition to a vast social harmony, emphasizing a continuity between the implicit art and order of nature and the
realization of divine art in man's social order. Between man
and nature there is a pastoral harmony, and its pattern becomes the model of a social harmony that redeems man's
world. The order of the flesh had been contained and transformed. Just as Pan's lust serves to produce the pastoral art
of Lodona's stream, the cruel vigor of the "sylvan chase" becomes the creative force of commerce. And to commerce we
may give A. N. Whitehead's ample definition: "every species
of interchange which proceeds by way of mutual persuasion."
This wedding of order and liberty becomes a prefiguration or,
as for Shaftesbury, a Promethean imitation, of a universal
order of charity.

In *The Rape of the Lock* we move from the nature-be-
come-art of the pastoral to the heroic-turned-artful.[7] The
world of Belinda is a world of triviality measured against the
epic scale; it is also a world of grace and delicacy, a second-
best world but not at all a contemptible one. Here Pope has
built upon a theme that plays against the epic tradition: the
mock-heroic world (in Dryden's version) of Virgil's bees is a
world that has some real, if extravagant, claim to the epic style.
The *Georgics* celebrate a mundane heroism and place it
against the special virtues of the martial hero.

The emphasis of the epic had, moreover, moved by Pope's
day—through Spenser and Milton—further and further toward
spiritual conflict. In *The Rape of the Lock* the primary quality
of Belinda is spiritual shallowness, an incapacity for moral
awareness. She has transformed all spiritual exercises and emblems into a coquette's self-display and self-adoration. All of
it is done with a frivolous heedlessness; she is not quite a
hypocrite.

> Fair nymphs, and well-drest youths around her shone,
> But ev'ry eye was fix'd on her alone.
> On her white breast a sparkling cross she wore,
> Which Jews might kiss, and Infidels adore (II, 5–8).

Our perspective closes more and more sharply, upon Belinda
as cynosure, and upon the sparkling cross that fixes attention

upon her beauty. The cross is a religious symbol turned to the uses of ornament, and by the rules of the little world of the poem it gains new power through this translation. At every point in the poem grace and charm supplant depth of feeling or heroic action; the only direct survivors of the old heroic virtues are the miniature playing cards. Here Pope's play with scale becomes most fascinating. Within the heroic frame of the mock-epic language we have the miniature world of belles and beaux, who live by an elaborate and formal set of rules. Within that small world is framed in turn the card game (with its further formalization of rules), where kings and queens, mortal battles and shameful seductions, still survive, as a game within a game.

The principal symbol of the triviality of Belinda's world is the machinery of sylphs and gnomes. The "light militia of the lower sky" are a travesty of both Homeric deities and Miltonic guardian angels. Like their originals, they have an ambiguous status: they exist within and without the characters. They are, in their diminutive operation, like those small but constant self-regarding gestures we may associate with a lady conscious of her charms. The sylphs who protect Belinda are also her acceptance of the rules of social convention, which presume that a coquette's life is pure game. The central action of the poem is Belinda's descent from coquette to prude, from the dazzling rival of the sun ("Belinda smil'd, and all the world was gay") to the rancorous Amazon who shrieks in self-righteous anger. It is Clarissa who vainly points to the loss. Her speech in the last canto is a parody, as Pope reminds us, of Sarpedon's speech to Glaucus in Book XII of the *Iliad*. For "the utter generosity of spirit, the supreme magnanimity of attitude" with which Sarpedon faces the loss of life, Clarissa offers to Belinda a substitute that is analogous:[8] within the scale of the playground world of the coquette there is the selflessness of "good humor," the ability to place value rightly and accept the conditions of life. This will permit Belinda to retain the radiance that has warmed and illumined her world.

Pope's use of scale has set up a double view of this play-world. It has the smallness of scale and fineness of organization of the work of art, yet like a game, it is temporary and threatens to break down. "At any moment 'ordinary life' may reassert its rights either by an impact from without, which interrupts the game, or by an offense against the rules, or else from within, by a collapse of the play spirit, a sobering, a disenchantment" (Huizinga, p. 21). Clarissa's speech offers a view of life as it must be when the playing has to stop. Thalestris offers the outrage of the spoilsport. "By withdrawing from the game [the spoilsport] reveals the relativity and fragility of the play-world in which he had temporarily shut himself with others. He robs play of its *illusion*—a pregnant word which means literally 'in-play' (from *inlusio, illudere,* or *inludere*)" (Huizinga, p. 11). Pope's play-world in *The Rape of the Lock* hovers between the trivial fragility of mere play (with its obliviousness to the possibilities of mature life) and the preciousness of a life ordered with grace, however minute its scale or limited its values.

In the dressing-table scene at the close of Canto I we see Belinda's beauty both as mere ornamentation governed by pride and as the realization of a genuine aesthetic ordering. The worship before the mirror of the "cosmetic powers" produces the appearance Belinda wishes to have and which she further adorns, her maid attending "the sacred Rites of Pride." With that word, the world pours in, diminished in scale:

> Unnumber'd treasures ope at once, and here
> The various off'rings of the world appear. . . .
> This casket India's glowing gems unlocks,
> And all Arabia breathes from yonder box.
> The tortoise here and elephant unite,
> Transform'd to combs, the speckled and the white
> (129–30; 133–36).

The spacious world can enter Belinda's dressing room only in a serviceable and diminished form. Arabia is compressed into its perfume; the unwieldy elephant and tortoise are transformed into the elegance of shell and ivory combs. The universe, the Indian philosopher tells us, is a great elephant standing on the back of a tortoise. John Locke had made much of the fable in his treatment of substance (*Essay of Human Understanding,* II, ch. 23, para. 2). This condensation of the vast into the small is at once reversed: the pins extend into "shining rows" or "files" of soldiers, and Belinda becomes the epic hero investing himself in armor as well as the godlike "awful Beauty." Here is the triumph of art: Belinda "calls forth all the wonders of her face" and gives them realization with her cosmetic skill. She is the mistress of the "bidden blush" but also the culmination of nature. Her art trembles on the precipice of mere artifice, but it retains its poise.

We can say, then, that the world of Belinda is once more a pastoral world, the world of the "town-eclogue." But it is filled with omens: balanced against Belinda's rites of pride are the Baron's prayers at another altar; balanced against Belinda's generous smiles are the labyrinths of her hair. As she descends the Thames, the "painted vessel" is the literal craft on which she sails and also Belinda herself—perhaps reminiscent of the "stately Ship / Of Tarsus . . . With all her bravery on, and tackle trim, / Sails filled, and streamers waving, / Courted by all the winds that hold them play"—the Dalila of Milton's *Samson Agonistes*. Belinda is at once the pastoral mistress ("Where'er you walk, cool gales shall fan the glade"), the power of harmony, and the imminent temptress and sower of discord. But her greatest power arises from the fact that she is not really aware of what she is leading the Baron to do or of what disaster may befall herself. Like Eve's, her very weakness increases her power for destruction, and the sylphs, lovely but variable, express her ambiguous self-consciousness—the sense of disaster that is also a sense of her power to call forth violence.

With the fall of her coquette's world, as the Baron snips her lock, we descend to the realm of anarchy, the Cave of Spleen, with its surrealistic atmosphere of fantasy and compulsions. Spleen is the anti-goddess; as Dulness is opposed to Light, so here the vindictive and self-pitying passions are opposed to good humor and good sense. This is surely one of the great cave or underworld passages, and we must call to mind the caves of Error and Despair or the dwelling of Night in Spenser to see its full value. Pope's special contribution is closer to the late medieval landscapes of Hieronymus Bosch: an erotic nightmare of exploding libidinous drives. The passions repressed by prudes find neurotic expression in mincing languor or prurient reproach; they scrawl, as it were, those graffiti that are a nasty travesty of love. The Cave of Spleen is one of the strongest pictures of disorder in the age: it gives us the measure of order, a sense of the strength of the forces that social decorum controls and of the savage distortion of feeling that it prevents.

The first effect of the entrance of Spleen into the upper world is Thalestris' skeptical questioning of the art Belinda has lavished upon herself:

> Was it for this you took such constant care
> The bodkin, comb, and essence to prepare?
> For this your locks in paper-durance bound,
> For this with tort'ring irons wreath'd around?
> (IV, 97–100.)

If we compare these harsh lines with the reverential rites of pride, we can see how false are the doubts cast upon the art of the dressing table under the strain of injured pride. The creative skill that brought nature to its full realization becomes for the prude and spoilsport a torturing of nature by a strained and cruel art. And Belinda herself becomes, in turn, like Lady Wishfort and Mrs. Marwood in Congreve's *The Way of the World,* or even Alceste in Molière's *The Misanthrope,* an affected and pharisaical "primitivist":

> Oh had I rather unadmir'd remain'd
> In some lone isle, or distant northern land . . .
> There kept my charms conceal'd from mortal eye,
> Like roses, that in deserts bloom and die
>   (IV, 153–54, 157–58).

Belinda is not unmindful of the fragrance she might have wasted, but she is professedly ready to renounce the whole game.

The game is, of course, in her world everything; we need not be put off by an effusion like, "O had I stay'd, and said my pray'rs at home!" (IV, 160.) What Belinda renounces and seeks to destroy, in her spleen, is the pattern of order by which she has lived and of which she was the moving force. It is always someone like Belinda who gives style and grace to a social pattern. If the heroic overtones of the poem constantly insist upon the comparative triviality of this pattern, they serve also to glorify it. Just as the brilliant detail of the Flemish painters gave a heightened reality to those bourgeois subjects that pre-empted the space of the saints, so Pope's almost dazzling particularity—in each case woven out of generalities of heroic splendor—insists upon the intense if miniature order of his society. The heroic virtues are transposed to the scale of charm, and one cannot resist quoting Burke's famous phrases about another such order:

> It is gone, that sensibility of principle, that chastity of honor, which felt a stain like a wound, which inspired courage whilst it mitigated ferocity, which ennobled whatever it touched, and under which vice itself lost half its evil, by losing all its grossness (*Reflections on the French Revolution,* 1790).

These words define what a code of civilized life must do. *The Rape of the Lock* leaves its moral judgments implicit in its double mock-heroic scale, but it makes of that scale an illuminating vision of art as a sustaining pattern of order. It is an art of "good humor," of tact and charm, and its symbol is the delicate beauty of a frail China jar. The metamorphosis at the close, in which the lock rises above the splenetic battle and becomes an enduring source of light, is more than a wry joke. Pope has shown in small scale the ferocities that such an order can mitigate. And if it is not the stain upon honor but upon brocade that is felt like a wound, there is at least a real correspondence between those worlds of transposed scale. The players of ombre are themselves not unlike the playing-card kings and queens, and their battles and intrigues are formalized into a pattern that is more real than the actors.

The incongruity of the mock heroic is dissolved in its even more surprising congruity, in its creation of an unheroic world of art and grace where the relative proportions are retained even as the total scale is sharply reduced. The poem does not rise to the elevation of *Windsor Forest,* for it does not seek to reconcile the least order with the highest. Instead it carries to new intensity the double vision that sees both the fragility and strength, the triviality and dignity, of art. (The elevated lock is, in a sense, the poem, shining upon beaux and sparks, but upon all others who will see it, too.) If this order remains an aesthetic one, below or beyond morality, it none the less insists upon the formal delight that is a dimension of all stable structures, whether cosmic harmonies or heroic codes, poems or patterns of civility. And it looks toward those more inclusive and morally significant visions of order that give weight to Pope's later work.

III. Character and False Art

In the poems of Pope we have considered there are three kinds of art: the art of Nature or of God; man's humble and reverent imitation of that in his own; and, finally, man's arrogant constructions in defiance of Nature. The last of these can be seen in the *Essay on Man,* with suggestions of the Tower of Babel; the Titans' piling Pelion upon Ossa in their effort to dethrone Zeus; the fallen angels' building of that travesty of heavenly splendor, Pandemonium, in *Paradise Lost;* and the "kings of the earth" of the Second Psalm:

> Oh sons of earth! attempt ye still to rise,
> By mountains pil'd on mountains, to the skies?
> Heav'n still with laughter the vain toil surveys,
> And buries madmen in the heaps they raise (IV, 73–76).

The point lies in the materialism and the *hubris,* the insensibility and the blasphemy.[9] The attempt to traverse the incommensurable distance that separates the order of flesh from the order of charity with heaps of earth is a telling instance of the constructions of false art.

Throughout his major satires Pope uses the mock order of false art as a symbol of moral failure. We can see this in his discussion of the splintered brilliance of false wit in the *Essay on Criticism:*

> Poets like Painters, thus, unskill'd to trace
> The naked Nature and the living Grace,
> With gold and jewels cover ev'ry part,
> And hide with ornaments their want of Art (293–96).

> False Eloquence, like the prismatic glass,
> Its gaudy colors spreads on ev'ry place;
> The face of Nature we no more survey,
> All glares alike, without distinction gay (311–14).

Here false art becomes all the more dazzling by sacrificing form to glitter: "one glaring chaos and wild heap of wit" (292), seeking to tyrannize over us by making an immediate appeal to the senses and closing off the more deliberate and demanding aesthetic response that is concerned with formal structure.

Pope's finest instance of the mock order of false art occurs in his second Moral Essay, the epistle *To Burlington* (1731). Originally called *Of False Taste,* the poem is an important document in the history of eighteenth-century sensibility, especially in the matters of architecture and landscape gardening. It celebrates the Earl of Burlington's classicism as a return to Roman manliness and severity, to public spirit and sober piety—a return from extravagance and ostentation, from the triviality of an art that has lost the sense of function in the pursuit of ornament. Burlington was, in effect if not design, the inheritor of Shaftesbury's artistic legacy. Like Shaftesbury, he renounced the baroque strain in Wren. Shaftesbury rejected "false and counterfeit . . . magnificence," and coldly dismissed two of Wren's great public works: the public can no longer bear "to see a Whitehall treated like a Hampton Court, or even a new cathedral like St. Paul's" (SC, 22). Burlington turned back to the work of Inigo Jones and Palladio, collecting and publishing their designs; and his own architectural inventions are closely based upon their example, although he moves even further back toward Roman models than they.[10]

Burlington inherited Shaftesbury's concerns in another, more striking way. His villa at Chiswick is an adaptation of Palladio's Villa Rotonda (given a saucer dome like that of the Pantheon), but the gardens, which were begun in 1715 and were not completed until 1736, became one of the earliest instances of the new interest in the "natural" garden. Shaftesbury, we may recall, admired the wildness of the natural scene for its authenticity. His devotion was to "the chief degree or order of beauty . . . that of the rational life, distinct from the merely vegetable and sensible" (SC, 20–21), but he found natural wildness free at least of the mock order of false art. Burlington, in turn, sponsored the irregular garden. It had at least some classical precedent. In 1728 Robert Castell published his *Villas of the Ancients,* a work sponsored by Burlington and probably available to him earlier. In it the garden of Pliny's villa is described, and, although it was largely regular, it contained areas of irregularity: the *pratulum,* where "nature appears in her plainest and most simple dress" and, particularly, the *imitatio ruris,* where "hills, rocks, cascades, rivulets, woods and buildings, etc., were possibly thrown into such an agreeable disorder as to have pleased the eye from several views, like so many landskips." Here again we have the dialectical interplay that we see in the literary criticism of the period. The return to a severe classicism is one statement, the irregular garden a counterstatement; they have in common a rejection of mock order and an imitation, in different ways, of a true order. Within the mathematical precisions of Chiswick House occur the varieties of form we find in the three rooms along the garden front (round, apsidal, and octagonal, in turn). Within the irregularities of the garden itself are those formal controls that are meant to be only glimpsed or sensed, without being sharply visible.[11]

In *To Burlington,* Pope questions the nature of taste: is it a discrimination of genuine pleasures or a conformity to fashion, a means of self-cultivation or of self-display? The fool does not buy for himself but at others' bidding and for others' eventual enjoyment; for he cannot possess these things with his own mind—

Think we all these are for himself? no more
Than his fine wife, alas! or finer whore (11–12).

The last line has incredible richness of suggestion. We are invited to contemplate a marriage that is little more than an act of acquisition by a man of wealth. His "fine wife" is another adornment or stage property, and it is not surprising if she is unfaithful. But in this world of display, one can achieve most conspicuous consumption with objects of luxury—the mistress must be even "finer" than the wife.

For the man who has no substantial self, who lives only for the creation of a public image, every act of self-display becomes an unknowing act of self-exposure. The proud worship of taste requires that man violate nature in order to satisfy his transient whim; in turning to his private will for a standard, he has lost touch with nature and has lost the stability of an excellence founded on something outside himself. Villario's formal gardens are pleasing enough, although suspiciously artful and pseudo-pastoral. But they are an imposition upon nature for the sake of a taste that is easily cloyed ("He finds at last he better likes a field"). Again Sabinus' son, fond of an "opener Vista," destroys the trees his father planted, and we find again the inversion of nature for the sake of an artificial taste:

> The thriving plants ignoble broomsticks made,
> Now sweep these alleys they were born to shade
> (97–98).

These lines contain what Donald Davie has called "a little tragic plot."[12] There is at least a suggestion of the heroic queen transported into drudging slavery, and this only reinforces the contrasts of living plants and stiff, dead broomsticks, or of "stretching branches" and rectilinear alleys. All of these themes are summed up in Timon's villa itself, where all is artful, dull, and unnatural. The interior crowns the effect: learning gives way to display, religion to comfortable self-flattery. In the chapel, the "pride of prayer" is overarched by ceilings "where sprawl the saints of Verrio or Laguerre." The grossness and overblown ripeness of the fleshy saints and of the "soft Dean" ("Who never mentions Hell to ears polite") point finally to an art that, in its essentially decorative or ostentatious end, is self-defeating, just as the scale of the dinner ("In plenty starving, tantaliz'd in state") is the frustration of true hospitality or service.

But Timon's pretensions accomplish what they least intend: service to many who are indifferent to his state, the laborers his "charitable Vanity" supports. The comic view is completed by the reclamation of the land from the usurper, as Nature regains her throne and produces a truer splendor:

> Another age shall see the golden ear
> Embrown the slope, and nod on the parterre,
> Deep harvests bury all his pride has planned,
> And laughing Ceres reassume the land (173–76).

The regal notes of *golden, nod,* and *reassume* effect a reconciliation of art and nature, of just rule and living energy. And again there is a suggestion of vast extent—the reaches of the estate are large vistas of grain—and of framed and ideal landscape. The *Essay* closes with a return to Roman building ("whate'er Vitruvius was before," "Imperial works") and to the constructive power of human art in its true sense—no less in control of nature ("And roll obedient rivers through the land") but serving "happy Britain" and creating a new harmonious order.

The divine force in nature is embodied in the "Genius of the Place," with its reminiscence of the classical deities who inhabit and inform both men and places. To consult the Genius of the Place is to serve nature rather than to coerce her; the true artist "helps" the hill to rise, "calls in the country," "joins willing woods." And that miraculous harmony one recognizes as a work of art seems to leap into being:

> Parts answering parts shall slide into a whole,
> Spontaneous beauties all around advance,
> Start even from difficulty, strike from chance;
> Nature shall join you; Time shall make it grow (66–69).

In contrast we have the sterile mock order of Timon's villa:

> No pleasing intricacies intervene,
> No artful wildness to perplex the scene;
> Grove nods at grove, each alley has a brother,
> And half the platform just reflects the other (115–18).

The topiary artist produces an "inverted Nature" by forcing artful forms upon the natural—"Trees cut to statues." And this is balanced by the profusion that loses all sense of design, "Statues thick as trees." The displacement of life is nicely caught in the final image of the impotent river god: "And swallows roost in Nilus' dusty urn" (126).

Milton's Eve must turn from her Narcissus-like love of her own "smooth wat'ry image" to love for Adam and learn "How beauty is excell'd by manly grace / And wisdom, which alone is truly fair" (IV, 490–91). So, too, Bernard Berenson remarks of Raphael that he was "not artist enough to do without beauty."[13] Here Burlington represents the standard of dignified severity:

> You show us, Rome was glorious, not profuse,
> And pompous buildings once were things of use (23–24).

We move back from the ornamental to the functional, and in a deeper sense from the aesthetic to the ethical.

> 'Tis Use alone that sanctifies Expense,
> And splendor borrows all her rays from sense (179–80).

The word *sanctifies* should not be underestimated; the light of Heaven now descends, through sense, to inform genuine art. Burlington, as artist, becomes himself a transmitter of the light of Heaven; it is but for kings to "call forth th' ideas of your mind" (195) and create works of authentic magnificence, "which alone is truly fair."

The theme of true magnificence draws together the use of riches and the problem of taste. Aristotle writes, in the *Nicomachean Ethics* (IV, 2):

> The magnificent man is like an artist; for he can see what is fitting and spend large sums tastefully. . . . Magnificence is an attitude of expenditures of the kind which we call honorable, e.g., those connected with the gods—votive offerings, buildings, and sacrifices . . . and all those that are proper objects of public-spirited ambition. . . . [The] magnificent man spends not on himself but on public objects . . . (trans. W. D. Ross).

In contrast for Aristotle is the man of "tasteless showiness." As Pope puts it, "never coxcomb reach'd Magnificence" (22). We are back to the "sons of earth" and "the heaps they raise."

The art that defies nature lies behind the central metaphor of the second Moral Essay, *To a Lady* (1735). The metaphor is drawn from painting, and it works in two principal ways: a discussion of the difficulty of painting the character of women, who are mercurial and unstable, and a criticism of the kind of painting they require. Running through the poem is an implicit analogy between the variability and ostentation of vain women and the broken light and color of dazzling but superficial painting:

> Pictures like these, dear Madam, to design,
> Asks no firm hand, and no unerring line;
> Some wand'ring touches, some reflected light,
> Some flying stroke alone can hit 'em right:
> For how should equal colors do the knack?
> Chameleons who can paint in white and black?
> (151–56.)

With these lines we may contrast those written twenty-three years earlier, to the painter Jervas:

> O, lasting as those colours may they shine,
> Free as thy stroke, yet faultless as thy line;
> New graces yearly like thy works display,
> Soft without weakness, without glaring gay
> (*Epistle to Mr. Jervas,* 63–66).

The kind of painting, then, that these ladies require, is precisely the kind that was regarded with distrust and alarm by such a critic as Shaftesbury: the Venetian school and its issue in Rubens.

Pope is alluding to the conflict between the claims of *disegno* and *colore* that culminated in the French academic debate between Poussinists and Rubenists. The doctrine that draughtsmanship and line have priority over color goes back at least as far as Aristotle's *Poetics,* where the primacy of plot over character invokes the analogy:

> Compare the parallel in painting, where the most beautiful colors laid on without order will not give one the same pleasure as a simple black-and-white sketch of a portrait (vi).

So Pope on "versifiers": "Their coloring entertains the sight, but the *lines* and *life* of the picture are not to be inspected too narrowly" (to Cromwell, 17 December 1710, *Correspondence,* I, 110). Colorist painting, with its broken areas, its touches and strokes, becomes the counterpart of the false architecture Pope treats in the epistle to Burlington:

> Load some vain church with old theatric state,
> Turn arcs of triumph to a garden gate (29–30).

A mere "dog-hole eked with ends of wall" becomes an entrance or "frontispiece" with the addition of a few touches of ornament and rustication:

> Then clap four slices of pilaster on't,
> That, lac'd with bits of rustic, makes a front (33–34).

Just as the dog-hole is dressed with pretentious sham, so the ladies in Pope's epistle try on various roles of historical or mythological painting:[14]

> Let then the fair one beautifully cry,
> In Magdalen's loose hair and lifted eye,
> Or dressed in smiles of sweet Cecilia shine,
> With simpering angels, palms, and harps divine (11–14).

Here the lines are worked out with a cruel incisiveness. What adverb can overwhelm its verb more than the self-conscious "beautifully" does the supposedly spontaneous "cry?" Or how better than with "in" suggest the assumption of a costume? And how more neatly catch the ambiguity of mock piety and self-display than in the sensual detail of the "loose hair," with Magdalen's humility in washing Christ's feet played off against the artful negligence of the lady? We can recall the iconography of the Magdalen's tear-filled eye and see it converted to histrionic imitation, which as readily turns to the rapt smiles of Cecilia. The lady is surrounded at last with all the furniture of divinity: cosmic harmony provides a musical setting, and angels can only simper their adoration.

The very grotesqueness of bad art has a fascination, for in the failure or misdirection of intention the ambitions of art are made all the more conspicuous; bad art cannot conceal art, and it becomes as a result monumental in its futility, its aspirations nakedly unrealized and imposingly asserted. So in the portraits of *To a Lady:* Atossa's vehemence and strain, her unconscious but unerring commitment to failure, her "brave disorder," which cannot come to terms with the world but still has neither integrity of aim or stable object of its own—these have a grandeur that approaches tragic stature. The forces at work within Atossa acquire more than human dimensions, and their magnification is insistently stressed. Such phrases as "by turns all womankind" or "all her life one warfare upon earth" create a vastness of scale that intensifies the shifting motives and unstable will. The vastness that cannot be composed becomes monstrous.

Yet, even as Pope creates this effect, he composes the picture; the thrusts of will and eddies of feeling are given a regularity of effect that Atossa cannot see. The implicit logic, to which Atossa is blind, is made inescapably neat:

> Strange! by the means defeated of the ends,
> By spirit robbed of power, by warmth of friends,

> By wealth of followers! without one distress
> Sick of herself through very selfishness! (143–46.)

The clarity of pattern makes Atossa's blindness seem all the more mechanical; every effort she makes accomplishes her defeat the more precisely. She becomes a near-tragic figure locked in a pattern of satiric transparency, and, like Timon's, her dreadful self-assertion is blandly assumed into a comic pattern as her wealth "wanders, Heaven-directed, to the poor" (150).

These lives are themselves failures of art; if Pope shows us "character as a creative achievement" in the *Essay*,[15] he shows us here the inability to create the stable self-knowledge which makes for a true self.

> Fair to no purpose, artful to no end,
> Young without lovers, old without a friend,
> A fop their passion, but their prize a sot;
> Alive, ridiculous, and dead, forgot! (245–48.)

Flavia's desperate thrusts are an instance. She is a woman who disdains every common thought and convention, who seeks for an intensity of experience that life can never give her. Her search, by its very nature, must be disappointed with every attainment, and she veers between impossible hope and utter despair. What casts her spirits down? "A spark too fickle, or a spouse too kind" (94). What does it mean? Does she fear her husband's pity? Or is he also unfaithful? Or does his loyalty stir her guilt? Or is he drearily trying to win her back? Or is he foolishly in the way? All kinds of guesses are possible, for "true no-meaning puzzles more than wit" (114). The formless work of bad art teases us with the forms it might have assumed. We cannot help taking for granted that nonsense is aspiring to meaning. But it turns out that we are looking at the wrong level. We cannot

> Infer the motive from the deed, and shew,
> That what we chanc'd was what we meant to do
> (*To Cobham*, Moral Essay I, 53–54).

Only in light of the ruling passion do the wild seem constant and the foolish consistent. The work which seems formless composes if one stands at the right distance. So with Flavia:

> You purchase pain with all that joy can give,
> And die of nothing but a rage to live (99–100).

The last lines fix compassionately on the helpless self-destruction that underlies the worldly wit and overrefinement.

But it is toward the order of a true work of art, a true character, that Pope moves. Character, Aristotle tells us, "is that which reveals the moral purpose of the agents" (*Poetics,* vi), and it demands the power of choice. The ladies we have seen so far act through involuntary passion, but at the close as we come to the Lady addressed (presumably Martha Blount), we move from intense femininity to a woman who is a "softer man." The Lady is capable of self-knowledge and self-control; even more, of generosity and tact. Pope looks back here, as in much of the epistle, to *The Rape of the Lock,* where a lovely order composed without true consciousness is easily lost. This Lady is "Mistress of herself, though China fall" (268). She becomes a fusion of the charm, variety, and energy of feminine passion, and the stability, directness, and strength of masculine reason. Pope has come close to defining the art toward which he has moved in his later satires, an art that goes beyond mere beauty and weds its aesthetic power to moral vision.

IV. The Poetry of Morality

> Late as it is, I put myself to school,
> And feel some comfort, not to be a fool
> (Pope, *Horace,* Epistle I, i).

Pope's *Imitations of Horace* were begun while he was still at work on the *Essay on Man* and *Moral Essays,* and it is questionable whether he saw them taking shape as parts of a new large work until he was well along with their composition. They are full of topical references, of answers to critics, of political attacks, and of self-vindication. But they form, nevertheless, a major work in their own right, and they mark the dominance of a new tone in Pope's work, the tone that emerges in the Socratic aspect of the *Essay on Man.* Pope writes at the close to Bolingbroke:

> urg'd by thee, I turn'd the tuneful art
> From sounds to things, from fancy to the heart
> (IV, 391–92).

In the *Imitations* Pope makes Horace the singing master of his soul.

We can best approach the *Imitations* by looking back for a moment to Shaftesbury. In a long letter to Pierre Coste, the French Protestant who had been part of Locke's circle, Shaftesbury sets forth a biographical approach to Horace's works. He sees three stages in Horace's career. The first is the young poet's "free republican state," when he followed the cause of Brutus and held a "suitable philosophy," which Shaftesbury calls "the Socratic, civil or social." This early commitment gave way as he won the patronage of Maecenas and Augustus; Horace's second stage Shaftesbury calls "his debauched, slavish, courtly state"—the period in which he moved toward Epicurean philosophy. Finally there arises "his third and last period, viz., his *returning, recovering state,* and his recourse to his first philosophy and principles, sorely against Maecenas and the court's desire, who would have kept him, and did all they could to do so, but in vain" (Rand, 360). Shaftesbury's Horace, of course, need not be Pope's. Yet this view of Horace's *sermones*—his late, conversational poems—as a movement back to moral severity and philosophical integrity is a dramatic conception that Pope uses in his imitations.

The drama of the satiric speaker is, in many ways, a stylized one. We are accustomed to read in many "program satires" (those works in which the satirist defends his art and presents his motives) that the satiric speaker cannot write in the high style of poetry, that he has turned from artifice to naked honesty, from "literature" to truth. Persius and Juvenal, too, contrast the dreary public recitations of epic bombast with their own anguished *cris de coeur* and biting coarseness. The satiric writer creates a speaker who is dramatically appropriate, who reveals the ethos which must animate the vision of the world that his satire will disclose. Rage or calm amusement, honest indignation or sardonic pleasure—whatever the tone or posture, it accounts for what is seen, just as the invocation of the muse prepares the epic speaker for the high style and subject to which he aspires. Maynard Mack has given us a set of categories by which to distinguish some of the principal roles the speaker assumes: the *"naïf,* the *ingénu,* the simple heart"; the *"vir bonus,* the plain good private citizen"; and "the public defender," the "satirist as hero." There are various ways in which these voices may "succeed one another, modulate and qualify one another, and occasionally fuse with one another." ("The Muse of Satire"; see Chapter I, note 5).

Yet, while we can see the stylization or the fictionality of
the satiric speaker, we cannot ignore the fact that, for a poet
as well known to his audience as Horace or Pope (or Chaucer
or Byron), there is a basis of historic fact under the fiction.
Pope, after presenting his satiric portrait of the corrupt and
effeminate Sporus, boasts:

> Be one Poet's praise,
> That, if he pleased, he pleased by manly ways
> (*Epistle to Dr. Arbuthnot,* 336–37).

The full import of the line is all the stronger if we know, as
everyone knew, how very small and twisted a body Pope had.
Manliness, Pope is making clear, resides less in swelling mus-
cle than in moral courage, and effeminacy less in Sporus'
gestures than in his passive subservience to the court and his
love of its soft pleasures. All through these *Imitations of
Horace* the dramatic role of the speaker serves to place Pope's
work in a long and dignified tradition that reaches back to
Plato's *Apology;* but the nature of the man who assumes that
role—the fact that it is also a well-known actual man named
Alexander Pope—gives new energy to the tradition.

Just as Yeats in his last poems finds a new voice that is still
remarkably his own by singing Swift's tunes (among others),
so Pope offers us the drama—superimposed upon that of the
satire itself—of a great poet learning a new "late" style, learning to do without much that he has already done supremely
well, freeing himself for a directness that rings with all it does
not need to say. Pope's *Imitations* have the force of what we
might call a poetry of renunciations, a poetry whose formal
freedom and personal intensity are given only with disdainful
sureness of poise. With all the careful protestations of humility
on the part of Pope's satiric speaker, his poetry has the
arrogance that Yeats gloried in, the arrogance of formal
mastery.

The plainness of style Pope affects, in the manner of Horace,
becomes the quietness of a man who finds his subject too
precious to risk any hint of inflationary rhetoric:

> Well, on the whole, plain prose must be my fate:
> Wisdom (curse on it) will come soon or late.
> There is a time when poets will grow dull:
> I'll e'en leave verses to the boys at school:
> To rules of poetry no more confin'd,
> I learn to smooth and harmonize my mind,

Teach every thought within its bounds to roll,
And keep the equal measure of the soul
    (Epistle II, ii, 198–205).

The withdrawal from "poetry" is like the withdrawal from the noise of the city ("Who there his Muse, or self, or soul attends?") to the "pensive Grot":

There all alone, and compliments apart,
I ask these sober questions of my heart (210–11).

The care that might have produced flowing verse must now go to the ordering of "inward numbers." We can hear through Horace an echo of Socrates:

Well then, these men, as I said, have spoken hardly one word of truth; but you shall hear from me the whole truth; not eloquence, gentlemen, like their own, decked out in fine words and phrases, not covered with ornaments; not at all—you shall hear things spoken anyhow in the words that first come. For I believe justice is in what I say, and let none of you expect anything else; indeed it would not be proper, gentlemen, for an old man like me to come before you like a boy moulding his words in pretty patterns (*Apology*, 17–18, trans. W. H. D. Rouse).

Pope achieves in the *Imitations* the poetry of morality. There is no poetic material that seems so unpromising to us today. We are prepared for a poetry of the disordered sensibility, the extreme state, the thrust beyond limiting forms. Juvenal can give us the plenitude of outrage: a torrent of uncontrollable images forces itself upon him, and he takes perverse pleasure in knowing that he has broken through every lie and kept alive the power of indignation. Alienation can be a measure of vitality; to be able to hate is at least still to feel. In Juvenal's outrage we can see the love of rhetoric and extravagant image even more; outrage becomes the release of poetic energy. Pope has something of this, but only so much as can be ordered in a larger structure.

Pope, like Yeats, is writing in full consciousness of the meaning that a new "late" style can have. Once the circus animals have deserted, as Yeats puts it, the poet must be satisfied with his heart. When Pope asks "sober questions" of his heart, he is exploring the problems of self-knowledge, and the *Imitations* are the most intimate and inward exploration Pope gives us of the life of moral choice. The use of the *per-*

sona—the semi-fictitious personality of the speaker—allows
Pope to dramatize the conditions out of which the self must
be made—the confusions and vanities, the rationality and impersonal passion. To do this, Pope surrounds the Horatian
text and the Horatian mode with other suggestions: the language of folly or vice fuses with the language of sin, the
intimations of serenity are touched with a hint of grace. The
center of these poems is the act of moral choice, and their
focus is the order of mind, but the order of mind may hold
within itself (as we have seen in Dryden) the dialectical struggle between the orders of charity and flesh.

A short Horatian epistle (I, vi), the famous *Nil admirari,*
can show us Pope's procedure. The poem turns upon the contrast of the philosophic eye and the sensual eye. The philosophic eye looks "through" the visible universe, undisturbed
by awful dimensions and power, for it sees and trusts the
"Ruler," the ordering power. The sensual eye is engrossed with
the visible; to "admire" is to wonder at the glitter and splendor
of the world.

> Admire we then what earth's low entrails hold,
> Arabian shores, or Indian seas infold?
> All the mad trade of fools and slaves for gold?
> Or popularity, or stars and strings?
> The mob's applauses, or the gifts of kings?
> Say with what eyes we ought at courts to gaze,
> And pay the great our homage of amaze? (11–17.)

The rapid intuitive movement of the philosophic eye is placed
in telling contrast with the strained effort born of "admiration"—the careering haste after exotic treasure, the traffic in
reputation and esteem to be awarded by populace or crown.
The "homage of amaze" becomes the superstitious worship of
the visible—in contrast to the faith of those who

> Look through, and trust the Ruler with his skies,
> To him commit the hour, the day, the year,
> And view this dreadful All without a fear (8–10).

Gradually Pope creates a cluster of terms (admire, amaze,
surprise, blaze) to convey the dazzle of the worldly and the
anxiety of the "unbalanc'd mind." The pursuit of wealth becomes a constant multiplication—as in a wilderness of mirrors
—of bright sensation:

Go then, and if you can, admire the state
Of beaming diamonds, and reflected plate;
Procure a Taste to double the surprise,
And gaze on Parian charms with learned eyes:
Be struck with bright brocade, or Tyrian dye,
Our birth-day nobles' splendid livery (28–33).

Awe varies proportionately with quantity. Pope beautifully
catches the industry of enjoyment: the deliberate cultivation of
fashionable taste, the long study that refines the response to
carved marble ("Parian charms"), the setting out to be
"struck." The slavery of pleasure is suggested in the last of
these lines: the brilliant garments worn for the royal birthday
become a mark of bondage as well as a proud ornament. In
this acquisitive society, where men struggle "For fame, for
riches, for a noble wife," the only meaning that is left to
"noble" is one of social status. It is a world of getting, not of
being; of admiring, not of seeing. Its light is the brilliant
flicker:

The greatest can but blaze, and pass away (47).

The poem comes to a brief rest as the poet offers a cure
for "the mind's disease": "Would ye be blest? despise low
joys, low gains" (60). But this kind of moral simplicity is
meaningless to a world that

virtue and a church alike disowns,
Thinks that but words, and this but brick and stones
(65–66).

At this point, as the moral advice is rejected, the motion is
renewed, more intensely than ever:

Fly then, on all the wings of wild desire!
Admire whate'er the maddest can admire (67–68).

The quantification of pleasure becomes flagrant heaping up:
"Advance thy golden mountain to the skies" (73). Wealth
acquires a rich wife, and wealth confers upon her beauty,
chastity, friendships. All value words become as characterless
as worn coins, and as convenient; so "A man of wealth is
dubb'd a man of worth" (81). But the mere possession of
wealth is no resting place; spurious dignities, once bought,
must be bought again and again—"A noble superfluity it
craves" (91), so that it can pay off its followers and dazzle
others with largess:

> If wealth alone then make and keep us blest,
> Still, still be getting, never, never rest (95–96).

One thinks of those lines in the *Essay on Man,* whose sense is
cruelly parodied here:

> Hope springs eternal in the human breast:
> Man never Is, but always To be blest (I, 95–96).

Pope has deepened the folly of misdirected awe until it has
become a counterpart of Hobbes's image of man as rest-
lessly and insatiably acquisitive.

This is not yet the worst. Pope darkens Horace at every
point. Where Horace's man shows pleasure in his craftiness,
Pope's shows the unpleasant laughter of contempt for those
he uses. Horace's glutton pretends to be a sportsman while
he buys his boar, but Pope's Lord Russell is a debauched
sybarite who yearns for any stirring of appetite and envies the
hunger and thirst of the poor he turns away to starve. Where
Horace's gluttons are likened to the forgetful hogs that are
Circe's captives, Pope's are elaborated further:

> Or shall we ev'ry decency confound,
> Thro' taverns, stews, and bagnios take our round,
> Go dine with Chartres, in each vice outdo
> K[innoul]l's lewd cargo, or Ty[rawle]y's crew,
> From Latian sirens, French Circean feasts,
> Return well travell'd, and transform'd to beasts,
> Or for a titled punk, or foreign flame,
> Renounce our country, and degrade our name? (118–25.)

Pope cites particular profligates in embassies as far apart as
Constantinople and Lisbon (whence Lord Tyrawley was to return, according to Horace Walpole, with "three wives and
fourteen children"); the peculiar fusion of refinement and de-
generacy looks ahead to the Grand Tour we see in the fourth
book of *The Dunciad.*

Both Horace and Pope find the alternative to admiration
in love and laughter, but Pope moves into this "solution"
through the figure of Rochester, the rake who died "after all"
a Christian, and he cites lines that present love as something
close to charity:

> If, after all, we must with Wilmot own,
> The cordial drop of life is love alone (126–27).

Rochester's lines, in the *Letter from Artemisa,* are worth
citing in full:

Love, the most gen'rous passion of the mind;
The softest refuge innocence can find;
The safe director of unguided youth:
Fraught with kind wishes, and secur'd by truth:
That cordial-drop heav'n in our cup has thrown,
To make the nauseous draught of life go down (40–45).

To the words of Rochester is added the wisdom of Swift's
Vive la bagatelle; the warmth of love and the playful self-
awareness of harmless laughter are fused into an image of
quiet goodness:

The man that loves and laughs, must sure do well (129).

It is offered tentatively and lightly, but its freedom from all
that Pope has opposed to it gives it the force of sane moderation and the accent of authenticity.

The *Imitations,* like the fourth epistle of the *Essay on Man,*
constantly try to distinguish between external and internal,
the claims of the world and the deep sources of self. This is a
movement back such as Robert Frost presents in "Directive"
—a burning away of detail, a recovery of wholeness and calm.
Pope, "public too long," tries to free himself of the "rhymes
and rattles of the man or boy," to retreat to simplicity:

What right, what true, what fit we justly call,
Let this be all my care—for this is all (Epistle I, i, 19–20).

He is impatient to escape "unprofitable moments"

That lock up all the functions of my soul;
That keep me from myself (40–41).

Simplicity is found in moving back from the "new court
jargon" of London's voice: "Get money, money still! / And
then let virtue follow, if she will" (79–80). We move back
through the "good old song" that children sing: "Virtue, brave
boys! 'tis virtue makes a king" (92). We move from the "modern language of corrupted peers" back to "what was spoke
at Cressy and Poitiers" (99–100). It is a double voyage in
time—toward the innocence of childhood and toward a more
heroic age.

One can select only a few of the contrasts through which
Pope explores the situation of the self and throws off the external that pre-empts its life. First, there is the contrast of
languages. Of his father he writes,

> Unlearn'd, he knew no Schoolman's subtle art,
> No language, but the language of the heart
>   (*Arbuthnot*, 398–99).

In contrast we have the timid advice of Fortescue, who is "learned in the law," and comes to a cautionary splutter of pure legality:

> Consult the statute: *quart*. I think it is,
> *Edwardi Sext.* or *prim. & quint. Eliz.*
>   (Satire II, i, 147–48).

There is the surrender of sense to sound in court panegyric, as the poet creates in words a stock baroque triumph, all noise and glory:

> Rend with tremendous sound your ears asunder,
> With gun, drum, trumpet, blunderbuss, and thunder?
> Or nobly wild, with Budgell's fire and force,
> Paint angels trembling round his falling horse?
>   (*Ibid.*, 25–28.)

There is the coy warble of pastoral flattery, a perfect dissolution of sense in liquids:

> Lull with Amelia's liquid name the Nine,
> And sweetly flow through all the royal line
>   (*Ibid.*, 31–32).

Nor do we need to go to the court to find the emptiness of conventional terms; all ask for indiscriminate praise:

> Each widow asks it for *the best of men,*
> For him she weeps, and him she weds again
>   (Epilogue II, 107–8).

There is also the contrast of prudent timeserving with naïve spontaneity. Walpole is the prisoner of his power and venality. The decent social man within is a sacrifice to the success the Prime Minister has chosen:

> Come, come, at all I laugh he laughs, no doubt;
> The only difference is, I dare laugh out
>   (Epilogue I, 35–36).

Poets are tactless:

> The season, when to come, and when to go,
> To sing, or cease to sing, we never know
>   (Epistle II, I, 360–61).

In contrast to the hesitation or reserve of dishonest wealth or power is the poet's freedom and vitality:

> I love to pour out all myself, as plain
> As downright Shippen, or as old Montaigne:
> In them, as certain to be lov'd as seen,
> The soul stood forth, nor kept a thought within
> (Satire II, i, 51–54).

> My head and heart thus flowing through my quill
> (*Ibid.*, 63).

> The feast of reason and the flow of soul (*Ibid.*, 128).

The business of getting demands constant activity, a busy motion that permits neither rest nor self-knowledge. Pope sets property itself in a whirl of movement from one transient owner to the next:

> What's property? dear Swift! you see it alter,
> From you to me, from me to Peter Walter;
> Or, in a mortgage prove a lawyer's share;
> Or, in a jointure, vanish from the heir
> (Satire II, ii, 167–70).

The free man is not a possessor, and hence not a prisoner:

> What is't to me (a passenger, God wot)
> Whether my vessel be first-rate or not?
> The ship itself may make a better figure,
> But I that sail, am neither less nor bigger
> (Epistle II, ii, 296–99).

And suddenly, at the close of a poem, property becomes a metaphor for all the external claims that keep us from ourselves:

> Let lands and houses have what lords they will,
> Let us be fix'd, and our own masters still
> (Satire II, ii, 179–80).

In the *Epilogue to the Satires* (originally published as *One Thousand Seven Hundred and Thirty Eight: A Dialogue Something Like Horace*) Pope achieves his strongest definition of self. He assumes in his own person the unremitting assertion of a moral view, and he makes his unnamed Friend the spokesman of all those attitudes that blunt, ignore, or discredit the moral view. The Friend tries at every point to escape the awareness Pope thrusts upon him, and in the course of the two dialogues that make up the poem he introduces virtually every objection that has ever been made to satire. One is more impressed by the steady tenor of his resistance than by the specific objections; and he succeeds only in stinging Pope to a brilliant defense.

" 'Tis all from Horace," the Friend complains of Pope's satire. Why—in effect—do it again? Yet Horace knew better than to rage like Pope:

> His sly, polite, insinuating style
> Could please at court, and make Augustus smile
>   (I, 19–20).

This chooses for praise exactly what Shaftesbury had denounced as Horace's "debauched, slavish, courtly state."

At every point, the Friend tries to turn the critic into a comforter, the teacher into an entertainer. For Pope to accept this is to move backward from things to sounds, to reverse the movement "from fancy to the heart." "Adieu, distinction, satire, warmth, and truth!" One can most easily lie in the inflated nonsense of court sermons and panegyric:

> The gracious dew of pulpit eloquence,
> And all the well-whipt cream of courtly sense
> . . . that easy Ciceronian style,
> So Latin, yet so English all the while (I, 69–70, 73–74).

Such mellifluous obscurity is at once tawdry, pretentious, and deceptive. Pope's travesty of it is comparable to Socrates' mockery of Phaedrus' devotion to the false rhetoric of Lysias.

Pope rejects the Friend's offer of a denatured satire that condones vice and makes all moral demands seem priggish. When he insists upon the power of satire to lash, the Friend suggests he attack only those out of power; they become eligible for whipping "exactly when they fall" (90). We have a new blunting of the moral end of satire—it becomes sheer vindictiveness. All it cannot reach now stirs the Friend's imagination. It is possible, if one has the right talents, to be one who never falls. The absolute courtiers find a messianic vision in their sovereign's smile, and they ascend to a serenity that is given only outside of time or change:

> no father's, brother's, friend's disgrace
> Once break their rest, or stir them from their place
> But past the sense of human miseries,
> All tears are wip'd for ever from all eyes,
> No cheek is known to blush, no heart to throb,
> Save when they lose a question, or a job (I, 99–104).

Isaiah's vision (25:8) is used to confer the glory of charity upon the order of the flesh, and heavenly transport is translated into the placid insensibility of flesh unvexed by the claims of spirit. The Friend has revealed his system of belief.

Once the worship of this world is fully set forth, it must be maintained. Pope offers himself as the defender of "the dignity of vice." If one worships this world, the world must be kept worthy of that worship. There has been a leveling of vice:

> Ye Gods! shall Cibber's son without rebuke
> Swear like a lord, or Rich outwhore a duke? (I, 115–16.)

The satirist must prevent Vice from becoming trivial. If all moral distinctions break down, the lowest will dare to be as vicious as the highest, and social distinctions will go as well. Virtue can do without worldly honor or splendor (since she claims allegiance to another order), but Vice cannot tolerate the fall of social status (it is the only Fall she recognizes):

> Vice is undone, if she forgets her birth,
> And stoops from angels to the dregs of earth (I, 141–42).

What is glorious in Lucifer is squalid in the petty criminal or gin-soaked ruffian. As Vice is equally open to all, she is all the more dependent upon appearances to give her dignity. Vice must always seek grandeur by imitating, however grossly in false art, the hierarchies and distinctions of Virtue. Otherwise she reaches one dead level of mere physicality, of undifferentiated appetite. The full tribute to the power of Vice can be paid only by the master of a moral imagination, who knows what she has overcome and debased. He alone can give her significance, and he gives it through the art of ironic satire.

In the second dialogue, the Friend's attempt to denature satire continues. It should be kept "general, unconfined" (14) and should not be allowed to "hurt a man that's rising in the trade" (35). Personal attacks will only "make men desperate" and prevent them from reforming (59–60). They tend to be specific and arbitrary—"Strange spleen to S——k!" (62).

At this point Pope begins an ascent very much in the spirit of Diotima's speech in the *Symposium*. Diotima describes to Socrates the ascending movement of the Platonic ladder of beauty:

> to begin from the beauties of earth and mount upwards for the sake of that other beauty, using these as steps

only, and from one going on to two, and from two to all
fair forms, and from fair forms to fair practices, and
from fair practices to fair notions, until from fair notions
he arrives at the notion of absolute beauty, and at last
knows what the essence of beauty is (*Symposium* 211,
trans. Benjamin Jowett).

Pope moves from mere personalities to worthy men ("Even
in a Bishop I can spy desert"), from worthy men to virtuous
friends, from virtuous friends to Virtue itself in any man:

> To find an honest man I beat about,
> And love him, court him, praise him, in or out
> (II, 102–3).

Once Pope has made his ascent to another order of being, he
can look down with scorn upon the great men of this world:

> Are they not rich? what more can they pretend?
> Dare they to hope a poet for their friend? (II, 114–15.)

To the poet who is wholly detached from commitment to the
power of this world, moral corruption loses its glamor; it
shows itself as mere filth. Pope describes its traffic in the image
of the Westphalian hogs that feed on each other's excrement.
The reaction of the Friend is the typical outrage of the respectable:

> FR. This filthy simile, this beastly line
>   Quite turns my stomach.
> P.   So does flattery mine.

One may compare a crucial passage in the *Gorgias:*

> SOCRATES: But what if the itching is not confined to the
>   head? Shall I pursue the question? And here, Callicles,
>   I would have you consider how you would reply . . .
>   if in the last resort you are asked, whether the life of a
>   catamite is not terrible, foul, miserable? Or would
>   you venture to say, that they too are happy, if they
>   only get enough of what they want?
> CALLICLES: Are you not ashamed, Socrates, of introduc-
>   ing such topics into the argument?
> SOCRATES: Well, my fine friend, but am I the introducer
>   of these topics, or he who says without any qualification
>   that all who feel pleasure in whatever manner are
>   happy, and who admits of no distinction between good
>   and bad pleasures? And I would still ask, whether
>   you say that pleasure and good are the same, or

whether there is some pleasure which is not a good?
(494–95, trans. Jowett.)

So Pope goes on:

> And all your courtly civet cats can vent,
> Perfume to you, to me is excrement (II, 183–84).

The issue is fully joined: it is precisely the glamor of saving appearances that shocks and nauseates the moralist. Pope can assume all the charges made against satire—its spleen, its spoil-sport naming of names, its intransigence—and shape them into the outward expression of a love of Virtue and an impersonal indignation at its suffering:

> Ask you what provocation I have had?
> The strong antipathy of good to bad.
> When Truth or Virtue an affront endures,
> Th' affront is mine, my friend, and should be yours . . .
> Mine as a friend to ev'ry worthy mind;
> And mine as man, who feel for all mankind
> (II, 197–200, 203–4).

The Friend makes a last thrust, "You're strangely proud," and Pope's disdain marks the poet in full acceptance of his high task:

> Yes, I am proud: I must be proud to see
> Men not afraid of God, afraid of me (II, 208–9).

Ridicule becomes a "sacred weapon," to be used with reverence but "honest zeal"; the splendors of court, so magnificent in the triumph of Vice, contract to "tinsel insects." The poem becomes an intense assertion of an order beyond that of the world where "other trophies deck the truly brave" (II, 236), a world with "other stars" than those that royalty wear, a world of "Honor not conferr'd by kings." This is surely the satirist at his most heroic, and Pope rises to the tragic stature of the last virtuous man in a degenerate world. But the Friend is not, after all, quelled:

> Alas! alas! pray end what you began,
> And write next winter more *Essays on Man* (II, 254–55).

The poem ends on a quizzical note. The durability of the Friend's devotion to this world makes Pope's heroic assertion a somewhat quixotic passion. The world will refuse to listen; it will deflect the meaning it cannot afford to recognize, or trivialize the moral view until it can be indulged without cost.

One critic sees in the opposition of the Friend and Pope that of the "political man" and the "moral hero," but this is to take politics in its lowest sense.[16] Swift (as I hope to show in the next chapter) also sees politics in opposition to intransigent morality; but to him politics is the ordering of the state so that duty and interest are not at odds. Here the politics of the Friend is the complete sacrifice of morality and the inversion of an order of charity so that it becomes an order of flesh.

In Pope the nature of the adversary always helps define the moral self. In the *Epistle to Dr. Arbuthnot,* Pope rises to self-definition through a series of "dialogues" with three adversaries, Atticus, Bufo, and Sporus. Atticus shows us a man of talent and charm who is flawed by vanity. He affects hauteur but registers fear; his company of followers becomes his magic circle of self-defense, for he can bear to have around him only men who do not threaten his insecure sense of superiority. The debasement is inevitable: a cultivation of the second-rate, a fear of excellence, a recourse to oblique attacks upon what he can neither reject nor admit. But if Atticus can "Bear, like a Turk, no brother near the throne," Pope avoids courts altogether and has kept, "like Asian monarchs" from the sight of fellow writers. If Atticus gathers wits and Templars (students of law were notorious for trifling literary ambition) about him, cultivates his "little Senate" and sits "attentive to his own applause," Pope can assert:

> I ne'er with wits or witlings past my days,
> To spread about the itch of verse and praise (223–24).

And so with Bufo, the false patron, who holds out the promise of reward in return for flattery, but who neither knows nor honors merit, Pope wishes to "live my own, and die so, too." He seems to tower "above a patron" in his indignation:

> I condescend
> Sometimes to call a minister my friend:
> I was not born for courts or great affairs,
> I pay my debts, believe, and say my pray'rs (265–68).

Once more, Pope's withdrawal from their world becomes a superb aloofness, the pride of a man whose moral habits are a passport to an order of experience the others have lost all power to reach. His stance is not without its own defensiveness: "condescend . . . to call a minister my friend" reveals a just pride stung into excess. But it serves to remind us of the dialectical occasion, of the fact that Pope's self-portrait is a warm response to others, not a cool inventory of self.

In other cases, the dialectic may take place within the self. At the close of his epistle to Bolingbroke (Epistle I, i), Pope turns to his "guide, philosopher and friend" reproaching him for not exacting the rigorous discipline that Pope needs. Anxious now "to be fool no more," Pope is still disturbed by the incoherence of his mind:

> When (each opinion with the next at strife,
> One ebb and flow of follies all my life)
> I plant, root up; I hold, and then confound;
> Turn round to square, and square again to round
> (167–70).

It is the self that is Pope's concern. Bolingbroke alone can make Pope what he himself has become:

> That man divine whom wisdom calls her own . . .
> At home, though exil'd, free, though in the tow'r;
> In short, that reasoning, high, immortal thing,
> Just less than Jove, and much above a king,
> Nay, half in heaven—

And then we have the collapse into the limiting body that must house this free soul:

> except (what's mighty odd)
> A fit of vapors clouds this demigod (180, 184–88).

We can see this pattern more concisely in the words Pope spoke in his very last days: "I am like Socrates, distributing my morality among my friends, just as I am dying." And then he added: "Ay, but I can say very little that's wise to you now" (cited from Spence's manuscript in *Correspondence,* IV, 525). The order of mind must mediate between flesh and charity; it must come to terms with both and see each in relationship to the other. Its ironic self-knowledge is the very center of a stable self that can admit the changes of time without losing its identity.

VI.

Swift: Order and Obligation

I. The Right and the Good

Swift has one of the most frighteningly unsentimental minds in literature. He is capable of playfulness, tenderness, rancor, touchiness, self-pity. He has sentiments, surely, and an excess of many. But he never confuses what we ought to do with what we want to do, the right with the good. (For my purposes, it is sufficiently precise to equate "the right" with obligation or duty, and the good with interest, inclination, or desire.)[1] The very idea of duty, as philosophers since Kant have observed, implies an inclination to be overcome. We may provide ourselves with "grounds" for our sense of obligation: we may accept the commands of a God who is to be loved with gratitude, we may wish to preserve the moral order that binds all human beings together by universal principles, we may feel that we are sustaining the society in which we have our life, and thus give the bleak requiredness of duty a dramatic basis. And we believe the cost of disobedience to be the loss of some important good. The dramatic scheme—whether it be theological or metaphysical, a cosmic or a social myth—gives us a stake in the preservation of the right by reconciling it with the good. As Bishop Butler observes, if the claim of "virtue" is to be saved from "open scorn" by men, "its very being in the world depends upon its appearing to have no contrariety to private interest and self-love" (Sermon XI).

Swift, more than any other writer of his age, refuses to celebrate the "grounds" of duty or obligation. He insists upon the right as something immediately evident, in an act of cognition, and he demands that we accept its claims in their stark immediacy:

> I look upon myself, in the capacity of a clergyman, to be one appointed by providence for defending a post as-

signed me, and for gaining over as many enemies as I can. Although I think my cause is just, yet one great motion is my submitting to the pleasure of Providence, and to the laws of my country (*Thoughts on Religion,* HD, IX, 262).

It is an uncompromising statement whose imagery may recall to a modern reader those strange and inexplicable posts and appointments of Kafka's fiction. There is a peculiar stress upon the pure obligation—appointed, assigned, defending, submitting, laws. Again, when Swift writes of cosmic Order, it is only to define the area of human responsibility that remains outside:

The motions of the sun and moon: in short, the whole system of the universe, as far as philosophers have been able to discover and observe, are in the utmost degree of regularity and perfection: but wherever God hath left to man the power of interposing a remedy for thought or labor, there he hath placed things in a state of imperfection, on purpose to stir up human industry, without which life would stagnate, or indeed rather could not subsist at all . . . (HD, IV, 245).

In this rigorous acceptance of obligation as distinct from, and opposed to, satisfaction, Swift recalls Pascal. Both insist upon disjunctions—discontinuities that eliminate moral confusions. "Without faith," Swift preaches in his sermon *On the Trinity,* "we can do no works acceptable to God: for, if they proceed from any other principle, they will not advance our salvation . . ." But he goes on in a vein quite different from Pascal: "and this faith, as I have explained it, we may acquire without giving up our senses, or contradicting our reason" (HD, IX, 168).

Faith, as Swift defines it, is essentially a disposition to act, "an entire dependence upon the truth, the power, the justice, and the mercy of God; which dependence will certainly incline us to obey him in all things. So, that the great excellency of faith, consisteth *in the consequence it hath* upon our actions. . . . Therefore, let no man think he can lead *as good a moral life* without faith, as with it . . ." (HD, IX, 164; my italics). The mind must accept the duties laid upon it by God, but it does not seek exaltation in His image. The pure in heart have "a daily vision of God" which confirms their beliefs; but Swift, in his own evening prayer, asks God only to "let us see so much of the excellencies of thy divine nature . . . as may make us hate everything in ourselves that is unlike to thee." So, too, for Swift the mysteries are inescapable; yet they serve no end in themselves but as a test of the fullness of man's faith, i.e., dependence. At no point does Swift seek to make religious experience intrinsically pleasurable; it must be accepted for what it is, revealed obligation.

Swift has scorn for presumption: "Miserable mortals! can we contribute to the *honor and glory of God?* I could wish that expression were struck out of our prayer-books" (HD, IX, 263). But he does not abandon trust in reason. It may be that "the reason of every particular man is weak and wavering, perpetually swayed and turned by his interests, his passions, and his vices" (HD, IX, 166). Yet it is only through his reason that man can achieve a moral existence; his task is to unbias his mind and attain impartiality as best he can—through the rejection of partisan zeal, through the test of what men have agreed upon through the ages, through conscientious observance of "those actions which scripture and reason plainly tell us to be good and evil" (HD, IX, 150). The individual reason must be squared with unequivocal laws, and only man's dependence upon God will give those laws sufficiently strong sanction to make them effective.

Although Swift sees the heart of religion in an inescapable obligation, he is prepared to recognize that this obligation is received in men's heads and hearts by a largely natural process. The divine may descend, but it descends among men of passion and interest. Religious disbelief, in Swift's eyes, is an almost invariable product of immorality; religion is contrary to the interest of profligates and frauds, and they will persuade themselves that it cannot be true. Hence, moral decency is a preservative of beliefs, just as belief in turn is the source of the only sanction strong enough to outweigh interest. Given man's fallen nature, the conflict between the right and the good must be minimized if morality is to be fostered. The priest must reveal how moral decency will further man's interest in Heaven, and the statesman must try to create a society where duty and interest are made as closely identical as possible. The art of politics is the art of moderating moral heroism, of making it unnecessary for the man who can never achieve it. It is one of the glories of Christianity for Swift that it demands no extraordinary individual powers; moral triumphs of the early Christians were "altogether the product of their principles and doctrine, and were such as the same persons, without those aids, would never have arrived to" (HD, IX, 249).

Swift, in these views, has something in common with Mandeville. Swift, too, can see the politician as the "artful manager" making a viable social harmony of men with limited minds and unlimited appetites. But there is a difference between an accommodation of morality to man's capacities and the creation of a beautiful social machine that can use any grade of fuel. Mandeville dismisses aspiration to the realm of private morality; within the state, he becomes the champion of whatever workably exists. Swift leaves much more room for public aspiration.

Swift's religious emphasis isolates the specifically moral and obligatory in Christianity, by insisting upon the immediate intuition of the right. He is, in fact, constantly posing the moral choice that must be made in the face of opposing interest or desire. In the words of Melville's Father Mapple, "if we obey God, we must disobey ourselves; and it is in this disobeying ourselves, wherein the hardness of obeying God consists" (*Moby Dick,* ch. IX). Swift, however, does not pit man against God; he pits man's desires against the reason by which man sees his duty. His central theme is the problem of moral cognition: to see one's duty is a simple act; yet all of man's powers are devoted to creating an escape. The reasonable is constantly possible, given man's nature; yet the unfailing ingenuities of rationalization confound each choice with specious arguments and false names. At times Swift is outraged by the stubbornness with which will persists in undoing mind and the readiness of mind to be seduced; at other times, he is fascinated by the artistry of falsehood or error—the charming patterns of harmless self-deception, the terrible patterns of delusive self-destruction, the disgusting patterns of self-debasement. Most great moralists become great pathologists, and the pathologist may fall so deeply in love with the clarifications his method brings that he transfers some of that love to the material itself. Swift admits the value of the passions which spur men to virtue. Of the love of fame he writes, it "requires but little philosophy to discover and observe that there is no intrinsic value in all this; however, if it be founded in our nature, as an incitement to virtue, it ought not to be ridiculed" (HD, IV, 244).

The end Swift keeps in mind is virtuous action. It may be the result of confusion or imperfect choice. Its sources in human nature may be as mixed as we have seen in Pope's *Essay on Man.* But, interestingly, while he readily condones mixed or imperfect motives that produce right action, Swift is always prepared to represent vice as choice—false, mistaken, but irrevocably a choice.

One of the principal dangers of a doctrine that places too much value on the nature of the action—the fulfillment of a duty—and too little on the motives that produce it is that bland conformity or low prudence may become the norm of behavior. Swift is aware of the danger, and he writes with beautiful irony (in *An Essay on the Fates of Clergymen,* 1728) on the power of "discretion" to make a career for itself in the church (or any institution). Discretion, as Swift defines it, is

> a species of lower prudence, by the assistance of which, people of the meanest intellectuals, without any other qualification, pass through the world in great tranquillity, and with universal good treatment, neither giving nor taking offence.

Such a gift is of value: "regularity and forms are of great use in carrying the business of the world." But the constant threat to any institution is that such discretion will displace "genius, learning, strong comprehension, quickness of conception, magnanimity, generosity, sagacity, or any other superior gift of human minds." Discreet men want wealth and power; they are self-centered and grasping, and they stifle excellence in order to maintain what they have won—"when a great genius appears in the world, the dunces are all in confederacy against him" (HD, XII, 38–39).

Swift's special problem is to recommend a life of decency and "common forms" that will preserve men from viciousness without capitulating to hypocrisy and mediocrity. He faces this issue most squarely—if not altogether successfully—in the *Project for the Advancement of Religion and the Reformation of Manners* (1709). In that pamphlet, which many readers have been unable to believe was not ironic, Swift recommends that the Queen promote morality by making it fashionable. Starting from the fact that much of the morality that survives at court is at best impure, Swift advances a political measure. The Queen can promote virtue "by making it every man's interest and honor to cultivate religion and virtue; by rendering vice a disgrace, and the certain ruin to preferment or pretensions" (HD, II, 47). Swift has no illusions: this will produce the appearance of virtue rather than the substance, and it will clearly increase hypocrisy. But Swift, in the manner of La Rochefoucauld, sees the deference of hypocrisy: "it wears the livery of religion; it acknowledges her authority, and is cautious of giving scandal." Even more, hypocrisy is hard to sustain: "a long continued disguise is too great a constraint upon human nature, especially an English disposition. Men would leave off their vices out of mere weariness, rather than undergo the toil and hazard, and perhaps expense"—this is Swift at his driest—"of practising them perpetually in private. And, I believe, it is often with religion as it is with love; which, by much dissembling, at last grows real" (HD, II, 57). Thus, Swift as politician concludes, "our duty, by becoming our interest, would take root in our natures, and mix with the very genius of our people" (HD, II, 59).

In proposing such a program, Swift is clear about the risks. We may feel that he is cheapening virtue by making it a ticket to preferment. Yet, as he explains, the current ticket was "fidelity to a present establishment," and this left no power of criticism or reform within the court. (As he wrote later in a sermon on *Doing Good*, "a man may be very loyal in the common sense of the world, without one grain of public good at his heart.") The infusion of moral behavior into court life may have unlimited consequences. The year before, in the *Argument against Abolishing Christianity* (1708), Swift in ironic guise had written: "as long as we leave in being a God and his providence, with all the necessary consequences which curious and inquisitive men will be apt to draw from such premises, we do not strike at the root of the evil." So, in the *Project*, keeping alive the language and forms of morality may keep alive as well an awareness of standards beyond those of the "present establishment."

Swift's interest in politics and morality raises the larger issue of his cast of mind. Swift grew up into the skeptical temper that we see in a great many later seventeenth century men— Halifax is another that comes to mind. There are various reasons for this: the Baconian criticism of scholastic thought, distrust of those unlimited sanctions that religious sects wrested from Scripture, concern with the preservation of a balance or mean in affairs of church and state. The pursuit of the middle way becomes, in the Restoration and Augustan periods, a dialectical strategy that we see in all fields of thought. It depends upon the making of nice distinctions, of separating out the valuable from the excessive in each position, and of finding a *rapprochement* between those valuable elements that are kept apart by poorly defined oppositions. This method of redefinition places great weight on limited and clearly ascertainable meanings; it rejects terms that are vague and emotive, explanations that are genetic rather than analytic. Swift places no reliance upon those myths that explain the origin of the state and attempt to build values into history. He refuses to speculate upon origins, "nor does he think any one regular species of government more acceptable to God than another." "Where security of person and property are preserved by laws which none but the whole can repeal, there the great ends of government are provided for, whether the administration be in the hands of one, or of many" (HD, V, 15).

With Hobbes, Swift recognizes that there must be an "absolute and unlimited" sovereign power within the state, but he distinguishes between the executive and the supreme magistrate, by which "is properly understood the legislative power." In a limited monarchy, Parliament remains the supreme magistrate in its power to determine succession or to depose the monarch; and Swift implies that Hobbes might have avoided his needless absolutism in the *Leviathan* if he had recognized this distinction (HD, II, 16).

In matters of church government, Swift again draws a distinction between the church's exclusive right to conduct its internal affairs and the supreme civil magistrate's right over the church as a temporal institution. The decrees of the civil power "may be against equity, truth, reason, and religion, but they are not against law; because law is the will of the supreme legislature, and that is themselves. And there is no manner of doubt, but the same authority, whenever it pleaseth, may abolish Christianity, and set up the Jewish, Mahometan, or Heathen religion. In short, they may do anything within the compass of human power" (HD, II, 74). This recognition of the power of positive law makes Swift an ardent defender of the interest of the church establishment; to admit Dissenters to parliamentary power is to invite disestablishment of the Church of England and Ireland.

What strikes us in these views is Swift's keen awareness of the limited nature of institutions and of the importance of power structures within the state. He can appeal to the law of nature or the law of reason, particularly in *The Drapier's Letters,* but he recognizes that the "wisest nations" with "the truest notions of freedom" believe that "there was no natural right in one man to govern another; but that all was by institution, force, or consent" (HD, II, 23). So Swift sees the English constitution, whatever its ultimate sources, as "an artificial thing, not fairly to be traced . . . beyond Henry I"

(HD, II, 84). This sense of the artifice of institutions accords with Swift's attitudes toward religious law as well. He declares at one point that "All government is from God, who is the God of order" (HD, IX, 238), and characteristically he recognizes divine will as an unquestionable authority whose mercy is not to be courted with selfish expectation of partiality. In his prayers for Stella at the time of her death, Swift—for all his intense grief—achieves a startling power of "unbiased" humility:

> Restore her to us, O Lord, if it be thy gracious will, or inspire us with constancy and resignation, to support ourselves under so heavy an affliction. Restore her, O Lord, for the sake of those poor, who by losing her will be desolate, and those sick, who will not only want her bounty, but her care and tending; or else, in thy mercy, raise up some other in her place with equal disposition, and better abilities. Lessen, O Lord, we beseech thee, her bodily pains, or give her a double strength of mind to support them (HD, IX, 254).

We can see in all of this Swift's readiness to dwell in an unconsoling vision. He can accept the groundlessness of the absolute claims upon man. He does not rely upon a system of Order to confirm the values or duties he accepts. Nor does he look to history for a messianic promise to strengthen his commitment to a cause. He is prepared to see a disheartening cyclical pattern in history that will bring total disregard of truth or justice for ages at a time; "there may be a peck of [virtues] in Asia and hardly a thimbleful in Europe" (To Bolingbroke, 5 April 1729, Correspondence, IV, 77). He can face the possibility that the church will undergo corruption and submit to disestablishment; that every political reform will be defeated: "If your scheme should pass into an Act, it will become a job, your sanguine temper will cool, rogues will be the only gainers. Party and faction will intermingle, and defeat the most essential parts of the whole design" (23 March 1733/4, Correspondence, V, 65). So, too, with the hopes of parents:

> religion will tell you, that the true way to preserve them [children] is not to fix any of them too deep in your heart, which is a weakness that God seldom leaves long unpunished: common observations showing us, that such favorite children are either spoiled by their parents' indulgence, or soon taken out of the world, which last is,

generally speaking, the lighter punishment of the two
(7 December 1727, *Correspondence,* III, 436).

Swift is always afraid of the disarming power of wishful-
ness. He warns against the dream that life can have any clear
and predictable meaning. "The common saying of life being
a farce is true in every sense but the most important one, for
it is a ridiculous tragedy, which is the worst kind of composition" (*Correspondence,* IV, 217).

Swift's pride in being free of illusion takes the form of
pessimistic overstatement. The effect of this attitude is twofold.
He can turn the more clearheadedly to the firm injunctions of
duty, aware of the fact that whatever order is achieved in one's
life is the result of one's own unremitting (if not always successful) vigilance and effort. Or he can fall into despair and
find in the hardheaded freedom from illusion a release from
all commitment. The second is a kind of self-indulgence that
Swift permits himself in his letters, and a recurring temptation
that he recognizes. But the fact that he gives it extravagant
utterance, and meanwhile continues to fight bitterly to defend
the "post assigned" to him, suggests that ironic safeguards are
being used to contain the mood of despair and make it a playful role. In the same way, Swift's tyranny over his friends
may at times suggest a displaced love of power; but it is controlled and shaped by a self-mocking sense of his own extravagance. The saving grace of lucid realism and unbiased
self-awareness allows Swift to play the "ridiculous tragedy"
with a feeling for farce as an ordering principle, *faute de
mieux.* "God be thanked," he writes Pope in his sixty-seventh
year, "I have done with everything, and of every kind, except
now and then a letter; or, like a true old man, scribbling trifles
only fit for children or schoolboys of the lowest class at best,
which three or four of us read and laugh at today, and burn
tomorrow" (1 November 1734, *Correspondence,* V, 100).

Because he is so little interested in the saving vision of Order and so firmly committed to the sense of obligation, Swift
in his role of moralist seeks out the most simple and unequivocal reminders of our duty. He constantly shows us that "either
our heads or our hearts are not as they should be" (HD,
II, 1). Men must see clearly what only a moral failure can
make them ignore. "There are solecisms in morals as well as
in words," he writes angrily to Steele, and the readiness to see
solecisms or errors at the heart of evil is Swift's way of directing moral questions to the central issue of cognition. A

man may best serve his country, in a time of party and faction, "by unbiassing his mind as much as possible"—this effort has as its chief recommendation that it is free of interest, of the "common design of making a fortune by the merit of an opinion." Moral cognition is earned by man's free use of his reason, and this freedom is achieved by discipline and painful efforts (as it is for Shaftesbury and Pope). The bulk of Swift's satire deals with the way in which the reason is cheated, subverted, betrayed, as readily by rationalism as by brutality. To construct a system is to absolve the mind of judgment and responsibility. Politics attempts this extrication from choice by making interest and duty agree. But rational systems are a spurious contrivance: they are built upon "solecisms," so that the claims of duty can be unobtrusively altered to accord with interest. They solve problems by cheating us of our moral existence. Politics circumvents the weakness of most men— particularly men in groups, where the worst prevails—but systems only promote that weakness by blinding the mind to the choices it cannot resign.

A small instance of this kind of system-building comes in *The Bickerstaff Papers*. After parodying Partridge's false claims to authority as an astrologer, Bickerstaff, with a wonderful insouciance, deduces the fact that Partridge can no longer be alive. Partridge's angry protestations are ineffectual; his mere existence cannot undo the elegance of Bickerstaff's demonstration. A more serious instance is the complacent assumption by the Moderns that they are superior to the Ancients. In *The Battle of the Books,* the Spider, who symbolizes the Moderns, builds a huge Gothic fortress spun out of his own entrails, its flimsiness concealed by its intricacy; he is startled and enraged to find the Bee bursting through it and destroying the comforting self-enclosure. Finally (in *A Modest Proposal*) one can see the power of system-building in the bland assumption that Ireland can be made subservient to England at the expense of all independent trade. If "people are the riches of a nation," as is true in a mercantilist economy of trade and export, where greater labor can produce greater wealth, then Ireland, which is allowed no freedom of export, must adopt the maxim literally and sell its babies as table delicacies for the refined appetites of the luxury trade.

Swift's ironic methods are means for restoring our awareness of choices. To make cognition the focus of his moral concerns is not, as I have tried to suggest, rationalism. Swift, like most Augustans, hates deductive system-builders. More than that, he does not for a moment suppose that men are wicked because they are ignorant or virtuous because they are rightly informed. When he mocks Bishop Burnet's warning that some pastors do not "know the depths of Satan," Swift notes that "a man may be *in the depths of Satan* without knowing them all, and such a man may be so far in Satan's depths to be out of his own. One of the depths of Satan, is to *counterfeit an angel of light*" (HD, IV, 78–79). So again he attacks Matthew Tindal's *The Rights of the Christian Church* as an "atheistical scribble, which would . . . serve as a twig for sinking literature to catch at":

> It must be allowed in their behalf that the faith of Christians is not as a grain of mustard seed in comparison of theirs, which can remove such mountains of absurdities, and submit with so entire a resignation to such apostles. If these men had any share of that reason they pretend to, they would retire into Christianity merely to give it ease. And therefore men can never be confirmed in such doctrine until they are confirmed in their vices (HD, II, 73).

The focus upon cognition is simply a way of catching moral corruption in that aspect where it demands the most tortured and ludicrous denial of reason. To catch the rationalization in its inconsistency is, after all, the method of Milton in Satan's great address to the Sun at the opening of Book IV of *Paradise Lost*. "I desire no stronger proof that an opinion must be false," writes Swift's Church-of-England Man, "than to find very great absurdities annexed to it" (HD, II, 22). Such a moral position does not demand remarkable sagacity and heroic wisdom of men: it insists, rather, as Pascal does, that the weakness of evil is best seen in its frantic flight from the inescapably true. This is not the agonized disappointment of a rationalist; it is the calculated point of view of a moral satirist.

II. The Energy of Imagination

Because Swift's emphasis is so sharply concentrated on cognition, his typical subjects are error, self-deception, and insanity. Characteristically, he sees intellectual and moral confusion as chosen: men fail to see clearly because their interests and passions make them prefer something more comfortable than truth. Swift's typical mode, therefore, is the ironic dramatization of the mind that chooses not to see. Such a mind may, and in fact usually does, have great energy. It is prompted by strong passions which capture the imagination, freeing it from the control of the reason and its adherence to truth. (The relationship of imagination to truth may be oblique, but its existence remains, for the Augustans, a test of all serious art.) Once the imagination is given rein, its fertility is enormous and its energy untiring.

Typically, in *A Modest Proposal* (1729), the fictitious author is a zealous "projector" (the type of enthusiast who, in W. H. Auden's phrase, commits a social science), anxious to impress the world with his sagacity, to outdo all previous schemers, and to win the undying gratitude of his native country. He concentrates intensely on finding a solution for Ireland's poverty which will accord with England's restrictions on trade, and the very fury of his ambition and concentration generates his scheme. The proposal itself has a strange combination of insane possession on the part of the speaker—one of those quiet men with a terrible glint in their eyes—and of savage representation of men preying upon each other in the respectable guise of mercantile policy. It is hard to think of this mad projector as himself responsible for what he espouses; but behind his words lie the whole fabricated world of economic abstractions, the whole moral chaos of people considering each other for their use rather than as ends (once the Irish sell their babies, husbands may be gentler to their wives, at least while they are pregnant). The English are convicted of imposing the inhuman conditions, the Irish of the brutalization of those who submit, the projector of the madness which is only the extreme and unguarded instance of moral blindness. What Swift has revealed is a hideous mock order whose plausibility and dedicated inventiveness conceal its moral failure, at least for a while.

In the greatest of the ironic tracts, the *Argument against Abolishing Christianity* (1708) we can see Swift's preparation for what Mandeville was to do a few years later. The fictitious author of this tract is, like the artful managers of *The Fable of the Bees,* a man cool in his detachment and able to see what those enmeshed in ideology are too preoccupied to notice. He writes, he tells us, at a time when the English are about to abolish Christianity because it opposes their "present schemes of wealth and power." Such a program assumes that men either believe or do not, but this is too simple a view. One must distinguish, the author points out, between real and nominal Christianity; the latter preserves all the outward forms and familiar names, without for a moment assuming that they have meaning. The society of England is too far committed to wealth and power to restore real Christianity; to do so

> would be to dig up foundations; to destroy at one blow *all* the wit and *half* the learning of the kingdom; to break the entire frame and constitution of things; to ruin trade, extinguish arts and sciences with the professors of them; in short, to turn our courts, exchanges, and shops into deserts . . . (HD, II, 27).

This is the threat of rigoristic Christianity that Mandeville broaches. It becomes Swift's way of opposing the right and the good; if we settle for the good, we must not for a moment confuse it with the right. And this is precisely the confusion that Swift's mock author exposes in his defense of nominal Christianity. He himself has no respect for the names, only for their possible usefulness; he is a social engineer of the Mandevillian type. And he can demonstrate beautifully that all the institutions and observances of Christianity—so long as they are freed of any meaning and, particularly, of their obligatory nature—can serve the worldly interests of a secular society. The Gospel system gives the wits harmless sport. The priesthood provides a modicum of literacy and (because it cannot afford luxury) a body of healthy "restorers of our breed." The churches provide useful meeting places for amorous or mercantile enterprise.

All through the tract there is wonderful play upon terms that have ceased to have meaning but still voice demands for power. Abolishing Christianity "would very much enlarge and establish liberty of conscience." The Church may be in great danger when the Christian religion is repealed; in fact, abolishing Christianity "may be intended as one politic step towards altering the constitution of the Church established, and setting up Presbytery in its stead." This marvelous concentration on the fate of institutions to the total disregard of their function or meaning is Swift's scornful view of a self-subsistent state as an end in itself, that is, of conservative secularism like Mandeville's. But even more, we see the conversion of those doctrines that should command and oblige us turned into instruments of conquest and domination.

In another tract, on the threatened repeal of the Sacramental Test (the English ministry sought to have the test removed first in Ireland, presumably with the hope that English public office in turn would be opened to Dissenters), Swift traces the march to power of the Dissenters, complaining at each new step of "persecution," until the complaint against injustice becomes a stratagem for gaining the power that (as Swift saw it) could disestablish the Church of England. In *A Tale of a Tub,* doctrine again becomes an instrument of self-aggrandizement; in *Gulliver's Travels* the Lilliputians fight bloody battles over the nominal issue of which end of an egg is proper to break. This is, in the words of the *Argument,* that "spirit of opposition that lived long before Christianity, and can easily subsist without it." What becomes terrifying is the way it turns Christianity to its own uses and makes of religion the pretext for conflict. The first of Swift's *Thoughts on Various Subjects* (1706) reads: "We have just religion enough to make us hate, but not enough to make us love one another."

The *Argument,* like the *Modest Proposal,* is meant to shock men into recognition: not simply recognition of values they have deserted or duties they have neglected, but of the way in which the mind constructs a coherent system as a refuge from moral cognition and an asylum from its obligations. To do this, the mind must first denature words—rob them of their meanings, make them attractive labels hiding unsavory mixtures, employ their force without their restrictions. Second, it must construct a new world in which these old sanctions gain a new source and a new import. In fact, of course, what Swift is describing is moral confusion and muddle, the embarrassing lapse that must be overlooked or covered by a saving name. But Swift insists upon treating the muddle as if it were a rational program; he expects a systematic structure and, of course, confers one. This brings to the surface what men have been keeping securely hidden, from themselves as well as others. By demanding that disorder take the form of an order, Swift makes inescapably clear the conflict of orders and the easy substitution of the lower for the higher. His irony is like Socrates' in requiring that we face what is more comfortably left unexamined, and the shock of ugly confrontation is doubled by the tone of disarming plausibility.

The ironic confrontation can be seen very clearly in the early *Discourse concerning the Mechanical Operation of the Spirit* (1704) which accompanied *A Tale of a Tub* and *The Battle of the Books.* The *Mechanical Operation* offers an analysis of religious enthusiasm, which it defines—with the ambiguity and sexual innuendo that are essential to the work—as "a lifting up of the soul or its faculties above matter." There have traditionally been, we are told, "three general ways of ejaculating the soul": inspiration (from above), possession (from below), and the natural process of strong conjunction or passion. Now a fourth method is set forth: "purely an effect of artifice and mechanic operation"—in short, self-induced trance or rapture. The working principle of this art is that "the corruption of the senses is the generation of the spirit," and so the technician of enthusiasm makes all efforts to "divert, bind up, stupify, fluster, and amuse the senses, or else justle them out of their stations." Religious enthusiasm has traditionally sought to overleap the senses in its flight to a supramundane realm. To the extent that the mystic has a discipline, he achieves an art of transcendence; and Swift provides a gross material counterpart—not only is it a mechanical operation (with the hint that it is a profitable trade), it demands a new meaning for "spirit." The "spirit we treat of here" does not descend from above but proceeds "entirely from within." It is aroused and contained by shutting up all communication with the objective external world; the senses are closed off, reason is denied any occasion for judgment, and the imagination is encouraged to create a new world in which glandular secretions will be spent in fantasies of power.

Norman O. Brown finds this process an anticipation of the doctrine that repression is the cause of sublimation.[2] Two comments are necessary. First, the process Swift is describing is conscious and deliberately imposed, as "repression" is not. Second, Swift sees the possibility of divine inspiration as a real one; this process of apparent "sublimation" does not produce truly higher forms but gross parodies of them.

What Swift shows us is the corruption of religious forms, as they are used to accommodate displaced erotic passion. Swift, unlike Freud, is primarily concerned with the decorum of the "higher" forms. He does, indeed, recognize the natural energies that go into them, but he is drawing a distinction between the lower and the higher, not marveling at their equivalence (as Mandeville does). Nor is Swift, like Freud, concerned about the cost that is paid for sublimation; he is an uncompromising if more naïve champion of civilization. Thus, when he sees his modern enthusiasts "abstract themselves from matter, bind up all their senses, grow visionary and spiritual," to the sound of a "continued gentle hum," he also sees that "the reasoning faculties are all suspended and superseded, that imagination hath usurped the seat, scattering a thousand deliriums over the brain." Swift does not, in short, relinquish the traditional terms that enforce distinctions of value.

Swift's emphasis is always fixed on the meeting of moral obligations. The powers that go into this process may be varied, but the ultimate concern of the moralist is that right use be made of them. Swift goes on, in the last part of the tract, to show the element of eroticism in the practices of religious fanatics (a fact that a respectable Englishwoman like Frances Trollope was to observe in American revival meetings a century or so later). The "thorn in the flesh serves for a spur to the spirit" in the "height and orgasmus" of their spiritual exercise. The point Swift is making is that, because this "sublimation" is so precarious, because it is a means of disguising rather than transforming, all of its higher expressions are short-lived, and the descent is as rapid as the ascent. "Too intense a contemplation is not the business of flesh and blood; it must by the necessary course of things, in a little time, let go its hold, and fall into matter."

We have seen Pope, in *Windsor Forest,* treating the hunt as the sublimation of those aggressions that might otherwise produce war. But the hunt is a self-contained game. Here Swift is presenting the infiltration of religious devotion by the precarious sublimations of sexual aggression. The devotions, however, are an obligation imposed from above, with their own decorum and their own high end, and sexual aggression has its appropriate expression in ordered forms. Just as the Freudian moralist may seek to cleanse us of false aspiration by showing that high is really low, so Swift as Christian moralist demands that we make the sanative distinction between high and low and free our sense of obligation from the confusions of the enthusiasts.

At one point Swift turns from the radical Protestants he is mocking to the larger confusions of all modern Christians. The simple dualism of wild Indians is crude—they adore two principles, the principle of good and that of evil—but it has a wholesome clarity that the more sophisticated Christians lose. The clarity is lost in the fervor of celebration; we spend so much effort on surrounding our principle of Right with sumptuous images of the Good that we end without principle:

> What I applaud them [the wild Indians] for is their discretion, in limiting their devotions and their deities to their several districts, nor ever suffering the liturgy of the *white* God to cross or interfere with that of the *black*. Not so with us, who pretending by the lines and measures

of our reason to extend the dominion of one invisible power, and contract that of the other, have discovered a gross ignorance in the natures of good and evil, and most horribly confounded the frontiers of both. After men have lifted up the throne of their divinity to the *Caelum Empyraeum*, adorned [him] with all such qualities and accomplishments as themselves seem most to value and possess; after they have sunk their *Principle of Evil* to the lowest center, furnished him with viler dispositions than any rake-hell of the town, accoutered him with tail and horns and huge claws and saucer eyes; I laugh aloud to see these reasoners, at the same time, engaged in wise dispute about certain walks and purlieus, whether they are in the verge of God or the Devil, seriously debating whether certain passions and affections are guided by the Evil Spirit or the Good.

And he cites Horace (Odes I, xviii, 10–11): "While greedy to satisfy their lusts they make little distinction (*exiguo fine . . . Discernunt*) between right and wrong (*fas atque nefas*)."

Nowhere do we get so clear a statement of Swift's distrust of the celebrative and the sublime. To see *his* kind of "celebration" we may turn to the last of his birthday poems for Stella, written in 1727. She is sick, and he is old; and Swift looks for "a Thought, / Which can in spite of all Decays, / Support a few remaining Days." He rules out the promise of immortality, and concentrates instead upon the "lasting Pleasure in the Mind" left by the performance of virtue. This

> by Remembrance will assuage,
> Grief, Sickness, Poverty, and Age;
> And strongly shoot a radiant Dart,
> To shine through Life's declining Part (31–34).
> Does not the Body thrive and grow
> By Food of twenty years ago? . . .
> And, is not Virtue in Mankind
> The Nutriment that feeds the Mind? (55–56, 61–62.)

Here, the consciousness of virtue is not made a pleasure more delicious than sensuous delight, as it tends to become in the sentimentalist's view; it is solid food, support and sustenance. The accomplished duties of the past "join to fortify your heart" (72); they are a source of courage for a future of unremitting duty and commitment.

I have stressed the element of obligation in Swift so strongly because it seems to me crucial to an understanding of his ideas of order. The opposition of duty and pleasure is traditional enough, but in Swift the idea of duty is an irreducible pres-

ence—not to be translated; hardly to be celebrated in its divine
source; never to be made to seem easy to perform, or even to
recognize. The difficulties in performance come of the drag of
sloth and the conflict of passion; they may be pitied or condemned. But the difficulties in recognition, while their source
may be the same, are a failure of an awareness that is simple
and distinctly human. They are ludicrous as well, the incrusta-
tion of the mechanical upon the living, in Bergson's phrase—
the reduction of supple intelligence to uncontrolled appetite
or compulsive mechanism. When the forces of compulsion
build a fantastic world with the wishful imagination, the failure
of intelligence is all the more ridiculous, and terrifying as well.
But that is the subject of my next chapter.

III. *Gulliver's Travels*

In *Gulliver's Travels* Swift carries the conflict of orders to
its sharpest expression. Lemuel Gulliver is the most famous
of Swift's masks or personae, and, as always, it is important to
see these masks in their fictional integrity first of all. Swift
may not be consistent in maintaining them; they become at
moments transparencies through which his irony shines in full
intensity, but much of the nonsense that has been written about
Swift's works derives from a failure to observe the character
of their spokesmen. Gulliver is obtuse in a plausible and often
attractive way. He is a matter-of-fact man, capable of minute
accuracy of detail in what he reports but equally capable of
total indifference to the "value tone" of experience. His dead-
pan style is consistent understatement through much of the
book. It is not knowing understatement such as we find in
Hemingway, conscious of all it refuses to mention. It is, rather,
unconscious irony—a style that is calculated (by Swift and not
by Gulliver) to reveal sharply just those values it fails to observe or mention; a style that gives itself away. Swift's spokesmen are always chosen for this useful service: they cheerfully
systematize, they avow what is commonly suppressed, they
scandalize where wiser or more cautious men would draw back
and reconsider.

Gulliver is invented as the hero of a comedy of incomprehension. This is only one dimension of *Gulliver's Travels*, but
it is an essential one. Why comedy rather than satire? Because,
in this one dimension, Gulliver embodies the incorrigible tendency of the mind to oversimplify experience, a trait that

takes, with equal ease, the form of complacency or of misanthropy. Given his tendency to see man as either a rational animal or an irrational beast, given his expectation that man will be essentially good or essentially evil, Gulliver can never comprehend the problematic nature of man as he really is. As Swift sees him, man is both blessed and cursed with the condition of *animal rationis capax*. Because he is capable of reason man can at least glimpse moral truth, because he is less than perfect in it he can lose the vision or pervert its meaning. The book raises the question of how much that we call civilization is an imperfect disguise of our lowest appetites (rather than a true sublimation or transformation of them), and also how far this civilization is necessary to the man who lives a purely moral life, adhering rigorously to the precepts of nature and reason alone (revelation apart). This is the same problem raised at least in passing by the *Argument against Abolishing Christianity*.

Finally, the book considers fundamental questions about the nature of politics, like the ideal reconciliation of duty and interest among the Houyhnhnms and the less perfect, but more humanly feasible, reconciliation in Brobdingnag. To these political orders are opposed such societies as that of the Lilliputians, which is elaborately administered disorder, the tyrannies of Laputa and Maldonada, and the savage democracy of the Yahoos. *Gulliver's Travels* is a tribute to the mixed state in which order is reconciled with freedom and yet made stable. To achieve such an order, one must come to terms with the nature of power, and the most essential feature of power is its tendency to become absolute.

Let us consider the political order. In Lilliput, Gulliver becomes the absolute weapon of an Emperor whose only wish is to conquer the world (that his world consists of two small islands makes the desire depressingly petty in its object but hardly petty in its intensity). The "spirit of opposition" governs the world of Lilliput; there is "a violent faction at home, and the danger [largely imaginary, a self-induced terror which unites the state, as in Orwell's *1984*] of an invasion by a most potent enemy from abroad" (I, iv). The occasions for dispute (like those for conquest) are so trivial as to be meaningless; the power drive creates its own pretexts. Within the state, the factions are rivals for influence and favor. Ministers are chosen by their agility—skill in walking a tightrope or jumping over sticks—and their subservience. The language of the court is a constant exercise in obfuscation. When the King's clemency is declared, his subjects run for cover. When Gulliver hastily puts out the fire in the Empress' palace by the quickest means available, the court accusation is a wonderful farrago of insinuation, self-importance, and intolerable legal jargon:

> Whereas . . . it is enacted that whoever shall make water within the precincts of the royal palace shall be liable to the pains and penalties of high treason: notwithstanding, the said Quinbus Flestrin [i.e., Gulliver], in open breach of the said law, under color of extinguishing the fire kindled in the apartment of his Majesty's most dear imperial consort, did maliciously, traitorously, and devilishly, by discharge of his urine, put out the said fire kindled in the said apartment, lying and being within the precincts of the said royal palace, against the statute in that case provided, etc., against the duty, etc. (I, vii).

Or again Gulliver is accused of preparing to make a voyage to Blefuscu, "for which he hath received only verbal licence from his Imperial Majesty."

What is even more telling than the crazy mock logic of Lilliputian politics is Gulliver's readiness to adapt to it. A bluff, well-meaning Englishman, twelve times their size and able to destroy them with ease, he becomes dazzled by the honors paid him and the high status he has won at court. Gulliver is restrained in part by oaths, in part by a sense of gratitude, but in part, too, by a naïve readiness to assume that power confers right. This becomes clear when, at the court of Brobdingnag, he reveals his belated schooling in Machiavellian statecraft and offers the horrified King the gift of gunpowder. Gulliver's disappointment at the rejection of this proposal is strong:

> A strange effect of narrow principles and short views! That a prince . . . should from a nice, unnecessary scruple, whereof in Europe we can have no conception, let slip an opportunity put into his hands, that would have made him absolute master of the lives, the liberties, and the fortunes of his people (II, vii).

In contrast to Lilliput, the Brobdingnagians have laws of no more than twenty-two words, and "to write a comment upon any law is a capital crime." Instead of a professional army they have a citizen militia, where "every farmer is under the command of his own landlord, and every citizen under that of the principal men in his own city, chosen after the manner of Venice by ballot" (II, vii). The militia fixes power in the whole body of the people rather than permitting the army to become an uncontrollable bloc such as we know in Latin-American politics today, and controls the disease that has attacked Brobdingnag, as it has every other nation: "the nobility often contending for power, the people for liberty, and the King for absolute dominion."

In the land of the Houyhnhnms we find an anarchy of reasonable creatures, such as William Godwin admired. The rational horses need no government; they immediately intuit their duties and perform them. Only in a rare instance, where a novel situation is created—as by Gulliver's presence—must they deliberate. They control any dissidence by rational persuasion and "exhortation," for they need no compulsion. George Orwell is interesting but, I think, mistaken when he sees in this exhortation the "totalitarian tendency which is explicit in the anarchist or pacifist vision of Society. In a Society in which there is no law, and in theory no compulsion, the only arbiter of behavior is public opinion,"—which, Orwell shrewdly remarks, "is less tolerant than any system of law."[3] This might be true if the Houyhnhnms cultivated a "general will," or if they carried on the kind of virtuous terrorism that in schools often goes by the name of "honor system." But there is no need to exert "continuous pressure" for conformity among the Houyhnhnms. They cannot but agree in all but an occasional matter, and even in the case Swift presents the Houyhnhnm master hesitates to assent only because of Gulliver's furious resistance to being sent away. Other critics have made similar objections about the religion of the Houyhnhnms. But one cannot call them conformists, as Orwell does, or Deists, as others do. Their reason inevitably produces agreement, and their piety is exemplary within the limits of their purely natural reason. We cannot blame them for finding fulfillment in what, for us, would be defects of liberty or failures of Christian faith.

Why should Swift have created these problems for us? Clearly he is demanding of his readers what he never grants to Gulliver, the power to make necessary distinctions. We must separate the intuitive rightness of the Houyhnhnms' choice from the tyranny of conformity, and we must separate natural piety from rationalistic or anti-clerical deism. Gulliver fails to make the most important distinction of all—between *animal rationale* and *animal rationis capax*. Only after long exposure to human folly and perversity does he give up the dream of man as a rational animal, but instead of coming to terms with what in fact he is, Gulliver immediately turns to truly rational animals, the Houyhnhnms, and hopes to become one of them. His pathetic whinny and canter betray the fantasy of a literal-minded convert.

The same kind of problem occurs in the realm of politics. Gulliver's account of English institutions to the King of Brobdingnag betrays the corruptibility they invite: English laws are extremely complex, and they "are best explained, interpreted, and applied by those whose interest and abilities lie in perverting, confounding, and eluding them" (II, vi). There is no reconciliation of duty and interest, but instead a systematic perversion of duty by interest. In his account of Europe to his Houyhnhnm master, Gulliver makes explicit all that he has earlier unconsciously revealed. Lawyers are now "equally disposed to pervert the general reason of mankind in every other subject of discourse, as in that of their own profession" (IV, v). This single instance is typical of all the rest. Gulliver has come to recognize the nature of corruption, but his recognition is so belated and so passionate that he despairs of all politics. When he writes an account of his travels, he expects the world to reform at once. But, in this case at least, we have a third possibility firmly sketched in: the reformed mixed state of the Brobdingnagians, which mediates between duty and interest, conformity and freedom, and accepts the need for a power structure but diffuses its control.

Parallel to the political issues in the book is the relationship of body and reason. In Lilliput, Gulliver's body is grosser than he can imagine (although he senses it), and the Lilliputians seem more delicate than in fact they are. In Brobdingnag the human body becomes monstrous, as Gulliver confronts with microscopic acuteness its ugliness and its noisome smells. In both the Struldbruggs and the Yahoos we see bodies that are completely without control or cleanliness; in fact, the Yahoos revel in filth and use excrement as a weapon. The body becomes a physical symbol of the power drives that are seen in the body politic; in Brobdingnag there is ugliness (simply more visible to Gulliver because of his diminutive size, as his own normal human ugliness was apparent to the Lilliputians) as there is cruelty and at least some measure of corruption (the farmer's turning Gulliver into a profitable show, the court dwarf's malice), but there is also a saving control of both corruption and physical nastiness. In the Struldbruggs old age has produced physical deterioration, avarice, contentiousness, and irrationality; in the Yahoos (who seem to have degenerated from an original couple, like the human race) there is sheer abandoned animality. The Yahoos are particularly nasty animals, it should be noted, not because Swift "in his fury . . . is shouting at his fellow-creatures: 'You are filthier than you are!'" (Orwell's view) but because they are a degenerate species, which neither possesses the instinctive controls of other animals (such as seasonal mating) nor preserves the faculties by which the human animal controls itself—its rational powers. Recent experiments have shown us animals that lose the power to identify with their proper kind and cannot acquire the traits of the kind they are raised among. Something of the sort has happened to the Yahoos; and their nastiness is only a further tribute to the importance of man's rational powers of self-control.

A third pattern, related to both politics and the control of the physical body, is that of simplicity and complexity. The Brobdingnagian laws are transparently simple; the Houyhnhnms need no laws at all. So it is with their cultures. The King, whose largeness of vision has the generosity of a Renaissance humanist, reminds us that Brobdingnag is a place of cultivation. But his people do not create books in great quantity; their largest library has a thousand volumes. In their writing "they avoid nothing more than multiplying unnecessary words, or using various expressions." They are skilled in practical arts, but utterly resistant to "ideas, entities, transcendentals, and abstractions." We see the reverse of this throughout the third voyage—the elaborate astronomy of Laputa is coupled with infantile superstition, the futile ingenuity of the experiments of Lagado is set against the simple adherence to traditional forms of Lord Munodi, the wisdom of Homer or Aristotle is swallowed up by the host of commentators that has battened on each. In place of the typical conqueror-heroes of history, Gulliver learns to admire the destroyers of tyrants and the defenders of liberty, the men who retrench corruption and win persecution in the process.

In the fourth voyage, the complexity of European civilization is traced in the Yahoos' savage behavior: they have a Prime Minister, they have court flirtations, they are acquisitive hoarders of shining stones, they become drunk and diseased, they even have a fashionable psychosomatic malady like the spleen. All the evils of civilization, and many of its professed glories, are caught in their elaborate behavior. In contrast, the Houyhnhnms perform "the necessary actions" of "a reasonable being" (IV, viii). They believe that "*reason* alone is sufficient to govern a *rational* creature"; they cannot even comprehend the nature of lies, let alone worse vices. "Neither is *reason* among them a point problematical as with us, where man can argue with plausibility on both sides of a question; but strikes you with immediate conviction, as it must needs do where it is not mingled, obscured, or discolored by passion and interest" (IV, viii). The consequences of perfect rational intuition are acute. They have no parental partiality nor do they mate except to bear children, and their choice of a marriage partner is based on cool eugenic principles. They accept death as natural ripeness and a return to the first mother. What are we to make of this passionless simplicity, where all is governed by the impartial virtues of friendship and benevolence?

In recent years critics have tended increasingly to find in the Houyhnhnms a satire upon the neo-Stoic humanism of Shaftesbury or the Deists. It is true that Swift mocks those who would base their lives on the belief that virtue is its own reward, but he does not mock the moral intuition that the Houyhnhnms live by. Of course, the Houyhnhnms are not human, and Swift never could have intended that we treat them as models. They are like that return to the System of the Gospels with which the *Argument against Abolishing Christianity* teases us. It would be disastrous to "our present schemes of wealth and power." But could we, in fact, return to primitive Christianity? In *A Tale of a Tub,* when the two brothers reject the corruptions introduced by the third, Jack performs a thorough reformation on his coat and tears it to shreds. Martin, on the other hand, preserves those additions that cannot be removed without destroying the fabric. So here, Swift mocks us with all we are not, with the simplicity and direct acceptance of obligation that is given all the more weight in the teaching of the Gospels (unknown to the merely "natural" Houyhnhnms), and with the close resemblance of our vaunted civilization to the bestiality of the Yahoos. But it is Gulliver, in his despair, who draws from this recognition the resolution to become a Houyhnhnm, and it is this that makes him shrink as if from a Yahoo when he encounters the generous and humane Portuguese sea captain who brings him back to Europe. At the last, even with his family, he is alienated, morose, contemptuous, although he has slowly begun to adapt himself once more to the human condition.

Swift is neither offering the Houyhnhnms as a model nor holding them up for satire. They have, it is true, some telltale complacency in the conclusions they draw without sufficient fact. But when Swift defends the ancient poets against ridicule, he points out that their moral teachings were altogether admirable within the limits of their awareness.

The Houyhnhnms would make a ludicrous model for man, but it is Gulliver who makes them that. They remain an embodiment—in alien animal form—of the life of unclouded moral intuition; a simple life because there are no passions to produce conflict or to generate "opinion." In most telling contrast to them is the Academy of Lagado, with its technical extravagance, its furious dedication to doing the unnecessary with the most dazzling ingenuity, its constant rediscovery of brute fact through ludicrous failure. The scientist who places the bellows to the posterior of a dog and inflates the beast until it explodes in a torrent of excrement serves as a link between the learning of Lagado and the filth of the Yahoos.

The Houyhnhnms represent the order of mind at its purest, free of rationalistic system-building or of pride in intellectual constructions. Conceived in this way, it contains much that is given to humans only in the order of charity—a moral sureness and serenity, a spontaneous goodness such as is bred in men by a "daily vision of God." But to achieve the equivalent in the world of men requires the arduous self-scrutiny, the courageous defiance of the world, the saving humility that Pope seeks to dramatize in the *Imitations of Horace*.

VII.

The Tragedy of Mind

I. Sound and Meaning

> Lightness changes to heaviness, transparence to thickness; the world weighs heavily; the universe crushes me. A curtain, an insuperable wall, comes between me and the world, between me and myself. Matter fills everything, takes up all space, annihilates all liberty under its weight. . . . Speech crumbles. . . .
>
> —Eugène Ionesco

The Augustans were deeply concerned with the breakdown of language. They saw it as a symptom of a decline of culture, and the greatest satires of the age have this as their central theme. The highest uses of language are the most inclusive: poetry draws upon all the possibilities of words, but it governs and directs their energy toward the framing of meaning. With the eclipse of the higher functions we move from the complex discriminations of meaning to language as a mere syntactic game, an exercise in words, as we say misleadingly, "for their own sake." Once the formal exercise becomes an end in itself, words have lost a crucial dimension; and meaning, if it survives at all, becomes a mere pretext. So it is with the students put to versifying in *The Dunciad:*

> Confine the thought, to exercise the breath;
> And keep them in the pale of words till death.
> Whate'er the talents, or howe'er designed,
> We hang one jingling padlock on the mind;
> A Poet the first day he dips his quill;
> And what the last? A very Poet still (IV, 159–64).

To eliminate the dimension of meaning is to eliminate the control of mind, and words are set on the downward path toward sheer noise. Without the power that brings the various functions of words under the command of meaning, there is no longer any way of discriminating between relevance and irrelevance, or of preventing rhetorical exercise from turning into the crassest kind of demagoguery. To corrupt language is, in effect, to surrender its control to the order of the flesh or to physical causation.

We can see these lower stages brilliantly set forth in the ironic works of the period. The irony turns on the crucial distinction between poetry (or rhetoric) as a making and poetry as the secretion or evacuation of pent-up feeling; between poetry as articulation of meaning and poetry as expressive noise; between poetry as "issue" (the creation of new living creatures) and poetry as "excrement." In *The Mechanical Operation of the Spirit* Swift treats the modern style of enthusiastic pulpit eloquence as the Art of Canting. This consists not in the communication of meaning but in the immediate force of words as pure sound:

> Thus it is frequent for a single vowel to draw sighs from a multitude; and for a whole assembly of saints to sob to the music of one solitary liquid. But these are trifles; when even sounds inarticulate are observed to produce as forcible effects. A master workman shall blow his nose so powerfully, as to pierce the hearts of his people, who are disposed to receive the excrements of his brain with the same reverence, as the issue of it. Hawking, spitting, and belching, the defects of other men's rhetoric, are the flowers, and figures, and ornaments of his. For, the spirit being the same in all, it is of no import through what vehicle it is conveyed.

Pope makes a comparable distinction in his ironic treatise on *The Art of Sinking in Poetry*. (It should be noted that both writers insist upon this collapse of control as a deliberate contrivance, an "art" of dehumanization.)

> It may be affirmed with great truth, that there is hardly any human creature past childhood, but at one time or other has had some poetical evacuation, and, no question, was much the better for it in his health; so true is the saying, *Nascimur poetae.* Therefore is the desire of writing properly termed *pruritus,* the "titillation of the generative faculty of the brain," and the person is said to conceive; now such as conceive must bring forth. I have known a man thoughtful, melancholy and raving for divers days, who forthwith grew wonderfully easy, lightsome, and cheerful, upon a discharge of the peccant humour, in exceeding purulent metre. Nor can I question, but abundance of untimely deaths are occasioned for want of this laudable vent of unruly passions. . . .

The decay of language, as I have said, is only one symptom of a cultural entropy.[1] We find a similar emphasis in our own age:

> Good writers are those who keep the language efficient. That is to say, keep it accurate, keep it clear. . . .
>
> Language is the main means of human communication. If an animal's nervous system does not transmit sensations and stimuli, the animal atrophies.
>
> If a nation's literature declines, the nation atrophies and decays. . . .
>
> It is very difficult to make people understand the *impersonal* indignation that a decay of writing can cause men who understand what it implies, and the end whereto it leads. . . .
>
> Nevertheless the "statesmen cannot govern, the scientist cannot participate in his discoveries, men cannot agree on wise action without language," and all their deeds and conditions are affected by the defects or virtues of idiom (Ezra Pound, *ABC of Reading,* Norfolk, Connecticut, pp. 32, 34).

> [The English language] becomes ugly and inaccurate because our thoughts are foolish, but the slovenliness of our language makes it easier for us to have foolish thoughts (George Orwell, "Politics and the English Language").

> We may say, then, that just as the first duty of a man *qua* citizen is to his country, so his first duty *qua* poet is to the language of his country. First, he has the duty to *preserve* that language: his use of it must not weaken, coarsen, or degrade it. Second, he has the duty to *develop* that language, to bring it up to date, to investigate its unexplored possibilities. So far as he expresses, in his poetry, what other people feel, he is also affecting that feeling by making it more conscious: in giving people words for their feelings, he is teaching them something about themselves (T. S. Eliot, "The Social Function of Poetry").

More than we, the Augustans saw man most fully realized in the achieved forms of a high culture which, as we have seen, include the "lower" elements, draw upon their energy, use and transform it. The energy of words as expression is absorbed into a disciplined rhetoric; the sound of words can amplify and refine their meanings. What, then, leads to the surrender of the control of mind? This is usually accomplished without awareness, in the course of our being preoccupied with something else. In the formal exercise, the reduction of poetry to versifying becomes the insensible substitution of the ingenious for the significant. In the forms of language released by enthusiasm, it is an attempt to pour forth in spontaneous utterance the spirit within; and the very spontaneity that is prized becomes the circumvention of mind. In the more urgent and debased forms of rhetoric, language becomes a technique for producing emotional "conviction"; the nature of the end that is sought precludes the use of those faculties that would frame rational persuasion. In each of these cases men are lulled into abdication of mind by the prospect of some desirable end. But this abdication only leads to a new captivity, for to surrender discrimination and control is to offer oneself as the victim of words.

In his early tract on *The Contests and Dissensions of Athens and Rome,* Swift shows the way in which each revolution that overthrows one tyranny produces another of a different kind so long as the controlling principle of a balance of power is forgotten. And Pope's treatment of Timon's villa shows how sumptuousness becomes the negation of true magnificence, just as its ostentatious details become the denial of true functional and organic form. So, too, when the critic with "a love to parts" in the *Essay on Criticism* celebrates an isolated beauty or damns a single fault with no standard of its relevance to a total design, his judgment is as defective as the art he denounces. In all three cases an essential ordering principle is ignored or subverted; with its loss there is a process of cultural entropy, a running down of higher forms into lower, a reduction of all fine articulations into the order of the flesh.

II. *A Tale of a Tub* (1704)

In *A Tale of a Tub* Swift makes this symptomatic fate of language clear by presenting a double theme: the misuse of words and the abuse of the Word. In the world of letters dominated by the Moderns, words serve to impress or express, and in the process they are freed of the restrictions of meaning. The Word of God is traced through the history of Christianity, as the churches convert its prescriptions into a license for their pursuit of temporal power. Three brothers, Peter (the Roman Catholic church), Martin (named for Luther but chiefly representative of the Church of England), and Jack (named for Calvin but inclusive of all radical Protestantism) are left coats by their father with the promise that the coats will last as long as the sons live and grow with them so as always to fit them. In the father's will (the New Testament) exact instructions are given for the treatment of the coats, and the brothers are commanded to remain together in one house. But the will must be committed to words, and the words in turn to the interpretation the three sons place upon them. At the very outset Swift has fused his two themes: the pride, self-seeking, and tortured wit of the Moderns is only a special case of the wresting of Scripture that is the history of the Word in the world.

The book is seemingly chaotic but subtly ordered. It abounds in prefatory material, digressions, apparent inconsequentiality, and bravura flights of specious wit; but under the surface there is an intricate linkage of images and themes and a peculiarly telling kind of unity. All the forms of self-assertion, whether literary, religious, political, or intellectual, are reduced, in the long run, to a damning sameness of pattern. In order to see this pattern we must consider the series of apparent contrasts that Swift reduces to identity.

The first of these is the contrast of ingenious artifice and brutish incompetence. We see the artifice in the language of the book, which is largely a parody of baroque intricacy and learned wit. Throughout the introductory material and the digressions this verbal intricacy is proudly brandished by a bumbling would-be Modern. He is of a somewhat earlier age, and he has learned the idiom in which men have described mysterious correspondences and celebrated the unlikely presence of God's design in the meanest of his creation. As a Modern, he has lost the piety that once informed this idiom, or rather, he has transferred it to a devout celebration of the wisdom and profundity of his contemporaries. They, alas, are so completely devoted to being original, and at the same time to winning effortless success, that their works are wretchedly slight. They desperately need a reverent interpreter. Their spokesman looks for hidden truths and veiled mysteries in the hackwork of pamphleteers, balladmongers, and hireling scribblers. The result of all this is a frenetic display of misdirected ingenuity, constantly kept in motion by a complacent trust in the greatness of the present.

Behind the credulous tale-teller lie the splendors of metaphysical sermons, the bathos of radical Puritans' reverence for the words of the Bible, and the acrimonious conflicts of scholarly editors, philosophical system-builders, theologians, and scientific theorists. All of these have in common the forcing of a text or of evidence. Their common achievement has been to make words malleable, easily shaped into the schemes the mind wishes to impose. Words cease to be norms that control men's thinking and readily feed the illusion of a mastery of experience. The conceits that run through *A Tale of a Tub* are almost invariably self-defeating. Wit somehow fastens upon inept analogies and is led where it could scarcely wish to go. But, so pleased is it with the speed of its movement and the distance it has traversed, it scarcely notices where it has landed.

Within the tale itself, the high artifice is the work of Peter, who uses the elaborate contrivances of interpretation to make the will say whatever he wishes. Once the brothers come up to town and fall in love with those noble ladies who represent covetousness, ambition, and pride, they find the will in conflict with the clothes religion that dominates the fashionable world. The worshipers of this sect revere a tailor as their creator, and they believe the universe itself "to be a large suit of clothes, which invests everything: that the earth is invested by the air; the air is invested by the stars; and the stars are invested by the *primum mobile*." The earth is adorned with "a very complete and fashionable dress": "how curious Journeyman Nature hath been, to trim up the vegetable beaux; observe how sparkish a periwig adorns the head of a beech, and what a fine doublet of white satin is worn by the birch." Man himself is not the microcosm of earlier philosophies but "a micro-coat . . . a complete suit of clothes with all its trimmings." For example, conscience is "a pair of breeches; which, though a cover for lewdness as well as nastiness, is easily slipt down for the service of both" (HD, I, 46–47).

The clothes religion is a worship of the outside of things, and dissolves the inside altogether. Everything is dress, and there is nothing left to be dressed. A few dissenters among the clothes philosophers try to meet this difficulty; they believe that man is "an animal compounded of two dresses, the natural and the celestial suit, which were the body and the soul: that the soul was the outward, and the body the inward clothing." Without the outward clothing (which was "of daily creation and circumfusion"), in which "we live and move and have our being" (cf. Acts 27:28), the body is "only a senseless unsavory carcase" (HD, I, 48). This is complicated irony: the last phrase seems orthodox enough, if a little too distrustful of unadorned nature. But the body and soul have reversed roles. The inward has become the outside; the "soul" is now worn as a covering over the body, as pure adornment. It is like the perfume the Brobdingnagian maids of honor wear to conceal their rankness, in a futile effort to accomplish with disguise what only cleanliness, or true restraint, could achieve. To the extent that anything has permanence in the world of the clothes worshipers, it is the body, which is given new disguises each day, in accordance with constantly shifting fashion. Shadow has replaced substance, verbalism has replaced the use of words as norms or law.

Verbalism is what permits Peter to destroy the efficacy of the will. If its statements explicitly reject adding fashionable ornament to the coat, the statements must be broken down into discrete words. If the words will not yield, they in turn can be dissolved into syllables or letters. When verbal manipulation can go no further, Peter has recourse to a second "will," oral tradition: "For brothers, if you remember, we heard a fellow say, when we were boys, that he heard my father's man say, that he heard my father say, that he would advise his sons to get gold lace on their coats. . . ." Thus Peter and his brothers are launched on a career of total absorption in the fashions of this world. When one of the brothers intrudes a rational reservation against Peter's practices, he is "taken up short, as one that spoke irreverently of a mystery, which doubtless was very useful and significant, but ought not to be over-curiously pried into, or nicely reasoned upon" (HD, I, 52, 53–54).

Throughout Section IV of the *Tale,* Swift elaborates the growing clutter of additions that Peter makes to the clear teaching of Scripture, until at last he kicks the brothers out of doors. Peter's arrogance grows with the mad abandon of his impositions on the Will; he demands at last that his brothers deny their senses and accept his assertions. He offers them a crust of bread as "excellent good mutton," and, when they protest (as the Anglicans did against the doctrine of Transubstantiation on the score that mysteries may transcend the reason and the senses but not contradict them), Peter offers "this plain argument: by G—, it is true, good, natural mutton as any in Leadenhall market; and G— confound you both eternally, if you offer to believe otherwise. Such a thundering proof as this left no further room for objection" (HD, I, 73).

Peter's is the way of artifice. Jack assumes the way of brutish incompetence. The commands of the will become "only secondary and subservient" to Jack's "hatred and spite." His motive is to rival Peter by undoing whatever his brother has taught, and he rips his coat to shreds under the pretext of restoring it to its original purity. Jack, like Peter, falls in with a system of belief (of which I shall speak below), Aeolism, that enables man to escape all restraint of his appetites. And like Peter he devises new institutions.

Finally, Jack and Peter become indistinguishable. The ingenuity of Peter's interpretations and the callow wilfulness of Jack's produce the same result; the patterns of psychopathology are complex, but the drives are simple and few. When Martin, who alone of the brothers finds a sound course, restores his coat, he realizes that his reformation must be a "work of time" cautiously performed. Some of the ornament can no longer be removed lest "the substance of the stuff should suffer injury" in the process. And this he accepts as "the right," that is, "the best method for serving the true intent and meaning of his father's will" (HD, I, 85).

A second theme that arises out of the Moderns' desire for novelty is the eventual equation of the fashionable with the time-bound or ephemeral. In a world where all that the Ancients have done must be rejected simply because it already has been done, there is a constant effort to keep outdoing oneself and others. The latest thing is by definition the best thing. The greater the competition, the shorter the life-span of each new work. The difference of a minute can make a reputation. When the tale-teller (himself a little old-fashioned, or he would not be involved in so unlikely an activity) tries to show Prince Posterity examples of the learning of the Moderns, all the evidence has evaporated. The tale-teller is left in a desperate act of faith: "I can only avow in general to your highness, that we do abound in learning and wit; but to fix upon particulars, is a task too slippery for my slender abilities."

The breakdown of all communication is not far off: "what I am going to say is literally true this minute I am writing: what revolutions may happen before it shall be ready for your perusal, I can by no means warrant" (HD, I, 21–22). As all words become bound to a certain occasion and a moment of time, meaning becomes "private." The last writer has a "despotic power over all other authors" before him; his very existence erases the past. To find meaning in him demands a refinement of interpretation that can uncover "a treatise of immense erudition" in any nursery fable. Or, a sympathetic reader can understand his author by placing himself in precisely the same posture; in the case of the *Tale,* we are told, it will require poverty, starvation, and disease to produce "a parity, and strict correspondence of ideas, between the reader and author" (HD, I, 27). There is no longer any need for words: the reader lives himself into the author's views.

A third theme which grows out of the first two is the paradox that the quest for excessive refinement may produce a certain grossness. The attempt to conquer time becomes a surrender to its tyranny. The attempt to reveal exquisite subtlety of meaning generates nonsense. The more credulous his celebration of hidden beauties, the more tasteless the critic may become. Wisdom is "a cheese, which, by how much the richer, has the thicker, the homelier, and the coarser coat: and whereof, to a judicious palate, the maggots are the best" (HD, I, 40). Judgments are mechanical or quantitative and feed complacency. The high aim may become, in the process, simply the honorific name for a low drive. Originality and reformation turn into self-indulgence. The refinements of art mean a release from its discipline.

It is in the doctrines of Aeolism that we see this best. This sect, founded by Jack, is an instance of ultrasupernaturalism, to use Ronald Knox's term for what enthusiasm seeks. The Aeolists find the spirit everywhere, but in their comprehensiveness, they break down all distinctions and worship the common principle of wind. "For whether you please to call the *forma informans* of men by the name of *spiritus, animus, afflatus,* or *anima,* what are all these but several appellations for wind, which is the ruling element in every compound, and into which they all resolve upon their corruption?" (HD, I, 95.) Not only does "the gift of Belching" become "the noblest act of a rational creature," but the erotic excitement of this worship is "such as, with due management, hath been refined from carnal into a spiritual ecstasy." We are back to the mechanical operation of the spirit, the confusion of low and high, of apparent refinement with a mere debasement of words.

Finally, as Phillip Harth has shown, Swift follows the example of earlier "Anglican rationalists" in equating religious enthusiasm and materialism.[2] Enthusiasm is only the most striking instance of a release from self-criticism. In its cultivation of excitement it may readily confuse the unspeakable with the ineffable. What Swift is treating here is the way in which the natural process (or, in the church, the temporal interest) swallows up and makes use of the higher forms by which men had thought to escape it. The higher forms must make their career within the natural process, submitting to its power but resisting its tyranny. Only a flexible awareness of being in the world but not of it, in the body but not simply physical, can escape this dialectic of subversion.

In the "Digression concerning . . . Madness" Swift brings together all aspects of the order of the flesh—the mechanical, the biological, political power, and military conquest. The central motif is the quest for happiness—or in the terms of the preceding chapter, the pursuit of the good at the expense of the right. Consider the case of conquest: a prince raises a great army and fleet with the apparent object of becoming a universal monarch. But "the movement of this whole machine had been directed by an absent female, whose eyes had raised a protuberancy, and, before emission, she was removed into an enemy's country. What should an unhappy prince do in such ticklish circumstances as these?" The unspent semen is converted to choler, ascends to the brain and induces dreams of "sieges, battles, and victories." This is not, clearly, "sublimation," but a conversion of the lesser desire to the greater; the desire is only magnified as it seeks substitute (not higher) forms. The desire for conquest in the realm of ideas, the creation of new systems of belief, is likewise a form of madness, "for what man in the natural state or course of thinking, did ever conceive it in his power to reduce the notions of all mankind exactly to the same length, and breadth, and heighth of his own? Yet this is the first humble and civil design of all innovators in the empire of reason." Again, there can be no way of explaining such zeal but by a physiological study of "vapors ascending from the lower faculties to overshadow the brain." The quest for happiness becomes, in simplest terms, the need for evacuation of an excess of vapors; frustration gives rise to phantasies, and phantasies in turn become programs of action. There is a tight chain of physical causation, in which happiness becomes the removal of pain.

Happiness is to be won by escaping from the "common forms," those norms of behavior that derive from our obvious duties. The removal of pain is the source of bold forays and worldly "heroism." The search for happiness may also be regarded as the pursuit of ease, "the perpetual possession of being well deceived." Happiness in the mind is won by choosing fiction over truth, imagination over memory. Happiness in the senses is won by seeing all things in "the vehicle of delusion" rather than "the glass of nature"; "if it were not for the assistance of artificial mediums, false lights, refracted angles, varnish, and tinsel, there would be a mighty level in the felicity and enjoyments of mortal men."

Having come to prize delusion and fiction as relief from the restraint of common forms and as a source of near-physical satisfaction, the tale-teller must protect them against the threat of reason. In his paranoid imagination reason takes on the frightening aspect of an officious surgeon who will look beneath the surface and reveal the defects within. Such "expensive anatomy" destroys all pleasing fictions; therefore, the tale-teller will make it unnecessary. He announces that "reason is certainly in the right, and that in most corporeal beings . . . the outside hath been infinitely preferable to the in." He recounts his own experiments: "Last week I saw a woman flayed, and you will hardly believe how much it altered her person for the worse." But this is a dismissal of, rather than a capitulation to, reason. The tale-teller gives in to reason in principle only to get rid of it in fact. The concentration on the woman's "person" is telling. It is the surface to which the tale-teller clings; he urges philosophers to "sodder and patch up the flaws and imperfections of mankind," as if the surface can become self-subsistent and rest securely on any inside or none at all. The Epicurean quest for happiness is what matters; the wise man will "content his ideas with the films and images that fly off upon his senses from the superficies of things":

> This is the sublime and refined point of felicity called the possession of being well deceived; the serene peaceful state, of being a fool among knaves.

Madness becomes a withdrawal into a private world or the parochial and time-bound world of fashion. It alternates between violent self-assertion and complacent delusion; the motive for action in each case is the recovery or preservation of sensuous pleasure. And in each case, the mind is thoroughly circumvented; fancy is astride reason, and fancy itself is under the dominion of the body. The "soul"—that is, all that might be called an intellectual or moral existence—has become a suit of clothes, and, as we see in a visit to Bedlam, it must be worn with an attention to fashion; the only difference between the inmate of Bedlam and the hero of his age is the timing of his behavior.

The astonishing vigor of *A Tale of a Tub* comes of its remarkable range, its bland equation of various intellectual activities, and its steady reduction of all of them to a few simple principles of physical compulsion and mechanical causation.

We are left with a world where, because the order of the mind has been rendered powerless, the order of the flesh can claim for itself the name of charity and offer a debased parody of its forms.

III. Martinus Scriblerus

Compared with Lemuel Gulliver or even with Pope's hero in *The Dunciad*, the fictitious author of *A Tale of a Tub* remains a shadowy figure, more a rhetorical stratagem than a character. In Martinus Scriblerus, Swift and Pope (in collaboration with Gay and Arbuthnot) created a full character who might embody mind in the process of self-destruction.[3] The Scriblerus *Memoirs* were left incomplete, but Martinus was invoked as the author of Pope's *Peri Bathous, or The Art of Sinking in Poetry* and as the patient, blundering editor of *The Dunciad Variorum*, the pseudoscholarly form in which Pope cast his satire in 1729. Henry Fielding was to create H. Scriblerus Secundus to edit the ancient tragedy of *Tom Thumb* as *The Tragedy of Tragedies* in 1742.

Martinus Scriblerus is a formidable master of systematic thinking; but his rational systems serve only to ensure that he will remain a thoroughgoing fool. He becomes, like Swift's Modest Proposer or Gulliver, a man oblivious to normal human feeling. He concentrates on the portion of reality that his system can admit. He is most composed and serene when he is ordering words as a critic, dismembering the text of Virgil in his *Virgilius Restauratus* and reducing the fullness of poetic meaning to the shallow clarity his mind can admit. He is delighted to be able to codify the bathetic, give a rationale to what others consider ineptitude, and to reduce the labors of art to an easy mechanical formula. All of this is done with an owlish solemnity and ponderous heaviness.

The *Memoirs* present us with the origin of Martinus' "gravity of deportment" and his startling appearance:

> His whole figure was so utterly unlike anything of this world that it was not natural for any man to ask him a question without blessing himself first. . . . But under this macerated form was concealed a mind replete with science, burning with a zeal of benefiting his fellow-creatures, and filled with an honest conscious pride, mixt with a scorn of doing or suffering the least thing beneath the dignity of a philosopher (*Memoirs,* Introduction).

We soon learn why he is in England. In his quest for "natural knowledge" in Spain, he heard of a lady "marked with a pomegranate on the inside of her right thigh, which blossomed and, as it were, seemed to ripen in the due season." Nothing could restrain Martinus until he saw the lady in her bath, but unfortunately he was discovered by her husband and suspected "of a crime most alien from the purity of [his] thought."

This nice mixture of superstitious awe, scholarly passion, and sublime single-mindedness has been inherited by Martin from his learned father, Cornelius. As an antiquary, Cornelius is devoted to all the forms of the past, as thoroughly and mindlessly as the Moderns are to those of the present. (It is Cornelius' brother Albertus who, like Lord Munodi in *Gulliver's Travels,* provides a norm: he is "clear of pedantry and knowing enough both in books and the world to preserve a due regard for whatever was useful or excellent, whether ancient or modern.") Cornelius sets about raising his son religiously according to the prescriptions of antiquity. When he obliviously orders for the wet nurse's dinner "the paps of a sow with pig," she leaves in dudgeon, "taking it as the highest indignity and a direct insult upon her sex and calling."

The problem of words emerges in the *Memoirs* when Cornelius procures Martin a companion, Conradus Crambe. Martin's understanding is "totally immersed in *sensible objects,*" Crambe's in words. The problems of universals immediately appear: Martin supposes "a Universal Man to be like a Knight of a Shire or a Burgess of a Corporation, that represented a great many individuals," and cannot free his mind of the particular Lord Mayor he has actually seen. Crambe, on the other hand, "swore he could frame a conception of a Lord Mayor not only without his horse, gown, and gold chain, but even without stature, feature, color, hands, head, feet, or any body. . . ." Between them, the two boys represent the nominalistic empiricism carried to an extreme by the new science and the ingenious scholasticism that thrives on verbal distinctions and treats universals as more real than particulars. Crambe's Treatise on Syllogisms is a beautiful instance of the kind of learned scholastic wit that punningly turns abstractions into concrete objects and living actors (the kind of wit that looks back to Rabelais or Donne and forward to Sterne and Joyce):

> He supposed that a philosopher's brain was like a great forest, where ideas ranged like animals of several kinds;

that those ideas copulated and engendered conclusions; that when those of different species copulate, they bring forth monsters or absurdities; that the major is the male, the minor the female, which copulate by the middle term and engender the conclusion (ch. VII).

All the puzzles that words create are brought to a climax in the episode of the double mistress. This burlesque of romantic fictions finds Martin in love with Lindamira, while he is loved in turn by Indamora. These two ladies comprise, unfortunately, a pair of Siamese twins ("how much soever our Martin was enamored on her as a beautiful woman, he was infinitely more ravished with her as a charming monster. . . . unable to resist at once so pleasing a passion and so amiable a phenomenon"). When Martin is charged with bigamy and incest, all the dazzling complexities of scholastic metaphysics and legal argument are fused. Martin's attorney pleads, since the ladies meet in the pelvic region and presumably have common sexual organs, that "if they made two individual persons, yet they constitute but one wife." Martin's case rests on the fact that the seat of the soul is in the organ of generation: "There the soul is employed in works suitable to the dignity of her nature and (as we may say) sits brooding on ages yet unborn." But his opponent scorns the impudence that would "degrade this queen, the rational soul, to the very lowest and vilest apartment, or rather sink of her whole palace."

The wit of the *Memoirs* depends on the absurdities that systems of thought (and therefore of words) almost inevitably generate. The legal fictions the laws require are upset by the stubborn refusal of particular creatures to settle mildly into the class memberships to which they are assigned. And the vivid physical detail, as it erupts into the conceptual world of legal abstraction, has a splendid power to destroy that world. The Judge assigns each of the two sisters (they are adjudged to be two) to her particular husband (Indamora is now married to a dwarf) and warns the husbands that

> being, as it were, joint proprietors of one common tenement, you will so behave as good fellow lodgers ought to do, and with great modesty each to his respective sister-in-law, abstaining from all farther familiarities than what conjugal duties do naturally oblige you to. Consider also by how small limits the duty and the trespass is divided, lest, whilst ye discharge the duty of matrimony, ye heedlessly slide into the sin of adultery.

As we see later in Sterne, the wholesome obscenity of the sexual cuts through the webs of finespun scholastic or legal reasoning, and the play on dead metaphors (e.g., sliding into sin) which wakens them to startling life reminds us of the traps and puzzles that are built into the most formidably refined jargon. The mechanistic materialists impose one systematic pattern of abstraction upon experience; the scholastic realists another. The dilemmas that arise from confrontation of their opposed schemes underline the stubborn fact that the soul *is* somehow in the body and scarcely extricable from it, that the mansion of love is, as Yeats tells us, pitched in the place of excrement. The breakdown of words is, after all, only the breakdown of our attempt to make words do more than they can, to create a fictitious world that is tidily rational.

In *The Art of Sinking in Poetry*, Martinus Scriblerus undertakes the public-spirited task of compiling an "art" of modern poetry: "how many promising geniuses of this age," he laments, "are wandering . . . in the dark without a guide." He has, therefore, "undertaken this arduous but necessary task to lead them as it were by the hand, and step by step, the gentle downhill way to the Bathos; the bottom, the end, the central point, the *non plus ultra,* of true modern poesy!" (ch. I). Martin sees poetry as a "trade" or "manufacture" that he is eager to promote; first of all, men must be taught more efficient methods of producing cheaper wares. No one expects of them what the Ancients asked of themselves. The Moderns may lack quality, but they can produce abundantly if they are released from the inherited standards that still inhibit them.

The eclipse of standards is managed by a systematic debasing of words. Modern taste is returning to the "first simplicity and innocence"—that of "the unprejudiced minds of children." Universality now means being "adapted to every capacity." In Horace's maxim that poetry wishes both to profit and please, the meaning of profit (*prodesse*) is gently shifted from "give profit" to "make profit." Thus, in the manner of Plato's sophist, the Moderns seek "to procure applause by administering pleasure to the reader." Horace's golden mean, *aurea mediocritas,* becomes the license for "mediocrity."

The treatise is a parody of Longinus' *On the Sublime;* the *Peri Bathous* of Scriblerus is a direct inversion of Longinus' *Peri Hypsous.* Genius becomes facility (ch. VI); for "choice and discrimination are not only a curb to the spirit . . . but also lessen the book" and reduce the author's profits (ch. VIII). The end of bathos is "to produce tranquillity of mind" (we think of Swift's "serene peaceful state of being a fool among knaves"). If passions must be roused, the most debased form excites most readily: "to move anger, use is made of scolding and railing; to move love, of bawdry." As for shame, "it is a silly passion, of which as our authors are incapable themselves, so they would not produce it in others" (ch. IX).

Throughout the treatise, we are shown ways of avoiding meaning while preserving its forms: "obscurity bestows a cast of the wonderful, and throws an oracular dignity upon a piece which hath no meaning." So later Fielding's Scriblerus Secundus will remark that "the greatest perfection of the language of a tragedy is, that it is not to be understood." This mechanical operation of the imagination produces a bathos that is the pride of the uncritical Moderns but can also be the calculated strategy of the satirist. Swift and Pope use bathos constantly to dramatize the collapse of mind in the very activities in which it takes pride. The *Peri Bathous* may be a catalogue of the failures of feckless bards, but it is also a catalogue of satiric techniques.

IV. *The Dunciad* (1728–41)

> [P]utting Shakespeare aside as rather the world's than ours, I hold Pope to be the most perfect representative we have, since Chaucer, of the true English mind; and I think *The Dunciad* is the most absolutely chiselled and monumental work "exacted" in our country. You will find, as you study Pope, that he has expressed for you, in the strictest language, and within the briefest limits, every law of art, of criticism, of economy, of policy, and, finally, of a benevolence, humble, rational, and resigned, contented with its allotted share of life, and trusting the problem of its salvation to Him in whose hand lies that of the universe ("Lectures in Art," Oxford, 1870, III, para. 70; *Works,* ed. E. T. Cook and Alexander Wedderburn, London, 1905, XX, 77).

It is too much, but it is Ruskin; and it will serve, as we approach the *Dunciad,* to remind us of its connection with the *Essay on Man* and the *Imitations of Horace.* The poem was first published in 1728, shortly after *Gulliver's Travels* and

The Beggar's Opera; Pope amplified it with Scriblerian prefaces and notes (*The Art of Sinking in Poetry* had been published in 1727) as *The Dunciad Variorum* in 1729. Twelve years later, he added to the first three books the fourth, as *The New Dunciad,* and replaced the poet-critic Lewis Theobald with the playwright-actor-laureate Colley Cibber as the chief of the dunces.

Aubrey Williams' fine study (*Pope's Dunciad,* London and Baton Rouge, 1955) has allowed us to see the full scope of Pope's greatest work. I should like to consider three aspects of the poem here: its concern with language, its myth of Dulness, and its approach to tragedy. First, however, I must say a word about the structure of the poem, as we now have it.

The first book gives us the hero, Bays, surrounded by the participants in the Lord Mayor's Procession, a pleasant *kermesse* of "Glad chains, warm furs, broad banners, and broad faces." These burghers in fancy dress and their duncelike bard are ludicrous; they represent the march of "Smithfield Muses to the ear of Kings," the surrender of court patronage to the cheapest and most meretricious of hacks and (in a larger sense) the surrender of aristocratic values to the commercial policies of the City. The Lord Mayor's procession to Westminster becomes the debased counterpart of Aeneas' bearing the gods and culture of Troy to Latium.

In the second book, the vortex spreads from Bays to the whole world of letters—booksellers (that is, publishers), patrons, would-be writers, hacks are all involved in epic games —where discus throwing, for example, is replaced by the contest of shooting one's stream of urine highest, with the first prize a loose lady-writer and the second her close counterpart, a chamberpot. In the third book the vortex opens wider: through the prophecies of Elkanah Settle, the old city-poet, we look back to the past and trace the coming of night through time and space. As cultures have died, culture itself has moved westward, from China to the Middle East, from there to Greece, thence to Italy, to France and Spain, at last to England and now—in prospect—beyond it to the West. The death of a culture is the progress of Dulness, and Bays is her prophet. Finally, in the fourth book we move from history into the mind itself and see the eclipse of its power and control. Dulness, as Pope's editor, Warburton, puts it, "admits something like each science" and accomplishes the insensible corruption that results in her complete triumph at the close.

Language in the *Dunciad* is always running down to non-sense, and from nonsense to sheer noise. The final noise is the great yawn from which all descends at last to sleep. At the acme, Cibber's poetry appears, involuted but essentially form-less:

> Maggots half-form'd in rhyme exactly meet,
> And learn to crawl upon poetic feet.
> Here one poor word an hundred clenches makes,
> And ductile dulness new meanders takes;
> There motley images her fancy strike,
> Figures ill pair'd and similes unlike.
> She sees a mob of metaphors advance,
> Pleas'd with the madness of the mazy dance (I, 61–68).

Pope's words are rich with import: *maggots* signify both grubs and perverse whimsies; the *feet* that support them are the metrical form that makes nonsense respectable. The malleability of words in puns ("clenches") and turns, the fool's motley of Cibber's fancy, the "mob" of metaphors that preserves only a semblance of order—all these signalize a fundamental breakdown of form. We get it as well in mismated genres ("Farce and Epic get a jumbled race") and the addled geography, with its symbolic abortions ("And heavy harvests nod beneath the snow"). This is Dulness' "wild creation," the first stage in the progress of her "uncreating word."

The monstrous is a consistent motif in the works of Dulness. Bays (that is, Cibber) is seen in the Cave of Poverty and Poetry, where

> Keen hollow winds howl through the bleak recess,
> Emblem of music caus'd by Emptiness (I, 35–36)—

a couplet happily glossed by an eighteenth-century editor as "bowel music." Bays' poverty is a result of his misapplication of talents, his desire to be what his gifts will never make him. We find him surrounded by "much embryo, much abortion" (I, 121), where his hot brains have overflowed like "running lead." His works, like all the works of Dulness, are unstable compounds:

> Prose swell'd to verse, verse loit'ring into prose
> . . . random thoughts now meaning chance to find,
> Now leave all memory of sense behind (I, 274–76).

The ultimate achievement of all this industrious plagiarism, intellectual laziness, and gross commercialism is that quintessential monster, "A vast, vamp'd, future, old, reviv'd new

piece" (I, 284). Cibber's guardian angel, Settle, later cries
with pleasure:

> Son, what thou seek'st is in thee! Look and find
> Each Monster meets his likeness in thy mind
>   (III, 251–52).

The reduction of language to noise comes during the epic
games. Dulness bids her followers learn "the wond'rous
power of Noise" (II, 222). Wherever dramatic art fails, spectacle may serve; where sense fails, trumpets or stage thunder
may fill the vacuity. In their games, the Dunces transform
themselves to noise:

> Twas chatt'ring, grinning, mouthing, jabb'ring all,
> And Noise and Norton, Brangling and Breval,
> Dennis and Dissonance . . . (II, 237–39).

Blackmore's triumphant bray fills and is echoed by the court
world, as Aubrey Williams shows (pp. 36–38); it subdues
sense with sound. Again in the third book, we have the howling of James Ralph to the moon ("Answer him, ye Owls!"):

> Sense, speech, and measure, living tongues and dead,
> Let all give way . . . (III, 167–68).

The apotheosis of noise occurs early in the fourth book with
the appearance of Opera. The fashion of Italian opera had
swept England in the 1720s and was the object of Gay's satire
in *The Beggar's Opera,* where Polly Peachum and Lucy Lockit
re-enact the deadly rivalry of imported divas. What Italian
opera means to Pope is made clear by what he sees it displace. Since "Rebellion will commence, / If Music meanly
borrows aid from Sense" (IV, 63–64), Dulness must banish
Handel to Ireland. Handel's crime has been "To stir, to rouse,
to shake the Soul"—to give music human import and moral
power. Dulness cannot tolerate his presence. Instead, she favors the "harlot form" of Opera, whose fiat is the undoing
of the Muses:

> Joy to great Chaos! let Division reign:
> Chromatic tortures soon shall drive them hence,
> Break all their nerves, and fritter all their sense:
> One Trill shall harmonize joy, grief, and rage,
> Wake the dull Church, and lull the ranting Stage;
> To the same notes thy sons shall hum, or snore,
> And all thy yawning daughters cry, *encore* (IV, 54–60).

For the Phoebus Apollo who leads the Muses, opera offers a

substitute Phoebus, who is Dulness' own. Scriblerus' note refers us to the French rhetorical term, Phébus, a figure in
which there is "an appearance of light glimmering over the
obscurity, a semblance of meaning without any real sense."

The culmination of the theme is in those startling reductions
and equations that provide the full satiric "recognition"—the
sudden disclosure of a relationship that simplifies and orders
experience with terrifying clarity. One such moment is the
boast of the tyrannous schoolmaster:

> . . . Since Man from beasts by Words is known,
> Words are Man's province, Words we teach alone . . .
> Plac'd at the door of Learning, youth to guide,
> We never suffer it to stand too wide
> (IV, 149–50, 153–54).

Words descend from the organon of reason to mere forms; the
student is assigned, as Shadwell is in Dryden's *MacFlecknoe*,
"some peaceful province in acrostic-land," and all the power
of art is frittered away in epigram. Pope immediately draws
the connection between language and society:

> For sure if Dulness sees a grateful day,
> 'Tis in the shade of Arbitrary Sway (IV, 181–82).

Some "gentle James," a pedant-king, can reduce the affairs of
state to scholastic games: "Give law to words, or war with
words alone" (IV, 178). And verbal ingenuity will ensure
that tyranny has its sanctions: "The Right Divine of Kings to
govern wrong" (IV, 188).

Another triumph of satiric recognition is the account of
the young Aeneas on his Grand Tour, where the process of
education is finally undone by the triumph of manners over
mind. The youth

> Dropp'd the dull lumber of the Latin store,
> Spoil'd his own language, and acquir'd no more;
> All classic learning lost on classic ground;
> And last turned air, the echo of a sound!
> See now, half-cur'd, and perfectly well-bred,
> With nothing but a solo in his head (IV, 319–24).

Dulness is a great anti-goddess. She recalls a primordial
deity like the Magna Mater, whose obscene worship was accommodated to urbane tastes in the Roman Empire, and also
Spenser's Night and Milton's Satan—a form of seeming grandeur that conceals an inner emptiness. Their end is the undoing of Order, and they are, to that extent, the embodiments

of the traditional view of evil as mere negation. When Duessa approaches Night in the first book of *The Faerie Queene,* she urges her on to the recovery of her ancient empire:

> Up then! up, dreary dame, of darknes queene!
> Go gather up the reliques of thy race,
> Or else goe them avenge, and let be seene
> That dreaded Night in brightest day hath place,
> And can the children of fayre Light deface
> (I, v, stanza 24).

(The Satanic elements in Dulness are fully set forth in Aubrey Williams' final chapter, "The Anti-Christ of Wit.") In Pope's poem Dulness is the

> Daughter of Chaos and Eternal Night . . .
> Gross as her sire, and as her mother grave,
> Laborious, heavy, busy, bold, and blind (I, 12, 14–15).

Her aim is to "blot out Order, and extinguish Light" (IV, 14), and her final triumph is as an anti-Logos, an "uncreating Word."

Behind the magnificence of the anti-goddess lies the brute force of inertia or sloth. In Plato's myth of the cave, the philosopher seeks "to unchain the soul and lead it up a steep and rocky trail into the light of the sun. But the soul resists this liberation, insisting that nothing exists but the life of the cave, clinging to its chains, weeping with anguish when forced to leave its beloved shadows, and struggle upwards into the painful brightness of reality."[4] Dulness is the incarnation of that darkness in which the soul elects to remain and chooses to call light. As Pope puts it in a note to I, 15 (written as by Bentley), Dulness "includes . . . labor, industry, and some degree of activity and boldness: a ruling principle not inert, but turning topsy-turvy the understanding, and inducing an anarchy or confused state of mind." All this energy is perfectly consonant with a moral inertia. As Helen Bacon observes about the myth of the cave:

> Plato's purpose is to show us men choosing between illusion and reality, and to reveal their complacency, anger, fear, suspicion, all the passions with which we defend ourselves against the knowledge of our own shortcomings. This *is* a drama, we might even say it is *the* drama of humanity (p. 417).

Dulness is less a real being than a projection of the moral inertia of the man who prefers the ease of remaining what he is to the pain of becoming properly human. The sleep that she offers is not simply a relaxation of intellectual faculties, but a freedom from moral cognition and, most of all, from moral effort. Her darkness is the darkness of the ooze into which her sons cheerfully plunge, of the womb toward which her laureate son, rocked on her lap, regresses. She provides her sons with the comfort of being less conscious and therefore less anxious. Her maternal indulgence fosters the infantile, encourages dabbling in excrement, and exclaims with delight at the least achievement.

While the dunces prance and gambol, Dulness herself moves with an irresistible viscosity through time and space. In history she is the constant relapse into barbarism, whether of Goths or Huns or the Moslem invaders of Byzantium. There is no better instance than her conquest of Rome, where the great sculpture and architecture of antiquity become the rubbish of an age without light: "Streets pav'd with Heroes, Tiber chok'd with Gods." The quarrying of Roman remains for building stones and the burning of marble for lime provide Pope with images of Dulness' power to bring all to "one dead level." The tasteless imposition of Christian names on classical statues becomes a symptom of a frightened and superstitious authority clinging to the forms of worship.

> . . . Peter's Keys some christen'd Jove adorn,
> And Pan to Moses lends his Pagan horn;
> See graceless Venus to a Virgin turn'd,
> Or Phidias broken, and Apelles burn'd (III, 109–12).

As Pope's note remarks, "the Goths scarce destroyed more monuments of antiquity out of rage, than these out of devotion. . . . In much later times, it was thought necessary to change the statues of Apollo and Pallas on the tomb of Sannazarius into David and Judith"—and there is disdain for false wit in the remarks that follow—"the lyre easily became a harp, and the Gorgon's head turned to that of Holofernes." So in his Epistle to Addison of 1715 he had written:

> Barbarian blindness, Christian zeal conspire,
> And Papal piety, and Gothic fire (13–14).

Dulness thrives on any cause that forsakes discrimination whether Goth or Christian, arrogant modernity or pious false wit.

In contrast to the formal beauty of the classical statues are the formless "full-fed Heroes" and "pacific Mayors" (III,

281). The dethronement of the Logos is marked by a bloating of the physical, and its typical sound is the snores of the surfeited. All vocation becomes play; all activity, relaxation; all relationships must be inverted:

> Till Thames sees Eton's sons for ever play,
> Till Westminster's whole year be holiday,
> Till Isis' elders reel, their pupils' sport,
> And Alma Mater lies dissolv'd in port (III, 335–38).

The masters of learning founder on the joys of the common room, while the busy sons of Smithfield move from the fair and the pantomimes—the grossest entertainments of the City —to bring the taste of the rabble to court. This double action, divided according to social class and levels of culture, is also an internal drama among the faculties of man. In his *Imitations of Horace,* Pope made this stronger, as he described a "Clergy, or a City feast":

> What life in all that ample body, say?
> What heavenly particle inspires the clay?
> The soul subsides, and wickedly inclines
> To seem but mortal, ev'n in sound Divines
>   (Satire II, ii, 77–80).

The play upon *body* and upon *sound* marks the inversion that has taken place, much like the evaporation of the soul in the clothes worship of *A Tale of a Tub. The Dunciad* reaches the culmination of this theme in the fourth book where the mysteries of Dulness—all the mysteries that survive in this physical world—are those of the *haute cuisine.* The ritual is conducted by a chef:

> On some, a Priest succinct in amice white
> Attends: all flesh is nothing in his sight (IV, 549–50).

The passage continues with a series of ingenuities of cookery (one of Plato's favorite examples of inverted art) that are also full of references to the sacred Christian mysteries, now lost except for this travesty. The last is the subtlety of dissolving two fowl to make a sauce for a third: "Three essential Partridges in one" (IV, 562).

The psychological meaning of Dulness is, clearly, the surrender of thought to sensation. Pope, like Socrates in Plato's *Gorgias,* uses the image of tickling to catch the most elementary nastiness of this abandonment to physical sensation. As the patron chinks his purse, the dedicators set to work, and with the physical stimulus come the maudlin fantasies:

> Now gentle touches wanton o'er his face,
> He struts Adonis, and affects grimace
> . . . Thus each hand promotes the pleasing pain,
> And quick sensations skip from vein to vein
> (II, 201–2, 211–12).

At last one youth more shameless than the rest finds the ultimate resource and the supreme titillation. He offers the patron his sister—

> As, taught by Venus, Paris learnt the art
> To touch Achilles' only tender part;
> Secure, through her, the noble prize to carry,
> He marches off, his Grace's Secretary (II, 217–20).

The dehumanization that seems fatuous as mere regression becomes loathsome in its fullest implications. The retreat into selfhood dissolves the self into a body that must be fed its diet of agreeable sensations at the expense of all who can be made to furnish them. All that survives of identity is the steadiness of appetite.

The social aspect of Dulness lies in the demand for power that all institutions make once they exist for their own sake. All through the poem, and particularly in the fourth book, runs a stream of allusions to England's current political corruption. When Silenus appears (an "Epicurean philosopher" from Virgil's Sixth Eclogue), he has the look of Walpole's Commissioner of Wine Licenses, a former journalist who sold out and became supervisor of the government-paid press. His account of the initiates in Dulness' mysteries sums up his own career and the age which fostered it:

> First slave to words, then vassal of a name,
> Then dupe to party; child and man the same;
> Bounded by Nature, narrow'd still by Art,
> A trifling head, and a contracted heart (IV, 501–4).

In Dulness' final words, she beams upon Walpole himself:

> Perhaps more high some daring son may soar,
> Proud to my list to add one monarch more;
> And nobly conscious, princes are but things
> Born for first ministers, as slaves for kings,
> Tyrant supreme! Shall three estates command,
> And make one mighty Dunciad of the land!
>   (IV, 599–604.)

These lines gain their point against the background of the rallying of hopes by Bolingbroke and others around the idea of a Patriot King, a man who might assume responsibility and rule for the entire nation. Walpole's systematic and unofficial absorption of political power had become the inversion of the idea of the mixed state. As "Tyrant supreme" he frustrated the aspirations of an opposition and reduced politics to intrigue—except in such isolated instances of heroic resistance as Swift's in *The Drapier's Letters*.

Finally, Dulness has a metaphysical dimension. She is matter claiming to generate form. Just as the soul is the *forma informans* of man (Dryden plays upon this in his portrait of Achitophel, whose fiery soul "o'er informs" his tenement of clay), so God is of the universe ("Whose body Nature is, and God the soul"). The Aristotelian fusion of soul and matter runs through all of Pope's poetry. It is the basis for his criticism of the Pythagorean aspect (as opposed to the moral and Socratic) of Platonism:

> Mad Mathesis alone was unconfin'd,
> Too mad for mere material chains to bind,
> Now to pure space lifts her ecstatic stare,
> Now running round the circle finds it square (IV, 31–34).

But Aristotelianism is even more fundamentally opposed—as Shaftesbury notes—to Epicureanism, that is, to a philosophy that credits the reality only of matter and sees all higher forms evolve through the chance collocation of atoms. Pope is like Dryden in that he insists upon the fusion of what descends from above with the matter to which it gives form; the rebellion of Absalom and Achitophel, we may recall, is a denial of that descent and an attempt to create seeming order from below.

In *The Dunciad* the worship of Dulness becomes a "love to parts," a distraction of the mind from unity into bits and pieces:

> The critic eye, that microscope of wit,
> Sees hairs and pores, examines bit by bit (IV, 233–34).

We may recall the *Essay on Man,* where God exists in all:

> As full, as perfect, in a hair as heart (I, 276).

It is precisely this ability to look through the material object to

see its relatedness that is lost by the dunces. They no longer
can see

> How parts relate to parts, or they to whole,
> The body's harmony, the beaming soul (IV, 235–36).

Again, we are reminded of the questions put in the *Essay:*

> But of this frame, the bearings, and the ties,
> The strong connexions, nice dependencies,
> Gradations just, has thy pervading soul
> Look'd through? or can a part contain the whole?
>   (I, 29–32.)

The pursuits of the virtuosi—collectors, botanists, lepidopterists
—become the fixation on the part as an end in itself. The collector values his mutilated statues or his coins above all human relationships:

> To headless Phoebe his fair bride postpone,
> Honour a Syrian prince above his own (IV, 367–68).

Men come to resemble what they love: the pursuit of the but-
terfly by a passionate collector becomes a counterpart to Eve's
narcissistic fascination with her own reflection in *Paradise
Lost:* "It stopped, I stopped; it moved, I moved again" (IV,
428).

> Yet by some object every brain is stirr'd;
> The dull may waken to a hummingbird;
> The most recluse, discreetly open'd find
> Congenial matter in the cockle kind;
> The mind, in metaphysics at a loss,
> May wander in a wilderness of moss (IV, 445–50).

The dunces must "Learn but to trifle" or, at most, in the manner of those who "believe and sleep," to free their religion
from all practical consequences: "To wonder at their Maker,
not to serve!" (IV, 458).

The ultimate stage of this involvement in parts and things
is the arrogance of the dogmatically rationalistic Deist. It is all
very well for others to be led inductively through the study of
nature to nature's cause. (This inquiry into final causes is defended, against Bacon, by a scientist like Robert Boyle: knowledge of the "uses of things" gives us "just cause of admiring
and thanking the Author of them" [*Works*, London, 1772,
I, 310].) The Deists have rejected inductive empiricism:

> We nobly take the high priori road,
> And reason downward, till we doubt of God
>   (IV, 471–72).

This is the method constantly ascribed to Descartes in contrast to Newton. Descartes became the forerunner of eighteenth-century materialism by conceiving a self-subsistent mechanical world parallel to, but no longer dependent upon, the operations of mind. It is, even more, the method of the system-builder in general, whether scholastic, Deist or whatever—the method of both Peter and Jack in *A Tale of a Tub.*

Once God has been reduced to a guarantor of a rationalistic system, the happiness of man as he is (not certainly as he should be, for all aspiration has been undercut) becomes the end of the universe. We have seen this pattern in the complaints of the interlocutor in the *Essay on Man,* who also is ready to

> Make God man's image, man the final cause,
> Find virtue local, all relation scorn,
> See all in self, and but for self be born (IV, 478–80).

These rationalists are, of course, the perverters of the order of mind; they make the mind independent of all below or above it and foist its systems on the whole of reality. In doing so, they open the way for unacknowledged passions within themselves to impose upon the mind. In depriving the mind's systems of any check against reality, they have allowed it to become phantasy, and its content is supplied by the appetites that remain unexamined in darkness. The God these men frame in their own image becomes Dulness herself:

> A God like Thee,
> Wrapt up in self, a God without a thought,
> Regardless of our merit or default (IV, 484–86).

Dulness ends as the blind principle of selfhood, an imagined Other men create to license their own appetites, the formless claiming to create its own form. What, in fact, is created is a travesty—the order of charity as it might be conceived by a fleshly imagination. The crucial breakdown is in the order of mind. The mind has been lulled into inactivity or flattered into arrogance. Its eclipse is ludicrous within each of the dunces we see, but awesome and tragic in mankind. The close of the poem emphasizes the loss—the tragic waste, in fact—and voices the consciousness of the one just man who survives in a world that has surrendered consciousness:

Thus at her feet approach, and secret might,
Art after art goes out, and all is night.
See skulking truth to her old cavern fled,
Mountains of casuistry heap'd o'er her head! . . .
Nor public flame, nor private, dares to shine;
Nor human spark is left, nor glimpse divine!
Lo, thy dread empire, Chaos! is restor'd;
Light dies before thy uncreating word
    (IV, 639–42, 651–54).

In these final lines, the ironic celebration has undergone a change. There is awe for the power of Dulness and tragic awareness of the death of mind. The second voice enters and takes over the poem at the close—the voice of the satirist as tragic hero. He exclaims, like Hamlet, "Oh God! a beast that wants discourse of reason / Would have mourned longer."

VIII.

Orders and Forms

1. Character and Causality

In Mandeville and again in Pope we see the problem of causality at the center of the conception of character. The uses of causality are different in each writer and in each form. The tragic hero is in conflict with some kind of necessity. He may struggle with the fates or with the secret cause within his soul. His catastrophe may be implicit in his virtues, as the cost of greatness, the inevitable weakness that besets the extraordinary man, even the weakness of having attempted too much. He accepts the fate he helped to make; in his power to recognize responsibility, to claim his error as his own, to see the continuity of the self he has made, he achieves a greatness we admire.

It is a stern and naked greatness, stripped of the comfortable pretexts and half-truths, the allowances and the self-pity men may feel their usual due. What he sees at last is the double causality, the chain of motive and action he has deliberately forged and the other chain of secret causes that now are manifest, the necessity of his nature or of his gods. The second chain has not been his own, for it has been secret; but he now accepts it as his own, as something which he could have missed only through a failure of mind or a failure of will. The tragic hero thus plays to the utmost the role of the self-caused man, the man who should have known better because he should have known all, the man whose every action is finally to be claimed as a choice, however mistaken.

The hero or mock hero of satire has a blindness comparable to that of the tragic hero, but the satiric hero can never acknowledge error, for he does not have the capacities to come to understanding. We, as readers or spectators, see through him from the outset; and this implies a blindness in him that is all the more dense. The satiric hero, therefore, does not evoke the sense of terror at the presence of the secret cause; for it is no secret to us and should not have been to him. He is culpable, and all his behavior is played out in a realm of responsibility he is never able to assume. He is, therefore, dramatized as a failure.

There are gradations between the tragic and satiric hero. Two cases come to mind at once: Achitophel and Cibber. Achitophel has terrible energy and a latent capacity for judgment, blotted out by the self-deceptions his restless nature demands. He is closer to a tragic figure than any other in Dryden's poem; in fact, he rises to tragic stature as much as he does through the contrast with Shimei, Zimri, and the rest of his followers. But Achitophel is fixed in a pattern that will never break; he is beyond self-discovery, more than Satan is in Milton's poem. Each is a victim of tremendous compulsions, and each must pay their cost in outrageous folly. What makes both in some measure tragic is that they have enough vestiges of greatness to make the mixture almost mysterious in its complexity; both, moreover, have an intensity of passion, a majesty of disorder, that invites the glorification Satan was to receive from later critics. Once intensity is elevated above order, Satan is a hero of authenticity, whose very inability to accept his fate becomes integrity. But such a view must blink the satiric devices Milton uses from the outset to detach our view of Satan from Satan's own, to give us a point of vantage that sees the father of lies deluding himself first of all.

In the case of Cibber, the very inversion of heroism, his universality makes him imposing; he is King of the Dunces, and his subjects give their free assent to his reign. In Cibber and his crew Pope is showing us the staggering catastrophe of the eclipse of the critical mind by the latent powers that are always present but usually under control. What we have is on the surface ludicrous comedy, but beneath is the mystery of the abyss that always underlies our scaffolding of culture and intelligence. The close of The Dunciad rises to tragic dimensions because its subject is the tragedy of mind, and Cibber becomes a dimension of the whole mind of man. The tragic hero of The Dunciad is the ordering mind that has created the poem. The last lines of The Dunciad are the final realization of Pope's conception of the satirist as tragic hero. In making satire a more profound and inclusive form than it had ever been before, the eighteenth century could express through it as much of the tragic view of life as could survive its distrust of cant and hollow gesture.

We are often told that the Augustans were incapable of writing tragedy, but much of what we call tragic consciousness is displaced into Augustan satire. And it is well to remember that the call for tragedy, especially in our own day, is often the call for a tribute to the grandeur of the human spirit. It can, all too easily, become an invitation to dishonesty. There is no greater temptation than to turn our immediate complaints into a tragic nemesis, our follies into cosmic evil. There is a robustness in the honesty that mocks man with his sub-tragic nature and taunts him with the needlessness of error. It is aware of what we might wish to be, but also of what we are. Both satire and comedy may see what tragedy sees and pass it by, outflanking it or including it in a longer perspective—the perspective that admits no ultimates and demands the drabber business of going on living. The tragic hero brings us all to a consciousness we can live with but not in; he splendidly takes upon himself more guilt than he has incurred and, having made this ritual sacrifice on our behalf, he leaves the task of living to those lesser characters who step forward and pick up the pieces. If this is mockery, it is meant to be respectful; I would simply point to the dangers of too jealous a devotion to the tragic experience and too casual a view of the comic or the satiric.

We have finally to consider the comic character, hero and butt. The comic butt remains essentially a satiric figure unless he is transformed miraculously into hero. Don Quixote undergoes such a transformation and becomes something like the divine fool of whom Erasmus wrote and of whom Dostoevsky was to write again. The comic hero may emerge from a pattern of repetitive compulsion, and escape into a kind of freedom that most of us lack. The Wife of Bath, to choose one, is fixed in a pattern of unending assertion of uncontrollable passions; and her use of the Bible or the Church Fathers, like her treatment of her clerkish husband or even her miraculous tale, reveals the same pattern of will overriding all that might brook or chasten it. Her arch enemy is the formulated principle, "auctoritee," and her manipulation of it is at once more ludicrous and more complex than any open and conscious rebellion. She is hardly her own master; she is like a vast unconscious natural force, as terrible and magnificent as climate itself. Her pattern ultimately is one of success; there is no controlling her, and we come to a sense that there is a rightness in her power. It is not merely intensity we can admire here, or the intransigence of Satan; she has a claim to our admiration like that of nature itself, in her spontaneity, her lack of the deviousness of such creatures as the Pardoner, in her demand to be recognized as God's work no less than the Parson or the Prioress. She breaks all our molds of morality and asserts a counter principle, dimly but insistently stated, of fecundity and earthiness. Like Falstaff, she corrects our ideas of order and reminds us of their limitations.

Such characters reappear in Squire Western who, in being the very antithesis of Allworthy, becomes an essential part of Fielding's definition of goodness in *Tom Jones*. The comic hero is less the victim than the elect, or both at once—fool and hero, hero because fool.

There is also another no less important kind of comic hero, the equilibrist—the man who without effort but with consummate, almost ludicrous skill, like the magician's, achieves success where it would seem impossible. Sometimes the equilibrist is a fool, like the Good Soldier Schweik and other such folk figures, too humble and stupid ever to be outmaneuvered. He may, on the other hand, be a man of great capacity, who enters into the world that might undo him, calls the turns and masters the intrigue with a defter counterplot. In his very effortlessness he is gyroscopic, always able to right himself. And this effortlessness or spontaneity seems close to the center of the comic vision. A frictionless ease in meeting the world's resistances marks the comic hero. If the world insists too much, he detaches himself from it and creates his own orbit, which may follow the world's or not, but has its own pattern. Whether we see the comic hero as a man with irresistible force or a man with ineluctable skill, we have a pattern of inevitable success, the very pattern of continued life and irrepressible survival. Sometimes the success may be entirely beyond the control and making of the comic hero himself; as the elect, he may be saved by the connivance of a providence, and his comic resolution becomes the assertion not so much of his human power as of a divine favor and generosity.

Causality, then, enters into our most fundamental conception of character, and it is expressed in our conception of plot. The confrontation of characters with some form of necessity is our problem, and it is this I want to examine in a group of works of the period, which illustrate the spectrum I have been presenting. The first group presents the plight of lovers in a hostile world and stresses the conflict of integrity and intrigue.

II. Integrity and Intrigue

All for Love embodies Dryden's characteristic tragic situation—the assertion of integrity in a world of conflicting claims or of sheer fortuitousness. Its action unfolds within the ideal time of the unities, a time more of logical sequence than of human duration and change. Its action is far more contrived than Shakespeare's *Antony and Cleopatra;* its characters are simpler and more symmetrically opposed to each other. Dryden's lovers die superbly, but they are victims of forces they hardly understand. Dryden's play occurs, one might say, within Antony; all the other characters represent divisions of Antony's soul: passions or commitments that make their claim upon him, each with seeming absoluteness and single-ness of purpose. Antony, therefore, never becomes a strong hero; he is so much the battleground of forces that he reaches fullness of assertion only at those moments, at the opening of the third act and the close of the play, when he is completely devoted to the highest of the claims upon him, Cleopatra's love.

The conflict between love and honor, so schematically presented in the rhetoric of the first two acts, is resolved by the opening of the third. Antony has chosen love and entered a new world of intrigue. The lovers accept their plight and rejoice in it. As Cleopatra crowns Antony, she has become his true fortune, he her soldier. They are a "brighter Venus" and a "greater Mars." Antony's speech is the central passage of the play:

> Receive me, goddess!
> Let Caesar spread his subtle nets like Vulcan;
> In thy embraces I would be beheld
> By heaven and earth at once,
> And make their envy what they meant their sport.
> Let those, who took us blush; I would love on
> With awful state, regardless of their frowns,
> As their superior god.
> There's no satiety of love in thee:
> Enjoy'd, thou still art new; perpetual spring
> Is in thy arms; the ripen'd fruit but falls,
> And blossoms rise to fill its empty place;
> And I grow rich by giving (III, i, 16–28).

The lovers are very much like Donne's, who have absorbed the world in each other, as in "The Sun Rising":

> She is all states and all princes, I,
> Nothing else is.

So Antony can bid the gods:

> Give to your boy, your Caesar,
> This rattle of a globe to play withal,
> This gewgaw world, and put him cheaply off:
> I'll not be pleas'd with less than Cleopatra (II, 443–46).

Yet Antony must say as well that the "boy pursues my ruin, he'll no peace" (III, i, 63). The world is implacable; the lovers accept its power, yet rise beyond it. Their slavery to each other, their entrapment in Vulcan's net, is for them both integrity and freedom. Their selflessness in love becomes indifference to the world and therefore control over it. Most of all, the generosity of their love—"I grow rich by giving"—creates a paradise for them even in their prison. They ascend even in captivity beyond the comprehension of the cold Octavius or the iron Ventidius. And in their ascent, so much like the canonization of Donne's lovers, they reduce all the others to much the same level.

The elevation of Antony and Cleopatra (essentially, of Cleopatra's Antony) is the more telling for the opposition it surmounts. In the first two acts, the claims of Rome and Egypt are balanced through the "rugged virtue" of Ventidius and the unheroic wiliness of the eunuch, Alexas. "Had I my wish," Alexas exclaims, "these tyrants of all nature, Who lord it o'er mankind, should perish,—perish, / Each by the other's sword . . ." (I, 71–73). In contrast, we have the Roman perspective of Ventidius:

> Oh, she has deck'd his ruin with her love,
> Led him in golden bands to gaudy slaughter,
> And made perdition pleasing . . . (I, 170–72).

Yet even in the first act, where Antony succumbs to the urgings of Ventidius, he is a fuller man than Ventidius, a man with a far greater range of emotion. He is capable of the ravings of a mad, pastoral lover, of the bitterest self-reproach, of godlike resolution against his love, but also of "soft humanity." In his greatness of soul and energy of passion, he is one with the Cleopatra who declares,

My love's a noble madness,
Which shows the cause deserv'd it. Moderate sorrow
Fits vulgar love, and for a vulgar man:
But I have lov'd with such transcendent passion,
I soar'd, at first, quite out of reason's view,
And now am lost above it. No, I'm proud
'Tis thus . . . (II, 17–23).

Here again we have the double awareness of the Vulcan's net passage: "lost above it." As Antony transcends Ventidius, so Cleopatra soars beyond Alexas, while he bears his "reason undisturbed" (II, 87). Their capacity for passion and generosity of spirit divide them from those lesser selves, their counselors, as well as from the coldness and prudence of Octavius, "Who dares not trust his fate for one great action." Again the image of soaring enters, in Antony's exasperated words:

Fool that I was, upon my eagle's wings
I bore this wren, till I was tir'd with soaring
And now he mounts above me (II, 138–40).

In the third act the world's claims confront Antony through the friendship of Dolabella, in a sense his own younger self, even more in Octavia and his children. Here the schematization is most rigid, as each claimant names his authority:

VENTIDIUS: . . . Emperor!
DOLABELLA: Friend!
OCTAVIA: Husband!
BOTH CHILDREN: Father!
ANTONY: I am vanquish'd: take me,
                  Octavia; take me, children; share me all
                  (III, 360–65).

In contrast to these increasingly mechanized claims is Cleopatra's renunciation of the world for Antony: "Now he is lost for whom alone I liv'd" (III, 467). Cleopatra meets the righteous Octavia with a mask of unsubdued pride, but as she drops it in solitude, her own "soft humanity," her capacity for generosity and her vulnerability, is the dominant note:

Then I till death will his unkindness weep
As harmless infants moan themselves asleep
(III, 481–82).

Correspondingly, the forces that act upon Antony and Cleopatra become more and more harsh, narrow, sordid. Ventidius falls to the level of Alexas in devising plots; Cleopatra submits reluctantly to her eunuch's counterplot. What has so far been moral conflict, growing more rigid and strait in the central act, has at last turned to intrigue and confused machination. Dolabella and Cleopatra cannot maintain the deceptions they are persuaded to undertake, and their integrity is thrown into new relief by their failure. Cleopatra's breast is "Transparent as a rock of solid crystal, Seen through, but never pierc'd" (IV, 201–2). Antony later describes himself as "a shallow-forded stream, Seen to the bottom" (IV, 436–37). But as Ventidius and Octavia spy, they see what they expect and want to see, proof of Cleopatra's promiscuity. Ventidius' Roman virtue comes close to savage rancor; he can behold Cleopatra's beauty "with a malignant joy"—"And, while I curse, desire it" (IV, 243, 244). The strain of Iago's embittered jealousy infects his torment of Antony, and he can malign Cleopatra—"every man's Cleopatra"—with Iago's suggestive nastiness: "You know she's not much us'd to lonely nights" (IV, 301).

In the course of the play, then, the lovers achieve heroic stature in their very defenselessness. Their abandon to love leaves them blind to others' cunning, and their integrity of heart renders them incapable of any worldly cunning of their own. Antony laments:

Why was I fram'd with this plain, honest heart,
Which knows not to disguise its griefs and weakness,
And bears its workings so outward to the world?
    (IV, 432–34.)

We may compare these words to Dolabella's earlier speech about men as "children of a larger growth":

And yet the soul, shut up in her dark room,
Viewing so clear abroad, at home sees nothing;
But, like a mole in earth, busy and blind,
Works all her folly up, and casts it outward
To the world's open view . . . (IV, 46–50).

Dolabella, in these words, discovers his soul's blindness; but he states a central issue of the play. The lovers are no longer blind to their appetites, but they have become the victims of plots that control them without their knowledge. Their generosity of spirit makes them curiously inflexible and unworldly. "Treason is there in its most horrid shape / Where trust is greatest . . ." (IV, 545–46). They are manipulated by the connivance, first of Ventidius, later of Alexas. The intrigue of the plot has thematic importance; it represents the "way of the world" that lovers "lost above it" cannot master. What gives the play strength is its insistence upon the double sense of "lost." The lovers have wrested their glory from the world, and they have lost all power in the world. They retreat more and more clearly, in the last act, into that realm of Metaphysical love where intensity outmeasures duration, and bondage to each other makes them monarchs:

> Think we have had a clear and glorious day
> And heav'n did kindly to delay the storm,
> Just till our close of evening. Ten years' love,
> And not a moment lost, but all improv'd
> To th' utmost joys—what ages have we liv'd?
> And now to die each other's; and, so dying,
> While hand in hand we walk the groves below,
> Whole troops of lovers' ghosts shall flock about us,
> And all the train be ours (V, 389–97).

In the close, the lovers at last "o'erleap this gulf of fate." They conquer themselves and the world and succeed to a new empire through death:

> See how the lovers sit in state together,
> As they were giving laws to half mankind! (V, 508–9.)

Death becomes a consummation of their love that makes them at last "Secure from human chance." The play fuses stoic power of spirit with the energy of passion and celebrates that energy at the expense of all worldly codes. Alexas, trembling for his life, offers a comic contrast to the lovers' boldness:

> Poor reason! what a wretched aid art thou!
> For still, in spite of thee,
> These two long lovers, soul and body, dread
> Their final separation (V, 134–37).

Dryden's play is a fine dialectical structure, establishing its initial contrasts of Rome and Egypt, surmounting these in the lovers' assertion of their unworldly love, then subjecting that love to the play of intrigue and counterintrigue until the world forces upon them the bolder assertion of death. The secondary characters have a pointed symmetry and schematization: Ventidius and Alexas are, in their different ways, so far beneath the lovers' generosity that they become counterparts; and Octavia and Dolabella are claimants upon an Antony who is no longer within their sphere. The play achieves the rigor of a Metaphysical poem in its opposition of giving and claiming, of soaring and netting, of love's conquest and worldly empire. And the lovers, less through robustness of individual character than through the tautness of situation, ascend from an all but foolish and ponderous rigidity to a massive integrity of will.

Flexibility, the power to accept and adapt to the world without yielding to it, marks the central figures of Congreve's *The Way of the World*. Here once more the lovers are confronted with a tangle of intrigue, but it is their skill in extricating themselves from it that we admire. They show the same skill in extricating themselves from the patterns of conduct the world imposes; their integrity is preserved by a tact that resists both the shallowness of affectation and the cruelty of blind passion. Mirabell and Millamant exist only within the framework of the play; their characters, like those of the lovers in *All for Love*, are defined by the symmetrical disposition of the other figures around them.

The most obvious foils are Witwoud and Petulant, who, like Fielding's Square and Thwackum, represent contrasting patterns of a common false wit. Petulant is the would-be man of candor, who masks no sentiment, however displeasing. He is, in fact, a bad actor even in that undemanding role, and he is soon exposed in all his vanity and hypocrisy as a man pretending to a more wholesome humor than he possesses. Witwoud is more obvious and yet more interesting. Congreve has presented him in greater depth, and he supplies the most brilliant epitome of wit without judgment. To that extent he is a fine embodiment of the way of the world in which he is a prominent parasite: his every gesture is designed to impress, and the bustling energy of the effort consumes all his powers. He is wholly dedicated to erasing his past and winning acceptance in the world of fashion on whatever terms it sets. Witwoud has his ugly traits, but he is so desperately affable, so fatuously self-congratulatory, and so transparently foolish, that he is at once somewhat shabby and altogether disarming. His harmlessness gives him a privileged status in the reader's eyes as it does in the ladies' cabals. He may remind us of the fictitious author of Swift's *Tale of a Tub*, again a desperate hanger-on, too dense to be guileful, too voluble to be subtle, a fool who gives away the game of the knaves he aspires to imitate. The cynicism of other men's epigrams, as Witwoud repeats them with an air of worldliness, becomes curiously abstract and unmotivated. When he says with a smirk, "a wit should be no more sincere, than a woman constant; one argues a decay of parts, as t'other of beauty," the effect is far different from that created by Fainall's more cruel and urgent remarks. The comparative ingenuousness of Witwoud's stylish malice underlines the strength and depth of Fainall's. Witwoud is a kind of industrious but incompetent apprentice in an inverted world. What Witwoud and Petulant dramatize so well is summed up in Mirabell's couplet at the close of the first act:

> Where modesty's ill-manners, 'tis but fit
> That impudence and malice pass for wit.

Lady Wishfort is, of course, the center of the plot. She is a tyrant, a hypocrite, and a lecherous old fool, but she exists more to be manipulated and hoodwinked than to control the situation. She, too, gives away the game by her overplaying; and there is at least a touch of pathos in the savagery with which she contests the ravage of age:

> FOIBLE: Your ladyship has frowned a little too rashly, indeed madam. There are some cracks discernible in the white varnish.
> LADY WISHFORT: Let me see the glass.—Cracks, sayest thou?—why I am errantly flayed—I look like an old peeled wall. Thou must repair me, Foible, before Sir Rowland comes, or I shall never keep up to my picture (III, i).

Like Witwoud, Lady Wishfort serves as a bathetic reduction of all the stratagems of this world. Foible remarks, "a little art once made your picture like you; and now a little of the same art must make you like your picture." Art rules nature in this world ("tenderness becomes me best—a sort of dyingness—you see that picture has a sort of a—ha, Foible! a swimmingness in the eye"). And Lady Wishfort is the kind of artist who so crushingly overwhelms nature that she somehow reveals it anew in unexpected ways. Her fondness for ratafia, her closet full of Puritan tracts, her avowed esteem for "decorums" —all these make her a torrential force of humor: her affectations and habits are borne on its surface like the debris that attests to the power of the current. In this way, Congreve frames a world in which the malice and polish are, after all, less universal than they seem. The situation anticipates that of the London of *Tom Jones,* where, beside such consummate scoundrels as Lady Bellaston, the would-be rogues like Lord

Fellamar and Jack Nightingale seem backward pupils in an exacting school. The full range of human warmth is suggested too, in the nuptials of Waitwell and Foible, the cheerful stolidity of Sir Willful Witwoud, and the generous lack of jealousy in Mrs. Fainall.

The figures who seem the masters of this world are Fainall and Marwood. It is they who have used the world with a hard and joyless egoism. Fainall, at the opening of the play, sets himself off from Mirabell by the quality of his temperament:

> FAINALL: . . . I'd no more play with a man that slighted his ill fortune than I'd make love to a woman who undervalued the loss of her reputation.
>
> MIRABELL: You have a taste extremely delicate, and are for refining on your pleasures.

The note of corruption that Fainall sounds allows us a glance ahead to such cold and perverse sensualists as Blifil; it establishes a character which is consistently presented. He can recall to his mistress the lies she has used in their behalf: "I meant but to remind you of the slight account you once could make of strictest ties, when set in competition with your love to me." And it is with reason that Marwood replies, " 'Tis false, you urged it with deliberate malice! 'twas spoken in scorn, and I never will forgive it" (II, iii). The disdain in which Fainall holds the world is best seen when he confronts Lady Wishfort with his demands, sparing her no humiliation, and finally—as he is defeated—turning upon his wife with all the malice of an outwitted Machiavel.

The case of Marwood is not much different; she wins more sympathy because the passions that possess her are less coldly egocentric. Her resentment of Mirabell's indifference has become a goad that makes her put up with a lover she seems half to hate. But, like Fainall, she flourishes in those moments when she can relieve her bitterness in the promise of pain to others; like Fainall, she needs to be revenged, and her need colors her plotting with a note of extravagant malice. She turns to an easy victim like Lady Wishfort with strong relish: "Here comes the good Lady, panting ripe; with a heart full of hope, and a head full of care, like any chemist upon the day of projection" (III, vii).

Millamant seems to sense this excess of Marwood's temper: in their scene together, she plays upon Marwood's jealousy with a cruel lightness that appears to be the only way to meet

the other's rage, and the song she calls for sounds the note of
Marwood's and Fainall's ambition:

> Then I alone the conquest prize,
> When I insult a rival's eyes:
> If there's delight in love, 'tis when I see
> That heart, which others bleed for, bleed for me.

I think that we can set Millamant's powers in this scene; she is
constantly unsettled herself by the intensity of Marwood's attitude, and she improvises until she finds the right level of malice herself to hold Marwood off and keep their relations on a
basis of ingenious insult. Even so, Marwood can scarcely
contain herself: "Your merry note may be changed sooner
than you think."

What gives the play its form is the way in which Mirabell
and Millamant can, through their own peculiar balance of wit
and generosity of spirit, reduce the bumbling Witwoud and
the mordant Fainall to the same level of false wit. Just as the
fools lack any depth of awareness and power of judgment, so
eventually the villains overplay their hands. Fainall and Marwood turn out, after all, to be victims of their own passions.
Their cynical manipulation of social convention is too assured; they cannot believe in the wit of others or in the capacity of others to elude their control. The way of the world in
which Fainall takes taunting pride is more complex than he
can understand, and his frustration, like Marwood's, exposes
the savage compulsions driving him. If at one point in the
play, Fainall's seems the most knowing view of the world, it
is finally revealed in its shallowness, a shallowness arising from
his disbelief in the reality of any being other than himself.

Mirabell and Millamant dramatize the true wit that is so
carefully and symmetrically defined through opposition. An
adequate performance of the play must present their strong
hold upon each other throughout and their resistance to the
claim that each has on the other's integrity. Unlike Dryden's
Antony and Cleopatra they do not glory in their oneness, nor
celebrate the world they have in each other. They are wary
and difficult, resenting the loss of judgment that love imposes
even as they accept it. "As for a discerning man, somewhat
too passionate a lover," Mirabell describes himself; "for I like
her with all her faults: nay, like her for her faults. . . . They
are now grown as familiar to me as my own frailties; and in
all probability, in a little time longer, I shall like 'em as well."
And Millamant's charming declaration: "Well, if Mirabell

should not make a good husband, I am a lost thing,—for I find I love him violently." These confidences do not prevent their careful and rational testing of each other and of their own chances for honesty in marriage. Millamant's affectations do not reveal her as artificial. They are clearly defensive maneuvers. She seems at every point to be inviting Mirabell to separate himself from this world and to free her from it.

In the famous proviso scene, they are fighting, humorously and banteringly but still generously, for a vision of marriage free from the cant and hypocrisy that surround them. These speeches, like the characters themselves, cannot exist except within the play that contains the Fainalls, Lady Wishfort, and Witwoud. They represent, like Mirabell's successful counter-plot, a rational intelligence playing upon the energies it cannot command but can at least direct. The lovers must find their proper order; it is hardly one of saintly abandon of the world —as in *All for Love*—nor is it simply the old order of the flesh of Fainall and Marwood given more shrewdness and lightened to rococo frivolity.

The triumph of the play is in the emergence of lovers who, through a balance of intense affection and cool self-knowledge, achieve an equilibrium that frees them of the world's power. They can use the world and reject its demands. They have assimilated the rational lucidity of the skeptical rake; they are awake to the world's ways and their own, but they are beyond any pained horror or need to wound those who have betrayed honesty. They accept what, through exploration, they have found in themselves; and they need only be sure that they can be both themselves and each other's. The quality that marks them is a critical acuteness—true wit—that is ready to submit to what, by all the rational tests they can manage, promises to be sincere and is, in any case, irresistible love.

In *The Beggar's Opera* we find once again a symmetrical disposition of characters. The play opens with a fine presentation of the inverted mercantile world of the Peachums. This world operates by the cash nexus alone, but it assumes its values with prim respectability. The tone of the play is extraordinarily complex, as William Empson has shown:[1] the Peachums present an outrageously straight-faced assertion of thorough acquisitiveness with all the false unction of bourgeois stuffiness. So straight-faced is their parody of the conduct of their betters that they create a world highly formalized and "rhetorical." Their speeches, like all those in the play, suggest

that no man can endure to think as little of himself as he deserves; all must console themselves with some form of righteous cant. Their use of this cant is so handsomely stylized
that it never quite seems the conventional self-deception men
need in real life; instead, it has, as they perform, a delicious
absurdity, with a constant undertone of bitter wit as one applies it to the actualities the play never directly admits.

This is, perhaps, a roundabout way of getting at a unique
effect. The play invites us at once to enjoy freedom from
moral judgment and accept the comic ease of this world,
where the "paradox of trade and morality" is so easily resolved into the values of trade and the gestures of morality.
In this aspect, it is like those comic and pastoral works (it was
undertaken, at Swift's urging, as a "Newgate pastoral") in
which the conflicts of moral existence are banished. Yet, at
every point, the play creates a satiric simplification of the conduct that governs the "high" world of Walpole and the court.
Neither of these aspects—the comic and the satiric—can be ignored. The pastoral simplicity is not virtue opposed to a corrupt and complex court, but corruption reduced to artless
ease, its humbug so effortless and thoroughgoing that it seems
to criticize only the ineptitude of actual hypocrites. One may
recall Pope's emphasis on the healthy freedom that dares
"laugh out"; there is a relief in the comparative decency of
frank assertion, even when it is presented by characters who
pretend not to recognize its import. Gay's method can, I think,
be traced back to such a work as Swift's *Argument against
Abolishing Christianity,* where the projector offers the comfortable meaninglessness of "nominal Christianity" in opposition to a strenuous and unreliable effort to legislate Christianity
out of existence. It is a method, as I have suggested, that
Mandeville used as well.

The Peachum household anticipates the family of Clarissa
Harlowe in its righteous distrust of the aristocrat: he is not
only dissolute, he is unpredictable, for he observes standards
they cannot admit. Polly stands out as a creature who is spontaneous and unguarded. She has been seduced by a mock
aristocrat who has lent her romances (the counterpart of
Millamant's reading in the Cavalier poets); they have opened
visions of a more generous life than her parents can conceive.
Polly's last words in the first act catch very well a self-drama-
tizing rhetoric, an unconscious identifying of herself with the
romance heroine: "O how I fear! how I tremble!—Go—but
when safety will give you leave, you will be sure to see me

again; for 'till then Polly is wretched." This note of the romantic and histrionic is present earlier, as Polly considers Macheath's possible end:

> Methinks I see him already in the cart, sweeter and more lovely than the nosegay in his hand!—I hear the crowd extolling his resolution and intrepidity!—What vollies of sighs are sent from the windows of Holborn, that so comely a youth should be brought to disgrace! I see him at the tree! The whole Circle are in tears!—even Butchers weep! (I, xii.)

There is a telling difference between this ardent mixture of alarm and erotic daydream and the crisp finality of Mrs. Peachum's, "Hang your husband, and be dutiful," or Peachum's sententious, "The comfortable estate of widowhood, is the only hope that keeps up a wife's spirits." Polly's emotion is more generous; it comes closer to the full range of human feeling than any other in the play, and it is reduced to a degree of comic unreality by its literary quality, its air of being something newly learned and not wholly mastered, however sincerely spoken. Gay makes romantic love a kind of child's masquerade in this world, as opposed to the more knowing game the elders seem to be playing.

But Polly herself suffers as the symmetry of the play develops. The second act gives us the world of the outlaw. The Gang are men who risk their lives for what they get. They depend upon each other for their safety, and their dependence builds a loyalty beyond the appeal of interest. They are at once more careless and more generous than the elder Peachums, and they live by a code of honor to which they trust their survival. It is in their swaggering boast of their purpose that their spirit of freedom is best stated:

> We retrench the superfluities of mankind. The world is avaritious, and I hate avarice. A covetous fellow, like a Jack-daw, steals what he was never made to enjoy, for the sake of hiding it. These are the robbers of mankind, for money was made for the full-hearted and generous, and where is the injury of taking from another, what he hath not the heart to make use of? (II, i.)

The opposition of avarice and generosity sets up the central contrast of the play and prepares us for Macheath's disclosure: "Polly is most confoundedly bit.—I love the sex. And a man who loves money might as well be contented with one guinea, as I with one woman" (II, iii). Just as Polly is free of the grasping avarice of her parents, so Macheath is free of the possessive loyalty of her love. He is a natural aristocrat, a man of style: "I must have women. There is nothing unbends the mind like them." And his treatment of his doxies shows a fine sense of tone, a feeling for the manner of address each must have. Macheath is even more unguarded than Polly: he is incapable of any surrender of his freedom. He has no higher use for it than to enjoy it, certainly; but his love of the sex, like his captaincy of a gang of outlaws, makes his life the more precarious. If his love of women be the "flaw" in his mock-tragic character, the pursuit of freedom is perhaps its more serious basis, and, curiously, the quality that makes him more romantic than any of Polly's daydreams. Gay insists upon him as a somewhat shabby seducer and a tavern swell, but the "high" note Macheath somewhat fastidiously borrows from Shakespeare ("If musick be the food of Love, play on," from *Twelfth Night;* and paraphrasing *Antony and Cleopatra:* "Was this well done, Jenny?") alludes to a vanished nobility as surely as do the gestures of the playing cards in *The Rape of the Lock.*

Once the symmetry of Peachum and Lockit is established, Macheath's solitary career is set between paired characters as tenacious as manacles: the mercenary fathers and the possessive daughters. "If you had been kind to me 'till death," exclaims Polly, "it would not have vex'd me—And that's no very unreasonable request (though from a wife) to a man who hath not above seven or eight days to live" (II, xiii). The girls are simpler, far less assured and deft in their intrigues, but they are in some measure their fathers' daughters. Macheath, on the other hand, for all his operatic self-dramatization and self-pity, comes to a stark awareness that is all but tragic. "That that Jemmy Twitcher should peach me, I own surpriz'd me!—'Tis a plain proof that the world is all alike, and that even our Gang can no more trust one another than other people. Therefore, I beg you, gentlemen, look well to yourselves, for in all probability you may live some months longer" (III, xiv). It is too much to say that he comes to accept his own nature as part of this world's, but the firm understatement would serve such a meaning in another kind of play.

Gay's lovers, then, seem to divide, Polly into the way of organized society, with its legal bonds and imprisoning institutions, Macheath into the way of outlawry, freedom from involvement, and therefore utter vulnerability. As Lockit puts it, "Of all animals of prey, man is the only sociable one. Every one of us preys upon his neighbours, and yet we herd to-gether." But the play cannot end so, and the beggar imposes upon it an ending such as the taste of the town requires. The beggar's manipulation is, in one sense, a symbolic selling out in key with the world he has presented.

But even before this last insistence upon artifice is made, Gay has overturned Macheath's moment of tragic eloquence with the introduction of four more wives, "with a child a-piece." Macheath dwindles from a noble solitary to a master of ineptitude, and the way is clear for a return to sentiment: "I take Polly for mine.—And for life, you Slut,—for we were really marry'd." We are back in the world of comedy, where the exceptional hero is as much fool as prophet, and where Polly's bungling goodness of heart finds its appropriate re-ward. The lovers are lovers, after all, and Macheath's seem-ing superiority to the captivity of marriage has been part of the somewhat tawdry swagger of a role too big to sustain. Polly, who has neither her parents' art nor Macheath's gran-deur, has captured this world for bourgeois romance. What gives the play part at least of its peculiar force is Gay's willing-ness to explore conflicting views to the uttermost; they must be resolved by contrivance, finally, but the contrivance seems, after all, the inevitable. Macheath is not "lost above" this world; but he has been allowed to enjoy the histrionic illusion for a while. And Polly is not simply the helpless victim of a savage world; she has the tenacity of her parents without their coldness. These characters never begin to know them-selves, nor do they control their fate; but Gay, like Fielding later, plays the just god in his creation.

III. The Mock Form

In the plays we have examined, rigidity can become a source of tragic grandeur at one level, of comic mechaniza-tion at another. The use of a single pattern with different ef-fects is inevitable in a literature that sees man as the "glory, jest, and riddle of the world." The first two terms converge on the third; man is a riddle because he is simultaneously glory and jest. The Augustans maintain the iridescence of the image of man; they deliberately create perspectives that shimmer into each other and apart again. The mock form is perhaps the finest means of achieving these double perspectives, and it is the most distinctive contribution of the age.[2] The mock form plays off a pure "view"—heroic, tragic, pastoral—against the befuddling reality from which it makes a sharp selection. The interplay of high and low, formalized and intractable, intended and accidental, has many forms, each with its own suggestions. I want to consider here the mock form in its satiric and comic aspects.

Two of the great satires of the Restoration present the forces that "wage immortal war with wit": *Hudibras* and *Mac-Flecknoe*. *Hudibras* anticipates Swift's *Tale of a Tub*; *Mac-Flecknoe*, *The Dunciad*. Concerned as these works are with wit in its largest sense—including imagination, maturity, and critical discrimination—they are first of all works of verbal criticism. The mock form begins by attacking a false language. We can see this tendency in all satire; Juvenal's first satire, for example, opposes the language of the heart to the fustian of unthinking epic imitation. And, to return once more to Plato, there is no more persistent motif in his earlier dialogues than mocking parody of false rhetoric. Dr. Johnson wrote of John Philips' burlesque, *The Splendid Shilling* (1701): "To degrade the sounding words and stately construction of Milton, by an application to the lowest and most trivial things, gratifies the mind with a momentary triumph over that grandeur which hitherto held its captives in admiration." The mock form is the most studied use of conflicting languages, and it becomes, with satire, the form in which Augustan writing finds its greatest range.

Hudibras is an attack on false wit that wittily imitates what it sets out to destroy. Its wit lies first of all in the verse. Butler's octosyllabic couplets are the perfect denial of a true verse form. Dryden found in rhyme a control over the exuberance of fancy, but Butler gives rhyme a splendid tyranny over verse form, pronunciation, and even sense:

> For rhyme the rudder is of verses,
> With which like ships they steer their courses
> (I, i, 463–64).

The four-foot line rushes toward the rhyme, and the complexity of the rhyme swallows up much of the short line:

> And pulpit, drum ecclesiastic,
> Was beat with fist instead of a stick (I, i, 11–12).

The effect prepares one for the complete unsettling of words, both as sound and meaning. The shocking analogies the Metaphysicals often justified by ingenious argument—Coleridge called them "witty logicians"—Butler achieves with an insouciant disregard of conventional restraints:

> He could raise scruples dark and nice,
> And after solve 'em in a trice;
> As if divinity had catch'd
> The itch of purpose to be scratch'd (I, i, 163–66).

The shocking analogy is usually converted by the Metaphysicals into an unexpected kind of celebration; the emphasis is on the relationship rather than the object, and the Metaphysicals employ the unlikeliest objects to define an intense commitment, a surpassing love, a transcendence of time and the world. In Butler the objects matter more, and we are constantly landing in debasing analogies. With dry common sense and extreme revulsion from the extravagances of verbal wit, Butler is turning its forms upside down.

In the same way, Butler's heroes—his fat, oafish Puritan Knight, Hudibras, and his radical Protestant squire, Ralpho—are inversions of the romance quest, snuffers-out of innocent sport, self-righteous little bigots, and self-important dunces. Their language constantly aspires to the most "romantic" and subtle philosophical vision. Ralpho is an adept in occult learning; with Pythagorean penetration

> He'd extract numbers out of matter,
> And keep them in a glass, like water . . .
> By help of these (as he professed)
> He had First Matter seen undressed:
> He took her naked, all alone,
> Before one rag of form was on (I, i, 553–54, 559–62).

Here, as later in the *Tale* or in the *Memoirs* of Martinus Scriblerus, the pure concept tumbles into a gross material image; the flight above matter becomes a wallowing in it. The Hudibrastic imagination converts downward; there is no latent heroism in Hudibras as in Don Quixote, only blundering officiousness. The form of Butler's poem constantly undercuts pretension; the language as well as the deeds is that of clumsy louts. Yet, at the same time, as in Swift's *Tale,* the louts are embodiments of a great social force, and their playing with ideas they never quite comprehend is a more serious and epidemic disease than mere clownishness. The fools cast grotesque and ominous shadows; and partly because those shadows constantly loom so high, Butler can make transparent sport of the manikins in the foreground.

In *MacFlecknoe* the august style of an epic incident is dislocated only slightly to accommodate the damaging terms:

> Shadwell alone my perfect image bears.
> Mature in dullness from his tender years:
> Shadwell alone, of all my sons, is he
> Who stands confirm'd in full stupidity (15–18).

The urbanity of Dryden's satire elevates its subject in order to dispatch it more thoroughly; the Nursery of young actors becomes "this monument of vanish'd minds," a phrase borrowed from Davenant's *Gondibert.* The force of *vanish'd* is all the more telling for conveying the dignity of the vanished past as well as the vapidity of the unhinged mind. *MacFlecknoe,* in a larger sense, catches the bathetic pride and mutual flattery of poetasters by elevating the epic hero to messianic grandeur:

> Heywood and Shirley were but types of thee,
> Thou last great prophet of tautology.
> Even I, a dunce of more renown than they,
> Was sent before but to prepare thy way (29–32).

Dryden is less interested than Butler in the furious energy and dangerous nonsense of his hero, more in the constant attrition excellence undergoes as its name is applied with insensible dislocation of its meaning to the venal and incompetent. Like Pope in *The Dunciad,* Dryden shows us how much can be preserved of the high forms while their meaning is eroded and lost. He does not, therefore, assume the tone of those he mocks for the sake of destructive parody; instead, he insists upon what has been lost and shows how minute are the outward differences between the travesty and the genuinely high.

From these examples of satiric mock form, we can turn to comic uses. The first begins, again, as a work of literary criticism. In a series of papers in the *Guardian* (April 1713; probably by Thomas Tickell) Pope's pastorals were ignored and Ambrose Philips' highly praised for their realism. Philips had followed Theocritus and Spenser rather than Virgil, and he had given images of actual rusticity at its best. For Pope, Philips' procedure was a neglect of the metaphorical nature of pastoral. Pastoral was not, as Pope saw it, the rendering of literal rusticity but "an image of . . . the golden age. So that we are not to describe shepherds as shepherds at this day really are, but as they may be conceived then to have been; when the best of men followed the employment." The question, as so often among the Augustans, involved the true nature of simplicity. Was simplicity to be attained by subtraction, that is, as primitivism; or was it properly to be found through discipline and art? Pope replied in a brilliantly ironic paper, printed unwittingly by the *Guardian* (27 April 1713), in which he offered true rusticity, with the dialect Philips affected carried to brilliant extreme:

> Rager, go vetch tha Kee, or else tha Zun
> Will quite be go, bevore c'have half a don.

At this point, presumably with Pope's encouragement, John Gay undertook *The Shepherd's Week*. In his Proeme, he mocks Philips' spurious Spenserianism: "as little pleasaunce receiveth a true home-bred tast, from all the fine finical new-fangled fooleries of this gay Gothic garniture," he offers "plain downright hearty cleanly folk." When he defends his own version of shepherds' language, Gay beautifully describes what Philips had produced:

> It having too much of the country to be fit for the court, too much of the court to be fit for the country; too much of the language of old times to be fit for the present, too much of the present to have been fit for the old, and too much of both to be fit for any time to come.

Gay's first target, like Scarron's or Butler's or Swift's, is a jargon that has lost touch with any living language, whether literary or literal. Gay composed six pastorals (the shepherds were allowed their sabbath) which, on the one hand, hold largely to Virgilian forms and, on the other, carry literal rusticity further than Philips' had done. The result is a brilliant interplay of the formality we see in Pope's pastorals with the most loutish side of rustic life: Gay chooses details deliberately, as Philips seemingly blundered into them, which will affront the high Virgilian forms. In a sense, he recovers some of the true spirit of Theocritus, who creates a humorous dissonance "between the bucolic simplicity of the pastoral and the literary refinement of the city" and, with deliberate irony, as Bruno Snell puts it, "makes his Sicilian shepherds live above their intellectual means."[3]

The effect of these poems is surprising. As Dr. Johnson wrote: "The effect of reality and truth became conspicuous, even when the intention was to shew them grovelling and degraded. These pastorals became popular, and were read with

delight, as just representations of rural manners and occupations, by those who had no interest in the rivalry of the poets,
nor knowledge of the critical dispute" (*Lives of the Poets,*
Gay). It is not so much that Gay's bumpkins are convincing
rustics as that they are curiously attractive. The affronting
details have a movement of their own, and the mock form
cuts both ways: if it protects the "pastoral vision" from a mis-
guided literalism, it also convicts the pastoral forms of a high-
minded vacuity by offering a world of robust animal energy.
Gay had Chaucer in mind as he was writing—he makes a sly
reference to *The Miller's Tale* in his notes to "Monday"—and it
is likely that not only the Miller's wife, Alisoun, but the widow's
barnyard of *The Nun's Priest's Tale* had some effect upon his
poem. Sparabella's lament, for example, in "Wednesday"
achieves a genuine country beauty:

> Though Clumsilis may boast a whiter dye,
> Yet the black sloe turns in my rolling eye;
> And fairest blossoms drop with ev'ry blast,
> But the brown beauty will like hollies last.
> Her wan complexion's like the wither'd leek,
> While Katherine pears adorn my ruddy cheek (51–56).

Her suicide is the purest bathetic anticlimax, it is true: after
considering every means,

> The prudent maiden deems it now too late,
> And 'till to-morrow comes defers her fate (119–20).

But that is as it should be: Gay's bumpkins—Hobnelia or
Grubbinol, Lobbin Clout or Cloddipole—never have enough
consciousness to be taken very seriously. At best, they are delightful children performing adult roles, and their unconscious-
ness is much of their charm. Marian's love lament in "Tues-
day" is grossly bathetic ("Ah, love me more, or love thy
pottage less!"), and its end is wonderfully apt:

> Thus Marian wail'd, her eyes with tears brimfull,
> When Goody Dobbins brought her cow to bull.
> With apron blue to dry her tears she sought,
> Then saw the cow well serv'd, and took a groat (103–6).

One could be fashionably portentous and speak of the bull as
the force of renewed life; it is enough to recognize that Gay's
rustics are continuous with the animals they tend. They remind us of that dimension of our own lives that is gratefully
earthy and unequivocally physical.

My brown Buxoma is the featest maid,
That e'er at wake delightsome gambol play'd.
Clean as young lambkins or the goose's down,
And like the goldfinch in her Sunday gown.
The witless lamb may sport upon the plain,
The frisking kid delight the gaping swain,
The wanton calf may skip with many a bound,
And my cur Tray play deftest feats around;
But neither lamb nor kid, nor calf nor Tray,
Dance like Buxoma on the first of May
        ("Monday," 49–58).

While Gay's humor keeps us outside and somewhat above
these characters they look forward—just as Macheath does—
to later, more Romantic figures. The dying Blouzelind's disposition of her few possessions ("My new straw-hat that's
trimly lin'd with green / Let Peggy wear, for she's a damsel
clean") is not so far from the narrow but intense feeling of
the people in Wordsworth's *Lyrical Ballads*. Wordsworth is
presenting them with defiance and daring us to deny their humanity (for which he was called obscure); Gay qualifies his
sympathy with a detached sense of their limitations, but there
is, at any rate, sympathy to qualify. And his account of folk
rituals, his interest in ballads and games, anticipates William
Collins' admiration for the superstitions of the Highlands. In
pushing down below the level where life is a matter of consciousness and choice, Gay comes upon that level where the
feelings and the body achieve their own artistry.

No writer seems to have read Gay with more sympathy or
to have used him so well as Henry Fielding. In *The Tragedy of
Tragedies* we encounter another mock form, a travesty of the
language of tragedy and the heroic play (see page 220).
Fielding shapes the story of Tom Thumb to admit a loving
giantess, Glumdalca, who loves in vain; a catastrophe in
which Tom is swallowed by a cow; and a heroine, Hun-
camunca, "of a very sweet, gentle, and amorous disposition,
equally in love with Lord Grizzle and Tom Thumb, and de-
sirous to be married to them both." Fielding beautifully mecha-
nizes the idiom of heroic tragedy. Doodle obligingly points out
both terms of his comparison with an inane delight in his verbal wit:

The sun himself, on this auspicious day
Shines like a beau in a new birthday suit:
This down the seams embroidered, that the beams (I, i).

Or Tom Thumb deftly fuses two of Dryden's extravagant figures to create lines like these:

> With those last words he vomited his soul,
> Which, like whipt cream, the devil will swallow down
> (III, ix).

The similes are constantly low and degrading, in the manner of Butler, but they create a countercurrent that is the most captivating element of the play. Grizzle defies his low station and defends his love for the princess with a telling argument:

> But love no meanness scorns, no grandeur fears,
> Love often lords into the cellar bears,
> And bids the sturdy porter come upstairs (II, v).

The sturdy porter, when he comes up, will find the chimney sweep; as Tom casts off "the bloody garment of battle" to claim his love, he exclaims:

> So when some chimney-sweeper all the day
> Hath through dark paths pursu'd the sooty way,
> At night, to wash his hands and face he flies,
> And in his t'other shirt with his Brickdusta lies (I, iii).

Against the background of this knockabout parody of the heroic play—with its echoes of a hundred latter-day Almanzors—Fielding creates the world of porters, chimney sweepers, Bridewell wenches (I, vi), apprentices vying for a whore (II, viii), seamstresses (II, ix), streets with swollen gutters and gushing spouts. The violent incompetence of the play suggests that the actors have written it themselves and drawn these images from their own lives. The heroic roles have fallen to urchins and clowns, and the streets of London are more vividly before us than King Arthur's court or even the tragic theater.

Hogarth painted at about the same time "Children playing *The Indian Emperor* before an audience" (1731–32, collection of the Earl of Ilchester, London); but they are eminently respectable children entertaining their families. Fielding's children have the rowdy delight that provides a low counterpart to the natural energy of the travestied heroes; and Fielding insists upon the wholesome obscenity that rejects the lifeless fustian of third-rate heroics. And in the midst of grotesque lowness there are sudden moments of beauty, as in the second of these lines:

>   Ha! the window-blinds are gone;
> A country-dance of joy is in your face,
> Your eyes spit fire, your cheeks grow red as beef (II, iv).

London, Mandeville's great bustling city, comes into Augustan poetry most tellingly in the mock pastoral and the mock georgic. Swift's *A Description of Morning* (1709) finds counterparts in the city for the conventions of pastoral; as Aurora leaves the bed of Tithonus,

>   Now Betty from her master's bed has flown,
> And softly stole to discompose her own (3–4).

The innocent shepherd becomes the corrupt gaoler:

>   The turnkey now his flock returning sees,
> Duly let out a-nights to steal for fees (15–16).

In place of gentle showers, we have apprentices sprinkling shop floors, in place of breezes the whirling mop, in place of birdsong the "cadence deep" of the coal seller and "shriller notes of chimney sweep." The little picture composes itself without much satire; people awaken together and form a harmony of which they are unaware. We end with the traditional schoolboys who "lag with satchels in their hands."

Most of these people are involved in some elaborate social situation: the maid who sleeps in her master's bed, the "slipshod prentice," the "duns at his Lordship's gate." All the creatures here are human, as are all the noises; but their unconscious harmony shows them as if they were birds or sheep, contributing their natural sounds without thought or concern. Again, we have moved below the level of full consciousness and choice, as we do in Mandeville's picture of London.

In *A Description of a City Shower* (1710), a poem he much preferred, Swift cites the *Georgics* as his model. It is a poem about managing life in the city, and, in the georgic tradition, it treats the common labor of man as a work of dignity. This encourages the heroic simile, and we have the beau pent up in his sedan chair while the rain pelts its leather roof:

>   So when Troy chair-men bore the wooden steed.
> Pregnant with Greeks impatient to be freed,
> (Those bully Greeks, who, as the Moderns do,
> Instead of paying chair-men, run them thro'.)
> Laoco'n struck the outside with his spear,
> And each imprison'd hero quak'd for fear (47–52).

The tone of Hogarthian swagger and squalor runs through the poem:

> Meanwhile the South rising with dabbled wings,
> A sable cloud athwart the welkin flings,
> That swill'd more liquor than it could contain,
> And like a drunkard gives it up again (13–16).

The elegant "poetic diction" of sable cloud and welkin builds toward the coarse descent in true burlesque fashion. And the poem suggests a harsh equation between the people drawn together by a sudden shower ("Triumphant Tories and desponding Whigs, / Forget their feuds, and join to save their wigs") and the torrent of rubbish swept down together through the open sewers:

> Sweepings from Butchers' stalls, dung, guts, and blood,
> Drown'd puppies, stinking sprats, all drench'd in mud,
> Dead cats and turnip-tops come tumbling down the flood
> (61–63).

But Swift is more amused than horrified by women in shops pretending "to cheapen goods" or the spruce young law student thriftily loitering under cover while he "seems to call a coach." He has caught the Londoners momentarily disarmed, their masks slipping if not dropped. And he describes the excrement of the city without the anguish of those young romantics who discover—in his later poems—that even their fair mistresses obey those few necessities that cannot be sublimated. Here Swift fits the grubby details within the pretentious forms he detests—the triplets with a final Alexandrine that Dryden had used so often in sublime effects—and makes of the verse form itself an example of those "artificial lights and false mediums" in which the soft imagination retreats from the actual where it can.

John Gay's city georgic is called *Trivia: or, The Art of Walking the Streets of London* (1716), and he confesses he owes "several hints of it to Dr. Swift." Gay devotes three books to the labors of getting safe and clean through the streets of the great city; and at every point he elevates the terrors of the streets to full epic height. Even the small dangers that beset one's footing are given the grandeur of generality:

> The sudden turn may stretch the swelling vein,
> Thy cracking joint unhinge, or ankle sprain (I, 37–38).

These epic terrors establish the humble heroism of the naïve honest man who walks alone through the streets of a busy scene of industry. In contrast to his walker's innocence is the sordid mercenary dishonor of those who roll by in threatening coaches.

Gay writes as a somewhat fatuous author, anxious for fame, whose poverty makes him one with his innocent. He identifies himself with his hero's honesty, eager to flatter the readers of his guidebook, and also ready to rationalize his own poverty as an excess of virtue:

> May the proud chariot never be my fate,
> If purchas'd at so mean, so dear a rate;
> O rather give me sweet content on foot,
> Wrapt in my virtue, and a good surtout! (II, 587–90.)

The poem has a complex tone. The author is one of those men who know the city so well because they have been poor in it; he seeks to impress the newcomer with his wisdom and the importance of his advice; he has genuine moral feelings but he has public sentiments, too, and no clear sense of which he is voicing. As a result, a note of ironic mockery is cast over the celebration of innocence; Gay seems really to be of the city and to love its vigor and color, for all the attitudes he strikes against its dangers.

The stalls spill over with riches; and Gay's London images have the same freshness that we find in *The Shepherd's Week:*

> The golden-bellied carp, the broad-finn'd maid,
> Red-speckled trouts, the salmon's silver jowl,
> The jointed lobster, and unscaly sole,
> And luscious 'scallops (II, 414–17).

> Walnuts the fruiterer's hand, in autumn, stain,
> Blue plums and juicy pears augment his gain
>   (II, 433–34).

>   where oyster-tubs in rows
> Are rang'd beside the posts; there stay thy haste,
> And with the sav'ry fish indulge thy taste:
> The damsel's knife the gaping shell commands,
> While the salt liquor streams between her hands
>   (III, 190–94).

The most characteristic note of the poem is the aesthetic response to the city's variety and energy. Gay sees the fish as color and form and smell; he precisely catches the vendors' hands immersed in their produce.

When Gay turns to what might be a scene of horror, he finds instead the brilliant accident, and he gives it shape by poising it with ludicrous aptness against the heroic myth that was once the vehicle of the marvelous. In the Great Frost of 1709–10, when the Thames was frozen over for three months, Doll, the applewoman, had the misfortune of falling through the ice:

> The cracking crystal yields, she sinks, she dyes,
> Her head, chopt off, from her lost shoulders flies;
> Pippins she cry'd, but death her voice confounds,
> And pip-pip-pip along the ice resounds.
> So when the Thracian furies Orpheus tore,
> And left his bleeding trunk deform'd with gore,
> His sever'd head floats down the silver tide,
> His yet warm tongue for his lost consort cry'd;
> Eurydice with quiv'ring voice he mourn'd
> And Heber's banks Eurydice return'd (II, 389–98).

Gay is delighted with the studied incongruity of Orpheus and the applewoman; his city creatures, like those of his mock pastoral, play out the traditional roles with coarse but charming indifference. Gay can see here, as in *The Shepherd's Week,* the pathos of their limited imagination and their contracted dreams. His little bootblack is full of maudlin self-pity, cast in a language of elegant inanity; but his meager aspirations have genuine pathos:

> At length he sighing cry'd; That boy was blest,
> Whose infant lips have drain'd a mother's breast;
> But happier far are those, (if such be known)
> Whom both a father and a mother own:
> But I, alas! hard fortune's utmost scorn,
> Who ne'er knew parent, was an orphan born!
>   (II, 177–82.)

> Had I the precepts of a Father learn'd,
> Perhaps I then the coach-man's fare had earn'd,
> For lesser boys can drive; I thirsty stand
> And see the double flaggon charge their hand,
> See them puff off the froth, and gulp amain,
> While with dry tongue I lick my lips in vain (II, 187–92).

The mock form opens up new dimensions of experience. Its emphasis on what these people are not is a way of discovering with sympathy and precision what in fact they are. Their submoral animal energy makes the large forms they cannot fill seem irrelevant. They point up in a new way the rigidity we have seen in Dryden's Antony and Cleopatra; and they remind us how much of life lies outside the realm of the preconceived forms. Just as Chaucer's Chauntecleer saves his life by changing from the pompous courtly hero to a wily peasant of a cock who can outwit a shrewd fox, so Gay's bumpkins and cits, and his London itself, insist upon the life that lies below high intention, with little mind for choice but an overwhelming power of survival.

Gay's London is a dangerous place for the innocent, but not so dangerous, we are made to feel, as Gay must sententiously pretend. It is a rewarding place for rogues, but against the sordid villains in high coaches we can set the brisk rascals who were to appear in *The Beggar's Opera*. It is most of all a brilliant spectacle of people and things—presented with all the hum and glisten of a great hive or the motion and shimmer of the pike pond. Gay is not interested in character here, and his people are much like his things; but he is interested in the force of their being, at whatever level, and its reality. His London is the home of the unheroic man (although he may, like Macheath, assume the airs of a hero, at least for a while). It embodies those vices the moralist must always chastise and seek to contain; it falls far short, as Mandeville insistently reminds us, of the order of charity. Yet it is the home of the "contingent, messy, boundless, infinitely particular, and endlessly still to be explained."[4] In *Hudibras* or *MacFlecknoe, A Tale of a Tub* or *The Dunciad* we see the satirist holding up to scorn the formless that offers itself as a substitute for the rationally controlled. In these comic works, the emphasis moves the other way, and exposes the hollowness of the tyrannical ideal—or shrugs it into inconsequence—and celebrates the energy that always overflows order or streams around its categories.

IX.

The Divided Heart

1. Defoe's Novels

The rise of the novel in the eighteenth century is the triumph of the particular, however we may explain the novel's coming into being. Two major tendencies feed into the central event. The mock heroic of Cervantes and his followers subjects the heroic image to the punishing presence of the commonplace. And the marvelous is naturalized as the saint's life, the rogue's picaresque career, the pilgrimage of the individual soul, are all enmeshed in the business of daily existence. The heroic may survive its punishment, but it takes on a new form. The allegorical translucency of the saint's life or of the pilgrim's progress may survive to some extent, but saint and pilgrim alike have now become first of all people with familiar names and addresses, with aunts and cousins, and the elaborate costume of a social existence. Saints become Clarissa Harlowes; pilgrims become Robinson Crusoes; and rogues become—instead of the resilient heroes of a hundred escapades —characters disclosed in the long, disorderly memoirs of Moll Flanders.

The triumph of the particular is the triumph of formal realism, a realism used to a different degree and for a different end by each of the great novelists of the century. The novel provides a spacious vehicle, with its slow rhythm of disclosure, its opportunities for dialogue, description, commentary. None of these is new in itself. They appear in epic, in romance, and in the genres of drama—but the mixture is new. The novel allows a rapid alternation between the character's internal thought and his action; between his view of himself and the author's view of him; between the intense scrutiny and the panoramic view. The novel gains fluidity by its prosiness. It sacrifices the concentration of poetic language for a new fusion of the poetic and the documentary, and for a more

thoroughgoing involvement of the significant in the circumstances where it must find its life and from which it must wrest
its values. The novel is the medium in which we can see the
spirit of man in its most problematic form—not in lucid contests of principle but (in Lionel Trilling's words) "as it exists
in the inescapable conditions which the actual and the trivial
make for it" (*The Opposing Self,* New York, 1955, p. 75).

Defoe's novels—written late in a career given over to jour-
nalism and pamphleteering—have always been a puzzle to
the critic. Defoe draws upon forms of autobiography as far
apart as criminals' sensational narratives of their careers and
Puritan preachers' records of their transactions with God and
the devil, factual narratives of sea discoveries, and pious
accounts of miraculous providences. Running through this
compound is the troubled conscience of a Puritan tradesman,
aware of the frequent conflict between the demands of commercial gain and those of spiritual salvation. It is this troubled
conscience that gives his characters their depth. They are
tremendously efficient and resourceful in meeting the difficulties of their "trade," and Defoe catches the excitement of
their limited but genuine art. But they are also nagged by doubt
and a sense of guilt, by an awareness of what they have ignored or put by in their single-minded commitment. These
pangs are not, in most cases, very effectual, but they are none
the less authentic. Defoe's characters participate, as often as
not, in what Iris Murdoch calls the "dialectic of those who
habitually succumb to temptation."

In the novels I shall consider Defoe gives us the great myth
of the isolated man bringing order out of unfamiliar materials
(the first part of *Robinson Crusoe*), the outlawry of a woman
whose social isolation makes her a freebooter in the center of
London (*Moll Flanders*), and the recovery of a man from
the life of crime into which he is plunged as a child (*Colonel Jack*).[1] All these characters aspire to some kind of morality; all have a glimpse of some idea of redemption. Without
these aspirations, they would be near successors to the picaresque heroes of countless jestbooks, coming through dangerous scrapes with wily dexterity. If the aspirations had fuller
control of their natures, they might become the heirs of those
spiritual heroes who find their way at last from the City of
Destruction to the Land of Beulah. But their lives remain
curiously unresolved and open. As Ian Watt has said, "Defoe
presents us with a narrative in which both 'high' and 'low' motives are treated with equal seriousness: the moral continuum

of his novels is much closer than was that of any previous fiction to the complex combination of spiritual and material issues which moral choices in daily life customarily involve" (*The Rise of the Novel*, p. 83).

Defoe remains a puzzle because he imposes little thematic unity on his materials. Usually the writer who is content to give us the shape of the tale itself has a shapely tale to tell; a tale with its own logic, its awakening of tensions and expectations, its mounting repetition, its elaborate devices for forestalling too direct a resolution, and its satisfying—perhaps ingeniously surprising—way of tying all its threads in one great stroke. Such a tale need not leave those gaps in its narrative that are occasions for us to consider its meaning or theme. In Defoe's narratives the inconsistencies are such that we want to find a significant design, yet they hardly accommodate our wish.

Some critics have found consistent irony in a work like *Moll Flanders* by trimming away troublesome details, hardening the central character, and importing a moral stridency Defoe does not invite. Dorothy Van Ghent finds in Moll "the immense and seminal reality of an Earth Mother, progenetrix of the wasteland, sower of our harvests of technological skill, bombs, gadgets, and the platitudes and stereotypes and absurdities of a morality suitable to a wasteland world." This seems to me at once a great deal more fastidious and more vehement than the attitudes that underlie Defoe's conception of his heroine. The fact that Moll measures her success by money does not necessarily mean that money is her only object. Nor does Moll's indifference to the sensuousness and concrete texture of experience make her "monstrously abnormal" (*The English Novel: Form and Function*, New York, 1953, p. 43).

Moll Flanders is the chronicle of a full life-span, told by a woman in her seventieth year with wonder and acceptance. In one sense, she is the product of a Puritan society turned to worldly zeal. Hers is very much the world of the Peachums, and in it Moll is the supreme tradeswoman, always ready to draw up an account, to enter each experience in her ledger as profit or loss, bustling with incredible force in the market place of marriage, and finally turning to those bolder and franker forms of competitive enterprise, whoredom and theft. To an extent, she is the embodiment of thrift, good management, and industry. But she is also the perverse and savagely acquisitive outlaw, the once-dedicated servant of the Lord turned to the false worship of wealth, power, success.

Her drive is in part the inevitable quest for security, the island of property that will keep one above the waters of an individualistic, cruelly commercial society. Born in Newgate, left with no resources but her needle, she constantly seeks enough wealth or a wealthy enough husband to free her from the threat of poverty and the temptations of crime. But she finds herself fascinated by the quest itself, by the management of marriages, the danger of thievery. When she has more money than she needs, she is still disguising herself for new crimes, disdaining the humble trade of the seamstress. When she finally settles into respectability, it is with a gentleman, not a merchant; her husband is a rather pretentious, somewhat sentimental highwayman, who is not much good as a farmer but is a considerable sportsman. Moll is no simple middle-class mercantile figure; nor is she another Macheath. Yet she has elements of both.

There is still another dimension of Moll Flanders. Her constant moral resolutions, her efforts to reform, her doubts and remorse cannot be discounted as hypocrisy or even unrealistic self-deception. Moll is a daughter of Puritan thought, and her piety has all the troublesome ambiguities of the Puritan faith. Her religion and morality are not the rational and calculating hypocrisy of the simple canter—the Shimei of Dryden's *Absalom and Achitophel,* for example. They are essentially emotional. She has scruples against incest, but they take the form of nausea, physical revulsion. She intends virtuous behavior and is astonished to discover her hardness of heart. Moll's life is a career of self-discovery, of "herself surprised," surprised by herself and with herself. Just as for the earlier Puritan, the coming of grace might be unpredictable, terrifyingly sudden, and very possibly deceptive, so for Moll the ways of her heart are revealed to her by her conduct more than by her consciousness, and even her most earnest repentance arouses her own distrust until it can well up into an uncontrollable joy. Personality is not something created or earned; the self is not the stable essence the Stoic moralist might seek. It is something given, whether by God or the devil, always in process, eluding definition and slipping away from rational purpose. Even at her happiest, with the man she has long missed, and in the late autumn of her life, Moll can think of how pleasant life might still be without him. It is a wayward thought, a momentary inclination, as real as her devotion and no more real.

What we find in Moll Flanders is not an object lesson in Puritan avarice or in the misuse of divinely given talents. Moll has all the confusion of a life torn between worldliness and devotion, but what remains constant is the energy of life itself, the exuberant innocence that never learns from experience and meets each new event with surprise and force. Moll, like the secularized Puritanism she bespeaks, has the zeal that might found sects as well as amass booty, that might colonize a new world as readily as it robbed an old one. And the form of the old zeal, now turned into a secular world, needing the old faith at least intermittently as the new devotion to the world falters with failure, gives us a pattern of character that is one of the remarkable creations of fiction. Defoe, we are told, seems not to judge his material; Defoe must be a brilliant ironist. Both assertions imply a set of values thinner and more neatly ordered than Defoe can offer. He is aware of the tension between the adventurous spirit and the old piety; he can see the vitality of both religious zeal and worldly industry; the thrifty efficiency and the reckless outlawry that are both aspects of the middle-class adventure; the wonderful excitement of technology as well as its darker omens. And seeing all of this, he does not seem to see the need to reduce these tensions to a moral judgment. Like Mandeville, who struts much more in the role, he is one of the artists who make our moral judgments more difficult.

Ultimately, one might call Defoe a comic artist. The structure of *Moll Flanders* itself defies resolution. In giving us the life-span, with its eager thrust from one experience to the next, Defoe robs life of its climactic structure. Does Moll face marriage to the brother of her seducer, a seducer she still loves? It is an impossible tragic dilemma. Yet the marriage takes place, the husband dies, the children are placed; and Moll is left taking stock as she enters the marriage market again. Does she face the dreadful fact of incest? This, too, passes away; she cannot reconcile herself to it, but she can make a settlement and depart in search of a new and illegal marriage. The commonplace inevitably recurs; we have parodies of tragic situations.

Moll herself is not contemptible in her insensitivity. She is magnificently unheroic; and yet there is a modest touch of heroism in her power of recuperation, her capacity for survival with decency. In her curiously meaningless life, there is a wonderful intensity of experience at a level where affection, inclination, impulse (both generous and cruel) generate all the motions that are usually governed, or perhaps simply accompanied, by a world of thought. We have Defoe's own account of this process in his *Serious Reflections of Robinson Crusoe* (iv):

> There is an inconsiderate temper which reigns in our minds, that hurries us down the stream of our affections by a kind of involuntary agency, and makes us do a thousand things, in the doing of which we propose nothing to ourselves but an immediate subjection to our will, that is to say, our passion, even without the concurrence of our understandings, and of which we can give very little account after 'tis done.

This way of reading *Moll Flanders* imposes its own straitening on the untidy fullness of the book. Ian Watt has made a decisive case for the comparative artlessness of Defoe; there are too many wasted emphases, too many simple deficiencies of realization to make the case for deliberate irony tenable. But one can claim for Defoe a sensibility that admits more than it can fully articulate, that is particularly alert to unresolved paradoxes in human behavior. Watt dismisses in passing the parallel of a work like Joyce Cary's *Herself Surprised*. There is point in this dismissal, for Cary has raised to clear thematic emphasis what is left more reticent in Defoe. Yet the relationship is worth exploration. Few writers have been so fascinated as Cary with the ambiguities of the Protestant temper. In a great many characters—among them the statesman, Chester Nimmo, in the political trilogy and the evangelical faith-healer Preedy in the last novel, *The Captive and the Free*—Cary studied the shimmering iridescence with which motives seem, from different angles, dedicated service and the search for grace or the most opportunistic self-seeking. Cary was not interested in "rationalization" but in the peculiar power achieved by the coincidence of religious zeal and imperious egoism. Preedy, for example, seduces a young girl and makes her virtually his slave; but he is convinced that his power to win her love is a sign of grace—that a love so undemanding and undeserved as hers can only be a sign of God's love in turn. Preedy is monstrous in one aspect, terrifying but comprehensible in another; the difference lies in what we recognize to ʰᵤ nis object.

Cary's effects are so adroit and so carefully repeated that

we have no doubt about calling them ironic. Defoe's are less artful and less completely the point of his tale. Yet his awareness of them seems no less genuine. Defoe's characters have secularized old Puritan modes of thought. Moll Flanders is constantly taking inventory and casting up her accounts as she faces a new stage of her life. Crusoe, too, keeps an account book, and, more like the earlier Puritans, an account book of the soul. The doctrine of regeneration, we are told, caused the Puritans "to become experts in psychological dissection and connoisseurs of moods before it made them moralists. It forced them into solitude and meditation by requiring them continually to cast up their accounts."[2] In the diary, particularly, the Puritan might weigh each night what he had experienced of God's deliverance or of Satan's temptation during the day. "It was of the very essence of Puritan self-discipline that whatsoever thoughts and actions the old Adam within had most desire to keep hidden, the very worst abominations of the heart, one must when one retired to one's private chamber at night draw into the light of conscience. . . . Having thus balanced his spiritual books, he could go to bed with a good conscience, sleep sound and wake with courage."[3]

The "other-worldliness" of Puritan theology was, as Perry Miller puts it, "a recognition of the world, an awareness of a trait in human nature, a witness to the devious ways in which men can pervert the fruits of the earth and the creatures of the world and cause them to minister to their vices. Puritanism found the natural man invariably running into excess or intemperance, and saw in such abuses an affront to God, who had made all things to be used according to their natures. Puritanism condemned not natural passions but inordinate passions" (p. 42).

This concern with the uses of things places emphasis not on their sensuous fullness but on their moral function, and the seeming bleakness of Defoe's world of measurables derives in part from this. Characteristically, when Defoe in his *Tour* praises the countryside, it is for what man has made of it: "nothing can be more beautiful; here is a plain and pleasant country, a rich fertile soil, cultivated and enclosed to the utmost perfection of husbandry, then bespangled with villages; those villages filled with these houses, and the houses surrounded with gardens, walks, vistas, avenues, representing all the beauties of buildings, and all the pleasures of planting. . . ." So, too, the natural scene of Crusoe's island "appeals not for adoration, but for exploitation" (Ian Watt, p. 70).

It is not the things we care about but the motives or energies they bring into play: they may satisfy needs, or call forth technical ingenuity, or present temptations. The physical reality of sensual temptation need not be dwelt upon, for moral obliviousness or self-deception is Defoe's concern (as in the account of Moll's going to bed with the Bath gentleman). If Moll's inventories seem gross, they may also be seen as the balance of freedom against necessity; poverty is the inescapable temptation to crime. And her inventories are, in an oblique sense, still account books of the spirit.

What might once have served the cause of piety becomes a temptation to exploitation. This is the dialectic of which Perry Miller speaks: the natural passion insensibly turns into the inordinate passion. Each of Defoe's central characters at some point passes the boundary between need and acquisitiveness, between the search for subsistence and the love of outlawry. And it is only in the coolness of retrospect that they can see the transgression. Defoe does not play satirically upon their defections; he knows these to be inevitable, terrifying so long as they can be seen with moral clarity, but hard to keep in such clear focus. His characters live in a moral twilight, and this leads to Defoe as a writer of comedy.

We must also keep in mind the essential optimism of the Puritan creed. The Puritans could not, Perry Miller tells us, sustain the tragic sense of life. "They remembered their cosmic optimism in the midst of anguish, and they were too busy waging war against sin, too intoxicated with the exultation of the conflict to find occasional reversals, however costly, any cause for deep discouragement. . . . Far from making for tragedy, the necessity [for battle] produced exhilaration" (p. 37). The battle against sin is not, of course, the only battle in which Defoe's characters are involved, but the struggle in the world demands the same intense concentration and affords the same exhilaration. If there is any central motive in Defoe's novels, it is the pleasure in technical mastery: the fascination with how things get done, how Crusoe makes an earthenware pot or Moll Flanders dexterously makes off with a watch. The intensity of this concentration gives an almost allegorical cast to the operation, as if Crusoe's craftsmanship had the urgency of the art by which a man shapes his own soul. It is beside the point to complain that these operations are "merely" technical and practical; undoubtedly the man who invented the wheel had beside him a high-minded friend who reproached him with profaning the mystery of the circle by putting it to such menial uses. The delight in mastery and in problem-solving may be a lower and less liberal art than those we commonly admire, but it is a fundamental experience of men and a precious one.

Even more, the energy of spirit that is concentrated in these operations is a source of joy. One might wish that Moll Flanders had founded a garden suburb with the force she gave to robbing a child, and at moments she feels so too; but the strength she brings to the demands of life is at worst a perversion of the spiritual energy the Puritan seeks to keep alive. It is in doing that he finds himself and serves himself, and Moll Flanders reaches the lowest point of her life when she falls into the apathy of despair in Newgate: "I degenerated into stone, I turned first stupid and senseless, then brutish and thoughtless, and at last raving mad as any of them were; in short, I became as naturally pleased and easy with the place as if indeed I had been born there." She loses her sense of remorse:

> a certain strange lethargy of soul possessed me; I had no trouble, no apprehensions, no sorrow about me, the first surprise was gone. . . . my senses, my reason, nay, my conscience, were all asleep . . . (VIII, 94).

In contrast is the recovered energy that comes with her repentance:

> I was covered with shame and tears for things past, and yet had at the same time a secret surprising joy at the prospect of being a true penitent . . . and so swift did thought circulate, and so high did the impressions they had made upon me run, that I thought I could freely have gone out that minute to execution, without any uneasiness at all, casting my soul entirely into the arms of infinite mercy as a penitent (VIII, 105).

These moments of spiritual despair and joy have their counterparts in her secular life as well. After the death of her honest husband, she is left in poverty:

> I lived two years in this dismal condition, wasting that little I had, weeping continually over my dismal circumstances, and as it were only bleeding to death, without the least hope or prospect of help . . . (VII, 199).

With the pressure of poverty and the temptation of the Devil, she commits her first theft and runs through a tortured circuit of streets:

> I felt not the ground I stepped on, and the farther I was out of danger, the faster I went. . . . I rested me a little and went on; my blood was all in a fire, my heart beat as if I was in a sudden fright: in short, I was under such a surprise that I knew not whither I was going, or what to do (VII, 201).

This is the energy of fear, but it is a return to life; and before many pages have passed, Moll is speaking with pleasure of her new art.

The benign form of this energy is that of the honest tradesman whom Defoe always celebrates: "full of vigor, full of vitality, always striving and bustling, never idle, never sottish; his head and his heart are employed; he moves with a kind of velocity unknown to other men" (*Complete English Tradesman*, II [1727], i, 106–7). As R. H. Tawney has written, "a creed which transformed the acquisition of wealth from a drudgery or a temptation into a moral duty was the milk of lions" (*Religion and the Rise of Capitalism*, London, 1926, ch. IV, iii). Yet, as Tawney recognizes, the older Puritan view of the evil of inordinate desires still survived. Defoe may call gain "the tradesman's life, the essence of his being" (*CET*, II, i, 79–80), but gain makes it all the harder for a tradesman to be an honest man: "There are more snares, more obstructions in his way, and more allurements to him to turn knave, than in any employment. . . . [For] as getting money by all possible (fair) methods is his proper business, and what he opens his shop for . . . 'tis not the easiest thing in the world to distinguish between fair and foul, when 'tis against himself" (*CET*, II, i, 33–34, 35). This candid recognition of the traps of self-deception leads Defoe to a considerable degree of tolerance. He cites the Golden Rule, "a perfect and unexceptionable rule" which "will hold for an unalterable law as long as there is a tradesman left in the world." But, he goes on, "it may be said, indeed, where is the man that acts thus? Where is the man whose spotless integrity reaches it?" He offers those tradesmen who "if they slip, are the first to reproach themselves with it; repent and re-assume their upright conduct; the general tenor of whose lives is to be honest and to do fair things. And this," he concludes, "is what we may be allowed to call *an honest man;* for as to perfection, we are not looking for it in life" (*CET*, II, i, 42).

More fundamental is the "paradox of trade and morality" that Defoe recognizes as well as Mandeville: "the nation's prosperity is built on the ruins of the nation's morals"; or, more cogently, "It must be confessed, trade is almost universally founded upon crime." By this Defoe means what Mandeville means: "What a poor nation must we have been if we had been a sober, religious, temperate nation? . . . The wealth of the country is raised by its wickedness, and if it should be reformed it would be undone" (*CET,* II, ii, 105, 108, 106). Of luxury, Defoe could write "However it may be a vice in morals, [it] may at the same time be a virtue in trade" (*Review* III, 65–66). As Hans H. Anderson (from whose study I have drawn several of these quotations) points out, Defoe does not try to shock his readers as Mandeville does by insisting upon the irreducible paradox; he tends to abstract issues and to exclude "ethical considerations by the simple expedient of restricting his discussion to what he called the 'Language of Trade.' "[4] But, although Defoe does not take pleasure in the difficulties he creates for the moralist, he shows a keen awareness of the difficulties his characters encounter.

When Robinson Crusoe voices his satisfaction with his island, he finds it a place where the dangerous paradox is happily resolved.

> I was removed from all the wickedness of the world here. . . . I had nothing to covet; for I had all that I was now capable of enjoying. . . . There were no rivals; I had no competitor. . . . But all I could make use of was all that was valuable. . . . The most covetous griping miser in the world would have been cured of the vice of covetousness, if he had been in my case; for I possessed infinitely more than I knew what to do with (I, 142–43).

In short, Crusoe's island is the utopia of the Protestant Ethic (as Ian Watt puts it[5]) in a double sense. It is a place where Crusoe holds undistracted to his work and where his work is rewarded; but it is a place, too, where his tradesmanlike energy remains innocent, with no danger of inordinate desires leading to dishonesty. Only in the overambitious project of the *periagua* does Crusoe exceed the limits of utility, and the only consequences are the futility of wasted effort.

All of Defoe's other major characters yearn at one time or another for this freedom from the "necessity" embodied in temptation. The only other character who comes close to Crusoe's freedom is Colonel Jack in his management of slaves. Jack is concerned with the exploitation of his fellow men. Jack's master, the slaveowner, must exact obedience in order to realize the value of his property, but he would prefer to win voluntary service. Jack introduces a policy of mercy that wins the obligation of gratitude from the slave, Mouchat, and thus Jack reconciles trade (or here expediency) with morality and eliminates cruelty:

> if they were used with compassion, they would serve with affection as well as other servants . . . but never having been let taste what mercy is, they know not how to act from a principle of love (X, 166–67).

Significantly, when Jack encounters a slave who will not learn this desirable lesson, he sells him off (X, 185); he can achieve his reconciliation only within the limits of the plantation, as Crusoe can his only in the isolation of his island kingdom. Both these scenes are, in effect, islands of ideal social order.

Later, when Jack is instructed in religious matters, he is made to see how God's mercy acts upon all men just as his own mercy has worked upon the slaves. The sense of mercy "seizes all the passions and all the affections, and works a sincere unfeigned abhorrence of the crime as a crime, as an offence against our Benefactor, as an act of baseness and ingratitude to Him who has given us our life . . . and who has conquered us by continuing to do us good when He has been provoked to destroy us" (X, 193). The "scholar" who instructs Jack proposes, somewhat in the spirit of Shaftesbury, that if men could see with full clarity the nature of both heaven and hell, "the first would have a stronger and more powerful effect to reform the world than the latter" (X, 194). This conception of a grateful man rejoicing in a merciful God is an ideal vision that Defoe would like to sustain. "But," as Jack remarks as he leaves home to wander in the world, "man is a short-sighted creature at best, and in nothing more than in that of fixing his own felicity, or, as we may say, choosing for himself" (XI, 107). We are back to Crusoe's "original sin" of leaving his father and the middle station of life, and in fact to all those expansive, restless efforts that are both the glory of the tradesman and the occasion for his temptations. The alternatives to this energy may be deadness of spirit or that serenity that at last confers "the leisure to repent." This leisure is given Defoe's characters intermittently in the course of their lives; only with age is it steadily achieved. Only after seventy-two years of a "life of infinite variety" does Crusoe fully "know the value of retirement, and the blessing of ending our days in peace."

Defoe's characters are all technicians, rational masters of their art, on one level, and creatures of impulse or obsession on another. When the young Robinson Crusoe hears his father's moving speech about the need to keep to the middle station of life, he is—as he tells us—"sincerely affected with this discourse . . . and I resolved not to think of going abroad any more, but to settle at home according to my father's wish." Then follows that verb that runs through Defoe's novels: "But alas! a few days wore it all off . . ." (I, 5). When a year later he goes to Hull, it is done "casually, and without any purpose of making an elopement that time"; yet on a sudden prompting he finds himself on board a ship bound for London. After escaping a dreadful storm that reveals all the horror and dangers of a life at sea, Crusoe is divided: he cannot face the shame of returning home, but he is still vividly aware of his career as a Jonah:

> An irresistible reluctance continued to going home; and, as I stayed awhile, the remembrance of the distress I had been in wore off; and as that abated, the little motion I had in my desires to a return wore off with it, till at last I quite laid aside the thoughts of it, and looked out for a voyage (I, 16).

This pattern is typical: the power of the impulse or obsession, the lack of clear decision; conflicts are settled in Crusoe or for him, not by him. Throughout his stay on the island, we see these fluctuations. Is the island a prison, or is it a deliverance from the sinful life he led in the world? Is the fate God has brought upon him an act of divine goodness, or is it fearfully inscrutable? All the trust he has achieved deserts him when he finds the footprint in the sand, and it is slowly regained. As he turns to Scripture and lights upon a telling verse, he finds comfort. "I thankfully laid down the book, and was no more sad," he tells us; and then adds, "at least, not on that occasion" (I, 175). There is always this note of reservation in Defoe's characters—as they prudently conceal some part of their fortune or story. It may be a note of mistrust, but, even more, it shows a sense, in the midst of joy or pleasure, that the mind of today need not be that of tomorrow, and perhaps cannot.

Moll Flanders, like Crusoe, is a creature of mixed and unstable motives. She goes to Bath, she tells us, "indeed in the view of taking what might offer; but I must do myself that justice as to protest I meant nothing but in an honest way, nor had any thoughts about me at first that looked the way which afterwards I suffered them to be guided" (VII, 106–7). It is sincere enough, but the moral twilight is clear, too. She lodges in the house of a woman "who, though she did not keep an ill house, yet had none of the best principles in her self" (VII, 107). When she has become the mistress of the gentleman she meets at Bath, she remarks that their living together was "the most undesigned thing in the world"; but in the next paragraph she adds: "It is true that from the first hour I began to converse with him I resolved to let him lie with me" (VII, 121). The surprise has come in finding that what she had been prepared to accept through economic necessity, she has encouraged through "inclination."

Earlier in America, when Moll discovers that she is married to her brother and the disclosure drives him to attempt suicide, she casts about:

> In this distress I did not know what to do, as his life was apparently declining, and I might perhaps have married again there, very much to my advantage, had it been my business to have stayed in the country; but my mind was restless too, I hankered after coming to England, and nothing would satisfy me without it (VII, 104).

Here, too, the motives are a wonderful mixture of concern, prudence, and impulse. What is most remarkable about Moll Flanders is her untroubled recognition of her motives, her readiness to set them forth with detachment, at least to the extent that she understands them. She recalls those Puritans who scrutinize their motives as if they were spectators beholding a mighty drama. When Moll robs a poor woman of the few goods that have survived a fire, she records:

> I say, I confess the inhumanity of the action moved me very much, and made me relent exceedingly, and tears stood in my eyes upon that subject. But with all my sense of its being cruel and inhuman, I could never find it in my heart to make any restitution: the reflection wore off, and I quickly forgot the circumstances that attended it (VIII, 14).

Fielding was to make something beautifully ironic of this kind of mixture of motives. Defoe uses it differently; candor disarms the moral judgment that irony would require. The stress is more upon the energy of impulse than upon its evil. And the energy is such that it can scarcely be contained by a single motive or be channeled long in a consistent course.

II. Clarissa and Lovelace

In Samuel Richardson's *Clarissa* (1748) the theme of the divided heart—or in Clarissa's own phrase, the "unexamined heart"—is given formal rigor and tragic consequences.[6] Clarissa's elevation of spirit arouses fear and jealousy in her family; and, as the Harlowes impose their will more and more cruelly, Clarissa finds herself drawn to Lovelace. Her desires to reclaim his faulty nature and to escape her family combine to make her Lovelace's victim. Once he has raped her, she puts beneath consideration all earthly solutions to her plight. She chooses to die, to become the bride of Christ; and her coffin becomes her marriage bed.

Lovelace is trapped by Clarissa in turn. He is a libertine who cannot endure the hindering of his will; he needs to control and subdue others, and he finds tremendous, almost sexual, pleasure in deceit and disguise. Yet there is an element of self-hatred in Lovelace, too, that attracts him to virtue. He must disprove its existence or be conquered by it, and he hardly knows which he wishes the more. The appeal of Clarissa is precisely her power to resist, and thus to conquer him; but he must test her to the utmost. If he can have her on his own terms, he will have preserved his old identity and shown up the claims of a higher order. If he is conquered by her, he will find a new identity; and it is clear that he half hopes this may happen. But the rape destroys both possibilities; in taking Clarissa by force, he has not conquered her will, and his effort to resolve the problem by offering her marriage only wins her scorn.

After the rape, Clarissa moves toward sainthood, and Lovelace discovers the emptiness of his satanism. She is now hopelessly "above" him. The orders of being have been completely sundered, and there is no possible reconciliation. The power of the book comes of the terrible force that each of these two characters exerts on the other. Each makes the other a supreme instance of a moral type. They are led to absolute self-assertion, and they "stand in contrast," as Alan D. McKillop puts it, "to many of the surrounding characters who are bogged down in convention and give automatic responses, facile and superficial answers to the questions that beset the principals."[7]

Lovelace is one of the great characters of English fiction,

and we can begin to understand him by looking back to the Restoration heroes. "Lovelace inherits the cynicism and the fluency of the fashionable libertine of Restoration comedy," McKillop observes. "But he is also the superman of the heroic play; he has the lawless egotism common both to the heroes and the villains of the genre."[8] Dryden is Lovelace's favorite poet, and he quotes from *The Conquest of Granada, Aureng-zebe, Tyrannic Love,* and *Don Sebastian.* Like the Restoration heroes, Lovelace has a skeptical distrust of the false order that the world conspires to maintain. Like Almanzor or Dorax, he despises cant and hypocrisy. Of the Harlowes he writes (I, 144): *"soul!* did I say—there is not a soul among them but my charmer's." His difficulties with them arise from his refusal to be "a sly sinner, an hypocrite." He scorns those *"tame spirits* which value themselves upon reputation, and are held within the skirts of the law by political considerations only" (II, 22). When he defends his conduct against his converted and repentant friend, Belford, he can point to the way of the world:

> Out upon me for an impolitic wretch! I have not the art of the least artful of any of your Christian princes, who every day are guilty of ten times worse breaches of faith: and yet, issuing out a manifesto, they wipe their mouths, and go on from infraction to infraction; commit devastation upon devastation; and destroy—for their glory! And are rewarded with the names of *conquerors,* and are dubbed *Le Grand;* praised, and even deified, by orators and poets, for their butcheries and depredations (IV, 451).

One need not take Lovelace's protestations at face value, but one must recognize an aspect of generosity in his defiant boldness. He is a liberal landlord who refuses to rack his tenants. He spends money lavishly, but never to the point of losing his independence of his family. He and Belford, even as libertines, recognize "the noble simplicity, and natural ease and dignity," of the Scriptures, and Lovelace finds Scriptural quotations in the works of modern authors who seek to appropriate them "like a rich vein of golden ore which runs through baser metals" (IV, 6). There are moral grounds, in short, for Lovelace's disdain of conventional respectability. Is he worse in his treatment of Clarissa than was "the *pious* Aeneas" in his behavior to Dido? Or the good Protestant Elizabeth in her behavior to Mary of Scotland? "Come, come,

Belford," he concludes, "I am *comparatively* a very innocent man" (IV, 30–31).

Much of this is pretext and self-justification, but by no means all. Like many libertines Lovelace has an impossible standard of goodness. When he cites Mandeville, he refers to him as his "worthy friend" (III, 145); and, like Mandeville, he makes the idea of virtue so remote and unattainable that men must despair of achieving it. But Lovelace is not so untroubled as Mandeville. While he glories in his contrivances and in his deception of Clarissa, he is still scarcely able to control his impulse to surrender to her. He snatches her hand and violently exclaims, "take me, take me to yourself; mould me as you please; I am wax in your hands; give me your own impression, and seal me for ever yours. We were born for each other!—you to make me happy, and save a soul—I am all error, all crime" (II, 81). He boasts to Belford that this is all play-acting, that he played the role so intensely because he could scarcely control his passion at the time (I, 98–99). But a few days later he finds himself proposing marriage "by an involuntary impulse, in defiance of premeditation, and of all his proud schemes" (II, 142). Later, he looks at Clarissa's tearful uplifted face and asks himself, "And can I be a villain to such an angel!—I hope not" (II, 187).

As libertine, Lovelace is consistently naturalistic. He invokes a barnyard analogy to describe the lover: "he struts over her with an erected crest, and with an exulting chuck-a chuck-aw-aw-w, circling round her with dropped wings, sweeping the dust in humble courtship" (II, 68). And while he dwells on his treatment of Clarissa as the taming of a caged bird, he invokes a larger view of natural cruelty, with Hobbesian overtones: "How usual a thing is it for women as well as men, without the least remorse, to ensnare, to cage, and torment, and even with burning knitting-needles to put out the eyes of the poor feathered songster" which "has more life than themselves (for a bird is all soul)" (II, 247). The cynicism with which Lovelace regards his fellow men ("Have I not often said *that human nature is a rogue,*" II, 498) betrays the bitterness of disappointment, even of moral outrage.

In his treatment of Clarissa, it is impossible to separate the sexual excitement Lovelace finds in her resistance from the moral excitement he finds in her virtue. He must prove to himself that she is only a woman, and women have never finally been able to resist him. But he senses the disaster that impends: "Why was such a woman as this thrown in my way, whose very fall will be her glory, and perhaps not only my shame, but my destruction?" (III, 146). And the torture increases. "By my soul, I cannot forgive her for her virtues! There is no bearing the consciousness of the infinite inferiority she charged me with. But why will she break from me, when good resolutions are taking place? The red-hot iron she refuses to strike—Oh, why will she suffer the yielding wax to harden?" (III, 154.) When the pressure of her virtue becomes more than he can endure, Lovelace resorts once more to the reductive explanation: " 'Tis pride, a greater pride than my own, that governs her" (III, 175).

When, after the rape, Clarissa refuses marriage, Lovelace at last confronts what he has both yearned and feared to see: "Such irresistible proofs of the love of virtue *for its own sake,*" he tells her, "did I never hear of, nor meet with, in all my reading" (III, 222). It is to this theme he constantly returns:

> Oh, my damned incredulity! That, believing her to *be* a woman, I must hope to *find* her a woman! Oh, my incredulity that there could be such a virtue (virtue for *virtue's* sake) in the sex, founded I my hope of succeeding with her (IV, 323).

Clarissa comes, at last, to accomplish her purpose of awakening him out of his "sensual dream" (IV, 437). He still fluctuates between the resurgent libertine, hectically defiant and skeptical, and the repentant worshiper, possessively trying to make Clarissa his own even after her death—"Clarissa Lovelace let me call her" (IV, 525). But he dies completely possessed by Clarissa, as much her captive as she had been his: "Look down, Blessed Spirit, look down!" (IV, 530).

Lovelace's pride and need to control others are only one aspect of his nature. The other is the vacuity his self-assertion and swagger have been used to conceal. The weakness of Lovelace's pride (Clarissa has remarked on this) is made clear in the final scenes. "Oh the triumphant subduer," he exclaims. "Ever above me! And now to leave me so infinitely below her!" He can examine his heart at last: "to bring her down from among the stars . . . that my wife, so greatly above me, might not despise me; this was one of my reptile motives, owing to my *more* reptile envy, and to my consciousness of inferiority to her!" (IV, 323.)

The character of Clarissa has been more fully explored by critics, and there has been growing agreement about the nature of Clarissa's "unconscious duplicities." We can never assume, Ian Watt points out, that any statement she makes "should be taken as the complete and literal truth." Until "the book is half done . . . we are fully entitled to suspect Clarissa herself of not knowing her own feelings" (*The Rise of the Novel*, p. 229). Or as Dr. Johnson put it, "there is always something which she prefers to truth." If Richardson seems at times to deny this weakness in his heroine, we can invoke Leslie Fiedler's formula: Richardson knows what she really feels "though he does not quite know he knows it." The result of this "happy state of quasi-insight" is that Richardson "never falsifies the hidden motivations of his protagonists" (*Love and Death in the American Novel*, New York, 1960, p. 31). Certainly one feels that Richardson is more accurate than his rather prim consciousness might have been expected to permit.

Clarissa is clearly attracted by Lovelace, and for good reason. His generosity and recklessness are in marked contrast to the tight, ritualized, status-seeking regimen of the Harlowes. Even his intrigues, which show him in a shabbier aspect, make him the counterpart of a Restoration comic hero in a world of shoddy hypocrites more culpable than himself. In such a world, Clarissa tries to maintain independence and freedom of choice. But she herself is a person of strong will, who terrifies her mother and is capable of a measure of malice to her genuinely malicious sister. One discovers only gradually the full degree of Clarissa's complicity in encouraging Lovelace's clandestine letters. Her motives are not necessarily what they seem to herself. Her friend Anna Howe can recognize Clarissa's incipient love for Lovelace before Clarissa is ready to face it. "Yet, my dear," Anna writes, "don't you find at your heart somewhat unusual make it go throb, throb, throb, as you read just here! If you do, don't be ashamed to own it. It is your *generosity*, my love, that's all" (I, 46).

Clarissa's "native generosity and greatness of mind" (as Anna Howe puts it, I, 45) only stimulate the repressiveness of the Harlowes. The ugly and rich Solmes whom the Harlowes would force Clarissa to marry is their own counterpart:

> Mr. Solmes appears to me (to all the world indeed) to have a very narrow mind and no great capacity: he is coarse and indelicate; as rough in his manners as in his person: he is not only narrow, but covetous: being possessed of great wealth, he enjoys it not; nor has the spirit to communicate to a distress of any kind. . . . Such a

man as this, *love!* Yes, perhaps he may, my grandfather's estate (I, 158).

Clarissa becomes the victim of the materialism as well as the willfulness of the Harlowes; she is left no room for self-assertion except in flight. Lovelace vows that his only object is "to restore [her] to her own free will" (I, 442).

The suffering of Clarissa becomes the cause of her greatness. She comes to recognize and acknowledge the feelings that have controlled her. Just as Lovelace is reveling in his successful deception of Clarissa, she is writing to Anna Howe of her trust in him and confessing her affection: "I think I could prefer him to all the men I ever knew, were he but to be always what he has been this day. You see how ready I am to own all you have charged me with, when I find myself out" (II, 225). But in the fragments she writes in distraction after the rape, she strikes a deeper vein. To her sister, she writes:

> I thought, poor proud wretch that I was, that what you said was owing to your envy.
> I thought I could acquit my intention of any such vanity.
> I was too secure in the knowledge I thought I had of my own heart.
> My supposed advantages became a snare to me.
> And what now is the end of all?

We are perhaps too eager today to see Clarissa accepting dark motives that have been hidden within her before. She does, certainly, acknowledge her pride and stubbornness of will as well as the appeal of Lovelace's frankness and generosity. But what she most dramatically accepts is responsibility for what has happened. She refuses Lovelace's offer of marriage, and she preserves her freedom now in the only way she can, by her readiness to die: "She who fears not death is not to be intimidated into a meanness unworthy of her heart and principles!" (III, 274.) "The man whom once I could have loved, I have been enabled to despise," she writes. "My will is unviolated." She has won through to integrity: "No credulity, no weakness, no want of vigilance, have I to reproach myself with. I have, with grace, triumphed over the deepest machinations" (IV, 186). As Lovelace puts it, "has not her triumph over me, from first to last, been infinitely greater than her sufferings from me?" (IV, 261.) Her triumph is completed, however, not with despising Lovelace but with forgiving him. It is a generous forgiveness in which she acknowledges once more that she "could have loved him" (IV, 306).

There is a danger, in reading Richardson, of allowing facile sophistication to displace more essential awareness. Richardson, like Defoe, seems a writer whose sensibility outruns his conscious art, and it is tempting to impose our own clearer designs upon what he has produced. Several critics have turned his novel into a great Puritan myth of love, as if we were to encounter, in Clarissa and Lovelace, after a long journey through time, the great ancestors. To do this is to import into the novel an historical awareness that may be enormously compelling, as it is in Leslie Fiedler's discussion, but that tends to obscure the response the novel demands in its own terms. We may prefer our historical myth to the novel Richardson wrote, but we should know we are making a choice. And I am not sure that it is the right choice.

The ambiguous motivations of Richardson's characters are the stuff of which tragedy is made, and we must respect this tragic possibility. Is it more apt to say that Clarissa "courts sexual violation as well as death" (Watt, p. 253) than to say that an Oedipal Hamlet courts failure as well as death? Perhaps. Richardson is no Shakespeare. Yet the evidence for Clarissa's unconscious desires looks more impressive when it is collected in lists of stock symbols than it does when it is examined in context. Again and again we have the savage irony of Clarissa's defense of her freedom exciting Lovelace's possessive desire. It is Lovelace who brings a febrile sexuality to the scenes he describes:

> she wildly slapped my hands; but with such a sweet passionate air, her bosom heaving and throbbing as she looked up to me, that although I was most sincerely enraged, I could with transport have pressed her to mine (III, 239).

This moment follows upon the notorious passage where Clarissa asks for death: "Then, baring, with a still more frantic violence, part of her enchanting neck, Here, here, said the soul-harrowing beauty, let thy pointed mercy enter" (III, 238).

Clarissa, six days after the rape, has just tried to escape from the brothel where Lovelace is holding her prisoner. He has seized her at the door and brought her back, "choked with grief and disappointment." Richardson has the dramatic shrewdness to make her desperation take the form of sexual provocation for Lovelace, and the force of the scene seems to me divided if one makes Clarissa a counterpart of Pope's Eloisa, a woman tempted by the very passions she is trying to fight. We must accept, with whatever difficulty, the fact that Clarissa, who at the outset was a robust and marriageable young woman of strong feelings, has begun the process of moving toward sainthood. She has accepted more than her share of guilt for making the abduction and the rape possible, and, having asserted an heroic degree of responsibility, she has begun the defense of her integrity that is the only expiation allowed her. McKillop has pointed out the importance in the last half of the novel of "isolation as an essential part of the tragedy of personality" (*Early Masters*, p. 74).

Clarissa displays a certain artistry in improving the pathos of her final situation; but the pathos comes from the inability of either Lovelace or, more important for her, the Harlowes, to recognize her nature. She has been driven by the world about her into the purest realization of the order of charity. Except for Belford, there is no one to see what she has become. Lovelace is all too aware at intervals of her terrifying superiority, but he must bury this haunting awareness by explaining it away in natural terms. He even hopes that she has become pregnant so that nature will overcome her austere principles, "all her cant of *charity* and *charity*." The Harlowes are locked up in the self-righteousness that is a nasty travesty of what Clarissa has genuinely attained. The loneliness of Clarissa's condition cannot be overstressed. If she prepares herself as the bride of Christ we need not shake our heads with post-Freudian condescension; she is herself making clear the disjunction between kinds of love, between the order of charity and Lovelace's order of the flesh or the Harlowes' love of power.

Richardson holds surprisingly well to the balance between Clarissa's triumph and her tragic catastrophe. One must think back to those protracted but intense scenes of family council, or to the confidences with Anna Howe, to recall how vividly Richardson has made Clarissa an actual personality. It is because she is so sharply presented in characteristic speech and gesture, strong in will and limited in self-awareness (far more limited than Anna Howe, and a forerunner of such later heroines as George Eliot's Dorothea Brooke and Henry James's Isabel Archer) that her emergence through suffering to sainthood seems a waste of powers as well as the discovery of new ones. Lovelace begins by regarding her quizzically, as a "charming frost-piece" and an exciting challenge. He ends in a state of absolute awe, with the dying word "Blessed." Clarissa has ascended above the possibilities of earthly life, and Richardson uses figures like Anna Howe and Hickman to make clear the severity, even cruelty, of this ascent as well as its glory. (One may recall T. S. Eliot's less successful treatment of a comparable instance, the bizarre martyrdom of Celia Coplestone in *The Cocktail Party*.)

Richardson has transformed highly particularized characters so that their dense and familiar social setting fades away in the course of the slow disclosure of consequences. The Harlowes and Lovelace represent a conflict of social classes, and Clarissa—like Polly Peachum—the rebellion of feeling against righteous bourgeois acquisitiveness. Unlike Polly, Clarissa is of divided mind; she still honors the filial relationship, even when her father has morally failed its demands. It is hard to make *Clarissa* into the great Bible of the bourgeoisie; the sinister nature of middle-class success has never been more harshly presented than in the Harlowes.

Nor can we properly draw out of Clarissa's defense of her integrity as a person a myth of bourgeois sexual morality. Dorothy Van Ghent has proposed that "Clarissa's whiteness, her debility, and her death are correlatives of the sterilization of instinct and the impotence that are suggested as the desirable qualities of family and social life" (*The English Novel*, p. 60). Leslie Fiedler has written brilliantly about those "secret scriptures" that the popular novel becomes, "holy books" in which "the Pure Young Girl replaces Christ as the savior, marriage becomes the equivalent of bliss eternal, and the seducer is the only Devil" (pp. 10–11). One can surely recognize the stereotypes that both critics trace back to their origins in Richardson, but the fact that they may have their origins there does not mean that they are what Richardson has created. Clarissa's withdrawal into sainthood is not offered as the pattern of the good woman in the world. There is little reason to assume "sterilization of instinct" in the marriages of Anna Howe and Hickman or of Charlotte Montague and Belford. Richardson's moralizing is oppressive, and he tends to displace charity into chastity; but the novel *Clarissa* succeeds in making charity its genuine concern and all else its "inescapable conditions."

X.

Fielding: The Comedy of Forms

"You see the man of education, the gentleman, and the
scholar, sporting with his subject—its master, not its slave"
—Byron, of Fielding.

"What an absurd thing, that fear of the self in literature:
fear of talking of oneself, of being interested in oneself,
of showing oneself. (Flaubert's need of mortification
made him invent that false, that deplorable virtue.)"
—André Gide.

I. The Energies of Virtue

Unlike Defoe and Richardson, Fielding shows no desire to
achieve minute realism. He does not provide the illusion of
actuality that allows the reader to participate immediately in
the lives of his characters. We may sympathize with Fielding's
characters, but we are always aware of them as characters
and of the novels as novels. Whatever we see in Fielding's
world is filtered through his own telling; his arrangement, his
commentary, and his idiom control our awareness throughout.
Coleridge speaks of Fielding's "unrealizing his story, in order
to give a deeper reality to the truths intended." "Unrealizing"
is a good term. It reminds us that Fielding was not a primitive,
clumsily extending the periodical essay into the novel; he was
almost what we would call today an anti-novelist, playing
games with an already established art of realistic narrative—
in Byron's words, "sporting with his subject—its master, not its
slave." A great writer finds his peculiar subject through his
form, and Fielding's games are what bring his subject into
existence. That subject is the problematic nature of human
goodness: the puzzles and confusions involved in defining it,
the deceptions made possible by the inwardness of virtue, the
curiously anti-heroic nature of its power, dependent on Fortune for its worldly success, easily hoodwinked and slandered,

generously reckless in its refusal to obey the world's law of succeeding by becoming its opposite.

Fielding is an Augustan writer first of all. He moves in a new direction; but more than any other figure he provides the fulcrum for the century. He is less intense and original than Swift before him or Sterne later, but he holds in remarkable balance the virtues of both. The central theme in Fielding's work is the opposition between the flow of soul—of selfless generosity—and the structures—screens, defenses, moats of indifference—that people build around themselves. The flow is the active energy of virtuous feeling; the structures are those forms that are a frozen travesty of authentic order. Fielding's satire builds upon the beautiful demonstrations by Swift and Pope of the logic of forms. *A Tale of a Tub* gives us a world of dress, in which the soul has dwindled to a suit of clothes worn with slavish adherence to the rules of fashion. *The Dunciad* gives the empire of vacuity, the usurpation of true Order by a goddess who exists only because she is worshiped. Fielding rarely elevates his theme to this level of mythical generality and dignity; he gives us, instead, a world of artifice and easy rationalization whose quintessence (as we see in both *Tom Jones* and *Amelia*) is the masquerade. Nor does this world require great villains. It is a disenchanting world where moral triviality can account for the horrors we commonly ascribe to demonic forces.

In his presentation of generosity Fielding goes beyond the typical balance of the Augustans. There are intimations of Fielding's theme in Gay's Macheath; and Pope—particularly in the Horatian Epistles—dramatizes "the flow of soul." But Fielding celebrates feeling in a more radical and unguarded manner. He takes from Shaftesbury the defense of a natural goodness in man that needs no threats or bribes and the celebration of an image of God as perfect goodness rather than as unsearchable mystery, formidable power, or irascible judgment. But Fielding frees Shaftesbury's neo-Stoic vision of its anticlerical or deistic implications. Instead, he fuses it with the views of those Latitudinarian churchmen who rejected Hobbes and offered a vision of man naturally delighting in good ("virtuously voluptuous," as Isaac Barrow put it) and strengthening his faith in the practical exertions of charity. "That man believes the gospel best," Archbishop Tillotson preached, "who lives most according to it."[1]

Fielding appeals to this natural goodness in man, but he also recognizes that man needs the sanctions of Christian revelation to give his good nature stability and confidence. Divine punishment and reward are not so much threat and bribe as the necessary corrective to the apparently meaningless injustice of the world. They justify goodness rather than coerce it. And once Fielding has established the radical simplicity of charity, he can say, in effect, with Pascal, "truth apart from charity is not God, but His image and idol, which we must neither love nor worship" (*Pensées*, 582).

Fielding wants to show that man is naturally prepared to lead a Christian life. A life of charity may make the severest demands upon him, but it makes its demands upon *him;* that is, upon man as he is naturally constituted and not as he becomes through some violence upon his nature or through some heroic sacrifice that only a few can hope to achieve. Therefore Fielding vehemently attacks those rigorists who make the possibility of achieving goodness seem remote or hopeless. (Mandeville seems to take sardonic pleasure in insisting upon the impossibility of attaining virtue, whereas Swift, as we have seen, tries to mitigate, through politics, the difficulty of meeting its inescapable obligation.) Those who "preach up mortification and self-denial," Fielding writes, "may insinuate that a man cannot be good and happy at the same time, and may deny all merit to all actions which are not done in contradiction to nature; but I say, with Dr. Barrow, *Let us improve and advance our nature to the utmost perfection of which it is capable,* I mean by doing all the good we can; and surely that nature which seems to partake of the divine goodness in this world is the most likely to partake of the divine happiness in the next. To speak a solemn truth, such natures alone are capable of such beatitude" (*Covent-Garden Journal,* ed. G. E. Jensen, New Haven, 1915, No. 29, I, 309).

This seems genial and optimistic, and to an extent it is. But the effect of it is to remove those pretexts by which men postpone accepting the clear injunctions of the gospels. "The camel has been discussed," André Gide once wrote, "the eye has been discussed, the needle has been discussed, and people have above all discussed to find out to what degree the rich man could or could not approach the kingdom of God. Yet what is more luminous than the word of the Gospel."[2] Like the Augustan satirists, Fielding sees the preposterousness of this evasion of goodness. And the methods of evasion are his constant object of scrutiny: the withdrawal into legality and dogma, the sophistry of bad faith, the careful preservation of a code too exalted to use. All these forms of self-justification Fielding renders with ironic courtesy; he is detached enough to make us see through them with ease, but he is attentive enough to their logic to make us respect its formal rigor. His subject is what Hazlitt calls "the farce of respectability," but the farce touches, too, in its elaboration of a mock order, on the Augustan theme of the tragedy of mind.

It is in the energy of virtue that Fielding finds men's fulfillment. *"In the energy itself* of virtue (says Aristotle) *there is great pleasure;* and this was the meaning of him who first said, *that virtue was its own reward. . . .* we may extend the observation of Aristotle to every human passion: for in what but in the energies themselves, can the pleasures of ambition, avarice, pride, hatred, and revenge be conceived to lie?" Their reward lies in "the labor itself," and why should this not be true, Fielding asks, of benevolence too. "Why should this most lovely of all mistresses be pursued, not for her native charm, but for the fortune which she is to bring us?" (*Covent-Garden Journal,* No. 29, I, 308.) This Shaftesburian emphasis does not, as I have said, preclude Fielding's belief in Christian doctrine. But, significantly, the Christian doctrine may only confirm the unlimited openness of virtue: "a glorious consideration to the virtuous man," Fielding wrote earlier (*Champion,* 4 March 1739–40, *Works,* XV, 230), "is that he may rejoice even in the never attaining that which he so well deserves, since it furnishes him with a noble argument for the certainty of a future state." Or, again, good-nature is "the only affection of the human mind which can never be sated" (*Works,* XV, 260). Fielding regards good-nature or charity much as his contemporaries were beginning to regard the creative imagination: as a force in itself more precious than any of its acts, and a force that could never be satisfied with those limited performances in which it expressed itself. The acts of goodness are essential, for Fielding, as a check upon hypocrisy or self-deception: the sentiments are not enough, for they fester into pride if they are not constantly put to practice. Yet it is not acts themselves that are the ultimate value but "the strong energies of a good mind" (*TJ,* XIII, i).[3]

This openness of virtue makes all morality problematic. Motives are hard to penetrate, even for their possessors. The existence of laws tempts men to self-righteous adherence to their letter rather than a generous pursuit of their spirit. What I have spoken of, in connection with Pope's *Essay on Man,* as the fluidity of relatedness is precisely what the existence of structures of order tends to block. Like Pope, Fielding finds a solution in the idea of the duty to the Whole. While he sees no necessary correspondence between rank and virtue, Fielding does accept the hierarchies of an existing social structure. His interest lies not in reordering society but in re-establishing the basis of its conduct. If men were genuinely subject each to the other, they would find their interest in the common good and would regard the powers of rank only as a greater responsibility to serve. The freezing of men into status (professions, classes) or the massing of them into mobs blocks this sense of oneness and mutual subjection. The task, as always, is to hold them to the claims they are so easily tempted to evade.[4]

But this solution, while essential in Fielding's thinking, does not hold the center of his attention. The problematic nature of morality does. His novels, whether or not he meant them to, shocked many of his contemporaries by disturbing their moral assurance. Miss Mulso (later Mrs. Chapone) writes with comparative assurance at first: "Is there not a tendency in all his works to soften the deformity of vice, by placing characters in an amiable light that are destitute of every virtue except good nature?" "Precisely," one can imagine Fielding replying. But Miss Mulso has a more fundamental difficulty—he is unsettling: "Fielding contrives to gloss over gross and monstrous faults in such a manner that even his virtuous readers shall call them frailties." We know that Lady Mary Wortley Montagu and Dr. Johnson were troubled too. William Cobbett, in 1829, could ask: "How is it possible for young people to read such a book [as *Tom Jones*], and to look upon orderliness, sobriety, obedience, and frugality, as *virtues?*"[5] The point, of course, is that each of these virtues can become a vice and does (they are an admirable catalogue of the qualities of Fielding's rogues)—so long as it is not informed by generosity and benevolence. Fielding has attempted nothing less than a fundamental redefinition of virtue—and to redefine it, he must dissociate the inessentials.

Fielding insists upon the difficulties. He demands that we take the full risk of dissociating true charity from moral conventionality. This becomes sharpest in his treatment of love. Presenting figures of innocence and goodness who are young, careless, naïve, and spontaneous—free of all the impostures of their graver elders—he insists, like Gay, upon the relationship between sexual warmth and charitable love. His fundamental concern is with generosity, and he builds up a contrast be-

tween the cold tight self-love of Blifil or the calculating debauchery of Colonel James and the natural vigor that, like the
heart itself, outruns the control of prudence. Joseph Andrews
preserves his chastity, but with more difficulty in the case of
Fanny than of Lady Booby. Tom Jones does not. Booth falls
into adultery. But what is common to all these instances is the
motif that is so clear in Dryden's heroic plays and *All for
Love*: only the man of strong feeling can achieve the generosity of spirit that rejects the partial and restrictive views of
more cautious or selfish men. This feeling need not take a
sensual form, as we see in Parson Adams or Amelia (neither
of whom disdains sexual pleasure, it should be noted); but in
the young hero it naturally does. Such vigor is a lesser force
than the fury of Almanzor or the towering splendor of Antony, but it is also fresher and more attractive—in Tom Jones,
at least—than its counterpart in Mirabell or Macheath. Fielding has transposed scale once more by introducing an element
not too far above the mock-pastoral rusticity of Gay's *Shepherd's Week*. Joseph and Tom may turn out to be gentlemen
after all, or nature's noblemen, but they are at home in the
pasture and they fight best with fist or cudgel.

Fielding is, like the Augustans, trying to define an ideal order of mind. It is in the order of mind, existing as it does
within that field of contrary attractions, between the order of
flesh and the order of charity, that the human situation must be
most clearly faced. If it can bring into harmony these seemingly disjunct orders, it will make possible a morality that is
both of this world and beyond it. The typical Augustan problem, as for Pascal, is to destroy the self-sufficient rationalism
that abstracts from experience those principles of which an
elegant logical structure can be built. Such rationalism becomes a source of pride that cuts man off from the pieties
and the sentiments that are rightly his, and its critics posit a
subtler, more intuitive order of mind that is at once head and
heart, thought and feeling. As Sterne preached later, "What
divines say of the mind, naturalists have observed of the body;
that there is no passion so natural to it as love,—which is the
principle of doing good" (*Sermons*, Shakespeare Head Edition, Oxford, 1927, I, 63). Nowhere do these puzzles become
sharper than in the nature of love, at once self-seeking and
self-transcending, predatory and generous, passionate and contemplative. Its capacity for conversion, from desire to disinterested reverence, has been the stuff of myth and philosophic
metaphor at least since Plato.

Fielding's treatment of love is another attempt to find an inclusive view of man's nature. Like Pope, he sees the reconciliation of self-love and the generous, outflowing love of mankind. In his famous chapter, "Of Love," in *Tom Jones* (VI, i), he judiciously sifts the elements that make up the "passion of Love." It is telling that he reclaims the term "passion" (as elsewhere he speaks of "the glorious lust of doing good" or "the heart that hungers after goodness") and separates the passion of *love* from "the desire of satisfying a voracious appetite with a certain quantity of delicate white human flesh." He grants that love, as he conceives it, will "call in the aid of that hunger" and that love heightens "all its delights to a degree scarce imaginable" to men who have mere sensual appetite alone. Love, moreover, seeks "its own satisfaction as much as the grossest of all our appetites." These concessions to the "mixed" nature of the passion of love go far beyond the emphasis we find in Shaftesbury (although not beyond Shaftesbury's full, balanced views) and are close in spirit to the inclusiveness we find in Pope's *Essay on Man*.

In return for these concessions, Fielding establishes his claims for the conversion of appetite. There exists "in some (I believe many) human breasts a kind and benevolent disposition, which is gratified by contributing to the happiness of others." This disinterested benevolence is a cause of "great and exquisite delight," which may be "heightened and sweetened by the assistance of amorous desires" but need not be. "Esteem and gratitude" fuse with the amorous desires and give them stability that can outlive youth and beauty (we may think here of Swift's poems to Stella). Fielding's argument is a homely version of the old reconciliation of the terrestrial and the celestial Venus; its emphasis is not the original Platonic one on the falling away of the lower order of appetite as the soul ascends but on the fusion in the active business of life of these orders. Shaftesbury had insisted upon man's natural capacity for the disinterested love of goodness and argued for it in the facts of aesthetic experience. Pope had shown man's inherent capacity for social love awakened by the necessities of forming a social order to curb his selfishness. This empirical bent is the reply to the Hobbesian or Mandevillian attempt to reduce all benevolence or seeming disinterestedness to a refinement or sublimation of appetite. Fielding, like his predecessors, insists upon a genuine duality, and, having established that to his satisfaction, he can accept and celebrate the mixture of disparate elements. Even more, he can draw upon the animal vigor of the barnyard and extend the esteem and gratitude to an acceptance of the teachings of the Gospels, and he can play ironically upon the lowness of both these extremes. Each affronts the self-righteous view of worldly respectability, for each confronts it with spontaneity and warmth, with a "passion" that needs no recourse to principles or argument.

Love, then, becomes one of the principal empirical tests Fielding uses to challenge the unthinking recourse to forms and principles. It is not, as Sir John Hawkins claimed, that he is "teaching that virtue upon principle is imposture, that generous qualities alone constitute true worth," but rather that principle without the generous qualities is readily subverted—wrested, like Scripture, and turned, like the will in *A Tale of a Tub,* to travesty.

II. The Subversion of Forms

Fielding the novelist is consistent with Fielding the moralist. The novelist plays against forms just as much as the moralist. "Playing against" may need a word of explanation. The comic writer and the comic actor achieve some of their best effects by maintaining the traditional forms of heroism or morality—which provide their world with a stable and secure familiar meaning—but treating them with an excess of gravity, a curiously upsetting literalness, a pleasure in the dilemmas they pose. The high rhetoric invites this touch of fatuity by its very height, as I have tried to show in discussing the Augustan mock form; and the systematic embarrassment of the traditional view is the stuff of comedy. In *The Tragedy of Tragedies* Fielding subverted forms with a high-spirited extravagance, but the forms he subverted were extremely susceptible to this treatment. The same may be said of *Shamela,* where he reduces Richardson's Pamela to a trollop with a simple-minded delight in her cunning. On one level or another this subversion of forms runs through Fielding's work; even when it is not used primarily as a comic technique, it represents a saving skepticism, a readiness to examine every possible imposture, even those that his heroes assume.

Let me illustrate. In *Jonathan Wild* the burden of the irony is carried by the villainy of Wild and his rapacious colleagues (as well as their counterparts in the high life of court). But once the innocent Heartfrees escape Wild's exploitation and are reunited with great joy, Mrs. Heartfree takes up her astonishing recital of her adventures. Her account is a parody of romance literature, but it also reveals the awakened vanity of a simple woman who has discovered her power over men. We can perhaps acquit her of deliberately torturing her husband with protracted accounts of attempts upon her virtue, but she tends to dwell on the compliments she has received.

> "If I mistake not, I was interrupted just as I was beginning to repeat some of the compliments made me by the hermit." "Just as you had finished them, I believe, madam," said the justice. "Very well, sir," said she; "I am sure I have no pleasure in the repetition. He concluded then with telling me, though I was in his eyes the most charming woman in the world, and might tempt a saint to abandon the ways of holiness, yet my beauty inspired him . . . (IV, xi).

And she goes on, unsparingly, apparently anxious to relive those moments of unfamiliar glory.

Something like this occurs in *Amelia* when Mrs. Atkinson tells her story to Amelia. Having raised her listener to a high pitch of curiosity, Mrs. Atkinson begins the long torture of delay and apology, pleased with her power over her audience, sure of the appeal of her subject. The tale reveals a good deal of pettiness in the teller, and the flood of emotions that are released demands draughts of cordial, glasses of water, and at least one violent convulsion fit that lasts "the usual time" (VII, viii).

This constant ironic reservation and readiness to overthrow whatever has grown suspect through hardening into formality link Fielding with some of our contemporary novelists. Kingsley Amis has spoken of his humor as "closer to our own than that of any writer before the present century," and has found "a Fielding revival" in the rejection by contemporaries of "the novel of consistent tone, moving through a recognized and restricted cycle of emotional keys." These novelists are comparable to Fielding in their attempt "to combine the violent and the absurd, the grotesque and the romantic, the farcical and the horrific within a single novel."[6] Amis overlooks the appeal of Fielding to writers like Stendhal and Gide, who achieved in considerable measure what the postwar English novel has attempted. But his point is important, and it is the kind of critical view that deserves the closest attention because it comes out of the problems of new literary creation.

The kind of writing that most closely resembles Fielding's today is the comic picaresque novel, like Amis's own *Lucky*

Jim, in which the hero makes up in honesty for what he lacks in respectability. His inability to live as prudently as others who are less honest and simply less alive produces a series of farcical scrapes. These are often painful, but they are so extravagantly elaborate and so ingeniously invented that our sympathy is displaced into laughter. The laughter is not without its edge—Lucky Jim's desperate efforts to save appearances are a tribute to the power of the conventions he has to live by in order to live at all. But the picaresque hero is at once a moral critic (like the satirist posing as *naïf* or *ingénu*), a careless innocent, and—in his comic resilience—a man saved by luck. Picaresque heroes are necessary whenever we wish to celebrate those virtues that cannot be—or simply haven't been —embodied in our morality. These heroes may be socially mobile men in an age of outgrown establishments, or they may be champions of values that society, by its very organization, necessarily represses. The resilience and survival of the picaresque hero is a survival of the values he stands for, values too closely involved with action to be put to sleep in Avalon. They must be seen in their readiness and their openness, and the picaresque work often concludes with the arc of a new gesture about to be made.

Yet it is not the picaresque hero alone that gives Fielding's novels their distinctive note, but the combination of naïve hero and sophisticated narrator. The fluid shifts of tone that we see in recent picaresque novels are produced by heroes (usually narrators as well) who are open to each new experience, variable and unpredictable, often self-mocking. In these novels the reader is left without a clear guide; he follows along as he can, prepared only for surprise. But in Fielding's novels the case is different. Tom Jones may be spontaneous and improvident, but he surprises himself more than he does the reader. We see him through the narrator's commentary, in a series of events that are clearly calculated and tellingly repetitive—so that he becomes a comic figure fixed in a limited pattern of response. We count on Tom's goodness and on his carelessness. It is the novelist, instead, who engages our curiosity. How will he bring it all off? How will he extricate his hero and, even more, his values? The novelist's relationship with the reader— itself, as Wayne Booth has suggested,[7] a subplot in the novel— is carefully modulated between doubt and trust, ironic aloofness and warm solidarity. The characters, hero and all, play out their roles within the space that Fielding creates and encloses in his relationship with the reader.

What is this relationship? Here we meet the problem we find in all Augustan irony. Ultimately, behind the work we see the historical author, the real personality behind the mask. In some cases, like Pope's late satires, where the author has become a public figure, our recognition of his actual traits may be essential. But generally before we come at that figure, we have the mask itself to meet. The Fielding who appears in his novels is, like Swift and Pope, a shifting series of personae; he is engaged in a constant dance of ironic postures. Behind them we may recognize a personality we can trust and accept, but we know him through his performance.

Let us consider a single instance of this. In the opening chapter of *Joseph Andrews* the author praises the power of example as opposed to mere precept: "A good man . . . is a standing lesson to all his acquaintance, and of far greater use in that narrow circle than a good book." This we can take on trust: "a standing lesson" is a little chilling and might seem an invitation to self-righteousness, but it need not trouble us. Fielding goes on, then, to consider the problem of making such a lesson available to the world at large, beyond the small circle of a good man's personal acquaintance; it is the writer who can achieve this end, and "by communicating such valuable patterns to the world, he may perhaps do a more extensive service to mankind, than the person whose life originally afforded the pattern." Again, this is plausible enough (Pope has done more for mankind than the Man of Ross), but it is disconcerting: the good man is now opposed to the writer of his history, and heroic goodness is made a less "extensive service to mankind" than the art of the biographer. We seem to be confusing values, and a phrase like "service to mankind" carries the seeds of the confusion. What, we ask, would the biographer have to represent without the "standing lesson" itself? The outside—the representation, the biography or legend —seems to be supplanting the active goodness that is so rare.

The subversion becomes clear as we move on to some examples of this "service to mankind": "John the Great, who, by his brave and heroic actions against men of large and athletic bodies, obtained the glorious appellation of the Giant-Killer." The nursery tales and romances are solemnly offered as the means by which "the reader is almost as much improved as entertained." This may be true; nursery tales do instill moral awareness. But the pompous claims begin to strike a false note.

This false note is now carried over to the two works Fielding offers as an "admirable pattern of the amiable"—Colley Cibber's *Apology* and Richardson's *Pamela*. All the implicit self-advertising of the "biographer or historian" is now lightly dropped on the shoulders of Richardson, who pretended to be working "from authentic papers and records." And Colley Cibber embodies the complete subversion of the relationship of "standing lesson" and "biographer." He is both at once, and "is by many thought to have lived such a life only in order to write it." The point of all this is that appearance and pretension have swallowed up the goodness they claim to serve, and Fielding has set the satirical keynote for his novel in the opening paragraphs.

Fielding is addressing his reader at two levels. He is speaking to the perceptive and good-natured man, but he is constantly teasing him with the possibility that he is not up to this candor. Readers, like other men, are conventional, snobbish, hypocritical; and, in any case, the morality of Fielding's novels is designed to unsettle accepted attitudes. If the reader is to achieve the flexibility and discrimination that Fielding's morality demands, he must be teased into a full exercise of his wits. Just as Fielding so often maintains an ironic courtesy toward his characters and hesitates over which motive to ascribe to them (meanwhile, of course, exposing the worst), so he is often embarrassingly tactful to his readers. His tact is the sort that makes its victim aware of how tenderly he must be treated, or, in other words, how little he can be trusted. The man who deserves to be trusted needs no tact; the banter of friends can be free and playful, and the author's irony will then only confirm his solidarity with the reader. But, in the process, there are few readers whose feelings are not tested and whose wit is not sharpened.

The structure of Fielding's major novels is a distinctive combination of elements. His comic plots are elaborate and contrived, but within them there is room for the casualness of picaresque incident; they have the artificiality of stage comedy and the leisurely looseness of a more realistic form. His heroes engage our feelings, surely, but they do not have enough consciousness to allow us to inhabit their minds very long or live there very fully. They do not stretch our awareness or offer the sense of limitlessness our own experience does. They have the measure of reality we confer upon many childhood memories: we can feel ourselves back into that simpler mind and know what it was like, but we cannot suppress our sense of what was not yet there. Tom Jones has traditionally been taken as a somewhat autobiographical character. Whether or not he was in fact, the book presents the effect of the mature author contemplating himself when younger—somewhat more equably than Byron does in *Don Juan*—with detachment but with warmth.

The presence of the author is an element that affects all the rest. He presents us with a microcosm to be contemplated, puzzled over, studied. As he puts it in *Tom Jones* (X, i), "This work may . . . be considered as a great creation of our own; and for a little reptile of a critic to presume to find fault with any of its parts, without knowing the manner in which the whole is connected . . . is a most presumptuous absurdity." This is a defense of the literary structure, but Fielding's deliberate echo of Pope's *Essay on Man* is telling: he points in the next paragraph to the "nice distinctions"—Pope calls them gradations—"between two persons activated by the same vice or folly as another." Fielding's novel is a world to be studied as God's creation is studied in the *Essay on Man,* and his diction throughout the book creates categories of discursive thought. We are made to apprehend Fielding's world conceptually. This device is often playful; the concepts are too inclusive to do more than mock the sorry things they denote. But we are always told as well as shown, or told as we are shown. Fielding keeps us constantly aware of the problem we have in coming to terms with a fluid world and an elusive spontaneous goodness by means of the concepts our minds have to make do with. Significantly, Fielding's minor characters talk a great deal; and they reveal in the process the treacherous nature of conceptual language.

Not only the language, but the arrangement of parts in Fielding's novels has a discursive form. Again and again characters are paired off to present false extremes. Or a cast of characters is led past Tom's bedside (as he recovers from the injury he sustained in rescuing Sophia) to cheer him or berate him, to exhibit different shades of love, benevolence, malice, or vindictiveness. Or all the characters execute a dance of attitudes around a single concept—love in *Tom Jones,* charity in *Joseph Andrews.* Characters are created to fill out a moral spectrum, and each gains from the presence of the rest: "the follies of either rank do in reality illustrate each other," as Fielding tells us (*TJ,* IX, i). We are teased and challenged once more by the problem of arranging these characters. Where shall we place Squire Western in any scale that runs from Allworthy to Blifil? But all these discursive effects would have little interest if they were not constantly played off against the narrative movement and our sympathies with the characters. Fielding is neither essayist nor realistic novelist, nor both in turn. He is rather both at once and therefore something different from either.

In such novels as Fielding writes, neither characters nor action can be allowed to escape the author's control. Fielding controls his characters by limiting them. In general, his heroes have more energy than reflectiveness, although all have their moments of dignified eloquence. The villains, in turn, are so transparent (but not to men like Allworthy) and so compulsive that we are left with an impression of moral shallowness more than depravity. There are bullies and braggarts, misers and hypocrites, but no one to say, "Evil, be thou my good." These characters are all dependent upon the social forms that give them a guise of respectability, and the forms—or dogmas or twisted meanings—become as responsible as the people who use them. Fielding brings this out through his symmetrical arrangements. He boasts, for example, of his description of "the different operations of this passion of love in the gentle and cultivated mind of the Lady Booby, from those which it effected in the less polished and coarser disposition of Mrs. Slipslop" (*JA*, I, vii). Again in the second book of *Tom Jones* he gives us "scenes of matrimonial felicity in different degrees of life." Here Mrs. Partridge's uncontrolled suspicions of her husband's relations with Jenny Jones produce Punch-and-Judy farce, while the hatred of Captain Blifil and his wife has a savage intensity that is possible only with a more refined etiquette. The Blifils' marriage is summed up in the widow's mourning:

> [She] conducted herself through the whole season in which grief is to make its appearance on the outside of the body with the strictest regard to all the rules of custom and decency, suiting the alterations of her countenance to the several alterations of her habit: for as this changed from weeds to black, from black to gray, from gray to white, so did her countenance change from dismal to sorrowful, from sorrowful to sad, and from sad to serious, till the day came in which she was allowed to return to her former serenity (*TJ*, III, i).

The word "allowed," ironic as it is, reminds us that, while the depth of malice may be directly proportionate to the complexity of forms, the forms themselves exercise a tyranny over the man who lives by them. We see something much like this in Restoration comedy; the case of Fainall in *The Way of the World* comes to mind, and the way in which Mirabell seizes the forms and turns them to a better purpose. Fielding's heroes do not attempt what Mirabell so handsomely carries off—or rather they bring new difficulties upon themselves when they do attempt it. Tom's proposal of marriage to Lady Bellaston succeeds in freeing him of a demanding mistress, but it rebounds against him when Sophia learns of it. Amelia sends Mrs. Atkinson to the masquerade in her place and eludes her would-be seducer, but she gives Mrs. Atkinson's indiscretion occasion to create new difficulties.

Another severe limitation Fielding places upon his characters is the importance that rumor and gossip play in determining their fate. We see Tom pursued along the road by malicious reports; Tom and Sophia kept at odds by the petty jealousy of their servants, Partridge and Honour. (Only rarely does the reverse work out, as when Tom's kindness to Anderson, the desperate highwayman, becomes known to Mrs. Miller and ultimately to Allworthy.) What gives Fielding's world its peculiar quality is that so much happens with so little design. There is a great deal of triviality—the snobbery of a Mrs. Graveairs, the weak swagger of a Beau Didapper, the autumnal lust of Mrs. Slipslop—some of it disarmingly grotesque, too mechanically incongruous to seem very menacing, but all of it building up through a crisscross of coincidence and a steady accumulation to formidable proportions. When Jack Nightingale seduces Nancy Miller, Tom must spell out to Nightingale the meaning of what he has done: "I do not imagine you have laid a regular premeditated scheme for the destruction of the quiet of a poor little creature, or have even foreseen the consequence: for I am sure thou art a very good-natured fellow, and such a one can never be guilty of a cruelty of that kind; but at the same time you have pleased your vanity, without considering that this poor girl was made a sacrifice to it" (*TJ*, XIV, iv).

Fielding's interest, then, lies less in the moral struggles within characters than in the ways in which selfishness finds refuge in forms. Lady Booby and Black George are both shown in formal deliberation, balancing alternatives with all the scruples of a high tragic character; but the formal deliberation also provides a comfortable disguise—from themselves—of the meanness of their motives. Fielding has taken over from Mandeville the close study of the way in which social forms

are learned. His delightful account of the young girl's schooling in coquetry (*JA*, IV, vii) derives from *The Fable of the
Bees* and turns all Mandeville's cruel insights upon Richardson's Pamela as well as Lady Booby. Fielding can use Mandeville's reductive analysis of motives to good purpose so long
as he is treating vanity and folly; it is Mandeville's similar account of the origin of moral virtue that he indignantly rejects.

Like Mandeville, Fielding has a detached appreciation of the
artistry of our vanities and passions, particularly as they make
use of social forms. One example will serve. Squire Western's
sister is a woman of shallow vanity, tall, ugly, unloved, who
has found her compensations not in prudery, like Bridget Allworthy, but in a studious devotion to the fashionable world.
She has "acquired all that knowledge which the said world
usually communicates; and was a perfect mistress of manners,
customs, ceremonies, and fashions." She has studied her plays
and romances, her historical memoirs and political pamphlets;
she has mastered "the doctrine of Amour" and the latest gossip—"a knowledge which she the more easily attained, as her
pursuit of it was never diverted by any affairs of her own"
(VI, ii). It is a wonderful picture of an empty woman feeding upon externalities and vicarious excitement. And, of
course, she speaks a dreadful gibberish of court lingo, diplo-
matic jargon, and military terms. The gibberish gives away
her innocent incomprehension of all she imagines she knows,
even as her pride in devious subtlety makes her parrot
the cynicism of the town. When Squire Western remarks,
"Allworthy is a queer b—ch, and money hath no effect
o' un," she can reply, "Do you think Allworthy hath
more contempt for money than any other man because he
professes more? Such credulity would better become one of
us weak women, than that wise sex which Heaven hath formed
for politicians." She is, of course, the most credulous of creatures herself. But all her affection for her brother and niece,
all her fundamental goodness ("a very extraordinary good and
sweet disposition") can produce, under the influence of fashionable forms upon her vanity, is the astonishing advice that
Sophia marry Blifil so that she may have Tom safely as a
lover (VI, v, end).

Such innocent depravity as Mrs. Western's—and it is not
much different from Jack Nightingale's or Lord Fellamar's—
shows the diffusion of responsibility Fielding creates in his
world. Actions follow from small vanities as often as from

deliberate evil. They may be the product of a chance meeting of characters who are in themselves ineffectual but become imposing in combination. Thus, when Sophia and Tom almost meet at Upton, they are kept apart by a series of accidents—yet in retrospect all that happens follows from the nature of the participants. Sophia's maid, Honour, exhibits all her pretensions in the inn kitchen as she loftily allows Partridge, who has come with Tom, to remain: "you look somewhat like a gentleman, and may sit still if you please: I don't desire to disturb anybody but mob" (X, iv). When Honour is sent by Sophia to call Tom, Partridge struts in turn: "One woman is enough at once for a reasonable man." His manner enrages Honour, who at once reports Tom's infidelity to Sophia and gives it as ugly a turn as possible. To make matters worse, Susan the chambermaid can relay Partridge's boasts "that your ladyship was dying for love of the young squire, and that he was going to the wars to get rid of you." This formidable array of pettiness provides a constant store of motives Fielding can bring into play with the slightest twist of coincidence. The result is that the coincidences that entrap the central characters seem only special cases of the prevailing conditions that surround them. This enables Fielding to use the most flagrant artifice without our losing touch with a plausible social reality.

Fielding's subversion of forms, at work throughout his novels, becomes most apparent in his comic resolutions, which can still outrage moralistic critics by their disdain for the full consequences of the heroes' frailties. Yet the artifice that resolves the near-catastrophe is the same as the artifice that creates it. Fielding weaves together blind and confused motives to bring his heroes to the brink of disasters they hardly merit. And the excess of these disasters makes them ludicrous, morally as well as dramatically. Fielding sharpens this by inventing, in both *Joseph Andrews* and *Tom Jones,* a travesty of the prototypical tragic nemesis, the dark mystery of unknowing incest. His point is that these terrors are not for such heroes as these; the incursion of the terrible into this world of limited consciousness and limited consequences is brilliantly unreal.

When Joseph and Fanny learn that they are apparently brother and sister, Fielding crowds the discovery scene with noisy emotion that suggests panic in a barnyard when a fox has entered. Joseph and Fanny grow faint and pallid, but little

Dicky Adams roars and Parson Adams falls to his knees to ejaculate many thanksgivings (*JA*, IV, xii). And Adams himself is to undergo, in the night farce of mistaken bedrooms, the test of being discovered by Joseph naked in bed with Fanny ("Hath he offered any rudeness to you?" Joseph asks in a rage). The novel never relaxes long enough to take the threat of incest seriously or to make more than ridiculous the resolutions with which it is met. Adams' advice is feeble enough, and it is followed by the vow of Joseph and Fanny of "perpetual celibacy." They plan, poor fools, "to live together all their days, and indulge a Platonic friendship for each other."

In *Tom Jones,* once the seeming fact that Tom has slept with his mother is revealed, we have tragic postures and a near-tragic speech: "But why do I blame Fortune? I am myself the cause of all my misery." But at this point the author intrudes to remind us how artfully he had managed the ninth book to prevent Partridge from meeting Mrs. Waters there. We are reminded not only of the fictionality of character and event, but of the absurdly intensified causality Fielding has created: "Instances of this kind we may frequently observe in life, where the greatest events are produced by a nice train of little circumstances; and more than one example of this may be discovered by the accurate eye, in this our history." Once more in *Amelia,* when the bailiff apprehends Booth outside Miss Matthew's lodgings just before he can return to Amelia, our attention is directed to the artifice that runs through all these novels and tightens causality to the point where it verges on the farcical:

> . . . there is no exercise of the mind of a sensible reader more pleasant than tracing the several small and almost imperceptible links in every chain of events by which all the great actions of the world are produced (XII, i).

We are made securely aware of the novelist in control, and we recognize that the terrible has been prepared as deftly and artificially as it will be overturned.

Is this cheating moral seriousness? Fielding has so arranged matters that there is no Thwackum-like punitive nemesis; he has subverted the form in which men have traditionally embodied their sense of guilt: their fear of the price that greatness must exact, their sense of the exposure to irretrievable error that comes of each new assertion of power or will. Tom has approached a tragic role throughout the last part as he assumes responsibility at each turn for what he has done. So here: "I am myself the cause of all my misery." And we can admire this, but we recognize the disproportion between the act and its consequences. Only a sinister deity would design such punishment, the kind of deity who invites prostration or defiance rather than trust. The fact that the tragic discovery is traditional does not, in short, make it appropriate; Fielding shrugs off the great tragic forms with a Christian cheerfulness. Dr. Harrison, when he writes to Booth and Amelia about their loss of her mother's fortune, congratulates them upon their happiness in each other. "A superstitious heathen," he goes on, "would have dreaded the malice of Nemesis in your situation; but as I am a Christian, I shall venture to add another circumstance to your felicity . . . that you have . . . a faithful and zealous friend" (*A*, III, x).

The result has its own kind of moral seriousness. Fielding insists upon the weight of folly and triviality that impedes the best and worst intentions. In the preface to his sister's *David Simple*, Fielding speaks of "the mazes, windings, and labyrinths, which perplex the heart of man to such a degree that he is himself often incapable of seeing through them" (*Works*, XVI, 10). In his own novels, his typical method is to place heroes of transparent and spontaneous goodness (they may have innocent follies and affectations, like Adams) amidst the mazes and windings of others' selfishness. These heroes need not succeed, and they come to recognize this fact; but they need not fail, either, in a world where evil often becomes self-defeating and Fortune seems to rule. Fortune is the name we give to the impenetrable intricacy of those "nice trains of little causes" or "small and almost imperceptible links in every chain of events." The links are, in most cases, the trivial obsessions of others, the inevitable accidents of countless jostling egos.

Fielding can reward his heroes because they do not seek a reward. He wishes to free our faith in Order, as Pope does, from any simple-minded expectation that goodness will find its reward on earth. The only reward it can find there is that it pays to itself: the pleasure it finds in doing good and in sustaining its integrity. Beyond that it seeks nothing, and, in seeking nothing, it has earned the reward the author confers. The comic resolutions are not devices for saving these heroes from facing moral consequences but rewards for their having done so. That the reward is externalized and paid in solid pudding rather than praise need not alter the point. That, too, is a way of reminding us that the malignant Fortune that hounds these characters and the comic providence that extricates them are only two aspects of the author himself, as they are of a benevolent deity. Those characters who can act as if there were such a God of course find Him:

> Earth smiles around, with boundless bounty blest,
> And Heaven beholds its image in his breast
> (*Essay on Man*, IV, 371–72).

III. Low and High

> It would have been useless for our Lord Jesus Christ to come like a king, in order to shine forth in His kingdom of holiness. But He came there appropriately in the glory of His own order.
> It is most absurd to take offence at the lowliness of Jesus Christ, as if His lowliness were in the same order as the greatness which He came to manifest. If we consider this greatness . . . we shall see it to be so immense that we shall have no reason for being offended at a lowliness which is not of that order (*Pensées*, 793).

These are solemn words to bring to Fielding's novels; yet their import is essential to an understanding of his lowness. I have argued for his constant subversion of forms, his deliberate overturning of rigid stances or systematized attitudes. Even the attitudes he espouses and the characters he admires submit to this untiring alertness to pretense. It is not simply the hypocritical or affected he attacks but the insensible conversion of active feeling into formal structure. The lowness of Fielding's heroes—the fact that in one sense or another they are dispossessed or disinherited—thrusts them into a situation where they have no props of status. The nakedness of Joseph, as he lies at the roadside after the robbery, is itself an extreme instance of the unprotectedness of these characters.

Not only are the characters without recourse to position; they are, by their nature, unable to foresee the malice of others. This inability is both worldly folly and the wisdom of charity. Parson Adams, we are told, "never saw farther into people than they desired to let him." Hypocrites like Peter Pounce were "a sort of people whom Mr. Adams never saw through." Allworthy, of course, carries on the pattern, and Dr. Harrison is no more beyond it than Booth and Amelia. In contrast, the selfish count on finding their own deviousness

in others and often as a result overshoot their mark, like
Fainall and Mrs. Marwood in *The Way of the World*. Fielding
is insisting upon the fact that goodness cannot be recognized
unless it is first felt within. This is a counterpart of the traditional Christian view that one cannot know God until one
loves Him. Until that love is felt, one's knowledge remains
fixed in categories of another order. There is no way of grasping the order of charity, one might say, with the categories
of the order of mind. The kind of awareness upon which
characters act seems deficient when it is interpreted in the
terms of another order. Dr. Harrison charges Booth with abus-
ing him by calling him wise: "You insinuated slily," says the
doctor, "that I was wise, which, as the world understands
the phrase, I should be ashamed of; and my comfort is that
no one can accuse me justly of it" (*A,* IX, iv). Characters
speak to each other in foreign tongues, although the words
they use are the same. It is Fielding himself who can entertain
all these levels of discourse at once, who can perceive how
men think in each order of being, and who can embody a
harmony of orders within himself.

Fielding's strategy is to dissociate orders—to give us figures
who upset our conventional expectations of "goodness and
innocence." In the preface to *Joseph Andrews* he sets forth a
doctrine of the "comic epic in prose" that steers a course between the conventional high heroism of romance and the
monstrous parodies of burlesque. He offers us "low" characters, and among them, "the most glaring in the whole,"
Parson Adams, "a character of perfect simplicity" whose goodness of heart "will recommend him to the good-natured." As
Stuart M. Tave has shown (in *The Amiable Humorist,* Chicago,
1960), Fielding's profession to write "in imitation of the manner of Cervantes, author of *Don Quixote*" is deceptive to
the modern reader, for Fielding is one of the pioneers in the
gradual recognition of the dignity of the foolish Quixote. Parson Adams is a challenge to the reader to discern an essential goodness within a sententious, vainly bookish, short-
sighted country clergyman. It is only near the close of the
novel that he can rise to the dignity of self-assertion in his
reply to Lady Booby:

> Madam . . . I know not what your ladyship means by
> the terms master and service. I am in the service of a
> master who will never discard me for doing my duty.
> . . . Whilst my conscience is pure, I shall never fear what
> man can do unto me (IV, ii).

The contrasts that run through *Joseph Andrews* are less sharp than those of *Jonathan Wild,* the dissociations less overtly satirical and emphatic. The strain of pastoral allows Fielding to use his setting as commentary; it reaches its culmination in Mr. Wilson's garden, where the freshness and vitality of the country (already so evident in Joseph and Fanny) take on dignity and serenity:

> No parterres, no fountains, no statues, embellished this little garden. Its only ornament was a short walk, shaded on each side by a filbert-hedge, with a small alcove at one end; whither in hot weather the gentleman and his wife used to retire and divert themselves with their children, who played in the walk before them. But though vanity had no votary in this little spot, here was variety of fruit, and every thing useful for the kitchen; which was abundantly sufficient to catch the admiration of Adams, who told the gentleman, he had certainly a good gardener. Sir, answered he, that gardener is now before you: whatever you see here is the work solely of my own hands (*JA,* III, iv).

When the visitors leave, Adams declares "that this was the manner in which the people had lived in the golden age," an echo of his obsession with classical learning, but also of Pope on pastoral poetry: "pastoral is an image of what they call the golden age. So that we are not to describe our shepherds as shepherds at this day really are, but as they may be conceived then to have been, when the best of men followed the employment." What gives *Joseph Andrews* its striking quality is that Fielding mixes this Virgilian note with the Theocritean of Gay's mock pastorals. The low energies of nature are given their animal vigor (though carefully distinguished from the urgencies of Lady Booby or Slipslop, let alone Beau Didapper), but they are made continuous with the warmth and generosity of a pastoral golden age and of the Christian charity that has drawn so much of its imagery from the life of the shepherd.

In *Tom Jones* the pastoral motive is also present, with the mock pastoral centering in Molly Seagrim and Squire Western. Western is the most startling creation in the novel; perhaps the finest English comic character to have emerged after Falstaff. He is a great baby, frankly selfish and uncontrolled, imperious in his whims, cruelly thoughtless, with the tyranny of a demanding child but none of the capacity to spin out of his appetites subtle schemes of domination or revenge, like Blifil and Lady Bellaston. When he bursts into the London scene, he brings with him the simplicity of the flesh at its most fleshly. He breaks through the code of honor, that most elaborate and attractive of worldly substitutes for goodness, as he breaks through the delicate modesty of Sophia ("To her, boy, to her, go to her"). Early in the novel we see his simplicity achieve the same ends as real astuteness. Thwackum and Square compete in praising Blifil, who has maliciously released Sophia's bird; Square sees in him another Brutus, Thwackum an exemplary Christian. "I don't know what you mean, either of you," Western breaks in, "by right and wrong. To take away my girl's bird was wrong in my opinion" (IV, iv). And it is he who defends Tom's effort to recapture the bird for Sophia. "I am sure I don't understand a word of this," he says to Square and Thwackum, still debating their moral doctrine.

> It may be learning and sense for aught I know; but you shall never persuade me into it. Pox! you have neither of you mentioned a word of that poor lad who deserves to be commended; to venture breaking his neck to oblige my girl was a generous-spirited action; I have learning enough to see that. D—n me, here's Tom's health! I shall love the boy for it the longest day I have to live (*TJ*, IV, iv).

It is only to be expected that Squire Western cannot sustain this noble intention. He has as little mind as any man can have; he lives in bursts of enthusiasm, maudlin affection, barbarous willfulness, sheer physicality. He pairs off with his sister—she all Whig politics and would-be townish smartness, he the typical hard-drinking Tory country squire. But Fielding does more with him than that. He uses him to embody animal energy without either the selfish cunning that builds upon appetites in some or the generous charity that fuses with appetite (and transforms it) in others. Tom stands between Western and Allworthy, able to participate in the worlds of both—an innocent carnality in Western and a rational charity in Allworthy—and to bring them together. It would be hard, in fact, to conceive of Tom without the presence of both Allworthy and Western in the novel.

One should observe as well how Jenny Jones, who is something of a prig at the outset, mellows into the generous, if irregular, Mrs. Waters of the later parts—in marked contrast to the vain and shallow Harriet Fitzpatrick. The progression of Tom's temptresses is significant. Molly Seagrim is coarse but pretentious, Lady Bellaston is refined and vindictive. Mrs. Waters strikes a balance between Molly's unmitigated (and slightly corrupt) low and Lady Bellaston's inverted high. She is capable—in the case of Tom—of a robust and unfastidious appetite:

> The beauty of Jones highly charmed her eye; but as she could not see his heart, she gave herself no concern about it. She could feast heartily at the table of love, without reflecting that some other already had been, or hereafter might be, feasted with the same repast (*TJ*, IX, vi).

But she is also capable—in the case of Northerton—of "that violent and apparently disinterested passion of love, which seeks only the good of its object" (IX, vii). Fielding allows her only a strong sensuality in her relations with Tom, but he makes her a woman who squares her passions with her conscience more boldly than the hypocrites around her. She defends, in Allworthy's presence, an attachment that has constancy without legal sanctions, and she values Tom's virtue at a greater rate than his freedom from vices. And, all the while, she retains her deep gratitude to Allworthy and recognizes in his goodness something that "savored more of the divine than human nature" (XVIII, viii). Fielding discriminates carefully between moral laxity and moral obliviousness—or, as Coleridge puts it, between what a man does and what he is.

Amelia is a weaker novel than *Tom Jones,* but it is clearly moving in a new direction. The fact that Billy Booth has a family depending upon him makes his irregularities less appealing than Tom's. His only sexual infidelity takes place at the opening of the novel, before our concern for his family has grown too strong. For the rest of the story he is suffering from remorse and the threat of Miss Matthews' revenge; we see more of the hangover than the intoxication. He is guilty of less attractive vices than Tom's; he is vain about keeping a coach, and he gambles disastrously when his family is near starvation. He is also older and shabbier than Tom; and he can do little for himself in the course of the novel. The center of attention is Amelia, his wife. Fielding makes their marriage the object of the world's attack, and Booth's moral dependence upon Amelia gives the marriage all the more significance. Amelia is as close as Fielding comes to a pure embodiment of the order of charity; she has traces of vanity, and she is sometimes handled with irony, but she is never made so ridiculous as Mrs. Heartfree. Still, Fielding seems to have gone back to the Heartfrees, that "family of love," reworked them in a new way, and perhaps offered them finally as a further qualification of the ethical doctrines of *Tom Jones*.

It is Amelia's Christian goodness—selfless, warm, readily forgiving—that sets the tone of the book. We hardly see Booth acting well on his own—except on the battlefield—as we see Tom Jones refuting the Gulliver-like misanthropy of the Man of the Hill, keeping Partridge in check, advising Nightingale, resisting the kind proposal of Mrs. Hunt. In this novel the generosity of goodness is much more strictly limited to the forgiveness of Amelia and the benevolence of that harsher, less amiable version of Adams, Dr. Harrison. And goodness is heavily beleaguered; under the stress of difficulties, Amelia tells her children hard truths. Good people will show love, "but there are more bad people, and they will hate you for your goodness" (IV, iii).

More than this, Fielding brings to the surface and faces what he cannot escape in the Heartfrees; the sentimentalism of Booth and Amelia in their innocence. The book opens with the savage injustices perpetrated by Justice Thrasher and the moral chaos of the prison itself. But it moves on at once to the two narratives of Miss Matthews and Booth. Miss Matthews is a brilliant instance of sentimental vanity; she is capable of stabbing her betrayer, and we have few doubts about her strength of will, but she voluptuates in a vision of herself as the creature of helpless passion. She can describe her method quite coolly in the case of her father. The kind old man had once caused Miss Matthews to miss a ball, and she fanned this memory until it could be revived at will in full strength. "When any tender idea intruded into my bosom, I immediately raised this phantom of an injury in my imagination, and it considerably lessened the fury of that sorrow which I should have otherwise felt for the loss of so good a father, who died within a few months of my departure from him" (I, ix). As Booth tells his own story, with torrents of tears, he inflames Miss Matthews' passion for him; and it bursts out in her brilliantly funny interruptions. But he is totally involved in his tale of how Amelia recovered from the accident wherein "her lovely nose was beat all to pieces."

Amelia's nose has become famous because Fielding failed, in the first edition of the novel, to make explicitly clear that it was restored, and the image of a noseless Amelia danced before critics' eyes. Even if we allow for an unfortunate oversight, the choice of a nose seems singularly inept. Amelia's suffering consists of having to hear false friends say that "she will never more turn up her nose at her betters"; and surely no author of Fielding's skill brought this kind of difficulty upon himself unintentionally. We can pity Amelia, but we cannot take her accident with quite the solemnity that Booth does. There is an undernote of laughter in more than Miss Matthews' sublime remarks ("a cottage with the man one loves, is a palace"). And there is surely laughter as well as pathos in Booth's account of his departure from Amelia:

> clinging round my neck, she cried, "Farewell, farewell for ever; for I shall never, never see you any more." At which words the blood entirely forsook her lovely cheeks, and she became a lifeless corpse in my arms.
>
> Amelia continued so long motionless, that the doctor, as well as Mrs. Harris, began to be under the most terrible apprehensions; so they informed me afterwards, for at that time I was incapable of making any observation. I had indeed very little more use of my senses than the dear creature whom I supported. At length, however, we were all delivered from our fears; and life again visited the loveliest mansion that human nature ever afforded it (*A*, I, 101).

Booth's sentimentalism helps explain his belief that man could act only "from the force of that passion which was uppermost in his mind, and could do no otherwise" (I, iii). Just as his sister Nancy dies, he learns that he may lose Amelia to someone else. "I now soon perceived how superior my love for Amelia was to every passion; poor Nancy's idea disappeared in a moment; I quitted the lifeless corpse, over which I had shed a thousand tears, left the care of her funeral to others, and posted, I may almost say flew, back to Amelia . . ." (II, v). It is necessary for Colonel James, his superior officer, to warn him—when he seems dangerously wounded—against going back to Amelia. James can appreciate "the comfort of expiring in her arms," but he points out the cruelty, too: "You would not wish to purchase any happiness at the price of so much pain to her" (II, v). The danger of Booth's temperament is obvious; as Fielding says, he is "in his heart an extreme well-wisher to religion . . . yet his notions of it [are] very slight and uncertain." He comes close to the error Dr. Johnson found in his friend Savage: "he mistook the love for the practice of virtue, and was indeed not so much a good man as the friend of goodness."

Amelia, far more than Booth, grows stronger under the stress of suffering. Fielding has designed the novel so that, at each point, we see Amelia—so much a human embodiment of pure charity—assailed by those who cannot understand her nature. She lives with a landlady who is little more than a procuress. She is tried by the designs of two rakes who have no comprehension of the sanctity of "wedded love." When Booth, too, seems to have lost all sense of the meaning of Amelia's love, she is close to despair. Amelia can, however, be freed from the temptations of sentimentality by devoting herself to others. When she joins Booth "she could not so far command herself as to refrain from many sorrowful exclamations against the hardships of their destiny; but when she saw the effect they had upon Booth she stifled her rising grief [and] forced a little cheerfulness into her countenance" (XII, ii).

Fielding allows Amelia's purity of character to emerge from the test of ridicule. Amelia is constantly seen in contrast with Mrs. Atkinson, who is good but vain and touchy, and whose story of her life exhibits a certain amount of partiality and self-justification. The angelic selflessness of Amelia is her primary quality, and it can afford to be seen in lights that make others ridiculous. Amelia's pathos is heightened by the very kind of extended simile that was once used to overwhelm a Deborah Wilkins or to mock a naïve Tom Jones; Amelia's quiet goodness can wear it with grace.

XI.

Sterne: Art and Nature

Sterne—whom I always regard as marking a stage in the growth of the modern self-consciousness. I used to say *Hamlet—Tristram Shandy—Faust.*
—Justice Oliver Wendell Holmes

. . . there is always in a genuine humor an acknowledgment of the hollowness and farce of the world, and its disproportion to the godlike within us.
—S. T. Coleridge

Candide is the poem of fortuitous existence, a bitter and enduring poem. —Alain

I. Chance and Choice: *Candide* and *Rasselas*

In Fielding's novels the resolutions depend upon the virtues of the heroes and the weakness of the villains, but these forces are insufficient in themselves to bring the action to a happy close. The central characters lack the strength to master their situations; they are caught in circumstances too complex and unpredictable to give their will sufficient purchase. It is a short step from a novel of flagrantly contrived resolution that calls attention to the incapacities of its characters to a novel that denies the possibility of resolution. Two works that appeared in England in the same year, 1759, the year of the first publication of *Tristram Shandy,* illustrate this further stage.[1]

Rasselas was published on April 19, 1759; *Candide* had appeared in a Geneva edition of January 15, and in two different English translations on May 19 and May 22. Sterne completed a draft of the first two volumes of *Tristram Shandy* by June and published them in December. In the ninth chapter he refers to "Candid and Miss Cunegund's affairs," and in a letter written, probably in October, to Dodsley he proposes bringing out in York "a lean edition" of his book —"in two small volumes, of the size of *Rasselas,* and on the same paper and type." The three works are curiously inter-woven.

Voltaire's *Candide* sets out to ridicule a despairing opti-mism. Its target is the philosophy that insists upon a meaning-ful universe at the expense of human hope and effort. Such a philosophy sees a rational structure in all that has happened or may happen; a divine purpose fulfilled in whatever befalls man; and it comforts us with the sense that our suffering is not without meaning. But in order to do so, it also seems cruelly to deny the reality of our suffering or at least the importance of our feeling; more than that, it prescribes resignation to a divine will whose purpose must include intolerable pain within its large gestures. The role of the individual is reduced to that of a minute element in a design he does not create but supports through pain.

There are possible ways of escape from this chilling opti-mism. One is to insist upon the tragic nature of history, the inevitable descent into pain which is involved in the descent into time: this is best dramatized in the dual figure of God as ordering justice and suffering mercy, Himself enduring the pain He must inflict and becoming the Redeemer even as He remains the Judge. Another way is to renounce a vision of Order that would see each moment of pain as inevitable, to surrender any hope of comprehending God's ways in this world. One might describe the pattern of *Candide* as the pro-gressive freeing of man from the illusion that his world will either foster his happiness or instruct him in his choices.

The action of *Candide* is even more elaborately contrived than Fielding's. But where Fielding's contrivance takes a prov-idential form, Voltaire's is a parody of such an order. There are numerous coincidences, but instead of reassurance they provide only the blank face of malignant fortune. Coincidence becomes catastrophic, the surprising re-encounters only a more insistent version of chance. Against this pattern of events are placed the fatuous systematizer, Pangloss, ready to extract a pattern of order from the most intolerable suffering, and Candide, respectful and docile, but impervious to meta-physical teaching.

At every point Voltaire stresses the resilience of the physi-cal animal. If Candide is driven on by the futile dream of a happy union with Cunégonde, the old woman servant is free of all such illusions. Compounded as she is of vanity and disil-lusion, warmth and selfishness, she can exclaim, "I have grown old (with only one buttock) in misery and shame, but

I have never forgotten that I am the daughter of a Pope. I have wanted to kill myself a hundred times, but somehow I am still in love with life. This ridiculous weakness is perhaps one of our most melancholy propensities; for is there anything more stupid than to be eager to go on carrying a burden which one would gladly throw away, to loathe one's very being and yet to hold it fast, to fondle the snake that devours us until it has eaten our hearts away?" (xii). Pangloss illustrates this reduction to sheer protoplasmic survival; flayed, burned, beset by every kind of torture and destruction, he goes on essentially unchanged, unable to learn from experience and equally unable to succumb to it.

This pattern of survival is one of the elements that gives *Candide* its great comic force. The pain and shame Voltaire seeks to demonstrate are obvious enough, and little is omitted to make their horror acute; but the senselessness of the pattern itself and of the characters who submit to it, whether cheerfully oblivious like Pangloss or darkly embittered like Martin, is as central to the work. In a baneful and ludicrous universe, the mechanism of an almost purely physical existence becomes benign. In a world that resists any control by thought, the absence of thought is a saving grace.

The mechanism is insisted upon. The rapidity and violence of the action carry along the players. Their only gestures of independence are the little vanities they insist upon, their obedience to forms or doctrines that have lost all meaning. Cunégonde is put out by the old woman's claims to misfortune: "unless you have been ravished by two Bulgars, had two stabs in your belly, and two of your country houses demolished; unless you have had two mothers and fathers butchered before your eyes, and beheld two of your lovers flogged at an auto-da-fé, I don't see how you can rival me, especially as I am a baron's daughter with seventy-two quarterings in my coat of arms, and yet have served as a kitchen-maid" (x). These trivialities in the principal characters are part of the senseless and perverse use of forms that governs the world at large. Whatever inhumanity occurs is sanctioned by the laws of warfare or accompanied by prayer; cruelty is ritualized, viciousness rationalized, as when the Jew, Don Issachar, and the Grand Inquisitor debate, in their apportionment of possession of their mistress Cunégonde, "whether Saturday night belongs to the old law or the new" (viii).

The sexual innuendoes that run through *Candide* are part of the pattern. The mechanism of sex is a constant force; the soldiers ravish, the Jesuits seduce, and the Oreillon maidens take their monkey lovers. Within the central characters, too, it becomes a simple, blind force. As Cunégonde tells of her terrible misadventures, Candide longs to see the scar on her left thigh. As Cunégonde sees Candide about to be flogged by the Inquisition, she is struck by the delicate bloom of his white skin. The whole restless search of Candide for Cunégonde is a parody of the romance quest, which is itself the sexual mechanism in its most sublimated form.

Most telling of all is the sureness with which Candide acts when he must. When he and Cunégonde are trapped by the Inquisitor, Candide makes up his mind "in an instant," his "reflections were clear and rapid," and "without giving the Inquisitor time to recover from his surprise, he ran him through and laid him beside the Israelite." Cunégonde exclaims, "A gentle creature like you to kill a Jew and a priest in the space of two minutes! What could you have been thinking about?" To this Candide replies, "A jealous man in love doesn't know what he is doing" (ix). Again, when he is struck across the face by the sword of Cunégonde's brother, the Jesuit, Candide instantly runs him through, and then weeps: "I am the best tempered man there ever was, yet I have already killed three men, and two of them were priests!" (xv).

In this kind of decision without thought Candide is freed from the impositions of the rational systematizers. In contrast are all the devices for justifying selfishness, immorality, and insanity: the laws of warfare, the hierarchy of the church, the Inquisition, and, most of all, the destructive complacency of Pangloss's rational optimism. Candide's companion, Cacambo, presents the detached and unheroic indifference to such systems: "You were going to make war against the Jesuits. Let's go and fight on their side instead. . . . When you don't get what you expect on one side, you find it on the other. Fresh sights and fresh adventures are always welcome" (xiv). Voltaire seems to suggest that life can be conducted successfully or decently only at a level below that of the system's grandeur. In Eldorado there is order, but it needs no justification beyond that of immediate intuition. What it does need is a trust in man's capacities, an indifference to those glories that distrust creates, and an acceptance of what is given with no tortured yearning for what is not. Eldorado has, of course, something of the mildly foolish and improbable simplicity that Swift gives to the life of the Houyhnhnms, and the "restless spirit" of man cannot endure it. But there is point in Candide's remark that "I have never seen men except in Eldorado" (xxii).

In the vexing conclusion of the book Voltaire gives us a reduced image of man's possibilities. All the characters have lost illusions (except, of course, Pangloss), charm, and hope. What they have left is little more than life itself, and their temptation to look beyond is firmly repressed by the philosophical dervish. "Will you kindly tell us why such a strange animal as man was ever made?" asks Candide. "What has that got to do with you?" said the dervish. "Is it your business?" When Pangloss proposes a metaphysical discussion, the dervish slams the door in their faces. There is no room for speculation, there is no occasion for dramatic choice; there is instead a tacit and unheroic acceptance of a plight that can at best be made endurable. And the way to accomplish this is through giving oneself to work. Work is given no moral dignity, but it can banish "boredom, vice, and poverty" (xxx). Some have found in the garden that Candide and his group come to cultivate the nobility of an example which may affect the world about them. But, whatever Voltaire's own dedication to reform, the tale itself hardly requires such a reading. *Candide* shows the need to strip away false ideals and falser rationalizations, to surrender the infectious dream of a glorious purpose, and to make do with the largely physical, scarcely rational, often intuitively sane creature that man is. If his physical appetites are all but ungovernable, they become so much the worse when they are institutionalized and systematized, and the more ruthlessly satisfied for their honorable disguise. The reduced image of man, less a creature of choice than he thinks, often the helpless victim of chance, is therapeutic: it frees man for reality.

Johnson's *Rasselas* is a quite different work. It has little of the overt levity and extravagance of Voltaire's book, it is much more sympathetic toward the futile speculation of its characters, and accordingly it catches more fully the tragic sense of man's trust in his mind. Johnson had sounded this note earlier: "It is necessary to hope, though hope should always be deluded; for hope itself is happiness, and its frustrations, however frequent, are yet less dreadful than its extinction" (*Idler*, No. 58). But if the note is tragic, the pattern of life that it implies has strong comic elements. The tale does much to cultivate these in its gently preposterous oriental setting, the self-mocking formality of its dialogue, the balance and antithesis of characters as well as of sentences, and the circularity of its total structure. The sustained ironic ambiguity of the tale catches everything in a shimmering light: the happy valley is both earthly paradise and cunning prison, the "hunger of imagination" stirs our appetite but denies us nourishment, the quest for a "choice of life" pre-empts the experience of life itself. Johnson so conducts his tale that his characters are frustrated but scarcely educated; like Voltaire's, they are left with a reduced image of life's possibilities, but they cling to fantasies. Unlike Voltaire's characters, they are not made to face the brutalization of frustrated hope, and, as Johnson says, "nothing is concluded."

One of the striking features of the tale is the interplay between Rasselas' youthful fatuity and Imlac's mature wisdom. Rasselas' sentimentality and self-indulgence are clear at the start, and Imlac's tone gives promise of mature decisiveness. But for all his experience and reach of awareness, Imlac can provide no answers. He knows the futility of the quest that Rasselas wishes to make, but he cannot resist joining it himself. Imlac seems to participate in the process whose end he already knows, as if being the spectator to another's desire were a palliative for the absence of his own. His discretion allows the prince and his sister to make their own troubling discoveries, but it is not discretion—simply the limit of his own capacity—that deters him from resolving their doubts. Doubt is the inevitable condition that follows upon the search for a choice of life. "Very few," Imlac points out, "live by choice. Every man is placed in his present condition by causes which acted without his foresight, and with which he did not always willingly cooperate" (xvi). It is Rasselas' foredoomed hope "to determine for myself," and his feeling that he has the world before him to contemplate and eventually to comprehend removes him from the engagement in experience that might end his quest.

Rasselas and his sister are too fastidious to accept the imperfection of a deluded or meaningless life, and too detached to experience the energy of such a life from within. "There are a thousand familiar disputes which reason never can decide; questions that elude investigation, and make logic ridiculous; cases where something must be done, and where little can be said." These observations Nekayah reaches from observing marriage, and she concludes: "There are goods so opposed that we cannot seize both, but, by too much prudence, may pass between them at too great a distance to reach either. This is often the fate of long consideration: he does nothing who endeavors to do more than is allowed to humanity. Flatter not yourself with contrarieties of pleasure. Of the blessings set before you, make your choice, and be content" (xxix). This provides a contrast to Rasselas' earlier expectation: "He thought it unsuitable to a reasonable being to act without a plan, and to be sad or cheerful only by chance. 'Happiness,' said he, 'must be something solid and permanent, without fear and without uncertainty' " (xvii).

There is more to be learned than this. Not only does the complexity of life elude rational choice, it mocks the stability of human sentiments. When Nekayah's companion, Pekuah, is abducted, the princess must accept the limits of her responsibility. Her self-reproach is cut off by Imlac; man can only do what he sees to be right, but he must resign his control over its consequences. Nekayah must face the limits of human grief. Imlac advises: "Do not suffer life to stagnate; it will grow muddy for want of motion; commit yourself again to the current of the world; Pekuah will vanish by degrees: you will meet in your way some other favorite, or learn to diffuse yourself in general conversation." As nature repairs itself, Nekayah begins "imperceptibly to return to common cares and common pleasures" (xxxv). In the same way the maddened astronomer must surrender the "luscious falsehood" to the daily concerns of human involvement (xliv). Man must come to accept his littleness and to give up the aspirations and guilt that come from a sense of uniqueness. Imlac advises the astronomer to remember always "that you are only one atom of the mass of humanity, and have neither such virtue nor vice, as that you should be singled out for supernatural favors or afflictions" (xlvi). One may recall the dervish's reply to Candide's concern about the role of evil in the world: "When His Highness sends a ship to Egypt, do you suppose he worries whether the ship's mice are comfortable or not?" The point of these remarks is different, and Johnson does not ridicule the conception of a providence at work in the world; but, like Voltaire, Johnson distrusts man's hope that he can understand that providence and, even more, man's assumption that he has understood it. At the close of Johnson's tale each of the characters dreams of some improbable happiness. Only Imlac and the astronomer "were contented to be driven along the stream of life, without directing their course to any particular port." But even this acquiescence is one of the wishes that all know well cannot be obtained (xlix).

Both these philosophical tales insist upon the dangerous

folly of man's high expectations for himself, whether of happiness or of the mastery of the idea of happiness. Both reject the trust in metaphysical speculation, especially that speculation that intoxicates us with a vision of a universe of rational order. Such a vision deflects attention from the local duties and charities that make our existence tolerable, and from the commitments of the heart that make for an authentic human order. Johnson gives more weight than does Voltaire to the power of speculative curiosity, and perhaps he sees more clearly the need for hope to impress itself upon our image of the world. Still, we may recall the final couplet of *The Vanity of Human Wishes,*

> With these celestial Wisdom calms the mind,
> And makes the happiness she does not find.

The stress is upon the difficulties and confusion of the search, the simple and immediate good the mind congenitally overlooks and overleaps, the comedy of misdirected effort and undeserved luck.

II. The Duality of Man

In Sterne, the opposition of chance and choice is carried further.[2] Sterne intensifies the causal pattern of ordinary life even more than Fielding, and his characters become the ludicrous victims of rigorously interrelated events. *The Life and Opinions of Tristram Shandy, Gentleman* is, among other things, a triumph of the "genetic method." Tristram's character is accounted for by the physical causes that operate upon him from the very moment of conception. With Mrs. Shandy's "unseasonable question" about the clock, "a foundation [has] been laid for a thousand weaknesses both of body and mind" —so that Tristram will "neither think nor act," as his father puts it, "like any other man's child" (I, ii, iii—all references are to volume and chapter numbers). The chain of causality that follows is brilliantly complicated; it reaches back into the history of the Shandy family and forward to the moment at which the book is being written. Walter Shandy's theories and his wife's stubbornness have produced a marriage settlement that exposes Tristram to the forceps of Dr. Slop: "so that I was doom'd, by marriage articles, to have my nose squeez'd as flat to my face, as if the destinies had actually spun me without one," and "a train of vexatious disappointments, in one stage or other of my life, have pursued me from the mere loss, or rather compression, of this one single member" (I, xv). Again, Walter's theory of names requires that his son be called Trismegistus, a name that Susannah the maid cannot master, and so it collapses into Tristram, the name Walter considers the most inauspicious. And the obsession of Toby Shandy with fortifications leads Corporal Trim to melt down for lead all the sash weights he can find, with the result that Tristram is circumcised by the sudden fall of a window—circumcised or worse, as Dr. Slop suggests in his desire to magnify the value of his treatment. As in *Tom Jones,* events flow from character but not from one responsible hero—rather from several characters brought into what the astrologers once called malign conjunction. And while the rigor of events causes temporary distress to Tom Jones or Sophia Western, here it works calamity upon the small body of Tristram, and upon the "opinions" that will be formed within it. The rigor of causality, the physical form it takes, the helplessness of the infant—all these give a new note to Sterne's novel.

The theme of human ineffectuality runs through all the main characters. The possibility of impotence hovers over all the Shandy males—whether in wounded groins, flattened noses, or a sheer distrust of feeling, like Walter's. But in a larger sense of impotence, Walter's mixture of irritability and love of far-fetched hypotheses produces constant frustration. Toby's shy, slow innocence and love of his game of fortifications keep him securely childlike. And Yorick's refusal to defend himself against slander and suspicion ensures that he will remain a perpetual victim of others' malice or envy. These disabilities of temperament are as crippling as Tristram's physical mis-adventures, and we see the two becoming one in the temperament of Tristram as author—unable to sustain connected narrative, fantastic and whimsical, emotionally undisciplined, as much the victim as the author of his book.

Or so Sterne pretends. He gives us—in Toby, Walter, and Yorick—curiously reduced versions of the great aspirations of soldier, scholar, and priest. They can, in fact, be seen as versions of the orders of Pascal. One might expect the order of flesh to be embodied in the soldier, but Toby's mildness is the denial of the search for power. His military force arises from tender loyalty, his elaborate operations on the bowling green are an end in themselves—a reduction of warfare to a harmless game, and his readiness to fight in behalf of his country is more than offset by his warm charity. So, too, in Walter we have all the towering structures and lofty rhetoric of the order of mind, but the systems are half-superstitious, half-playful—the harmless obsessions of an eccentric amateur. In Yorick we come to the order of charity, but Yorick's disdain for the world is ruefully ludicrous and self-mocking. The vestiges of greatness adhere to the professions, but not to these men. Tristram shares in their unsuccess. He holds all the orders in ironic perspective, but, unlike the narrator of Fielding's novels, he is not securely ironic. He alternates between defiance and deception, appeal and assault. He is intensely histrionic, as if he knew that none of the roles he assumes may be sustained for very long at a time, that none in itself will suffice, that the very shifting of roles is necessary to the full act of awareness.

Throughout his work Sterne plays off the crippled body or temperament, seen from the outside as the ludicrous victim of circumstance, with the expansive mind, which tries to convert all it apprehends into the stuff of its obsessions. We see this most clearly in Toby, who is baffled by words and tortured by the difficulty of handling maps until he hits upon the expedient of recreating his vision on the bowling green. There he builds, in small scale, the world in which his mind lives. It is a world he can control and reshape at will, and all the furniture of the larger and less real world about him (notably the sash weights of young Tristram's nursery window) is transformed into the gear of his imaginary battlefield. There warfare becomes a pure tactical game, abstracted from cruelty and suffering. The innocuousness of the game helps to set the scale, as with the game of ombre in Pope's *Rape of the Lock,* but the game is also the perfect vehicle for obsession—complex, absorbing, and self-contained.

Walter's mind expands into hypothesis. "It is the nature of an hypothesis, when once a man has conceived it, that it assimilates every thing to itself as proper nourishment; and, from the first moment of your begetting it, it generally grows the stronger by every thing you see, hear, read, or understand" (II, xix). And Walter, like the Spider in Swift's *Battle of the Books,* has a horror of anything—whether the intrusion of stubborn fact or the exposure of miscalculation—that will destroy his fabric: "error, Sir, creeps in thro' the minute holes, and small crevices, which human nature leaves unguarded" (II, xix). Walter's predilection for seeing things "in his own light," "out of the high-way of thinking," makes his intellectual systems as self-contained and obsessive as Toby's game.

Walter is so tenacious in his opinions, we are told, that he "would intrench and fortify them round with as many circumvallations and breastworks, as my uncle *Toby* would a citadel" (III, xxxiv).

In a more general way, Walter is infatuated with words. When he discovers, for the sake of his son, a "North-west passage to the intellectual world" through the mastery of auxiliary verbs, we see a brilliant reduction of all his ambitions to their essence. The use of auxiliary verbs, he tells Yorick, "is, at once to set the soul a going by herself upon the materials as they are brought her; and by the versability of this great engine, round which they are twisted, to open new tracks of enquiry, and make every idea engender millions" (V, xlii). And Walter triumphantly builds his world of words:

> A WHITE BEAR! Very well. Have I ever seen one? Might I ever have seen one? Am I ever to see one? Ought I ever to have seen one? Or can I ever see one?
>
> Would I had seen a white bear! (for how can I imagine it?)
>
> If I should see a white bear, what should I say? If I should never see a white bear, what then?
>
> If I never have, can, must or shall see a white bear alive; have I ever seen the skin of one? Did I ever see one painted?—described? Have I never dreamed of one?
>
> Did my father, mother, uncle, aunt, brothers or sisters, ever see a white bear? What would they give? How would they behave? How would the white bear have behaved? Is he wild? Tame? Terrible? Rough? Smooth? (V, xliii).

Like the priests of Pope's Dulness or the ebullient Conrad Crambe of the *Memoirs of Scriblerus,* Walter has succeeded in confining the mind to words alone.

The conflicts that inevitably ensue between rival obsessions are like the sudden confrontation of two rival orders that meet in a common term. There can, it is true, be moments of communication. When Trim mistakes Walter's auxiliaries for troops, Toby, for once, can see the error: "The auxiliaries, Trim, my brother is talking about,—I conceive to be different things." Even Walter is astonished. "You do? said my father, rising up" (V, xlii). Toby's customary role is to switch the train of ideas from the track of Walter's obsessions to his own; he does it guilelessly enough, for he cannot credit the reality of Walter's world enough to sense the difference. This comedy of incomprehension can become very complicated, as comedy tends to do. After his son Bobby's death, Walter reads aloud Servius Simplicius' consolatory letter to Cicero, with its references to travels in Asia (where Walter had once gone as a merchant). Toby takes the letter as Walter's own and asks when it was written. "Simpleton! said my father—'twas forty years before Christ was born." Toby's warm sympathy is aroused; he is convinced that Walter is maddened by grief, and he prays silently for his brother with tears in his eyes. And Walter, in turn, is pleased with the tears, which he takes as a tribute to his moving delivery (V, iii).

The most startling and brilliant treatment of this comedy of the mind locking itself up in its own world is Trim's reading of Yorick's sermon. Trim's brother Tom has been a captive of the Inquisition for fourteen years, and as Trim reads the sermon—with its images of the Inquisition's victims—all distance between himself and the world he is evoking breaks down:

> 'To be convinced of this, go with me for a moment into the prisons of the inquisition.'—[God help my poor brother *Tom*.]—'Behold *Religion,* and *Mercy* and *Justice* chained down under her feet,—there sitting ghastly upon a black tribunal, propp'd up with racks and instruments of torment. Hark!—hark! what a piteous groan.' [Here *Trim*'s face turned as pale as ashes.] 'See the melancholy wretch who utter'd it,'—[Here the tears began to trickle down] 'just brought forth to undergo the anguish of a mock trial, and endure the utmost pains that a studied system of cruelty has been able to invent.'—[D—n them all, quoth *Trim,* his colour returning into his face as red as blood.]—'Behold this helpless victim delivered up to his tormentors,—his body so wasted with sorrow and confinement.'—[Oh! 'tis my brother, cried poor *Trim* in a most passionate exclamation, dropping the sermon upon the ground, and clapping his hands together—I fear 'tis poor *Tom*] (II, xvii).

Even when Trim cannot go on with his reading and Walter takes over, Trim cannot bear to leave. Trim's is a case of ludicrous obsession and yet of admirable intensity of feeling. His power of sympathy breaks through all the forms of language and achieves a terrifying immediacy. The pathology of his response is clear enough: in its naïve form, it is the child's cry of warning at the play; and in its more obsessive form, it is the sending of letters and gifts to fictional characters of television programs. Trim shows us the folly of the obsessive imagination, but since his obsession arises from an intense sympathy for his brother, he shows us also the glory of feeling overleaping the restraints of the literal and the rational.

Sterne carries the duality of man to its ultimate expression. He comically exaggerates the outside view of man as a physically determined creature, the sport of chance or mechanical causation, the lonely product of a valueless material world. He exaggerates no less the inside view of man as a creature of feeling, convinced phenomenologically that he has a soul, creating the world in which he chiefly lives by the energy of his own imagination. The disjunction is as violent as Pascal's. Each man exists at once in what Thomas Browne called "divided and distinguished worlds." Nor does he find the reconciliations the Augustans sought in an order of mind supple enough to participate in orders above and below and firm enough to hold them together in harmony. Sterne envisages such a balance, as his sermons make clear, but in his fiction he exploits the imbalance, the fluctuation, the crazy veering between "delicacy" and "concupiscence." The Augustans always make the balance an indefinable and elusive point. It is stated by negations, caught in the delicate poise between the excesses of statement, protected by strategic retreat from every attempt to fix it in formula. We see it as the fulcrum of a thousand different antitheses, in the tone of a voice engaged in dialectical play, or the ironic self-corrections of stance. For all the challenges of Fielding's narrator, we feel that he personifies this balance. We are never allowed this much security in Sterne. The central order of mind drops out of view (although it can still be felt in the play of intelligence and comic detachment), and we are left with radical alternations of derision and sentiment.

Love for Sterne, as for Fielding, is the clearest instance of duality. Walter Shandy cites the two Venuses of Plato and his Renaissance commentators: "The first, which is the golden chain let down from heaven, excites to love heroic, which comprehends in it, and excites to the desire of philosophy and truth—the second, excites to *desire,* simply" (VIII, xxxiii). We see the puzzles in Toby's question whether he is simply irritated by a blister in his "nethermost part" or in love with the Widow Wadman—"till the blister breaking in the one case—and the other remaining—my uncle Toby was presently convinced, that his wound was not a skin-deep-wound—but that it had gone to his heart" (VIII, xxvi). We see them in the Beguine's tender treatment of Trim. She rubs his wounded leg, "till at length, by two or three strokes longer than the rest—my passion rose to the highest pitch—I seiz'd her hand—" This conversion of irritation to passion, Tristram concludes, "contain'd in it the essence of all the love-romances which ever have been wrote since the beginning of the world" (VIII, xxii). We see the incongruity most sharply in Slawkenbergius' tale, where the doleful courtly lover rides sighing through Strasburg, obliviously exhibiting his astonishingly large and obscene nose. He remains sublimely engaged in his tender and exalted sentiment, while the spectacle of his nose titillates the mass of Strasburgers to a carnival of erotic frenzy and the graver ones to the heat of scholastic dispute.

Sterne is equally willing to trace the highest and most stately activities down to the erotic energy they sublimate, and to overturn the stateliest structures so that their precariousness becomes clear. The large-nosed stranger alternately addresses his beloved mistress (up there and far away) and his refractory mule (down here and close): "O Julia, my lovely Julia! —nay I cannot stop to let thee bite that thistle—that ever the suspected tongue of a rival should have robbed me of enjoyment when I was upon the point of tasting it" (IV, opening section). Or we have the termination of Julia's tender farewell: "'Tis a bitter draught, Diego, but oh! 'tis embitter'd still more by dying *un*——." Slawkenbergius, the scholarly editor, "supposes the word intended was *unconvinced*, but her strength would not enable her to finish her letter." The pathos of the unfinished letter descends nicely into sexual innuendo, just as when Diego writes his ode in charcoal, we are told that "he eased his mind against the wall." Sterne keeps alive the Augustan irony about "poetical evacuation." He is as much aware of the convertibility of terms as the conversion of sentiments; whatever goes up can also come down.

We can see Sterne's distrust of systems and forms again in his mockery of scholastic debates about baptism. At what point does the embryo become a person? If the child can be baptized in the womb with an injection-pipe, why can't we extend this marginal area and simply baptize the spermatozoa all at once, "after the ceremony of marriage, and before that of consummation?" (I, xx). Sterne constantly satirizes our tendency to take our mental abstractions for real entities, a tendency deeply built into all of our systems for achieving moral or legal consistency. The danger is that we become reluctant to sacrifice a system to the suppleness or novelty of experience. We become attached to our words and preserve them at any cost. When Walter cannot make sense of a text, he "decides to study the mystic and the allegoric sense,—here is some room to turn a man's self in" (III, xxxvii). It is an amiable crotchet in Walter and a good instance of the way in which men turn the search for meaning into the delights of conundrum. But Sterne wishes us, I think, to remember as well such results as the exertions of the three brothers in Swift's *Tale of a Tub* on their father's testament, when words become forms behind which interest can hide. The mild obsessions of Walter and Toby are innocent comic versions of something much worse in designing men, who welcome the opacity of forms. Sterne's central characters are transparent men, in whom the soul stands naked, so that one can trace "all her maggots from their first engendering to their crawling forth" (I, xxiii).

Sterne does all he can to subvert words and forms. He plays upon the unexpected implications of words and makes a casual analogy go round and round on all fours. He topples the jargon of courtly love or stoical pride. He mocks the delicacy of nuns who split an obscene word into syllables, each taking half, in order to get it said to a stubborn mule. (One may recall that Swift's three brothers, when they cannot twist words to their will, break them into syllables, which prove more malleable.) He infects words with obscene suggestions, which, once released, spread like a plague and corrupt every simple reference to noses, whiskers, or crevices. He exploits typography, as he reproduces the form of a contract, in order to make clear (as Pope does with legal abbreviations) how much the authority of the law depends upon formality or mystery. And all this is related to the self-consciousness that is constantly subverting the larger forms of the book itself—insisting upon it as a printed thing, exploiting the arbitrariness of chapter divisions, calling attention to the artifice of fictional time or to the process of reading itself or, most of all, to the author's exercise of control. Readers of fiction are generally eager to surrender themselves to belief; so long as a novel is conducted with sufficient skill, its conventions are rapidly accepted. Sterne insists upon making us conscious of all we have commonly taken for granted. By pretending incompetence or indecision, by teasing us with false leads or cheating our logical expectations, he exposes the forms at every point. Fielding's subversion of his artistic form is his ultimate commentary on the moral life he is treating. Sterne's is that and something more; his book is more generally philosophical than Fielding's. Sterne moves from the problems of ethics into the general theory of knowledge; his satire is moral, but his comedy is epistemological.

III. The Art of the Natural

At the heart of Sterne's work is a central paradox that runs through the eighteenth century and receives its fullest statement in Denis Diderot's *Paradoxe sur le comédien* (written in the 1770s and published in 1830). Diderot's actor is the man who must be free of emotion in order to call up emotion in others:

> At the very moment when he touches your heart he is listening to his own voice: his talent depends not, as you think, upon feeling, but upon rendering so exactly the outward signs of feeling, that you fall into the trap. He has rehearsed to himself every note of his passion. He has learnt before a mirror every particle of his despair (trans. W. H. Pollock, as *The Paradox of Acting,* New York, 1957, p. 19).

Diderot's paradox is the culmination of a dialectical process one can see in his *Salons* and even more clearly in *Rameau's Nephew* and *Jacques the Fatalist,* a dialectic of art and nature.[3]

Rameau's nephew is the intransigent "natural" man, who insists upon his selfishness and uncontrollable passions. He makes the point that moral restraint and dedication are unnatural; they require a position—as he puts it—"which would cause me trouble and which I could not hold" (88). His energies are enormous and undisciplined; his talents are spilled in vile pantomime; his art is an unstable mixture of brilliance and nonsense. He challenges the decorum of moral men: "Just imagine the universe philosophical and wise, and tell me if it would not be devilishly dull" (35). At least he is nakedly what he is: "Neither more nor less detestable than other men, he was franker than they, more logical, and thus often profound in his depravity" (76). "The important point is that you and I should exist, and that we should be you and I. . . . The best order, for me, is that in which I had to exist—and a fig for the most perfect world if I am not of it" (16).

The music the young Rameau defends against his uncle's is a "natural" music in which "the animal cry of the passions [dictates] the melodic line":

> We call out, invoke, clamor, groan, weep, and laugh openly. No more witticisms, epigrams, neat thoughts—

they are too unlike nature. And don't get it into your head that the old theatrical acting and declamation can give us a pattern to follow. Not likely! We want it more energetic, less mannered, more genuine (71).

Rameau's nephew represents the vitality and the formlessness of the natural, both its honesty and its shabby cruelty. The *Moi* who confronts him may be somewhat stuffy in contrast, but he defends the freedom of Diogenes the Cynic, "the philosopher who has nothing and asks for nothing." Art holds its own against nature.

Diderot is fond of pushing to extremes the unnaturalness of morality, and he draws from that demonstration an ambiguous conclusion. In the *Conversation between a Father and His Children* (1772), the father insists upon maintaining the law even when to do so creates unhappiness for everyone; and his son, the philosopher, argues against him for the "natural": "Isn't the natural wisdom of humanity many times more sacred than that of some lawgiver? We call ourselves civilized, yet often we behave worse than savages. . . . Pure instinct, unhindered, would have led us straight to our goal" (283). The issue is drawn but hardly settled; the father's moral simplicity, unnaturally devoted as it is to law, has a strength that the son's arguments hardly damage.

In *Jacques the Fatalist* this problematic relation of morality and nature is presented differently. Jacques professes a doctrine that denies all meaning to morality, but he cannot live by it. Jacques is persuaded that actions follow inevitably from their causes, that whatever will happen is written in the Great Scroll, and that no action, therefore, has moral value.

> According to such a system, one might imagine that Jacques rejoiced and sorrowed about nothing. Such, however, was not the case. He behaved very much as you and I. . . . Often he was inconsistent, like you and me, and subject to forgetting his principles, save in those few circumstances where his philosophy clearly dominated him. It was then he would say: "That had to be, for that was written up yonder." He tried to prevent evil; he was prudent, yet all the while he had the greatest scorn for prudence. When the inevitable accident happened, he reverted to his old refrain, and was consoled by it. For the rest, he was a good fellow, frank, honest, brave, affectionate, faithful, strong-headed, but more than all these, talkative . . . (167).

Here unhindered instinct, for all the overlay of doctrine, has its own morality, more active and energetic than that of the master, who insists upon his freedom but hardly acts.

In *Jacques the Fatalist,* which resembles *Tristram Shandy* in several important respects and borrows from it, Diderot is exploring several problems in which ethics shades off into metaphysics. Jacques, like Voltaire's Candide, acts well when he acts without regard for his theories. And through Jacques and his master, we explore the issues of freedom, and especially men's habit "of confusing the voluntary with the free" (as Diderot put it in a letter of 1756 to Landois). Diderot wants to preserve an inclusive and problematic view of choice. Its role is crucial even though it is determined by all that a man has been and known. Diderot tries to avoid the fatalism that denies that man can ever be a moral agent and the radical libertarianism that separates a decision from its conditions and sees it as a pure act of will.

Related to this problem of man's nature is that of the world's order. Pangloss, with his doctrine of "sufficient reason," finds a tight causal sequence in all events that conforms to human values and produces good out of evil. He vulgarizes the optimism we see in Pope's *Essay on Man* by insisting that the good is an external, tangible one, realized in the world. (Pope insists only upon the necessary limitations on any one individual's external happiness in a design that must sacrifice each individual in some degree to every other, and he tries to induce the contentment that can arise from identifying the will of the self with the welfare of the whole.) Diderot and Sterne do not present in their fiction the possible Order that lies behind apparent disorder, but, like Pope, they study the pathology of false expectation.

In Pope it is pride that lies behind the demands of self-hood; in Diderot and Sterne, the error is not moral failure but simply the limitations of man's categories of thought. Both writers are willing to acknowledge a rightness of choice that rises out of the "heart" when thought is suppressed or side-stepped. Both are willing to recognize the dangers of formal thinking, where all is "reasoned, formal, stiff, academic, and flat" in contrast to the exuberance of natural energy finding its own form. "The license of his style," Diderot says of Montaigne, "is practically a guarantee to me of the purity of his habits" (*Jacques,* 206). And this license of style—the subversion of narrative or discursive forms—makes, in turn, for the celebration of those non-verbal, spontaneous movements of psychosomatic wisdom—gestures.

Neither Diderot nor Sterne, it should be noted, is content to give unqualified trust to the heart or to the natural. Both see something ludicrous and unstable (and Diderot also something terrible) in the natural, and both insist on the paradox of nature and art. The natural heart can achieve a spontaneous artistry that puts to shame all deliberate endeavors; yet, it may turn out, in another view, that the natural can be attained only by the calculated surprises of art, the deliberate disordering of forms and the artful pretense of spontaneity. The balance the Augustans tried to hold between the natural and the artificial, the "true" and the histrionic, breaks down in Sterne; there is interplay but hardly fusion. In this respect Sterne recalls some of the qualities of baroque art.

It was F. W. Bateson who first applied the term "baroque" to English literature of the later eighteenth century. Like the baroque art of the century before, the art of Sterne (and others of his age) deliberately splits open the harmonies of classical form. High baroque art in Italy leaves nothing undone "to draw the beholder into the orbit of the work of art."[4] Bernini's statues, in Rudolf Wittkower's words, "breathe, as it were, the same air as the beholder, are so 'real' that they even share the space continuum with him, and yet remain picture-like works of art in a specific and limited sense" (101). In Bernini's bust of Scipione Borghese (1632) "the head is shown in momentary movement, the lively eye seems to fix the beholder, and the half-open mouth, as if about to speak, engages him in conversation" (98). The effect is a breakdown of familiar limits. As the beholder finds himself "drawn into the orbit of the work," he asks himself, "What is image, what is reality? The very borderline between the one and the other seems to be obliterated" (106).

Inevitably, when realism is so intense that it has become illusionistic we become aware of its artifice and theatricality. Illusionism breaks through the familiar conventions, stable and unobtrusive as they often remain, upon which most art depends; and in doing so, it calls up awareness of the conventionality of all art. Sterne's age is far different from Bernini's, however. The breakdown of artistic distance in Bernini becomes an approach to religious mystery, a dissolution of rational coolness and an involvement of the senses in the full experience of ecstatic transcendence. The theatricality we see in Sterne is turned upon itself, and it is closer to what Wittkower sees in the late baroque, where we find an interesting double movement—in one direction toward the example of stage design, in the other toward the new celebration of the sketch as opposed to the finished work. Wittkower also draws a connection between the new interest in the sketch and the new taste for painters, like Magnasco in the eighteenth century, who use a broad brush and depart from the conventional realism of the finished surface. We have moved from art as illusion to concern with the processes of art.

Diderot in his *Salon* of 1767 treats the question of our pleasure in the sketch. It has, he begins, "more life and less defined forms. As forms become more accurately defined life departs. In dead animals, dreadful objects to our sight, the forms are there, but life is gone." He tries that most common of explanations: the sketch pleases us because "it leaves our imagination free to see what we like in it, just as children see shapes in the clouds, and we are all more or less children." He goes on, however, to make a significant comparison, to which I shall return in connection with Sterne's use of music: "It is the same difference as that between vocal and instrumental music; in the former we listen to what it says, but in the latter we make it say what we choose." When he turns to Greuze, Diderot considers the problem again. "A sketch is generally more spirited than a picture. It is the artist's work when he is full of inspiration and ardor, when reflection has toned down nothing, it is the artist's soul expressing itself freely on the canvas. His pen or skilful pencil seems to sport and play; a few strokes express the rapid fancy, and the more vaguely art embodies itself the more room is there for the play of imagination." And once more Diderot turns to the example of instrumental music.

What matters for Sterne is the shift of attention from the embodied work to the energy of the artist, from the formed—in Shaftesbury's distinction—to the forming, from the creation to the immanent creator. It is this concern, I think, that accounts for the double interest in the artifice of art and the process of artistic creation. In the eighteenth century, a number of instances come to mind—some of which I deal with in the next chapter—like Hogarth's device of formal notation reducing human postures or frames to geometrical forms, out of whose suggestions figures could be formed anew; Gainsborough's gathering of rocks and bits of moss from which to paint full landscape scenes in his studio; Alexander Cozens' method of developing a landscape drawing from an ink blot. In all these cases the artist cultivates an arbitrary beginning, suggestive but vague, from which the inventive process can take its start. Or one can cite Reynolds' use of "quotations," partly witty allusion, partly suggestive model—Mrs. Siddons as a Michelangelo Sibyl or prophet, Garrick between Tragedy and Comedy like Hercules at the Crossroads, infants in the grand postures of prophets and judges. In the case of Reynolds we can see most clearly the link between awareness of the artificial and the arbitrary and the double vision of the mock form, where the Augustans had allowed artifice freest and most conspicuous play. The divorce between apparent form and apparent subject was at the heart of the mock form, and the play of imagination was therefore most frankly play.

Sterne's interest in gesture draws together many of the tendencies of the age. It led, first of all, to his being likened (by Ralph Griffiths) to "the delicate, the circumstantial Richardson himself." Sterne's gestures, so meticulously presented, allow the reader that "play of imagination" Diderot valued in the sketch. Sterne himself wrote of the "true feeler": "His own ideas are only called forth by what he reads, and the vibrations within, so entirely correspond with those excited, 'tis like reading *himself* and not the book." The gesture, like music, combines formal clarity with suggestiveness; it gives the reader the experience of having his unconscious movement sharply defined before him. Gestures have much the same function for the artistry of feeling that suggestive forms may have for the painter. This artistry of the heart is an essential theme in *Tristram Shandy,* and we see it most clearly in the untutored movements of Corporal Trim. As he prepares to read the sermon aloud, he assumes precisely the posture that reveals Hogarth's "line of beauty," the serpentine curve whose movement "along the continuity of its variety" Hogarth had praised in *The Analysis of Beauty* (1753) and presented on his title page (where he also cited Milton's "Curl'd many a wanton wreath," the description of Eve's hair).

Sterne ponders Trim's curious infallibility:

> How the duce Corporal *Trim,* who knew not so much as an acute angle from an obtuse one, came to hit it so exactly;—or whether it was chance or nature, or good sense or imitation. . . .

The description is minute and fussy:

> He stood,—for I repeat it, to take the picture of him in at one view, with his body sway'd, and somewhat bent forwards,—his right-leg firm under him, sustaining seven-

eights of his whole weight,—the foot of his left-leg, the defect of which was no disadvantage to his attitude, advanced a little,—not laterally, nor forwards, but in a line betwixt them;—his knee bent, but that not violently,—but so as to fall within the limits of the line of beauty;—and I add, of the line of science too;—for consider, it had one eighth part of his body to bear up;—so that in this case the position of the leg is determined,—because the foot could be no further advanced, or the knee more bent, than what would allow him mechanically, to receive an eighth part of his whole weight under it,—and to carry it too.

The full account of Trim's stance makes clear the holistic nature of Sterne's concern with gesture. The gestures become part of a composition:

Corporal *Trim*'s eyes and the muscles of his face were in full harmony with the other parts of him;—he look'd frank,—unconstrained,—something assured,—but not bordering upon assurance.

We see Trim at last "with such an oratorical sweep *throughout the whole figure,*—a statuary might have modell'd from it" (II, xvii).

This feeling for the *gestalt* of the whole figure is important in Sterne. In the account of the Monk of Calais in *A Sentimental Journey* we have an artistic rendering again:

The rest of his outline may be given in a few strokes; one might put it into the hands of any one to design; for 'twas neither elegant or otherwise, but as character and expression made it so. . . .

When the Monk pleads the poverty of his order, he does it with "so simple a grace, and such an air of depreciation was there in *the whole cast of his look and figure,* I was bewitch'd not to have been struck by it—"

In the phrases I have set in italics, we can see the emphasis upon the unifying power of expression. Gesture, by its very muteness, calls forth sympathetic imagination and demands an attention to the whole figure. "There are a thousand unnoticed openings," says Walter Shandy, "which let a penetrating eye at once into a man's soul; and I maintain it, added he, that a man of sense does not lay down his hat in coming into a room,—or take it up in going out of it, but something escapes, which discovers him" (VI, v).

Trim's funeral sermon on Bobby provides another instance of the eloquence of gesture:

> —'Are we not here now';—continued the corporal, 'and are we not'—(dropping his hat plumb upon the ground—and pausing, before he pronounced the word)—'gone! in a moment?' The descent of the hat was as if a heavy lump of clay had been kneaded into the crown of it.—Nothing could have expressed the sentiment of mortality, of which it was the type and fore-runner, like it,—his hand seemed to vanish from under it,—it fell dead,—the corporal's eye fix'd upon it, as upon a corps,—and *Susannah* burst into a flood of tears.
>
> Now—Ten thousand, and ten thousand times ten thousand (for matter and motion are infinite) are the ways by which a hat may be dropped upon the ground, without any effect.—Had he flung it, or thrown it, or cast it, or skimmed it, or squirted, or let it slip or fall in any possible direction under heaven,—or in the best direction that could be given to it,—had he dropped it like a goose—like a puppy—like an ass—or in doing it, or even after he had done, had he looked like a fool,—like a ninny—like a nincompoop—it had fail'd, and the effect upon the heart had been lost.

What is clear in these brilliant descriptions of gesture is that Sterne is more than a realist. He records them with an exactness that goes far beyond the demands of conventional realism, and he brings to description the analytic apparatus of the art or drama critic, as if he were judging the performances by their effect. Scattered through the book are allusions to the formal criteria of criticism:

> My father instantly exchanged the attitude he was in, for that in which Socrates is so finely painted by Raffael in his School of Athens; which your connoisseurship knows is so exquisitely imagined, that even the particular manner of the reasoning of Socrates is expressed by it (IV, vii).

The formal categories of criticism are necessary to express the exquisite rightness of the least detail. Yet, as usual, the critics are too clumsy and arrogant to do justice to their subject; their heads are "stuck so full of rules and compasses." When Garrick suspends his voice in the epilogue, he breaks the rules of the "grammarian."

> But in suspending his voice—was the sense suspended likewise? Did no expression of attitude or countenance fill

up the chasm?—Was the eye silent? Did you narrowly look?—I look'd only at the stopwatch, my Lord.—Excellent observer!

And what of this new book the world makes such a rout about? [i.e., *Tristram Shandy*]—oh! 'tis out of all plumb, my Lord,—quite an irregular thing!—not one of the angles at the four corners was a right angle.—I had my rule and compasses, &c. my Lord, in my pocket.—Excellent critic! (III, xii.)

But the language of criticism, for all its limitations, is necessary to show the artless art of Walter's rhetoric or Trim's oratorical postures, to catch Toby's benign oval of a face, or the eloquent "venereal" eyes of the Widow Wadman. The author may be forced to translate gesture into words, as he paraphrases the Widow's blushes "for the sake of the unlearned reader" (IX, xx). Still, words and critical categories can only approximate the supple expressiveness of Nature:

She, dear Goddess, by an instantaneous impulse, in all *provoking cases,* determines us to a sally of this or that member—or else she thrusts us into this or that place, or posture of body, we know not why—But mark, madam, we have amongst riddles and mysteries—The most obvious things . . . have dark sides . . . and even the clearest and most exalted understandings amongst us find ourselves puzzled and at a loss in almost every cranny of nature's works (IV, xvii).

What Sterne does with gestures, he does again with sound. Walter's rational systems prove to be eccentric twistings of thought and language, but his earnest sophistry becomes effective in its musicality. When he argues down an opponent, he falls into "that soft and irresistible *piano* of voice, which the nature of the *argumentum ad hominem* absolutely requires" (I, xix). It is language that has become expressive sound that fascinates Sterne. Phutatorius' reaction to the hot chestnut in his breeches produces "Zounds," conveyed in "a tone of voice, somewhat between that of a man in amazement, and of one in bodily pain." Those with "nice ears" can "distinguish the expression and mixture of the two tones as plainly as a *third* or a *fifth,* or any other chord in musick" (IV, xxvii). Dr. Slop's assertion that there are seven sacraments produces Toby's "Humph!"—"not accented as a note of acquiescence, —but as an interjection of that particular species of surprize, when a man, in looking into a drawer, finds more of a thing than he expected." And Dr. Slop "who had an ear, understood my uncle Toby as well as if he had wrote a whole volume against the seven sacraments" (II, xvii). The Widow Wadman's eye, finally, recalls those nuances of expression that turn words to music:

> 'twas an eye full of gentle salutations—and soft responses —speaking—not like the trumpet-stop of some ill-made organ, in which many an eye I talk to, holds coarse converse—but whispering soft—like the last low accents of an expiring saint (VIII, xxv).

IV. Tragic and Comic: Maria or the Dance

Tristram as artist embodies all the problems and paradoxes of Sterne's work. Sterne has built upon Locke's treatment of the pathological association of ideas and uses it to present his characters as comic victims of both chance and obsession. Chance rules when Mrs. Shandy is so inopportunely reminded of the clock; obsession when Toby returns (at the least hint) to his ruling passion or hobby-horse. Sterne sees a certain grandeur in the use of obsession to convert all experience to the stuff of its private world. In Tristram himself we see the malady of association and the finest instance of the artistry of the associative process.

In 1794 Walter Whiter was to set forth a commentary on Shakespeare based on Locke's principle of association of ideas. The metaphorical combinations of word or image he wished to study were those that are not naturally connected with each other and therefore seemingly irrational. They had to be understood by unfolding the processes of mind in which they originated. They "were not formed by the invention, but forced upon the fancy of the poet," who "is totally unconscious of the effect and principle of their union" (*A Specimen of a Commentary on Shakespeare*, 1794, p. 71).

This might be taken as a partial description of Tristram's unconscious artistry. But Tristram is acutely conscious of the aberrations of associative thought, and he welcomes the accidental with the assurance that it will form part of the unity of his mind and work. He risks being ingenuous; he is ready to be surprised by his feelings and to submit himself to them as they well up from below consciousness. He abruptly recalls—in the midst of their solid life in the narrative—the deaths of Trim and Toby (VI, xxv). Such an eruption of feeling produces an apparent digression, but it serves beautifully to lend a proper note of weakness and unconscious pathos to Toby a few pages later when he explains his devotion to warfare:

> For what is war? what is it, *Yorick,* when fought as ours has been, upon principles of *liberty,* and upon principles of *honour*—what is it, but the getting together of quiet and harmless people, with their swords in their hands, to keep the ambitious and the turbulent within bounds? (VI, xxxii.)

Tristram, in one aspect, is the artist willing to give the unconscious its free play and to co-operate with it. He is also, in another aspect, the calculating manipulator of his own feelings and his readers'. The accidental and unforeseen turn out to be the inevitable and necessary as our conception of the structure of his work grows to meet its challenge. There are countless instances of Tristram's deliberate effort to surprise feelings in himself, to control them, or to complicate them. What in the long-nosed knight-errant of Slawkenbergius' tale is the solemn yoking together of ludicrously disparate ideas becomes in Tristram the cool play of wit, shaping feeling with the detached humor of a free mind, enjoying the comic bathos of a "delicious mixture" of contraries. The death of Le Fever is a famous instance of pathos caught up by saving self-consciousness (but not simply cancelled by it, surely): As

> Nature instantly ebb'd again,—the film returned to its place,—the pulse fluttered—stopp'd—went on—throbb'd—stopp'd again—moved—stopp'd—shall I go on?—No (VI, x).

As Yorick puts it in *A Sentimental Journey,* "In transport of this kind, the heart, in spite of the understanding, will always say too much." The peculiar tone of Sterne comes of his readiness to say too much and his alertness to see that it is too much. The histrionic openings of several of his sermons (including the one in *Tristram Shandy*) represent this wave of generous feeling that rises and then breaks with ironic self-correction.

In the remarkable seventh volume of *Tristram Shandy* the apparent artlessness of uncontrollable feeling breaks into the structure of the book. This violent disruption of the narrative, which brings Tristram up to the near-present and sends him careering in flight from death, adds a dimension of meaning to the entire work. The note of death has been sounded earlier in the laments for Bobby and Tristram's sudden recollection of Trim and Toby's deaths; here it becomes a central motif directly felt and faced, and it prepares us for the comic defeat of Toby's amours in the books to follow. Tristram's flight from the "long-striding scoundrel of a scare-sinner, who is posting after him" is also a flight from what Byron later calls the moral North and what Sterne calls Freezeland or Fog-land. It is a flight to the "clear climate of fantasy and perspiration, where every idea, sensible and insensible, gets vent," where "all flesh is running and piping, fiddling, and dancing to the vintage, and every step that's taken, the judgment is surprised by the imagination" (VIII, i).

The specter of Death gives focus to the sense of the disorder that has earlier been comically presented as contretemps and muddle. Death is not moderated here by Christian comfort; it is the mythical dancer with a grin of finality. And the closeness of Death makes Tristram acutely aware of what is intensely and authentically alive. He refuses to sketch the architectural monuments of Montreuil but turns for a subject to the innkeeper's daughter: "who measures thee, Janatone, must do it now—thou carriest the principles of change within thy frame" (VII, ix). In reply to Bishop Hall's traditional celebration of the serenity of rest, Tristram asserts, "so much of motion, is so much of life, and so much of joy—and . . . to stand still, or get on slowly, is death and the devil—" (VII, xiii). He moves away from formality and imposture, from the perverse Christianity that calculates the total space left in Hell for damned souls to inhabit, and turns to the warm life of returning pagan gods.

Tristram is so disenchanted with a religion of cold formality that he can risk seeing its forms as the denial of energy—an energy that must be found by the flight from formality and perhaps, in time, although he does not say so, brought back into it by men who have achieved generosity of spirit. Sterne wrote to Mrs. Montagu in 1764, "such rapidity of motion is a proof of my leanness at least—and as vivacity is often miscalled wit—why not of my spirituality also—Mark! by spirituality I mean nothing *ecclesiastical* or in the least analogous to church affairs. I use the word in your own good-natured sense—and heaven forbid I should look further. . . ." This is lightly said, but it is telling that the motion tends to become life itself, spinning away humbug and hypocrisy, reaching its culmination in a warm dance of generous feeling.

When Tristram joins the peasant dance in Languedoc, the "sunburnt daughter of Labour" gives him a piece of string to tie up a tress of her hair. "It taught me to forget I was a stranger—The whole knot fell down—We had been seven years acquainted. . . . The sister of the youth who had stolen her voice from heaven, sung alternately with her brother—'twas a Gascoigne roundelay

> Viva la joia!
> Fidon la tristesse!"

"Viva la joia" is in Nannette's eyes, and "a transient spark of amity shot across the space betwixt us. . . . Why could I not live and end my days thus? Just disposer of our joys and sorrows, cried I, why could not a man sit down in *the lap of content* here—and dance, and sing, and say his prayers, and go to heaven with this nut brown maid?" (VII, xliii.)

In a letter written at about the same time (16 November 1764) there is a similar note. Sterne wrote to his banker and friend, Robert Foley, of a place where he might spend "every winter of my life, in the same lap of contentment, where I enjoy myself now—and wherever I go—we must bring three parts in four of the treat along with us—In short we must be happy within—and then few things without make much difference—This is my Shandean philosophy." Earlier in the same year (5 January 1764) just after a "scuffle with death," Sterne wrote, "I shall not die but live—in the meantime dear Foley let us live as merrily but *as innocently* as we can—It has ever been as good, if not better than a bishoprick to me—and *I desire no other—*" These remarks are more than banalities; they help one to see the peculiar weight and quality of *joia* in Tristram Shandy, even as he dances off, "changing only partners and tunes."

The joy is something man creates for himself. As he thinks of his uncle's amour, Tristram is "in the most perfect state of bounty and good will" and feels "the kindliest harmony vibrating" within him, "so that whether the roads were rough or smooth, it made no difference; every thing I saw, or had to do with, touch'd on some secret spring either of sentiment or rapture." It is at that moment that he meets Maria, "sitting upon a bank, playing her vespers upon her pipe, with her little goat beside her." Her banns were cruelly forbidden by the local curate, and she has become insane. Now she plays "an evening service to the Virgin" on the pipe she has mysteriously, even miraculously, learned to play. Tristram leaps out to sit beside her and follows her eyes as she looks alternately at her goat and at him. "Well, Maria, said I softly—What resemblance do you find?" (IX, xxiv.)

Sterne has given a typically ludicrous counterpoint to the pathos, but he has set forth in Maria's heartbroken vespers the alternative to the pipe and taborin of the joyous dance. Maria's faith is no simple matter. It somewhat consoles her for the pain of her existence, somewhat expresses her mad grief. It is in both cases dissociated from the world about her. When we see her again, through Yorick's eyes in *A Sentimental Journey*, "Affliction had touch'd her looks with something that was scarce earthly." The alternative to Maria's grief is the peasant dance, whose erotic energy and innocent joy create the warmth of involvement. It holds Death at a distance and reveals something like charity in its unquestioning and untroubled joy. Sterne has carefully separated out the innocence of this joy from the anxious proprietary questions of the Widow Wadman about Toby's wounded groin, just as he has separated the vespers of Maria from the ill-natured formalism of the church (as we see it, for example, in Dr. Slop's defense of the Inquisition).

Fielding tried to fuse the three orders of Pascal into a new mixture that drew energy from man's animal vigor and brought charity down to human benevolence. Sterne's values are not much different, but the order of mind has become an elusive element, half obliterated in the artistry of feeling, half refined away to histrionic cunning. Sterne carries further than Fielding the method of playing against a form. I would cite the program of Eugène Ionesco as a counterpart:

> Onto a senseless, absurd, comical text one can graft a *mise en scène* and an interpretation which are grave, solemn, and ceremonious. [Walter warns Toby, who is about to court the Widow Wadman, "that there is no passion so serious, as lust. Stick a pin in the bosom of thy shirt, before thou enterest her parlour."] On the other hand, in order to avoid the ridiculousness of easy tears, of sentimentality, one can graft upon a dramatic text a clownesque interpretation, underline by farce the tragic sense of a play ("Discovering the Theatre," p. 11).

"For the modern spirit," Ionesco continues, "nothing can be taken entirely seriously, nor entirely lightly." The comic and the tragic "do not mix completely with each other, they coexist, they repulse one another constantly, each setting the other into relief; they criticize each other, mutually deny each other, constituting through this opposition a dynamic balance, a tension" (p. 12). Sterne, like Ionesco, has used an almost diabolic artistry to bring about the rebirth of naïvety. In the process he makes clear how much of art must be artifice, and how much of all men's thought is shaped by arbitrary conventions, rigid categories, specious terms. Just as Ionesco makes his scenery move around his actors and embodies the absurdity of his characters in grotesque physical presences, so Sterne brings to the surface the inherent ludicrousness of all schemes of ordering. He assumes the manner of an egocentric and tyrannical author, who at every point seems to lose control of the suggestions of his words, the movement of his memory, and the direction of his narrative. As author he enacts the confused state in which he finds man. But like any good actor he remains in fact detached from his role and in control of his audience. He insists upon the fact of his performance; and the histrionic becomes the guarantee of sanity and the recovery of the natural.

XII.

The Theatre of Mind

1. Actor and Audience

During his grand tour, James Boswell became "sulky" one evening at dinner and "railed against the French." His remarks offended his host, a French artillery captain, who denounced him as a scoundrel. A duel threatened, and Boswell strengthened his resolution by calling up in imagination all that might support his sense of honor: the dignity of his family, his national loyalty as Scotsman, his character as a man.

> I must do myself the justice to say that I was fully determined for the worst [he wrote later in his journal]. Yet I wished that the affair could be made up, as I was really in the wrong. I felt myself in the situation which I have often fancied, and which is a very uneasy one. Yet, upon my honour, so strong is my metaphysical passion that I was pleased with this opportunity of intimately observing the working of the human mind.[1]

Boswell was an exceptional man, but in the last sentence we can see a characteristic of the age: the self-consciousness of a mind turned at once upon the world and upon itself, constantly surprised by what it discovers in the self and as constantly eager to induce the self to reveal its mysterious feelings. "A man cannot know himself better," Boswell had written two years before, "than by attending to the feelings of his heart and to his external actions. . . ." So, while attending church (where he heard a sermon on "By what means shall a young man learn to order his ways") he is surprised at what he finds in himself:

> What a curious, inconsistent thing is the mind of man! In the midst of divine service I was laying plans for having women, and yet I had the most sincere feelings of religion. . . . I have a warm heart and a vivacious fancy. I am therefore given to love, and also to piety or grati-

tude to God, and to the most brilliant and showy method of public worship (28 November 1762).

As one might expect, particularly in a young man with literary ambitions, Boswell conceives of himself in terms made current by writers he admired. This last passage catches the "generosity" of Fielding's Tom Jones, as the first one catches the method of Tristram Shandy. Frederick Pottle has observed that Gay's Macheath dominates the early London journal, and there are moments, too, where Boswell plays the role of the Spectator and sustains the "native dignity" of his mind through the example of Addison.

Boswell is a good example of the deliberate artist working upon the materials of his own feelings. He values his "genius for poetry, which ascribes many fanciful properties to everything," but he can keep it "within just bounds by the power of reason, without losing the agreeable feeling and play to the imagination which it bestows" (15 November 1762). Bowing thrice before Edinburgh's "lofty romantic mountain" (as he leaves for London) and feeling a "warm glow of satisfaction" in his "agreeable whim and superstitious humour," he illustrates the distinctive excitement of his age in the "pleasures of imagination."

In one of the earliest poems to find the subject of poetry in the poetic energies of the mind Mark Akenside had written of man's power

> to behold in lifeless things,
> The inexpressive semblance of himself,
> Of thought and passion
>   (*The Pleasures of Imagination*, 1743, III, 284–86).

In a note to the passage Akenside called this procedure "the foundation of almost all the ornaments of poetic diction." As he wrote later, "The ambitious mind / With objects boundless as her own desires / Can there converse" (1765, II, 21–23). It is this theme—the poet as his own subject—that I wish to use as an approach to the poetry of the middle and later eighteenth century. The poet becomes both actor and audience. He contemplates himself as he stands in the theatre of nature, finding in its mute and "inexpressive" forms the life of his own thought and passion. He may, as he tests and studies his feelings, become histrionic—watching with detachment the passions he has worked up in himself. As he celebrates the powers of mind in their superiority to outward and corporeal

forms, he may become visionary. As he exercises the creative
and evocative power of emotion, he may call into being those
personified presences that only passion can animate. Or, as he
exemplifies the philosophic eye, he may become at once minutely particular and rapturously transcendent, moving between close attention to the object and a sense of its part in
the cosmic order. This variety of styles may be said to serve
a common impulse, just as Gothic, Chinese, or rococo architectural forms may equally (and almost interchangeably) satisfy a desire for irregularity that is more constant than any
of its vehicles.

If there is a danger in subsuming all these styles under one
common impulse, as I have proposed, there is still a great need
to establish the identity of the period and to characterize it,
at least tentatively, in terms that are not a mere denaturing
of what precedes or follows. The case of Johnson might be
cited. In most ways, he is one of the great Augustans; but he
participates none the less in the curious self-awareness of the
age. W. J. Bate has written with great sensitivity about the
histrionic element in Johnson, so visible in his overstatement,
his mimicry, or the self-mocking formal sententiousness of a
work like *Rasselas*. "For the exactness with which Johnson
senses motives, blows them up, and then punctures them after edging them into the absurd are largely based on his own
self-perception. . . . Johnson's latent sense of the comic involves a self-burlesque" (*The Achievement of Samuel Johnson*, New York, 1955, p. 123). And there are remarks, such
as the following on prayer, that open up—like *Rasselas* itself—
vistas of skepticism against which to set the massive assertions:

> to reason too philosophically about prayer does no good.
> To be sure, you cannot think it makes God alter his
> purposes. But by producing good effects on the mind of
> him who prays, it disposes the mind in such a manner
> that the thing prayed for is insensibly attained.[2]

II. The Graveyard Scene: Edward Young

Perhaps the best place to observe the histrionic note of
mid-century poetry is in what Boswell called "a mass of the
grandest and richest poetry that human genius has ever produced"—Edward Young's *Night Thoughts* (1742–45). Young's
method becomes clear if we compare him with Pope. First,

the great passage that opens the second epistle of the *Essay on Man* (1733):

> Know then thyself, presume not God to scan;
> The proper study of mankind is man.
> Plac'd on this isthmus of a middle state,
> A being darkly wise, and rudely great:
> With too much knowledge for the sceptic side,
> With too much weakness for the stoic's pride,
> He hangs between; in doubt to act, or rest;
> In doubt to deem himself a God, or beast;
> In doubt his mind or body to prefer;
> Born but to die, and reasoning but to err;
> Alike in ignorance, his reason such,
> Whether he thinks too little, or too much:
> Chaos of thought and passion, all confused;
> Still by himself abus'd, or disabus'd;
> Created half to rise, and half to fall;
> Great lord of all things, yet a prey to all;
> Sole judge of truth, in endless error hurl'd:
> The glory, jest, and riddle of the world!

And a corresponding passage in Young:

> How poor, how rich, how abject, how august,
> How complicate, how wonderful, is man!
> How passing wonder He, who made him such!
> Who centred in our make such strange extremes!
> From diff'rent natures marvelously mix'd,
> Connexion exquisite of distant worlds!
> Distinguish'd link in being's endless chain!
> Midway from nothing to the Deity!
> A beam ethereal, sully'd, and absorpt!
> Tho' sully'd and dishonour'd, still divine!
> Dim miniature of greatness absolute!
> An heir of glory! A frail child of dust!
> Helpless immortal! Insect infinite!
> A worm! a God!—I tremble at myself,
> And in myself am lost! At home, a stranger,
> Thought wanders up and down, surpriz'd, aghast,
> And wond'ring at her own: How reason reels!
> O what a miracle to man is man,
> Triumphantly distress'd! what joy, what dread!
> Alternately transported, and alarm'd!
> What can preserve my life? or what destroy?
> An angel's arm can't snatch me from the grave,
> Legions of angels can't confine me there (I, 68–90).

Pope's lines, among his most brilliant, draw upon the paradoxes of Pascal's double infinity and fix the rivalry of orders in the antitheses of the heroic couplet. Young makes more violent use of paradox. The movement of lines 79–81 (beginning with "An heir of glory!") is toward sharper and more shocking juxtapositions, which contract from a full phrase to a single adjective and noun, and at last to the bare terms *worm* and *God*. At this point, Young breaks off. His rhetorical argument has gone as far as it can. Words fail, and he shifts—in a way that is most important—from generalized irony to the personal predicament. He writes out of his condition, as one immersed in it and struggling toward meaning. When he returns, at the close, to the large scheme of the cosmos, the verbs have become fiercely kinetic and the paradoxical self has become a center of titanic struggle.

Young's poem asks to be set beside Pope's. Perhaps because the anonymously published *Essay on Man* had once been attributed to him by many, he defends his own poem—in the first of its nine long "nights"—by opposition to Pope's:

> Man too he sung: *immortal* man I sing;
> Oft bursts my song beyond the bounds of life;
> What now but immortality can please?
> O had *he* press'd his theme, pursu'd the track
> Which opens out of darkness into day! (I, 453–57.)

Pope's poem, in Young's view, dwells in mundane light. It deals with man's earthly happiness and does not confront man directly with the prospects of eternal reward and punishment. Young's interest is in the light of eternity; he withdraws into that night where man is alone beneath the spectacle of the firmament. He has turned away from the social world and rejected all human achievements as "childish toys." He will settle for nothing less than infinity. George Eliot[3] (in her famous denunciation "Worldliness and Other-Worldliness: The Poet Young," 1857) is affronted by Young's "deficient human sympathy," his "impiety towards the present and visible" (78). All that she admires in Cowper (or Wordsworth) finds its contrary in Young's effort to startle, to dazzle, and to terrify: he "knows no medium between the ecstatic and the sententious," and his poetry is "a Juggernaut made of gold and jewels, at once magnificent and repulsive." His religion she sums up as "egoism turned heavenward" (3–4, 67).

Against this we have Boswell's testimony that he "who does not feel his nerves shaken, and his heart pierced by many passages . . . must be of a hard and obstinate frame." Young's poem may have had special appeal for Boswell; it is addressed to a young "man of pleasure and the world" (named Lorenzo), and conceived in terms Boswell might well have applied to himself. Lorenzo is the embodiment of worldly grace and wit, but he must be brought to despise the world and venerate his soul. Young makes use of typically Pascalian themes—the two infinities (IX, 1573–86), the *deus absconditus* ("Triune, unutterable, unconceiv'd, / Absconding, yet demonstrable, great God!" IX, 2290–91), the rival orders. The vehemence of his conceits derives from his constant separation of orders. When he portrays a devout Christian ("A man on earth devoted to the skies"), Young rings all the changes:

> He sees with other eyes than theirs: where they
> Behold a sun, he spies a deity;
> What makes them only smile, makes him adore.
> Where they see mountains, he but atoms sees;
> An empire, in his balance weighs a grain
> (VIII, 1081, 1107–11).

It is this kind of wit that leads George Eliot to speak of Young's "radical insincerity as a poetic artist": "The grandiloquent man is never bent on saying what he feels or what he sees, but in producing a certain effect on his audience" (51). In "proportion as morality is emotional, it will exhibit itself in direct sympathetic feeling and action. . . . A man who is perpetually thinking in monitory apothegms, who has an unintermittent flux of rebuke, can have little energy left for simple feeling" (69).

One need not defend Young against George Eliot: her principles of judgment would lead her to condemn far better poets. What matters is the kind of poetry he is trying to create. It is endlessly hortatory and ejaculatory, and it suffers from the effort to sustain intensity too long ("So long on wing," as he puts it, "and in no middle climes"). The effort forces Young into all kinds of devices—Senecan pointedness; extended conceits ("Let burlesque go beyond him," Johnson remarked of these); an imagery of bursting, soaring, and plunging. "No poet," Marjorie Nicolson has written,[4] "was ever more 'space intoxicated' than Edward Young, nor did any other eighteenth-century poet or aesthetician equal him in his obsession with the 'psychology of infinity'—the effect of vastness and the vast upon the soul of man." "There dwells a noble pathos in the skies," Young wrote, "Which warms our passions, proselytes our hearts" (IX, 1632–33). And his paradoxes begin from the ever-present awareness of death:

This is the bud of being, the dim dawn,
The twilight of our day, the vestibule. . . .
Embryos we must be, till we burst the shell,
Yon ambient azure shell, and spring to life
(I, 123–24, 132–33).

The darkness of night becomes the possibility of new life. Others may adore the sun, Young writes:

Darkness has more divinity for me;
It strikes thought inward; it drives back the soul
To settle on herself, our point supreme!
There his own theatre! There sits the judge.
Darkness the curtain drops o'er life's dull scene
(V, 128–32).

This kind of paradox can culminate in such a line as

The King of Terrors is the Prince of Peace (III, 534),

a line that permits Blake, in his illustration, the great pictorial irony we see in his illustrations to Job: the threatening figure of Death who has appeared with his dart through earlier plates assumes the benign countenance and gestures of the Christ.

Young emphasizes the emptiness of the life to which Lorenzo is committed—its chanciness, futility, constriction:

Shall sons of aether, shall the blood of heav'n,
Set up their hopes on earth, and stable *here,*
With brutal acquiescence in the mire? (VII, 54–56.)

Young is calling forth from Lorenzo his sense of his own divinity—"Man's misery declares him born for bliss; / His *anxious* heart asserts the truth I sing" (V, 60–61). The tone ranges from satire to rapture:

Or own the soul immortal, or invert
All order. Go, mock-majesty! go, man!
And bow to thy superiors of the stall;
Thro' ev'ry scene of *sense* superior far (V, 290–93).

Only the awareness of eternity and of the divine in man "restores bright order" and "re-inthrones us in supremacy / Of joy, ev'n here" (V, 316–18). And, typically, this becomes kinetic imagery: "Man must soar. / An obstinate activity within, / An insuppressive spring, will toss him up," for "souls immortal must for ever heave / At something great" (V, 389–91, 399–400).

Unlike Pope, who tries to show man reasonable aspiration within his present state, Young's aim is to launch the soul into flight: "The soul of man was made to walk the skies" (IX, 1016). All of Lorenzo's worldly ambitions must be translated into another order and converted to a desire for eternity. Young offers eternity as the fulfillment of the latent energy within man rather than as a more traditional death and rebirth; the movement of the poem is the bursting out of constrictions, expansion into infinite space, progress toward unreachable perfection. The images of the heavens yield an atmosphere in which the soul

> Freely can respire, dilate, extend,
> In full proportion let loose all her powers;
> And, undeluded, grasp at something great.
> Nor as a stranger, does she wander there,
> But, wonderful herself, through wonder strays;
> Contemplating their grandeur, finds her own
>   (IX, 1020–25).

The heavens present an order in disorder. " 'Tis comprehension's absolute defeat"; yet it is "Confusion unconfus'd" —"All on wing! / In motion, all! yet what profound repose" (IX, 1105, 1115–17). We return to Milton's great imagery of the cosmic dance—the "circles intricate" and "mystic maze" (IX, 1130). This energetic order corresponds to the order within man. Young sees man as always grasping, dilating, in some form or other moving: "The mind that would be happy must be great" (IX, 1379).

> The visible and present are for brutes,
> A slender portion, and a narrow bound!
> These reason, with an energy divine
> O'erleaps; and claims the future and unseen!
>   (VI, 246–49.)

One of the interesting consequences of Young's themes is his treatment of vision. When he seeks to free Lorenzo from the world, he demonstrates its poverty by showing what man brings to it. The powers within man descend from a divine source and confer beauty on the visible world. The senses

> Take in, at once, the landscape of the world,
> At a small inlet, which a grain might close,
> And half create the wondrous world they see.
> Our senses, as our reason, are divine.

> But for the magic organ's powerful charm,
> Earth were a rude, uncolor'd chaos, still.
> Objects are but th' occasion; ours th' exploit. . . .
> Like Milton's Eve, when gazing on the lake,
> Man makes the matchless image man admires
>   (VI, 425–31, 435–36).

This doctrine of creative perception clearly goes back to the same kind of Neo-Platonic sources upon which Shaftesbury draws. It is the moment of transcendent vision, however, that concerns Young more; and this is involved with the compelling power of feeling. Here is the instance of man contemplating the Crucifixion:

> Who looks on that, and sees not in himself
> An awful stranger, a terrestrial god? . . .
> I gaze, and, as I gaze, my mounting soul
> Catches strange fire, Eternity, at thee,
> And drops the world—or, rather, more enjoys:
> How chang'd the face of nature! how improv'd!
>   (IV, 494–95, 499–502.)

In both these senses of vision, Young seems to have had some influence on his illustrator, Blake. The bursting of the "ambient azure shell" is an image we find again in Blake; another is the "self-fetter'd" soul (Blake's "mind-forg'd manacles"). And Blake's *The Gates of Paradise* recalls these lines:

> How, like a worm, was I wrapt round and round
> In silken thought, which reptile Fancy spun!
> Till darken'd Reason lay quite clouded o'er
> With soft conceit of endless comfort here,
> Nor yet put forth her wings to reach the skies!
>   (I, 133, 157, 158–62.)

Young anticipates the image of natural man enclosed in a cavern as well as the image of the cocoon: "Through chinks, styl'd organs, dim life peeps at light" (III, 450). These "influences" are not important as such, but they serve (and Blake's illustrations serve even better) to show us how Young could be read in his own century. His gloom and melancholy are far less important than his insistence upon man's expansive grandeur of spirit and upon the dramatic experience of self-discovery. He builds on the doctrine of divine punishment and reward, but his ultimate emphasis is on the energy that sanctifies the passions—their "grandeur . . . speaks them rays of an eternal fire" (VII, 527–30)—and informs the order of charity.

III. The Theatre of Nature: James Thomson

Young emphasizes throughout the *Night Thoughts* that the infinity of space and the intensities of light are internal dimensions of man as well (like Milton's Heaven and Hell). The firmament is "the noble pasture of the mind, / Which there expatiates, strengthens, and exults" (IX, 1037–38). In James Thomson's *The Seasons* (1726–28, revised continuously until 1746), while the imagery is far more minutely accurate and concrete, it has much the same function. Thomson draws not only from nature itself, but from Scripture, from Virgil's *Georgics,* from the great account of creation in the seventh book of *Paradise Lost*—and from Shaftesbury's *Moralists.* One of his early poems is, in effect, an adaptation of Shaftesbury, and his interest in Newtonian science could readily be accommodated to Shaftesbury's doctrines of cosmic harmony. Just as Theocles takes his friend on a circuit of all the regions of the earth to show the range and complexity of nature's order, so Thomson writes four poems on the seasons which explore the Arctic north, the torrid equatorial zones, and all between.[5]

In *Paradise Lost* Milton created a poetry of nature that drew its force from the whole cosmos of the poem. Even in those passages of free and intense phantasy where Milton catches the energies of creative goodness, the cosmic and moral themes of the dramatic action are involved:

> The grassy Clods now Calv'd, now half appear'd
> The Tawny Lion, pawing to get free
> His hinder parts, then springs as broke from Bonds,
> And Rampant shakes his Brinded mane; the Ounce,
> The Libbard, and the Tiger, as the Mole
> Rising, the crumbl'd Earth above them threw
> In Hillocks; the swift Stag from under ground
> Bore up his branching head . . . (VII, 463–70).

These are images of creatures bursting into life, dragging themselves from the womb of earth, rising into light like branching trees, yet with a swiftness that confounds our conception of the slow growth of a tree. They are defiant and jubilant images. In the spirit of the sublime, they overwhelm our familiar conceptions and demand the reach of imagination that is appropriate to their great theme. Here more successfully than anywhere else Milton outweighs the energy of the fallen angels with its divine counterpart, and the power of destruction just seen in the war in Heaven—"Heav'n ruining from Heav'n" —with the energy of ascending life.

But the great epic action has disappeared from Thomson's *Seasons*, nor has it yet been replaced—as it was to be in Wordsworth's *Prelude*—by a single dramatic movement toward a consummation of man and nature. At the heart of Wordsworth's poem is the deep underpresence that waits to be perceived and recognized, to be brought to the surface of awareness, and to be created anew in the consciousness. In Thomson we have only the beginnings of such a theme. The subject of his poem is not the poet himself but the divine order within the created world. But, once the epic narrative has given way to a descriptive and meditative structure, the movement of the poem reflects the movement of the poet's mind. The very arbitrariness of design, the constant shift between observation and reflection, makes us aware of the associative mind at work. His subject, moreover, is the natural scene, and the muteness of landscape throws the poet back on himself. Thomson teases images that are only partly claimed by general meanings and have, as a result, a suggestiveness and openness that bring a new quality to poetry.

The design of *The Seasons* can best be seen in the *Hymn* that Thomson appended to the four poems. The seasons are the aspects of the "varied God"; beneath their changes lies the art of God, but it can be perceived only with subtle and reverent perception—"Deep felt" (22)—lest man fail to discriminate "Shade unperceiv'd so softening into shade, / And all so forming an harmonious whole." The Hymn evokes the choir of all created things (as in Book V of *Paradise Lost*)— each creature animating every other:

> Bleat out afresh, ye hills; ye mossy rocks,
> Retain the sound; the broad responsive low,
> Ye valleys, raise; for the Great Shepherd reigns,
> And his unsuffering kingdom yet will come (72–75).

The poet, finally, withdraws into his own consciousness; the outwardness of a given scene is of secondary concern:

> Since God is ever present, ever felt,
> In the void waste as in the city full;
> And where He vital breathes there must be joy. . . .
>   I cannot go
> Where Universal Love not smiles around
>   (104–7, 111–12).

And at last there is the movement toward self-transcendence—
or is it Shaftesbury's rational ecstasy?—and the silence of communion:

> But I lose
> Myself in Him, in light ineffable!
> Come then, expressive silence, muse His praise (116–18).

In the poems of *The Seasons* there is a double movement—
the descent of God in plenitude and the ascent of man's mind
in recognition of Order. Between the two stands the challenge
that lies at the outward edge of plenitude before the ascent
can begin: the threat of the ambiguous or the meaningless.
Thomson presents this threat as the extreme of heat or cold,
the predatory cruelty of wolf or serpent, the utterly inhuman
or hostile—or the internal confusion and betrayal of passionate
and jealous love, as in *Spring*. These are limiting cases that
test man's faith in Order; once they are met and passed by,
the movement of ascent (or, in another figure, the movement
back to the One from the borders of emanation) can commence.

Thomson is, as his language shows, particularly concerned
with number; plenitude always confounds our powers of
measure, and few adjectives are so frequent in Thomson's
poetry as "innumerous." Blake was to write, among his "Proverbs of Hell": "The roaring of lions, the howling of wolves,
the raging of the stormy sea, and the destructive sword, are
portions of eternity, too great for the eye of man." And Thomson, even more frequently, creates phrases to distinguish the
eye that can look at eternity from the mere sensual eye. Newton is "All intellectual eye," "all-piercing sage," with "well
purg'd penetrating eye / The mystic veil transpiercing," he
"whose piercing mental eye diffusive saw / The finish'd university of things" (*A Poem Sacred to the Memory of Sir
Isaac Newton*, 1727). *The Seasons* are full of phrases like
"philosophic eye" (opposed to "the grosser eye of man"), the
"skilful eye" or "watchful eye," the "exalting eye," the
"raptur'd eye," the "mind's creative eye."

The opening lines of *Winter* were cited by the painter Constable "as a beautiful instance of the poet identifying his own
feelings with external nature."[6] They give us the external and
the internal—"vapors and clouds and storms" that "exalt the
soul to solemn thought / And heavenly musing." The glooms
are "kindred," the horrors "cogenial"; and the interanima-

tion that we find in Milton's "Proserpin gath'ring flow'rs /
Herself a fairer Flow'r" recurs in Thomson's

> Pleas'd have I wander'd through your rough domain;
> Trod the pure virgin-snows, myself as pure (10–11).

Winter is a force of both destruction and purification. The
white desert of unrelieved snow is the denial of life; but the
severe test of endurance creates the stern virtues of those
who meet it. Winter includes the external threat of annihilation and the social threat of oppressive indifference; and its
desolation may call up resistance and fortitude. The poem
weaves back and forth between physical and moral, between
external and internal.

Throughout *Winter* the outward scene dissolves into the
responses it calls forth. The first storm awakens the "pleasing
dread" of sublime emotion (109), the sudden calm that succeeds the second brings the serenity of contemplation:

> Let me shake off th' intrusive cares of day,
> And lay the meddling senses all aside (207–8).

The pattern of ascent is prefigured here, in the freedom of
the poet from the formlessness of a life committed to the
world and from its round of futile repetition. He prays to be
saved from "every low pursuit," to rise to

> Sacred, substantial, never-fading bliss! (222.)

The bleakness of the snow which erases forms and destroys
life gives way to the icy cruelty of the "gay licentious proud,"
and that in turn to the wolves who descend from the Alps,
"Cruel as death, and hungry as the grave" (393). The "smoth-
ering ruin" of the avalanche that overwhelms the small societies of man (422–23) leads to the retreat of the poet to the
study of those heroes who represent the tenacity of the human
spirit. He holds

> high converse with the mighty dead—
> Sages of ancient time, as gods rever'd,
> As gods beneficent, who bless'd mankind
> With art and arms, and humaniz'd a world (432–35).

The political heroes are lawgivers, defenders of liberty and
martyrs to tyranny, men of "awful virtue," down to Ham-
mond, the newly dead friend and patriot. And from these
heroes Thomson ascends to the principles themselves which
actuate such virtue:

That portion of divinity, that ray
Of purest heav'n, which lights the public soul
Of patriots and of heroes (595-97).

From the contemplative we move to the social—the "rural gambol" and the more sophisticated pleasure of the city—only to close in upon the figure of Chesterfield, at once polite and virtuous, a man of wit and noble passion, the reincarnation of the classical heroes in a modern world.

In the last portion of the poem we confront the ambiguities of winter. It clarifies, purifies, invigorates: it produces the wholesome sports of Europe and the noble simplicity of the Goths and Scythians. But as we move farther north into the land of ice we see the frozen death of the merchant adventurer, and we descend to the "gross race" of rudest men who scarcely sustain life at all, "sunk in caves" (941). Still, the intrepidity of the explorer survives in the magnificence of Peter the Great, whose "active government" called a "huge neglected empire . . . from Gothic darkness" (950-54). Peter becomes the heir of ancient heroes; he animates the vast land and makes it "one scene of art, of arms, of rising trade." He represents the moral response to the challenge of winter, the moral power of vigorous action which its severity exacts.

In the picture of the thaw with which winter ends, Thomson brings back the threat of confusion. The terror of the icebergs is likened to the sinister threat of the whale in *Paradise Lost,* whose slumbering body the "Pilot of some small night-founder'd skiff" mistakes for an island, anchoring his vessel with deceptive security. Milton's whale is a figure for Satan, and Thomson is returning to the problem of evil at the close of his poem. In the earliest version he refers to "th'eternal scheme / The dark perplexity, that mystic maze, / Which sight could never trace nor heart conceive" (379-81). In the later version the optimism is firmer: "The great eternal scheme / Involving all, and in a perfect whole / Uniting, as the prospect wider spreads" (1046-48). Winter brings about the triumph of virtue and with it comes the promise of redemption:

The glorious morn! the second birth
Of heaven and earth! Awakening Nature hears
The new-creating word, and starts to life
In every heighten'd form, from pain and death
For ever free (1042-46).

The prospect of imperfect life on earth is widened to include the hope of heaven:

> The storms of wintry time will quickly pass,
> And one unbounded spring encircle all (1068–69).

We are close to the conclusion of Pope's *Essay on Man:* in attaining virtue, man creates Eden anew and escapes the cycles of Time; the breadth of his vision (and, Pope would say, love) opens Eternity to him.

While this pattern is essential to our understanding of *The Seasons,* it does not entirely account for its successes. The pattern prepares us to sense each experience as implicitly moral in significance. In fact, the large structure might encourage one to look for little allegories or emblems in particular scenes, and Thomson occasionally confirms this view. But his landscape is more suggestive and elusive than this. He foreshadows Wordsworth in giving himself up to a scene, accepting its mysterious power over him, describing with the exactness of awed attention the least movement he sees. All his best landscapes involve tension and movement. It may be the tension of anticipation, as all nature waits for the descent of rain or the breaking of a storm. It may be the movement into the deep recesses of shade and quiet. It may be the bursting force of a descending stream, roaring through a broken channel until it spreads over the valley below. What do these tensions and movements signify? It is hard to give them any simple moral import, or even a determinate psychological one. They accommodate meanings or feelings we bring to them. Like an abstract form—musical or pictorial—they articulate patterns of tension that underlie or are embedded in much of our experience.

To some extent, Thomson is finding new vehicles for religious experience and putting behind him the landscape of symbols we see in the Metaphysical poets. He insists upon a scientific understanding of the operations of nature; and this attempt to see the splendor that streams through natural process makes for a minuteness of detail and at times a deliberate pursuit of the "unpoetic." Reynolds in his Eleventh Discourse (1782) warns the landscape painter to content himself with "shewing the general effect" of what he himself knows anatomically: "for he applies himself to the imagination, not to the curiosity, and works not for the virtuoso or the naturalist, but for the common observer of life and nature." But Thomson, like Constable later, is filled with a natural piety that watches for the revelation that lies in the minute natural process. Constable, for example, praises a winter piece of Ruysdael that shows an exact knowledge of the atmospheric changes that "will produce a thaw before morning." "The occurrence of these circumstances," Constable adds, "shows that Ruysdael *understood* what he was painting." On the other hand, when Ruysdael paints *An Allegory of the Life of Man,* "there are ruins to indicate old age, a stream to signify the course of life, and rocks and precipices to shadow forth its dangers;—but how are we to discover all this?" (318–19.)

This gritty fidelity to natural fact, which we find again in Wordsworth, underlies Thomson's ecstasies—just as Constable's studies of skies underlie his use of them as "the chief organ of sentiment" (85). Man, Constable said, "is the sole intellectual inhabitant of one vast natural landscape. His nature is congenial with the elements of the planet itself, and he cannot but sympathize with its features, its various aspects, and its phenomena in all its aspects" (329). Earlier he had written his wife of a visit to Suffolk: "Everything seems full of blossom of some kind and at every step I take, and on whatever object I turn my eyes, that sublime expression of the Scriptures 'I am the resurrection and the life,' seems as if uttered near me" (73). And of a painting of a "Boat Passing a Lock" he wrote to Fisher: "it is silvery, windy, and delicious; all health, and the absence of everything stagnant, and is wonderfully got together . . ." (141). This movement from close observation to intense feeling, and one might say *only* from close observation of the actual, is a distinctive contribution of Thomson, and it is his poetry that Constable cites more than once (as does Turner) in the catalogue entries for his exhibited paintings, and in the letterpress of *English Landscape,* the volume of engravings made of his work by Lucas.

But tracing the lineaments of design in nature or finding in it the vehicle of religious sentiment is too restricted an account of what Thomson does. Thomson has often been praised for his remarkable feeling for light, but one can say as much for his sense of space (in a passage Constable cites):

> As from the face of heaven the shattered clouds
> Tumultuous rove, the interminable sky
> Sublimer swells, and o'er the world expands
> A purer azure (*Summer,* 1223–26).

Or, in the account of Hagley, we move with Lyttleton to a height,

from whose fair brow
The bursting prospect spreads immense around:
And snatched o'er hill and dale, and wood and lawn,
And verdant field, and darkening heath between,
And spiry towns by surging columns marked
Of household smoke, your eye excursive roams—
Widestretching from the hall . . .
To where the broken landscape, by degrees
Ascending, roughens into rigid hills
O'er which the Cambrian mountains, like far clouds
That skirt the blue horizon, dusky rise (*Spring,* 949–61).

What Thomson catches in these scenes is that curiously indefinable sense of the "import" of space—the kind of sense the
architect must try to articulate in planning effects, different
as they must be from these. In the first passage, we are involved in breaking free of limits as we move above the violence of the great clouds into the blue vacancy of endless
space that "swells" and "expands" with exaltation and freedom. In the second passage we break out of the trees into
the freedom of the prospect. We give ourselves to the motion
of freedom with "bursting prospect" and "spreads immense
around"—words that characterize not the scene so much as
the experience of coming upon it. The following lines emphasize the stretch of sight, the high view that looks down upon
hill and dale, wood and lawn, and (securely anchored to the
hospitable hall) looks over the slight traces of towns. And just
as the "eye excursive" pushes to the edges of the horizon,
the scene composes with the ascent of rough hills and the
enclosing bowl of faint mountains. This second landscape has
something of pictorial composition, but what gives it peculiar
force is the motion contained and bounded by these last
images. The passage picks up suggestions from its context:
we are following Lyttleton and his Lucinda walking through
grounds where

Nature all
Wears to the lover's eye a look of love;
And all the tumult of a guilty world,
Toss'd by ungenerous passions, sinks away.
The tender heart is animated peace.
. . . it pours its copious treasures forth
In varied converse . . . (*Spring,* 936–42).

The landscape, at once extensive and peacefully protected,
gives one the spatial feel of this sentiment—its expansive "ani-

mated peace." The sentiment finds definition in the landscape that embodies it.

Landscape can call emotion forth by offering a vehicle with its own formal properties and its own power of suggestion. If man finds himself, in Constable's terms, congenial with the elements of the planet itself, he can lend himself imaginatively to those elements, filling out these movements with the impulses of his own nature. His study of landscape becomes a release of his own feelings into forms which will shape them; it allows him, in other words, to project feelings that might otherwise have no mode of expression and to order them in ways that a moral system might not admit. This is important. We need not assume that there is a natural movement from Protestant individualism to sentimentalism to pantheism; these terms are too categorical to serve many particular instances.[7] Thomson's sentimentalism is much greater in his narrative episodes than in his descriptive passages, and we need hardly infer from the sympathies with the phenomena of nature of which Constable speaks a doctrine of pantheism. What we have is something less systematic and more interesting: the discovery of a vehicle that opens up a range of feelings otherwise without expression and shapes them into a subtle unity which eludes any received canons of art.

One more example will illustrate the pattern we find in Thomson. In *Summer* there is a splendid passage on the "raging noon," when light has become a "dazzling deluge" that forces the eye to the ground, only to be met there by "hot ascending steams / And keen reflection pain." The heat is felt in the depth of the parched soil and the "throbbing temples" of the poet, who draws from it an "emblem" of a fevered world of vice. The "tempered mind serene and pure" of the virtuous man seeks its counterpart in the cool caverns of the forest-covered mountainside. Withdrawal into the shelter of "lofty pines" and "venerable oaks" brings new vigor: "The fresh expanded eye / And ear resume their watch." Below him the poet sees the meandering stream "scarcely moving" among reclining cattle and beside the sleeping herdsman—a nicely composed scene of indolent repose. Into this scene moves a flight of "angry gadflies" to disturb the cattle into bellowing motion. And this in turn admits the fierce motion of "the horse provoked":

> While his big sinews full of spirits swell,
> Trembling with vigor, in the heat of blood

Springs the high fence; and, o'er the field effus'd,
Darts on the gloomy flood with stedfast eye
And heart estrang'd to fear: his nervous chest,
Luxuriant and erect, the seat of strength,
Bears down the opposing stream; quenchless his thirst,
He takes the river at redoubl'd draughts;
And with wide nostrils snorting skims the wave
    (*Summer*, 507–15).

As the poet plunges once more into coolness and darkness, the intensity of the horse's motion evokes a contrary intensity of "awful listening gloom." The recess of meditation becomes a sacred place where "ancient bards" have had ecstatic visions in which angelic visitors descended.

    Deep-rous'd I feel
A sacred terror, a severe delight,
Creep through my mortal frame (540–42),

and the voices speak of their gradual ascent through "stormy life" to "This holy calm, this harmony of mind" (550). The poet wakens from the "airy vision" to the sound of water. He traces the growth of a stream as it collects into "one impetuous torrent" that "thundering shoots" down the steep, dashing to foam on rocks below, sending up a "hoary mist," then roaring into separate channels until it spreads "Along the mazes of the quiet vale" (606).

The violent chiaroscuro of brilliance and blackness, the contrast of throbbing sunlight and gelid caverns, the fierce energy of the horse and the holy power of the visionary figures, the downward rush of the stream from the high recess through the turbulence of the waterfall to the quiet vale where the cattle browse—all of these form an indistinct but suggestive dialectical pattern. One feels that the force of outward energy that is caught in the heavy heat or in the frenzied motion has been absorbed into the seraphic vision, cleansed of its fever and raised to prophetic power. This absorption of the natural scene into man looks back to Addison's remark that "a spacious horizon is an image of liberty" and forward to Blake's "When thou seest an Eagle, thou seest a portion of Genius; lift up thy head!"

iv. The Sublime

Thomson and Young, more than any other poets of the century, helped prepare the way for the theories of the sublime and the picturesque. These new doctrines mark a revolt against the tyranny of beauty. The idea of beauty, as we see it in the Augustans, is essentially one of unity in variety, the *concordia discors*. Its metaphor of harmony pervades all realms of experience—cosmic Order, the "inward numbers" of the moral self, the "according music of a well-mixt state." In Pascalian terms, it is the reconciliation and interpenetration of the discrete orders of man: the order of charity and the order of flesh find their integration within the order of mind. The typical Augustan compromise, the poise within the antithesis, is a strategy of inclusiveness. As soon as anyone tries to reduce the poise to a fixed attitude, the harmony to a formula, he is met with a tactical retreat. For every assertion there will arise a counterassertion, for every excess a counterexcess; extremes can be refined away indefinitely, lest a stance be reduced to a doctrine.

The new categories emerge by limiting the meaning of beauty. Beauty ceases to be a term for all aesthetic experience; it is restricted to a specific area. We can see this most clearly in Addison's *Spectator* papers on the Pleasures of the Imagination (1712). Addison, it has been argued by Jerome Stolnitz,[8] sets the note for the century to follow by establishing a distinctively aesthetic experience, characterized by disinterestedness. The pleasures of the imagination are distinguished from those of both sense and knowledge. They are "not so gross as those of sense," and they are more immediate and "less refined" than those of knowledge. They are "innocent pleasures" (*Spectator,* No. 411). Addison devotes himself to the imagination, Stolnitz suggests, "because imagination provides a habitat for disinterestedness."

In *Spectator,* No. 412 Addison constructs a triad of terms: the Great (which was to become the sublime), the New or Uncommon (which was to become the picturesque), and the Beautiful. He defines the experience of the Great partly in psychological and partly in formal terms. The Great includes works of nature that produce "pleasing astonishment," a "delightful stillness in the soul at the apprehension of them." "The mind of man," Addison goes on, "naturally hates everything that looks like a restraint upon it, and is apt to fancy itself under a sort of confinement when the sight is pent up in a narrow compass. . . . On the contrary, a spacious horizon is an image of liberty. . . ." Having moved to a formal account of the sublime as grandeur or immensity (in effect, the breaking out of limits), Addison draws an analogy with religious experience: "Such wide and undetermined prospects are as pleasing to the fancy, as the speculations of eternity and infinity are to the understanding." (In the following paper, Addison suggests that the contemplation of God's nature is, in fact, the "final cause" of the aesthetic experience of the Great.)

The New or Uncommon also reclaims experience that the Beautiful cannot contain. Man's curiosity is gratified by the Uncommon, which "bestows charms on a monster, and makes even the imperfections of nature please us." We are clearly moving toward the reclamation of the ugly, and this would require a new basis of judgment, perhaps a psychological one; but Addison carries his examples only as far as the variety of rivers, fountains, and waterfalls, "where the scene is perpetually shifting. . . ." Elsewhere the new basis of judgment begins to appear. The Beautiful is that which "strikes the mind with an inward joy, and spreads a cheerfulness and delight through all its faculties." This psychological approach introduces a note of relativism ("Every different species of sensible creatures has its different notions of beauty"), and the traditional formal criteria of beauty—symmetry and proportion, and "just mixture and concurrence" of elements—are made less important than the love of one's species.

Once aesthetic experience becomes a psychological state— notably, one of disinterested pleasure—it can join with Shaftesbury's emphasis upon wildness in the contemplation of Order. Order may be seen, as Thomson shows, in cosmic harmony, but it may also be sought at the very boundaries of disorder, where we feel the limits of all conventional human categories and are struck by the immensity of God's design. Men have always been struck by the gap between God's authentic and incommensurable Order and the often deceptive and artificial order of human institutions. What becomes strikingly new in this period is man's readiness to find an exemplar of God's authentic Order in the vast system of nature, and, even more, to associate the plenitude of the system with the idea of political liberty. Marjorie Nicolson, in *Mountain Gloom and Mountain Glory,* has shown how the "natural sublime" preceded the "rhetorical sublime." The revival of Longinus confirmed the "Aesthetics of the Infinite" that the seventeenth century had discovered. For men like Henry More (and the followers of Shaftesbury later) in man's "divine discontent lay his greatness. He grew with what he attempted to comprehend. Mind and spirit released from finite bonds, he became in part the thing he sought" (p. 147).

Sir Thomas Browne had (as Miss Nicolson points out, pp. 70, 264–65) looked for God's Order in "nature's narrow engines" rather than her "prodigious pieces," and Erasmus Warren (in *Geologia,* 1690) sought God in "the beauty of aspectable things." But the later eighteenth-century theorists depress the value of beauty unless it can be fused with sublimity. They tend to characterize beauty by drawing one or another element out of erotic experience. Edmund Burke emphasizes the smoothness and insensible transitions of feminine curves, Uvedale Price youthful freshness as well. Thus Burke can transfer all the roughness and severity of grandeur to the sublime, Price all the "character" that marks maturity or age to the picturesque. The sublime and the picturesque grow out of the dissatisfaction with too simple an idea of order. The sublime tries to come to terms with the irregular and energetic in their most overwhelming forms; it makes the experience of transcendence the material of aesthetics. The picturesque starts from the irregular and intimate and moves toward the pleasure in texture, the complex presentation of what we sometimes call "felt life."

In Mark Akenside's *The Pleasures of Imagination* (1742; revised version, 1770) we have a poem that derives its terms from Addison but brings to them the system of Shaftesbury. Akenside tries to "mix the Stoic with the Platonic philosophy," as he writes to a friend (David Fordyce, 18 June 1742), and he connects Stoicism with the sublime, Platonism with the beautiful. He imagines the Stoic genius a mature man, of "manly sternness and simplicity" seated on a rock looking at a stormy sea, "regarding the noise of the thunder and the rolling of the waves with a severe defiance." The Platonic genius is a fair virgin muse, seated in a garden beside a canal, contemplating the bright sun only in "his milder image reflected from the water." Akenside explores the psychological nature of imaginative experience in his poem, but he fits the discoveries of empirical philosophy into a Platonic system much like Shaftesbury's. In fact, Akenside makes very clear how Shaftesbury and Hutcheson can use Locke but "convert" his findings, much as Pope does Mandeville's.

Man enters the "boundless theatre" of the created world, but only as into a discipline from which he may ascend to heaven:

> Else wherefore burns
> In mortal bosoms this unquenched hope,
> That breathes from day to day sublimer things,
> And mocks possession? wherefore darts the mind
> With such resistless ardor to embrace
> Majestic forms, impatient to be free . . .
> Proud to be daring? (1744; I, 166–74.)

There is a progression of kinds of beauty—a Platonic ladder
—from mere color to geometric form, thence to vegetable and
animal, finally to intellectual form:

> Mind, mind alone . . .
> The living fountains in itself contains
> Of beauteous and sublime (I, 481–83).

No landscape can achieve "the high expression of a mind";
no mountain can rival the majesty of Brutus freeing Rome of
Caesar's tyranny. The forms that "brute, unconscious matter
wears" (I, 527) cannot compare with "the moral species."
The "ambitious mind / There sees herself . . . / and medi-
tates, well pleas'd, / Her features in the mirror" (I, 533–37).

Akenside can accept Locke's doctrine of secondary qualities and explore the association of ideas, "the different images
of things," as he puts it, "By chance combin'd" (III, 312–13).
But it is clear that he sees the mind merely finding its proper
realm through empirical experience; there lie latent within it
ideas and capacities that are prior to all experience and await
the occasion of their exercise.

> What then is taste, but these internal powers
> Active, and strong, and feelingly alive
> To each fine impulse? a discerning sense
> Of decent and sublime, with quick disgust
> From things deform'd, or disarrang'd, or gross
> In species? This nor gems, nor stores of gold,
> Nor purple state, nor culture can bestow;
> But God alone. When first his active hand
> Imprints the secret bias of the soul (III, 515–23).

In the process of self-discovery, mind moves from "outward things" where she has become accustomed to "meditate the charm / Of sacred order" and "seeks at home / To
find a kindred order" (III, 602–4). And when "the forms /
Of servile custom" or "sordid policies" try to "bow her down /
To tame pursuits," she disdains them and "appeals to Nature" for the authentic order of the Eternal Maker:

> we feel within ourselves
> His energy divine: he tells the heart,
> He meant, he made us to behold and love
> What he beholds and loves, the general orb
> Of life and being: to be great like Him,
> Beneficent and active (III, 624–29).

In the later version of his poem, Akenside makes the Platonism more obvious: the mind is given "forms which never deign'd / In eyes or ears to dwell, within the sense / Of earthly organs" (1765; II, 103–5). These are the counterpart in man of the "uncreated images of things" the Eternal One loved and with "his vital smile / Unfolded into being" (1744; I, 66, 72–73).

What Akenside makes clear is the theme that Wordsworth was to give its ultimate statement:

> Our destiny, our being's heart and home
> Is with infinitude, and only there;
> With hope it is, hope that can never die,
> Effort, and expectation, and desire,
> And something evermore about to be
> (*Prelude,* 1850, VI, 604–8).

This emphasis upon the vital energy of the mind, its divinely sanctioned powers, makes its traffic with the world a constant process of self-discovery, as the inadequacy of the senses leads to their eclipse and to the sublime transcendence of them by the mind that feels infinity within itself. Akenside, like Young and Thomson, stresses the "philosophical" or the "attentive" eye, the organ that comes to recognize its own creative role in perception.

The recognition of a transcendental self that lies behind its empirical experience is one of the most intense expressions of the self-consciousness of the age. It absorbs and transforms much of the interest in association of ideas. In the subtlest of associationists, Archibald Alison (*Essays on the Nature and Principles of Taste,* 1790; third edition, 1812, II, 423), we find once more the assertion of an ultimate Platonism: "the beauty and sublimity which is felt in the various appearances of matter are finally to be ascribed to their expression of mind." "Our minds, instead of being governed by the character of external objects, are enabled to bestow upon them a character which does not belong to them" (II, 428). "I believe," Alison wrote, "there is no man of genuine taste who has not often felt, in the lone majesty of nature, some unseen spirit to dwell, which, in his happier hours, touched as if with magic hand all the springs of his moral sensibility, and rekindled in his heart those original conceptions of the moral or intellectual excellence of his nature, which it is the melancholy tendency of the vulgar pursuits of life to diminish, if not altogether to destroy" (II, 438). And we can look all the way back to Longinus, the first century theorist of the sublime, for a similar Platonic note:

> Nature has appointed us men to be no base or ignoble animals, but when she ushers us into the vast universe . . . she implants in our souls the unconquerable love of whatever is elevated and more divine than we. Wherefore not even the entire universe suffices for the thought and contemplation within the reach of the human mind (*Longinus on the Sublime,* trans, W. Rhys Roberts, Cambridge, 1935; ch. XXXV).

The most influential discussion of the sublime in the century is Edmund Burke's *Philosophical Enquiry into the Origin of Our Ideas of the Sublime and Beautiful* (1757). Burke's treatise, as J. T. Boulton has shown in his edition (1958), draws together much of the thought of the preceding fifty years. Burke approaches the sublime as a problem of physiological psychology, and his description of the experience of the sublime is one that can serve as the meeting place of quite varied metaphysical schemes. Burke bases the sublime upon the aesthetic counterpart of the experience of terror—that is, an experience of terror or one that "operates in a manner analogous to terror"—"at certain distances and with certain modifications" that prevent the experience from becoming an immediate and inartistic state of emotion. We must be secure in order to have a disinterested, aesthetic response to danger (I, vii).

The experience of terror "robs the mind of all its powers of acting and reasoning" (II, ii) by fusing the threat of danger with the obscurity of unlimited or undefinable power. Whatever unsettles the mind with its staggering force or overwhelming dimensions creates the effect of the sublime: the general privations of "vacuity, darkness, solitude, and silence" (II, vi); vastness or infinity; the evidence of tremendous effort or labor. Burke is ingenious in showing how great light or great darkness, deep silence or violent sound, can equally produce the sublime, for either extreme "amazes and confounds" the imagination, in a "staggering and hurry of the mind" (II, xvii).

In his discussion of words, Burke tries to free poetry from the demand increasingly made by critics who were in revolt against Augustan wit—for example, Joseph Warton—for "clear, complete, and circumstantial images."[9] This stress upon pictorial particularity grows out of the desire to create immediate sympathy between reader and object—to turn men from readers into spectators, as Warton put it. It also grows out of the emphasis upon poetic enthusiasm; the poet who feels deeply will summon up a vivid picture of what holds his attention. He will give himself to the scene without the analytic play of detached wit that marks the descriptions of Pope, and he will call forth from the reader as well a complete surrender to sympathetic imagination.

Burke must defend his view of the sublime from such an emphasis, and he does so by insisting upon the artifice of art. Poetry is composed of words, and words do not simply evoke pictures. They are conceptual as well as pictorial, and a phrase like Milton's "universe of death" cannot be explained by any narrow imagistic doctrine. In discussing obscurity as a source of the sublime, Burke asserts: "A clear idea is . . . another name for a little idea" (II, iv). The boundlessness of the sublime is better conveyed by words than by the images of painting. "We yield to sympathy, what we refuse to description." Our sympathetic imagination need not fix on the image; it requires, rather, that the speaker "call in to his aid those modes of speech that mark a strong and lively feeling in himself. Then, by the contagion of our passions, we catch a fire already kindled in another" (V, vii). Burke, in short, transfers the power of sympathy from imagery to dramatic utterance; words reveal the workings of the mind rather than its object.

The emphasis on the working of the mind comes to qualify the stress upon the image. The "pure poetry" of which Joseph Warton writes becomes identified with what Addison had called the "fairy way of writing." It is, Mrs. Barbauld writes, "conversant with an imaginary world, peopled with beings of its own creation. It deals in splendid imagery, bold fiction, and allegorical personages."[10] The clarity of the image is less important than the force of mind behind it; and this force is shown most tellingly at the point where the image dissolves into suggestions of infinity or calls into form apprehensions of something that cannot be properly seen—or seen only in a state of visionary power. Milton supplies us with examples of the image at the point of dissolution—in effect, transcending itself. The alternative, the image fixing, however dimly, a mysterious or infinite force, is seen in the personification. The personification is achieved only by the mind at the limits of its power, exploring dim realms or even creating its own fictions. What Collins calls the "shadowy tribes of mind" are mythic personages who arise on those occasions in which mind finds its most intense exercise. If the sublime is the art of transcendence, the personification is among its characteristic works.

Burke's treatment of the sublime makes inescapably clear that a new mode of poetry is being discovered in this period. The seeming contradictions of Warton's demand for circumstantial imagery and Burke's denial of the power of the image are resolved when we see that both are trying to specify the proper vehicle of the energies of mind. The stretch of mind is sometimes to be found in its power to make vivid the remote and exotic; sometimes in the dramatic presence of natural genius, in the folk-poet or the "original." Even the apparent contradictions of the spontaneity of genius and the artifice of poetic art give way as we recognize the emphasis on the artistry of nature or the unconscious, on the one hand, and the emphasis on poetry as a release from the quotidian and practical, on the other. The natural genius attains at once what lesser artists achieve only through extensive labor. The artifice of poetry, as summed up in Gray's famous remark that the "language of the age is never the language of poetry," becomes a way of creating an autonomous realm in which the exalted mind finds its own idiom and its appropriate objects.

Both seemingly primitive and highly artful poetry may have in common abrupt transitions (as in the ballad in one case or the Pindaric ode in the other) that demand an act of sympathetic imagination in the reader to follow and comprehend. The cultivation of mystery and obscurity is to be found in language as well as in imagery. Thomas Warton as editor writes of the towers and battlements "Bosom'd high in tufted trees" of Milton's *L'Allegro:* "Modern seats are seldom so deeply ambushed. They disclose all their glories at once: and never excite by concealment, by gradual approaches, and by interrupted appearances." In discussing a description (of the bonnet of Camus) in *Lycidas,* he applies this standard to poetry: "Perhaps the poet himself had no very clear or determinate idea: but, in obscure and mysterious expressions, leaves something to be supplied or explained by the reader's imagination."

Once the poet seeks to write the kind of poetry that is "more spiritous, and more remote from prose than any other" (as Edward Young regarded the ode as early as 1728), he moves inevitably to the histrionic. Cultivating extreme states of mind, voicing them in passionate, energetic speech, he runs the danger of seeming (as Johnson wrote of Gray's odes) to have "a kind of strutting dignity," to be "tall by walking on tiptoe." His art and struggle, Johnson concluded, "are too visible, and there is too little appearance of ease and nature" ("Gray" in *Lives of the Poets*). For all Johnson's objections to this, he is pointing to what a new mode of poetry set out to achieve. Bishop Lowth described the poetry of the Bible in terms that precisely match these qualities of the fashionable poetry of the day. The "language of reason" he characterized as "cool, temperate, rather humble than elevated, well arranged and perspicuous." But the "language of the passions" is "totally different: the conceptions burst out into a turbid stream, expressive in a manner of the internal conflict; the more vehement break out in hasty confusion; they catch (without search or study) whatever is impetuous, vivid, or energetic. In a word, reason speaks literally, the passions poetically."[11]

v. Ruins and Visions

In 1717 Pope published *Eloisa to Abelard,* a heroic epistle in the manner of Ovid. Of all Pope's poems this most clearly anticipates the forms of later eighteenth-century poetry, and no other, consequently, so sharply reveals the difference between Pope and his successors. The poem presents Eloisa years after her separation from Abelard; each has gone to a convent, but now her passion is reawakened by a letter of Abelard's that has fallen into her hands. "This awakening all her tenderness," Pope explains, "occasioned those celebrate letters (out of which [this poem] is partly extracted) which give so lively a picture of the struggles of grace and nature, virtue and passion." Pope's Eloisa is a moving and, to some degree, a terrifying figure in the style of Dryden's Nourmahal or—Austin Warren has suggested—Racine's Phèdre. Her passion infiltrates all the divine images she opposes to it and colors even the vision of grace with erotic natural passion. She carries with her the kind of hell that is comically presented in the Cave of Spleen.

This force of passion has an effect very close to what is

admired as the power of imagination in later critics. A dominant emotion forces images into coalescence. But Pope conveys the moral shock of this coalescence, rather than an exultation in the fusing force. Pope elaborates a sympathetically rugged setting—"grots and caverns shagg'd with horrid thorn" (20), "moss-grown domes with spiry turrets crown'd / Where awful arches make a noon-day night" (142–43). Out of the darkness of this melancholy retreat Eloisa rises in visions of brilliant light and divine rapture. She imagines the happier plight of the "blameless Vestal":

> Grace shines around her with serenest beams,
> And whisp'ring Angels prompt her golden dreams.
> For her th' unfading rose of Eden blooms,
> And wings of Seraphs shed divine perfumes;
> For her the Spouse prepares the bridal ring,
> For her white virgins Hymenaeals sing;
> To sounds of heav'nly harps, she dies away,
> And melts in visions of eternal day (215–22).

In contrast she feels within herself the compulsion of lust:

> Provoking Demons all restraint remove,
> And stir within me ev'ry source of love.
> I bear thee, view thee, gaze o'er all thy charms,
> And round thy phantom glue my clasping arms
> (231–34).

> Thy image steals between my God and me (268).

Her desperate conflict makes her call upon Abelard to "oppose thy self to heav'n; dispute my heart. . . . Snatch me, just mounting, from the blest above" (282, 287)—and then to recoil once more toward the hope of grace. But what are we to make of her final resolution? She makes her escape into her vocation; but, even as she seems to triumph, her vision is infected with Abelard's claims. As she bids him pay the "last sad office" at her death, she cries, "Suck my last breath, and catch my flying soul!" Her only escape seems to lie in the destruction of the body, "That cause of all my guilt and all my joy" (338); and the last phrase makes clear how willed and inadequate her resolution remains. So, upon her death, she prays, may "streaming glories shine" on Abelard, "And Saints embrace thee with a love like mine" (341–42).

For contrast, we can take Thomas Warton's *The Pleasures of Melancholy* (written at seventeen, published two years later in 1747). Warton's poem draws upon the language of Milton's minor poems (Pope's does, too, but much less heavily); and

like Gray, Warton wishes to avoid "the language of the age."
His poem, unlike Pope's, involves little conflict. The poet gives
himself enthusiastically to Melancholy. He sits beneath "yon
ruined abbey's moss-grown piles . . . While sullen sacred silence reigns around" (28, 32), or walks among the pines
"where mus'd of old / The cloister'd brothers" (38–39). What
is striking is the way in which the adolescent poet feeds on
darkness and destruction. He voluptuates in all that Eloisa
dreads, and in fact claims for her—"whose mind / Had lan-
guish'd to the pangs of melting love" (96–97)—"more genuine
transport" among the tombs and shrines than any worldly
woman can begin to know.

He seems to revel in the terrors of night—the conspiratorial
murder, the pilgrim astray in a desert where monsters howl
and the "black-descending tempest ceaseless beats." It is almost as if he draws power from the destructiveness of night
and the pain of others. Nor is this feeling altered by his account of the "soft thrillings of the tragic muse." His review of
catastrophic dénouements culminates in the pleasures of sympathy—"My big heart melts in sympathizing tears" (225).
Once again we are more struck by the feeding upon suffering
than the capacity for feeling. The characteristic note of the
poem is given earlier, when the poet wakens in the middle
of the night. He finds all others lying "in mute oblivion" and
reflects "that through the still globe's awful solitude, / No
being wakes but me!" (57–58).

The young Thomas Warton is trying on a role that derives
its sense of power from various kinds of renunciation—even
Christ's in the temptations of *Paradise Regained*. Out of these
renunciations comes the posture of an isolated man of refined
feeling, discovering his powers in the very process of striking
attitudes. It is a precociously skillful poem, but it is frivolous
without lightness, self-conscious without self-awareness. It
might be given the title Auden gave to an early work, "Letter
to a Wound"; Warton is paying tribute to the value of disease
—to the intensity of feeling and imaginative power that may
be gained from morbidity. He points ahead to the more vehement pursuit of blackness in the Gothic novel.

We can see the movement from Augustan detachment to
the involvement in sensibility by considering a sequence of
odes. In *Alexander's Feast* (1697) the "power of music"
(Dryden's subtitle and theme) is embodied in Timotheus, who
yields the tribute of his greatness, in the last stanza, to St.

Cecilia: "He rais'd a mortal to the skies; / She drew an angel down." The first six stanzas show Timotheus playing his lyre at the court of Alexander. He exercises absolute influence over his listeners; and the hypnotic magic of his performance is made clearer by the constant shift between contrary passions. Alexander is presented at the outset in all his magnificence:

> Aloft in awful state
> The god-like hero sate
> On his imperial throne.

But as Timotheus plays, Alexander begins to exhibit the somewhat comic aspects of a puppet. As the crowd cries out, "A present deity," we have the dry account of Alexander's response:

> With ravish'd ears
> The monarch hears,
> Assumes the god,
> Affects to nod,
> And seems to shake the spheres (37–41).

As Alexander becomes flushed with his own greatness, he fights his battles again in his intoxicated mind: "And thrice he routed all his foes; and thrice he slew the slain" (68). Timotheus' power becomes clear:

> The Master saw the Madness rise . . .
> But while he heav'n and earth defy'd,
> Chang'd his hand, and check'd his pride (69–72).

By the next stanza, Timotheus (who has moved Alexander to tears) is the "mighty master" (93); and at the close of the sequence Alexander has seized a flambeau, fired by revenge, while his mistress Thais leads the way, "And like another Helen, fir'd another Troy." The power of music is the clever technician mastering the master of the world; the emotions of Alexander and his court are seen from the outside, grotesque in their rapid alterations, tremendous in their compelling force, but all at the expense of the mind and dignity of those aroused.

In Pope's *Ode for Music on St. Cecilia's Day* (published 1713; dated 1708 by Pope) there are notable resemblances to Dryden's ode, but now it is Orpheus rather than Timotheus who embodies the power of pagan music and finally cedes his eminence to Cecilia: "His numbers rais'd a shade from Hell, / Hers lift the soul to Heav'n." The shift to Orpheus is important, for the power of music now rises from the suffering of the poet himself. Pope sets forth the spectrum of passions that music arouses, but in the second half of the poem music is expressive rather than coercive:

> Now with Furies surrounded,
> Despairing, confounded,
> He trembles, he glows,
> Amidst Rhodope's snows

And as Orpheus dies singing of Eurydice, his passion is echoed by woods and water, by rocks and "hollow mountains" (117).

In Gray's *The Bard* (1757), the passions are those of the last of the Welsh bards, who sits "on the summit of an inaccessible rock," hurls his prophecies down on the English invaders who have put all his fellow bards to death, and finally "precipitates himself from the mountain." The Bard sees, with prophetic vividness, the death of Edward I; the long succession of monarchs that ends with the return of Britannia's true issue, the Tudors; and his own triumph in the eventual rule of Elizabeth and the resurgence of poetry with Spenser, Shakespeare, and Milton.

> Fond impious man, think'st thou you sanguine cloud,
> Rais'd by the breath, has quench'd the orb of day?
> (135–36.)

Gray's Bard is an assimilation of political liberty, poetic power, the grandeur of moral passion, prophetic vision. The mountains of Wales are the outward symbol of these internal forces, which reduce the "crested pride" of Edward to pettiness. The Bard, for all his magnificence ("Loose his beard and hoary hair / Streamed, like a meteor, to the troubl'd air"), is, like the Delphic priestess, the anguished vehicle of powers that descend mysteriously upon him:

> Visions of glory, spare my aching sight;
> Ye unborn ages, crowd not on my soul! (107–8.)

We have moved from the cool mastery of Timotheus through the personal suffering of Orpheus to the indignant prophetic voice of the poetic imagination itself.

In William Collins' *The Passions, An Ode for Music* (1746) music works directly upon the passions, and they enact the feelings they represent. We have left behind historical or mythical characters for the forces of character themselves. The passions achieve their own musical art: fired by music, "rapt, inspired," they seize her instruments:

> Each, for madness rul'd the hour,
> Would prove his own expressive pow'r (15–16).

The "all-commanding power" or "diviner rage" of music—"warm, energic, chaste, sublime!" (106) is embodied in the "expressive power" of the passions—each achieving a purity of state and compelling the world in turn. As Joy plays (Sterne's "Viva la joia!" was yet to come):

> Love fram'd with Mirth a gay fantastic round,
> Loose were her tresses seen, her zone unbound,
>   And he amidst his frolic-play,
>   As if he would the charming air repay,
> Shook thousand odors from his dewy wings (90–94).

Although it does not belong to this group, Collins' *Ode to Evening* (1746; revised 1748) introduces further elements of the sublime. In this poem, as W. K. Wimsatt has shown in others,[12] the location of Evening—"chaste Eve"—becomes a problem. She is addressed as a goddess ("O nymph reserv'd," "maid compos'd"), but she seems to be identified with the landscape itself. We learn of her "folding-star arising" (to mark the close of day and the driving of sheep into their fold), of her "shadowy car." But the folding-star has a soft light, a "paly circlet," and the ambiguous light of Evening is diffused through the landscape. In the earlier version of the poem Collins writes:

> Then let me rove some wild and heathy scene,
> Or find some ruin midst its dreary dells,
>   Whose walls more awful nod
>   By thy religious gleams.

This is altered in a telling way. The light is no longer Evening's; it is mediated through reflection:

> Then lead, calm vot'ress, where some sheety lake
> Cheers the lone heath, or some time-hallow'd pile
>   Or upland fallows gray
>   Reflect its last cool gleam (29–32).

Evening is absorbed into the placid lake, and the lake in turn casts its reflected light over heath, ruin, and fallows; the diffused light is part of the softer, more gently melancholy scene. And two stanzas later the poet looks over the landscape and

marks o'er all
The dewy fingers draw
The gradual dusky veil (38–40).

Is Evening a divine person who governs the scene or is she immanent in the scene itself? The ambiguity is typical not only of Collins but of Blake in his early season poems. We are moving away from the self-conscious act of imagination toward religious celebration, from the art of transcendence to the worship of an immanent Presence.

VI. The Garden and the Wild: The Picturesque

Speaking of Thomas Hardy, T. S. Eliot noted that "he makes a great deal of landscape; for landscape is a passive creature which lends itself to an author's mood. Landscape is fitted too for the purposes of an author who is interested not at all in men's minds, but only in their emotions; and perhaps only in men as vehicles for emotions" (*After Strange Gods,* New York, 1934, p. 59). Like many of Dr. Johnson's remarks, this is an outrageous judgment that points to an important fact. We can see the conception of personality altering in later eighteenth century poetry, and we recognize the alteration by the changes in its forms of self-dramatization. Thomson explores modes of feeling by projecting emotion into landscape, and makes new modes of feeling possible by giving them symbolic forms in which to act. Many of the later eighteenth century writers—Sterne and Voltaire, Fielding and Diderot—explore the immediate act of artistry the feelings achieve, the intuitive rightness of impulsive acts. These writers are breaking out of a received tradition of rationalism (which they also dramatize, more satirically) and offering alternative views with a dialectical sense of what they oppose. They are no more renouncing mind than Eliot is renouncing emotion; they are interested in the complex interplay or even the indissoluble identity of the two. There can be no question of this when we look at the body of their work. To see man as part of landscape, continuous with it and bound to it by sympathies, is not to reject mind but to deepen our conception of its role in the total man.

This is not the book in which to treat at length the growth of garden theory in the eighteenth century. The revolution that leads from the formal garden to the picturesque landscape involves the authority of Milton (whose Eden was often cited as an example), the teaching of Addison, and the active influence of Pope. The garden, like Thomson's larger landscape, is the creation of forms in which feeling can exercise itself. Feeling is too narrow or vague a word. The garden is an occasion of an aesthetic awareness and a theater of thought; it suggests meanings as much as it starts trains of sensation or sentiment. In Pope's *Windsor Forest* we can see the meaning of landscape as microcosm; it is a memory of Eden, where all impulses are harmonized with the least sacrifice of each, where the energies of man are given play (in the hunt) without the cruel consequences of disorder, where the contemplative mind finds communion with the past and launches forth into visions of the future. *Windsor Forest* is still, to a large extent, an emblematic garden, however. In the later epistle *To Burlington,* Pope uses the harmony of the garden and the proper piety of man toward nature as the ground for his image of pride in the Timons and other petty titans. The epistle links aesthetic with moral sanity—through their common recognition of an objective reality outside man's will, an order that transcends human art. This theme, so dominant in Shaftesbury, lingers in garden theory. As Nikolaus Pevsner puts it,

> the free growth of the tree is obviously taken to symbolize the free growth of the individual, the serpentine path and rivulet the Englishman's freedom of thought, creed, and action, and the adherence to nature in the grounds, the adherence to nature in ethics and politics ("The Genesis of the Picturesque," *Architectural Review* 96 [1944] 146).

The defense of the "garden of liberalism" may take various doctrinaire forms, but its harmony is clearly one with the "according music of a well-mixt state."

But the moral basis of garden theory gives way to a more fundamentally aesthetic theory. The symbolic representation of which Pevsner speaks is, ultimately, a response to those forms—metaphors, images, proportions—that shape our moral thought as well. Our thinking about values depends, for the most part, on fundamental images—archetypes, if one wishes—and our changes of value, like the changes in our conception of man, involve a return to the realm where the images are generated and reshaped. The period with which this chapter deals is one of those great moments of change when the return to the aesthetic bases that underlie, at least in some measure, our cosmic and moral thought frees men to find new forms without having to face up to their consequences. Such freedom is essential. Too much concern with the moral and social outcome of one's fundamental metaphors blocks the imaginative movement, the trying-on of roles and attitudes, that allow men to discover what in fact they want to be. There is time for such scrutiny later, when there is something new to scrutinize; and then new grounds will be found for new experiences.[13]

The movement in garden theory is toward the psychological garden. Horace Walpole wrote of Stowe: "all these images crowd upon one's memory, and add visionary personages to the charming scenes, that are so enriched with fanes and temples, that the real prospects are little less than visions themselves" (7 July 1770). "This then," writes H. F. Clark,[14] is the essence of the new art, the 'real prospects' appear as 'little less than visions.'" We can see this development sharply in the accounts of William Shenstone's *ferme ornée*, The Leasowes. Shenstone shows more strain than perhaps any other gardenist of the age. His resources were limited, and he was put to elaborate devices to achieve his ends. He had enormous ambitions for a small estate, and he took great pleasure in having distinguished callers (when Thomson and Lyttleton are to come down from neighboring Hagley, he laments, "I fancy they will lavish all their praises upon *nature,* reserving none for poor *art* and *me*"). Shenstone's *Unconnected Thoughts on Gardening* and Dodsley's description (among others) of The Leasowes exercised great influence. The *Thoughts* carry over some of Pope's moral emphasis. Shenstone carefully distinguishes "nature's province": the "shape of ground, the disposition of trees, and the figure of water must be sacred to nature; and no forms must be allowed that make a discovery of art." Whatever thwarts nature in her own province is "treason"; art must enter there only "clandestinely and by night." But Shenstone does not discount art: "Apparent art, in its proper province, is almost as important as apparent nature"—so long as their provinces are "kept distinct." This means, in effect, that art decides whether the natural scene lends itself to the beautiful or the sublime, and, without violating the intrinsic character of the scene, shapes it accordingly.

Shenstone's estate was an elaborate composition of views and retreats. He carries on the method we can see in Pope's advice to his friends, but he carries it to the point where it becomes a new form. Shenstone was adamant about his visitors' entering at the proper point so that they might undergo the planned succession of varied experiences. Mottoes were placed on urns and seats to induce the proper Virgilian associations with a given prospect; memorials invoked the presiding spirit of the place. Hagley, Lyttleton's estate, used temples and memorials "combined with scenes expressing the character of the friendship and the personality of the friend"—a "scene that 'held the eye' for Thomson . . . for Pope, 'a gay, irregular, sylvan walk,' and for gentle Shenstone, 'a quiet and sequestered recess' " (Clark, p. 162). We are obviously moving toward virtuosity in manipulating nature.

In 1770 a clergyman and schoolmaster, William Gilpin, made his tour of the River Wye with "a new object of pursuit":

> that of not barely examining the face of a country; but of examining by the rules of picturesque beauty; that of not merely describing, but of adapting the description of natural scenery to the principles of artificial landscape.

Gilpin is the father of the picturesque; he sets about seeing nature under the aspect of art, bringing to the untouched landscape a will to see it as a series of potential works of pictorial art. In this, he carries to a new pitch of self-consciousness what is latent in the descriptions of Pope and Thomson and what gardenists had sought on a small scale in their improvements. Gilpin does not expect nature to provide him with finished works of art. She is, he remarks, "always great in design, but unequal in composition." In terms that recall Shaftesbury (and Shenstone) he explains: "She works on a *vast scale;* and, no doubt, harmoniously, if her schemes could be comprehended." The artist works in a small span, where he lays down "the principles of picturesque beauty, merely to adapt such diminutive parts of nature's surface to his own eye, as come within its scope." The painter who "adheres strictly to the composition of nature," therefore, "will rarely make a good picture." For composition "is the foundation of all picturesque beauty" (*Three Essays,* 1792, p. 70).

Gilpin observes those scenes in which nature approaches the compositions of art. He looks constantly for a harmony that softens hard regularity: it may be the work of fog, of "beautiful obscurity," of color, of light and shade. His taste in painting is that of a colorist. When he looks at Raphael, he exclaims, "What harmony can arise from a conjunction of red, blue, and yellow, of which the draperies are composed, almost in raw tints?" (*Lake Tour,* II, 236).[15] Reynolds finds Gilpin's picturesque "applicable to the excellences of the inferior schools." There is, he feels, nothing of what Gilpin calls the picturesque in Michelangelo or Raphael, "whereas Rubens and the Venetian painters may be said to have nothing else." The picturesque, in short, is "incompatible with the grand style" (Letter to Gilpin, 19 April 1791). Gilpin admires the grand style, too, but its uniformity and simple boldness do not satisfy him. He wants a mixture of the greatness of the sublime with the varied harmony of beauty. A rock alone is "bleak, naked, and unadorned. . . . Tint it with mosses and lichens of various hues, and you give it a degree of beauty. Adorn it with shrubs and hanging herbage, and you make it still more picturesque. Connect it with wood and water and broken ground, and you make it in the highest degree interesting."

Since art can provide the composing unity, and nature the rich variety, Gilpin moves back and forth—sometimes praising nature at the expense of art, sometimes the reverse. All depends on where he starts. When he sees the play of sunlight and shadow on one of the great formal crescents of Bath, it seems "like an effort of nature to set off art," as "a mere mass of regularity [becomes] the ground of so enchanting a display of harmony and picturesque effect" (*Wye Tour,* 94). Even when nature "deviates" toward regularity, she does it with a "negligent air of greatness" (*Lake Tour* I, 170); a calm lake proves to be *"tremblingly alive* all over: the merest trifle, a frisking fly, a falling leaf, almost a sound, alarms it" (*Lake Tour* I, 100). When Gilpin turns to works of art, he looks for "ruggedness." If the body represented is smoothly regular, it is better seen in action than at rest; better still, "agitated by passion, . . . its muscles swoln by strong exertion," its face marked by "energetic meaning" or "force of expression." And in representing what he sees, the painter should use a "free, bold touch" but (here Gilpin is more conservative than some) not call attention to the act of execution itself (*Three Essays* I, 10–17).

Gilpin is troubled by the aestheticism he falls into. Having broken down the distinctions between art and nature, he moves, unlike the moralist, toward considering all objects for their visual effect. He laments that picturesque ideas run "counter to utility": a ruined tree is far more picturesque than a healthy one (*Remarks on Forest Scenery,* 1791, I, 7), a loitering peasant than an industrious mechanic. And such destroyers as Henry VIII and Cromwell have adorned the countryside with picturesque ruins. When the scene moves toward grandeur, it is enhanced by those Salvator Rosa types—"figures in long, folding draperies; gypsies; banditti; and soldiers—not in modern regimentals" (*Lake Tour* II, 46). Gilpin is looking for images of energy, and their intensity outweighs their moral import, so long at least as the pursuit remains purely aesthetic.

One of the interesting consequences of Gilpin's views is the way he looks at human scenes. How shall one create a picturesque village, he asks, and he doubts that it is possible "for a single hand" to do it.

> Nothing contributes more to it than the various styles of building, which result from the different ideas of different people. When all these little habitations happen to unite harmoniously, and to be connected with the proper appendages of a village—a winding road—a number of spreading trees—a rivulet with a bridge—and a spire, to bring the whole to an apex,—the village is complete (*Lake Tour* I, 22).

He is interested also in the harmony accidentally achieved by crowds. In "managing a crowd, and in managing a landscape, the same general rules are to be observed." There must be massing into unity but variety within it. "Figures must be contrasted with figures; and life, spirit, and action must pervade the whole" (*Wye Tour,* 77). Gilpin draws from his correspondent, the poet Samuel Rogers, some fine instances—Sterne-like in their observation—of this aesthetic view:

> I have seen a ragged shepherd boy . . . throw himself down in an attitude that Raphael would not have disdained to copy—& I have often stopt to admire the form and graceful step of a girl . . . with a brown pitcher on her head (*Samuel Rogers and William Gilpin,* ed. Carl Paul Barbier, London, 1959, p. 22).

One of the consequences of the picturesque (which has an interesting relationship to the mock forms of the Augustans) is the democratization of subject matter. Sir Uvedale Price, the theoretician of the picturesque, is fascinated with the Dutch painter Ostade. Ostade's low subject matter has a curious correspondence—from the point of view of the picturesque —with the high subjects of Claude. "The porches and posts of the one answer those purposes [variety without loss of harmony] as effectually as the porticos and columns of the other; projecting roofs, sheds with brackets, and rails have in another style the effect of cornices and balustrades: the vulgar flower-pots of Ostade take the forms of urns and vases in Claude: his winding staircase, of magnificent flights of steps; it is the fable of Baucis and Philemon." This is the same kind of problem that troubled Gilpin: the picturesque eye becomes indifferent to the nature of subject matter. And at this point we move to a new stage.

Price tried to create a systematic doctrine in his *Essay on the Picturesque* (1794; volume II in 1798) by making the picturesque a third aesthetic category, to supplement the sublime and the beautiful. To do this, he went back to Addison's basis for the New or Uncommon—curiosity. The picturesque "corrects the languor of beauty or the tension of sublimity." By intricacy, variety, and partial concealment it excites a play of mind, "loosening those iron bonds, with which astonishment"—as in Burke's sublime—"chains up its faculties" (I, 89). Sublimity, Price points out, encourages the uniformity of a single bold effect; the picturesque thrives on varied particulars. It can be light and playful, and, unlike the sublime, it can mix with and improve the beautiful. In effect, the picturesque is the "characteristic" elevated to an aesthetic principle. Shaftesbury, it may be recalled, speaks of the characteristic nature of a cock or a bull and makes out of it a concrete universal—the embodiment of a distinctive kind or species. Price shows a similar interest: "We are amused and occupied by ugly objects, if they be also picturesque, just as we are by a rough, and in other respects a disagreeable mind, provided it has a marked and peculiar character" (I, 199).

To widen the basis of aesthetic theory, Price appeals to the instance of painting, where composition may mold into a subtle harmony a great variety of objects and forms. Price wishes to restore to cultivated landscape the richness of texture it had enjoyed in the designs of Kent and the painted landscapes of Claude and Poussin. But this appeal to painting is a way of defining a complex harmony within nature; Price is not trying to make landscape reproduce familiar pictorial compositions or draw its values from the associations of such paintings. He provides a catalogue of picturesque objects, whose intricacy and variety make them aesthetically interesting although they fall outside the canons of both the sublime and the beautiful. Among these are classical architecture in ruins (its formality and symmetry broken); Gothic architecture intact; such intricate structures as cottages, stables, and old mills; water with a broken surface; rugged and mossy trees; shaggy goats, deer, or asses (rather than sheep or horses); gypsies and beggars; noble statesmen in age and exile. What do these have in common? They are neither smoothly formal nor awesomely grand; they have strong individual "character"—"mellowed and consecrated by time, and varied by accident" (II, 164), or irregular in growth and filled with animation. These objects do not fit readily into categories of high and low; their value comes in many cases from their power of endurance and from the way in which experience has inscribed itself upon them. Price grants them an aesthetic dignity for which theory had made no provision, and their elevation is—as he put it—"the fable of Baucis and Philemon."

The picturesque vision admits the scene that absorbs much seeming irrelevancy into a dense structure. Here is one such scene that Price records (and it reminds him in turn of an image in the *Iliad*):

> It was a place where a small cascade had worn a bason in the natural rock: I came suddenly upon it at a turn of the road; it was almost surrounded by women busily employed, but gaily, laughing, talking and singing, amidst the noise of beating clothes, and the splashing of the water. Some of the clothes were spread out on the low rocks near the bason, and partly hanging down their sides; others were in bundles on the ground, or on the heads of those who were carrying them away; while their different shapes, folds, and colours, the actions and expressions of the women, the clearness and various motions of the water, the whole seen on a beautiful summer evening, made the greatest impression on me as a picture: but it also struck me as the most delightful image of peace and security . . . (II, 364–65).

This picture of humble occupations recalls the pastoral, but suggests even more the new interest in scenes of varied life that we see in the poetry of Goldsmith, Cowper, and sometimes Crabbe—scenes in which human characters compose as naturally and organically as the parts of a landscape, held together by common feeling and shared life, set among the houses and fields whose character they have created:

> Sweet was the sound when oft at evening's close,
> Up yonder hill the village murmur rose . . .

> The swain responsive as the milk-maid sung,
> The sober herd that lowed to meet their young,
> The noisy geese that gabbled o'er the pool,
> The playful children just let loose from school,
> The watch-dog's voice that bayed the whispering wind,
> And the loud laugh that spoke the vacant mind.
> These all in sweet confusion sought the shade,
> And filled each pause the nightingale had made
>   (*The Deserted Village* [1770], lines 113–24).

Another striking instance of picturesque vision is a passage in George Crabbe's "The Borough" (1810) on the stains in the church tower. Price is full of observations on the inimitable tints of the stains of time, and here Crabbe, with his scientific training, presents the "living stains" of minute vegetable matter that seems like the very surface of the flint:

> Seeds, to our eyes invisible, will find
> On the rude rock the bed that fits their kind;
> There, in the rugged soil, they safely dwell,
> Till showers and snows the subtle atoms swell,
> And spread th' enduring foliage;—then we trace
> The freckled flower upon the flinty base;
> These all increase, till in unnoticed years
> The stony tower as gray with age appears;
> With coats of vegetation, thinly spread,
> Coat above coat, the living on the dead:
> These then dissolve to dust, and make a way
> For bolder foliage, nursed by their decay:
> The long-enduring ferns in time will all
> Die and depose their dust upon the wall;
> Where the wing'd seed may rest, till many a flower
> Show Flora's triumph o'er the falling tower
>   (Letter II, "The Church").

The interest in the "freckled flower" is partly visual awareness, partly, as Crabbe makes clear, a feeling for the slow and imperceptible growth that marks the unique object in its peculiar circumstances of place and time. The character of the church tower is only a special case of the character of all individuals, whether persons or nations, institutions or cultures. The historicism of the later eighteenth century draws upon the metaphors of vegetable growth in the discussions of genius (for example, Edward Young's *Conjectures on Original Composition*, addressed to Richardson and published in 1759). The awareness of the mysterious play of accident is as strong in Burke's discussion of the growth of the English constitution. In criticism of the rational planning of the revolutionaries in

France, Burke uses the analogy of the slow growth of a great tree for the historical unfolding of the English state, and by means of that analogy introduces the piety that reveres the dignity of age, the sanctity of the natural, and the vitality of the living.

The picturesque, as the term has survived today, calls to mind pictures in doubtful taste and garish color of Italian hill towns, Swiss chalets, Balkan peasant dances, and sunsets behind desert palms. We are properly suspicious of the sentimentalism that attributes artistic merit to the pleasant associations that may be stirred by their subject matter. But terms like "romantic" have undergone a comparable debasement. The picturesque need not suggest banal complacency or Late Biedermeier coziness. We may be offended or amused by Diderot's praise of Greuze's paintings; yet we can see in Diderot and Sterne, among others, an experimental interest in the power of feelings to call forth play of mind. There are unquestionably excesses—so strong that we feel our responses coerced and react with laughter or contempt—in much of the poetry as well as the painting of the time. Perhaps the bad poetry of the period is exceptionally bad because it has open to it the devices of cheap success. But we must make the kind of distinctions that have recently been brought to Victorian art and literature.

First, we must distinguish between kinds of association. Association of ideas is a hypothesis that, in its fullest form, seeks to account for all mental processes; and we must distinguish between those images whose indeterminacy admits a great range of association and those that are tied (although not limited) to particular associations. For example, the landscapes of Thomson—apart from the meanings that are suggested by the context—give us forms of space and of light, patterns of tension and harmony, that underlie any specific content we may give to them. The fact that these forms are located in landscape gives them concreteness but tends to empty them of specific human content. This makes them suggestive without making them distinctly symbolic.

In the gardens of Shenstone and others, landscape features are deliberately tied to a specific content by mottoes or memorials. This governs our response and, at least temporarily, limits it. But one can allow the response, once the key is set, to become more general and indeterminate as it fixes in the landscape itself. The more specific association, in other words, can be amplified into the kind that is stimulated by Thomson's landscape. This need not happen, of course, and a tightly "literary" association may govern all our response. Still, one must recognize the possibilities.

In the same way, a personal association may be aroused and recorded—as in those poems that mark a return to scenes of childhood—which involves the sense of funded experience and the disparity between an early response and the later, more self-conscious one, part of whose very nature is that it *is* a "return." The sense of loss—if that is what is felt—or the sense of continuity and reassurance may again become amplified and generalized. It may point up features of the landscape and waken associations with those forms; or it may define a psychological state into which we can enter and which we can generalize into the pattern of numerous experiences we have felt in other places and at other times. The personal need not be wayward, and it may disclose associations of the most universal sort.

The first kind of association I have mentioned is one that we find most architects (of either buildings or landscape) taking into account: the sense of security given by certain spatial relationships; the peculiar liberation as we move from narrow corridors to large bright open spaces, as in the movement from gateway to court or from a low barrel vault into a high domed space; the tension between formal proportions and loose, natural forms, whether rococo ornament or living plants. "In the castle," Uvedale Price writes, "every thing proclaims suspicious defiance; the security of strength and precaution. A commanding, or at least an uncommanded situation; high solid walls and towers; the draw-bridge, the portcullis; few apertures, and those small; no breaks nor projections that would interfere with strength and solidity" (II, 263–64). Clearly, this is not a castle seen entirely as a functional structure; yet so many discussions of function tend to deny some functions for the sake of others or dogmatically to make some functions by-products of others. What seems otiose or superficially decorative may prove to be more subtly essential than we imagine until we have removed it.

What becomes apparent in all these creations of elysiums and Arcadian landscapes is the strong sense of the play of mind that was involved in the experience of them. To create, as Shenstone does, a series of varied aesthetic and associative experiences is an exercise not only in landscape gardening but in the psychology of perception. The element of artifice that is so strong in the landscape garden is akin to what we find in the cultivation of exotic styles in architecture, in the decorative arts, and in poetry. It is clear that William Collins' *Persian Eclogues* or Goldsmith's Chinese letters or Montesquieu's *Persian Letters* earlier are not authentic transpositions, any more than so-called Rococo Gothic or—for all the scholarship they embody—Gray's Norse and Welsh poems.

It is easy to be patronizing toward the frivolity of these enterprises, but what seems to us mere frivolity (and certainly must have been in many cases) was often the detached experimental playfulness of men testing the nature of sensibility and the powers of response. If it seems decadent aestheticism, especially as compared with the pieties of the Romantics or of the nineteenth-century Gothic revivalists, we must be careful to respect its freedom and its boldness. The detachment is essential to the sense of trying on roles and testing the emotions they might induce. Gray could recall that, when he wrote his great odes, "I felt myself the bard." The histrionic lies somewhere between the utter detachment and calculation Diderot describes in his *Paradoxe* and the complete identification the doctrine of sympathy might imply. Sympathy allows us to become the character we create, to enter into his feelings, however extreme or bizarre. Detachment is the saving self-consciousness that tells us what we are doing and allows us to contemplate ourselves in the process of doing it. This detachment seems "insincere" to an age that prizes only sympathy and gives it a religious and metaphysical basis; but we might better think of Sterne and call it ironic.

There is something to be said for an age that shows more interest in the nature of belief than in specific beliefs, more concern with the processes of art than with its products. One might risk a grand generalization and say that such a period excels in the decorative arts, where styles can be tried on and put off, where history can be searched for new costumes or settings. Each costume or setting imposes a role to be played out with the histrionic excess that marks a lightness of commitment. But, at the same time, the very range of styles that are tried on makes one all the more aware of the nature of style itself, of the reciprocal play between character and dress, emotion and setting. If faiths are accepted as conventions, the study of convention itself may produce a new faith in the imagination.

But such generalizations are at best correctives to other generalizations, equally grand and equally forced. Let us consider instead a specific instance of taste that runs through the poetry, painting, and architecture of the day—the interest in ruins. The ruin emerges as a subject for painting in the backgrounds of Nativity scenes, and during the seventeenth century the landscape with ruins has a great vogue. In the eighteenth century we have the creation of artificial ruins as ornaments of landscape gardening.

The appeal of ruins has many bases.[16] They reveal the "unimaginable touch of time," in Wordsworth's phrase. They embody moral lessons about the transience of all human works. They stir us to pleasant melancholy as we meditate the lives that once were spent among these stones. They reveal—as Crabbe shows—the gradual fusion of the artifact with nature, so that the sharp angles or clean curves of art crumble into the picturesque irregularity of hedges or rocks. Conversely, they present the assertion of art against the power of nature— the heroism of the lonely column asserting human order and transforming the landscape like Wallace Stevens' jar in Tennessee. They offer exercises in imaginative construction, as the mind seeks to trace out the building from the fragments. They awaken memories of the paintings of Claude or Poussin. And they evoke the aesthetic experience those painters made use of—the play of vertical accents against horizontal, of white or ocher stone against green landscape, of regular forms against the hollows and thrusts of natural landscape. We are reminded by Sir John Summerson that the appeal of ruins is "in origin, an aesthetic appeal, though it may be, and very often is, interpreted in sentimental terms":

> The building has become comprehensible as a single whole—no longer an *exterior* plus one or more *interiors* but a single combination of planes in recession, full of mystery and surprise, movement behind movement; and since it retains all the character of architecture—a structure designed for use—it suggests its own participation in life: a fantastic participation. The doors and windows in a ruined building accent the drama of human movement, of through-going, out-looking and raise it to a transcendental plane. . . .
>
> The art of preserving ruins is a kind of play-acting and must be appraised in that spirit. But it is a mistake to suppose it mere sentimentality. It is—as play-acting should be—an affair of taste and imagination (*Heavenly Mansions*, London, 1949, pp. 236, 238).

Play-acting is not an activity that wins our prompt respect.

Yet it is a natural occupation in a period when the metaphors men live by have become detached from old systems of belief and have not yet been absorbed into new structures. It serves a period when the orders of being seem to have at most a problematic relationship, neither clearly reconciled nor clearly discrete, where the order of mind survives as the process of art, and the larger Order that art once sought to imitate turns out to be something it perhaps creates. Play-acting is simultaneously aware of the conditioned and the creative, of man as the product of natural forces and man as the producer of imaginative structures.

XIII.

Blake: Vision and Satire

I. The Vision of Innocence

William Blake's *Songs of Innocence* were engraved by 1789. Not until five years later were they incorporated into *The Songs of Innocence and Experience, Shewing the Two Contrary States of the Human Soul.* Partly because the *Songs of Innocence* have found their way into the nursery, partly because the *Songs of Experience* include some of Blake's most brilliant poems, there has been a tendency to discount the *Songs of Innocence* or to save them by reading them as highly ironic poems, each with its own built-in contraries. This produces strained readings and obscures the full import of Innocence as one of the "two contrary states." We must first take the *Songs of Innocence* in their own right, and by doing so we can make better sense of the *Songs of Experience.*

What the contrary states mean is shown in two poems Blake enclosed in letters to his friend and patron, Thomas Butts, the first on 2 October 1800, the second two years later, on 22 November 1802.[1] In the first the themes of Innocence are restated in the language of vision. Blake achieves an ecstatic transcendence on the shore at Felpham and looks down upon his mortal Shadow and his wife's. His eyes "Like a Sea without shore / Continue Expanding, / The Heavens commanding." All Heaven becomes one man, Jesus, who purges away "All my mire & my clay" (as in "The Little Black Boy" or "The Chimney Sweeper") and enfolds Blake in his bosom, saying:

> This is My Fold,
> O thou Ram horn'd with gold,
> Who awakest from Sleep
> On the Sides of the Deep.

The lion and the wolf, whose "roarings resound," the "loud

Sea & deep gulf"—all of them threatening—now become, for Jesus, "guards of My Fold."

> And the voice faded mild.
> I remain'd as a Child;
> All I ever had known
> Before me bright Shone.

This draws together visionary perception and childlike innocence, and makes visionary transcendence a discovery of the protected world of the divine sheepfold, where seeming evil is absorbed into a pastoral version of Order.

In the second of these poems we encounter the trials of Experience. Blake is torn with conflicting obligations; "the duties of life each other cross."

> Must Flaxman look upon me as wild,
> And all my friends be with doubts beguil'd?

Blake resolves the conflict by defying the sun and looking through its earthly form:

> Another Sun feeds our life's streams,
> We are not warmed with thy beams . . .
> My Mind is not with thy light array'd,
> Thy terrors shall not make me afraid.

The defiance makes all the natural world shrink and grieve, but Blake moves forward with triumph into the world of vision:

> The Sun was hot
> With the bows of my Mind & the Arrows of Thought—
> My bowstring fierce with Ardour breathes,
> My arrows glow in their golden sheaves.

"Now," he concludes, "I a fourfold vision see . . . Tis four-fold in my supreme delight." He has wrested vision from grief, and won through to a trust in his powers (pp. 816–18).

The *Songs of Innocence* cultivate a tone of naïvety, but we must recognize that what is spontaneously discovered by the child has in fact been earned by the poet's visionary powers. It is not easy to achieve Innocence, and one does not reach it by a simple process of subtraction. While the *Songs of Innocence* insist upon the naïve vision, they show, in their own way, as much calculation as the more radical of Wordsworth's *Lyrical Ballads*. Wordsworth's subjects are children, displaced persons or wanderers; humble people who live in dwellings all but indistinguishable from nature; morally displaced persons such as criminals and idiots—those rejected or oppressed by society; poets as social misfits and dreamers; and, most generally, people who have not entered and for some reason have fallen out of the social pattern. Wordsworth's treatment of them is a bold assertion of the dignity of their elementary feelings. Coleridge speaks of the "daring humbleness" of Wordsworth's language and versification, and we know that their challenge was felt and resisted by early critics. Blake's *Songs of Innocence* are more traditional in their literary and religious associations and more remote from such stubborn commonplaces of life as swelling ankles, idiot sons, and the love of property. But, like Wordsworth's poems, and, in fact, like most pastorals, they create a vision that risks one-sidedness. Such a vision teeters on the verge of calling to mind all it excludes, and Blake has given us what Innocence excludes in the *Songs of Experience*. But pastoral can teeter without falling into overt irony, and its assertion is all the more defiant for that poise.

The defiance is the poet's. The innocents themselves remain indifferent to all that crowds in upon us. This indifference is not ignorance, any more than it is in Wordsworth's "We Are Seven," where the child insists that her dead brother and sister are still in the midst of their family. The childlike trust becomes a metaphor for the more strenuous faith and defiance of doubt that all may achieve.

The landscape of Innocence is a fostering, humanized landscape. It echoes human songs and laughter; it accepts and sympathizes with every feeling. The "Laughing Song" is one of the simplest of the *Songs*, but Wordsworth found it worth copying into his commonplace book in 1804. It closes with the invitation to participate:

> When the painted birds laugh in the shade,
> Where our table with cherries and nuts is spread,
> Come live & be merry, and join with me,
> To sing the sweet chorus of "Ha, Ha, He."

The language is somewhat archaic ("painted birds"), the form reminiscent of Elizabethan lyrics, and the poem closes tellingly with the call to "sing the sweet chorus." The harmony of shepherds (the song first appears written in a copy of *Poetical Sketches* as *Sung . . . by a Young Shepherd*) and maids, of man and nature, is caught in the very meaningless exultation of the "Ha, Ha, He." If one calls it witless exultation, one has only underlined the point: this is the least self-conscious of sounds, the pure merry note. So it is with "Spring." Animal sounds, "infant noise," and the sounding flute are all part of one song; and child and lamb play together with no sense of difference. Music is only one manifestation of the reciprocal warmth that marks all relationships (every creature is related to every other); the nurse is trustful and indulgent, old John on the echoing green participates in the laughter of the children at play. There is neither jealousy nor restriction; darkness brings safe repose and satiation. The "happy Blossom" welcomes both the merry sparrow and the sobbing robin, rejoicing in its power to accept or comfort each alike.

In "The Lamb," the harmony grows out of a deeper union:

> I a child, & thou a lamb,
> We are called by his name.

Each creature is a member one of another because of their common membership in God's love and the body of His creation. This participation in one life is nicely stated in "The Shepherd," where the freedom of the shepherd ("From the morn to the evening he strays") is consonant with his watchfulness, for he is himself a sheep watched over by his Shepherd with generous love. The condition of peace is security without restraint. The participation is extended in "The Divine Image" to "every man of every clime," for every man—"heathen, turk, or jew"—is "Man, his child and care."

In "Night" all these themes come together. The moon sits in "heaven's high bower" like the happy blossom. The darkening fields are left by sleeping lambs to the "feet of angels bright." As in *Paradise Lost,*

> Millions of spiritual Creatures walk the Earth
> Unseen, both when we wake, and when we sleep
> . . . oft in bands
> While they keep watch, a nightly rounding walk
> With Heav'nly touch of instrumental sounds
> In full harmonic number join'd, their songs
> Divide the night, and lift our thoughts to Heaven
> (IV, 677–78, 684–88).

Blake's world of Innocence is not, however, Paradise. The angels cannot always control wolves and tigers, or deny them victims; but the victims are received, "New worlds to inherit."

> And there the lion's ruddy eyes
> Shall flow with tears of gold,
> And pitying the tender cries,
> And walking round the fold,

> Saying "Wrath, by his meekness,
> And by his health, sickness
> Is driven away
> From our immortal day.
>
> And now beside thee, bleating lamb,
> I can lie down and sleep;
> Or think on him who bore thy name,
> Graze after thee and weep.
> For, wash'd in life's river,
> My bright mane for ever
> Shall shine like the gold
> As I guard o'er the fold" (33–48).

The regeneration of the lion, so that he can now "remain always in Paradise," is a perhaps unconscious but eloquent reply to Mandeville's comment on Milton (see p. 123). As the angels pitied the howling wolves and tigers, the lion can now pity the tender cries of the sheep. It is a splendid assertion of the power of meekness, as the gold of the lion's "bright mane" becomes an aureole.

But pastoral celebration does not contain all that Blake wishes to say. "The School Boy," while it seems spoken in trust of parents' understanding, is a lament against restriction. It is one of the peoms that await the coming into existence of the *Songs of Experience,* where, five years later, it was placed. Other poems are less clear cases. "Holy Thursday" presents the Ascension Day "anniversary" of the charity school children. The "grey-headed beadles" who lead the children into St. Paul's are mentioned first, and they may seem like threatening figures with their "wands white as snow." But the children flow like a river, they are like flowers, they have a "radiance all their own," and they raise their choral voice "like a mighty wind" or "like harmonious thunderings the seats of Heavens among." And, as is usual in these poems, the closing lines have gained meaning from the whole poem. Now the formidable beadles take their place below the angelic children:

> Beneath them sat the aged men, wise guardians of the poor;
> Then cherish pity, lest you drive an angel from your door.

The last line seems pat and inadequate to those who are on the watch for irony; yet it converts the aged men to the counterparts of Abraham and Lot, who entertained angels at their door and were shown favor.

In "The Little Black Boy" the pain of being born with a

different face is genuine and acute. Blake enters imaginatively into the condition of the boy and his mother. She supplies a consoling vision that makes the suffering temporary and even a source of pride. By showing her boy that the body is a "cloud" that absorbs the beams of God's love and vanishes after a short term of trial, she turns upside down the standards of the world around him. This can save his sense of worth. His body is better adapted than the white boy's to bearing God's love (God is here conceived much as in Milton, where He dwells in "unapproached light" which the angels can bear to behold only when they veil their eyes with their wings). And all bodies are the instruments by which we are trained to live in the spirit.

The poem ends with a reversal like the one that sets the ominous beadles below the angelic children of "Holy Thursday." The little black boy sees himself with the English child in heaven:

> I'll shade him from the heat, till he can bear
> To lean in joy upon our father's knee;
> And then I'll stand and stroke his silver hair,
> And be like him, and he will then love me.

One can see pathos, surely, in the fundamental desire to "be like him"—the lack of any image of oneself that can give repose or self-respect. Yet there is also a strain of mature understanding or even pity in the recognition that the white boy can bear less love and can give less love—that he needs to wait for the black boy to be like him before he can recognize their oneness in a common father. We may deplore the comparative quietism of this, but we must recognize a faith that permits the boy to live with the inevitable without surrendering to it.

"The Chimney Sweeper" descends farther into suffering, and the plight of the sweeps is as grim as can be conceived. What the poem is saying, nevertheless, is that the naïve faith we see in Tom's dream is the means of survival. In a "Song by an Old Shepherd" Blake had written:

> Blow, boisterous wind, stern winter frown,
> Innocence is a winter's gown;
> So clad, we'll abide life's pelting storm
> That makes our limbs quake, if our hearts be warm (64).

The chimney sweep, Tom, dreams that thousands of sweepers are "lock'd up in coffins of black," when

> . . . by came an Angel who had a bright key,
> And he open'd the coffins & set them all free;
> Then down a green plain leaping, laughing, they run,
> And wash in a river, and shine in the Sun.

The Angel is like those in "Night" who receive the wolves' victims, "New worlds to inherit." Here the new world is the miserable child's vision of a heaven—green plains, a river to wash in, sunlight, play, a father. The old world is still there when Tom awakens, but Tom and his companions have a "winter's gown":

> Tho' the morning was cold, Tom was happy & warm;
> So if all do their duty they need not fear harm.

The last line stings with irony as we think of the duties left unperformed by the boys' elders, and it has pathos if we take it to imply that Tom expects virtue to be rewarded in the world. But it is also a daring assertion of naïve faith, the faith that will inevitably be rewarded in its own terms, with an assurance of spirit that can transcend its worldly conditions. This naïve faith has both the precariousness and the strength of a pastoral vision: it seems too fragile to survive suffering, yet it somehow does survive, more vivid and intense than the world it transcends.

I have spoken of these assertions as metaphors for adult existence, and we can see their counterpart in Blake's letters:

> . . . now I have lamented over the dead horse let me laugh & be merry with my friends till Christmas, for as Man liveth not by bread alone, I shall live altho' I should want bread—nothing is necessary to me but to do my Duty & to rejoice in the exceeding joy that is always poured on my Spirit (To William Hayley, 7 October 1803).
> . . . as none on Earth can give me Mental Distress, & I know that all Distress inflicted by Heaven is a Mercy, a Fig for all corporeal! Such Distress is My mock & scorn (To Thos. Butts, 11 September 1801).

In "The Little Girl Lost" and "The Little Girl Found" we come to the borderland between Innocence and Experience. Blake moved these poems from one group to the other, and this convertibility helps us understand the relationship of "contrary states." In the two border poems, the seeming forces of evil prove to be as gentle and fostering as parents—perhaps through the influence of the sleeping maid, whose innocence creates a precinct of "hallow'd ground." The lion's "ruby tears" flow with pity for her unprotectedness: her weakness and her trust disarm the beasts of prey. In the second poem the lion reveals an angel within, and his cave becomes a palace; the parents who brave the wilds for the sake of their lost child are rewarded with a new freedom and security:

> To this day they dwell
> In a lonely dell;
> Nor fear the wolvish howl
> Nor the lions' growl.

They live in a world where evil has no power, however it may seem to threaten others.

If we stress the faith that is strong enough to transcend the power of the world, these poems clearly fall into the pattern of Innocence. If, on the other hand, we stress the adversity to be overcome and the courage with which it is faced, they move toward Experience, although they remain the most triumphant of the *Songs of Experience*. Seven-year-old Lyca wanders into the "desart wild" and is lost. Significantly, she is concerned not for herself but for her parents' grief. She confidently summons the moon to guard her and goes to sleep. The beasts of the wild play around her body, licking her and weeping with pity, until at last they accept her as one of themselves, loose her dress, and carry her to their caves. In "The Little Girl Found" we see that Lyca's parents do indeed grieve and search for her (as parents in Innocence do). After seven days of anxiety and distress, the mother can go no farther and is carried in her husband's arms. They too encounter a lion, which seems to stalk them. But suddenly he licks their hands and becomes a "Spirit arm'd in gold" (like the lion in "Night"). He leads them to his palace where Lyca lies sleeping among "tygers wild."

The strength of Experience comes of its ability to sustain or recover the faith of Innocence. The state of Experience is one of suffering, but we have already seen much of that in Innocence. More significant is the attitude taken toward suffering: those who are frustrated and corrupted by it, surrender; those who seek their freedom and keep their vision alive, rebel. In some poems only the condition of suffering is given: these contribute to that composite image, the contrary of the pastoral vision of Innocence, of a world to be met with either despair or defiance. In "A Little Girl Lost," Ona is terrified by the father whose "loving look" is the face of the punitive moralist, professing (sincerely enough) anxiety for his stray-

ing child, but scarcely concealing the self-pity of the rigid law-
maker. In "A Little Boy Lost" the Cordelia-like protestations
of the boy lead to his torture and murder by the priests.

In other poems the surrender is clear. In "The Angel"
and "My Pretty Rose Tree," life is rejected for the sake of
chastity or possessiveness; and the result is armed fear or resentment. The "Nurse's Song" is the expression of anxiety and
envy; the repressive nurse is projecting doubts of her own self
into the lives of the children. In "The Sick Rose," the secrecy
of love becomes disease. The "crimson joy" suggests the
rose's complicity both in passion and in secrecy; disguise destroys from within. We see this more clearly in "The Lilly,"
where the modest rose and the humble sheep protect themselves with a thorn and a threatening horn; whereas the lily's
open delight in love makes her whiteness incapable of stain,
as is the case with Oothoon later in the *Visions of the Daughters of Albion.*

The central distinction between honest wrath and stifled or
corrupted energy is given in the opening poems of the *Songs
of Experience.* "Introduction" announces the visionary Bard

> Whose ears have heard
> The Holy Word
> That walk'd among the ancient trees,
>
> Calling the lapsed Soul,
> And weeping in the evening dew;
> That might controll
> The starry pole,
> And fallen, fallen light renew! (3–10).

"Controll" here still carries the sense of "contradict" or "disprove." The Holy Word is the Poetic Genius within man summoning the dawn of revived life. "Earth's Answer" comes out
of "grey despair"; Earth's locks are as gray as those of the
virgin who resists love in "The Angel." She can see only the
God she has created for herself:

> Prison'd on wat'ry shore,
> Starry Jealousy does keep my den:
> Cold and hoar,
> Weeping o'er,
> I hear the Father of the ancient men.
>
> Selfish father of men!
> Cruel, jealous, selfish fear!
> Can delight,
> Chain'd in night,
> The virgins of youth and morning bear? (6–15).

Are we to take Earth's words as a just condemnation of the Holy Word, or is Earth's despair the counterpart of the resentment of Adam and Eve in their fallen state, before they recover the power to love and recognize that their Judge is also their Redeemer? The latter seems the more plausible.

"The Tyger" is the best known of Blake's songs and the most frequently and elaborately interpreted. The phrase "fearful symmetry"—whatever its possible symbolic suggestions—is clearly the initial puzzle: the "symmetry" implies an ordering hand or intelligence, the "fearful" throws doubt on the benevolence of the Creator. The "forests of the night" are the darkness out of which the tiger looms, brilliant in contrast; they also embody the doubt or confusion that surrounds the origins of the tiger. In the case of "The Lamb," the Creator "calls himself a Lamb. / He is meek, & he is mild; / He became a little child." In "The Tyger" the Creator again is like what he creates, and the form that must be supplied him now is the Promethean smith working violently at his forge. The last alteration we have of this much altered poem insists upon the likeness of Creator and created: "What dread hand Form'd thy dread feet?" The tiger is an image of the Creator; its "deadly terrors" must be His.

The most puzzling stanza of the poem is the next-to-last:

> When the stars threw down their spears,
> And water'd heaven with their tears,
> Did he smile his work to see?
> Did he who made the Lamb make thee?

The first two lines are the crux of the poem. Are the tears the rage of the defeated, or the tears of mercy as in a later Notebook poem, "Morning"?

> To find the Western path
> Right thro' the Gates of Wrath
> I urge my way;
> Sweet Mercy leads me on:
> With soft repentant moan
> I see the break of day.
>
> The war of swords & spears
> Melted by dewy tears
> Exhales on high;
> The sun is freed from fears
> And with soft grateful tears
> Ascends the sky (421).

Here we have come through wrath to mercy, through night to

dawn. This progression appears again in *Jerusalem,* where Los, the imaginative power, considers his task as visionary poet. Los is seeking to make error visible so that it may be thrown off, and his satiric task requires him to adopt the "forms of cruelty."

> I took the sighs & tears & bitter groans,
> I lifted them into my Furnaces to form the spiritual
> 　sword
> That lays open the hidden heart. I drew forth the pang
> Of sorrow red hot: I work'd it on my resolute anvil . . .
> I labour day and night. I behold the soft affections
> Condense beneath my hammer into forms of cruelty,
> But still I labour in hope; tho' still my tears flow down:
> That he who will not defend Truth may be compell'd to
> 　defend
> A Lie: that he may be snared and caught and snared and
> 　taken:
> That Enthusiasm and Life may not cease . . .
> 　　(9:17–20, 26–31).

The "spiritual sword / That lays open the hidden heart" is a counterpart of the tiger we see in the *Songs of Experience.* The wrath serves the ultimate end of redemption and becomes one with mercy. If the God of apparent wrath is also the God of forgiveness, the tiger's form is only superficially "fearful." In the words of Pope:

> Nor God alone in the still calm we find,
> He mounts the storm, and walks upon the wind
> 　(*Essay on Man,* II, 109–10).

"The Tyger" dramatizes the terrors of the shocked doubter, but it moves with assurance—in the stanza I have quoted—to an assertion of faith (faith in the oneness of God, in the goodness of wrath, in the holiness of prophetic rage). When the last stanza repeats the first, but for the alteration of "could" to "dare," the question has been answered. The inconceivable of the first stanza has become the majestic certainty of the last: the daring of the Creator—whether God or man—is the cleansing wrath of the tiger.

The honest wrath that is celebrated in "The Tyger" is the open and healthy response to suffering. In contrast, as we have seen, is the tortured brooding of the bound infant who sulks upon his mother's breast, or the viciousness that comes of "unacted desires" in "A Poison Tree." In "London" this

pattern of externally imposed suppression (the swaddling bands
of the infant, the binding with briars by priests in black gowns)
or internal self-imposed repression (the armed fears of the
virgin, the secret love of the rose) becomes a general condition whose meaning is evident only to the visionary poet. He
alone sees and hears what others take for granted.

> In every cry of every Man,
> In every Infant's cry of fear,
> In every voice, in every ban,
> The mind-forg'd manacles I hear.

The power to penetrate the conventional sounds—whether
street cries, oaths, infants' wails—makes the self-imposed tor-
tures of man not simply audible but visible. The cry of the
soot-covered chimney sweeper appalls—blackens as much
as shocks, convicts as much as arouses—"every black'ning
Church" (blackening with the guilt of its indifference far
more than with soot). So too the "hapless Soldier's sigh"
brands the palace he has been suffering to defend with the
guilt of causing his pain; and—sound made visible—"Runs in
blood down Palace walls."

> But most thro' midnight streets I hear
> How the youthful Harlot's curse
> Blasts the new born Infant's tear,
> And blights with plagues the Marriage hearse.

The visible stain has become a virulent infection, and its
power is caught in the terrible poetic condensation that sees
the marriage coach as already a hearse. The existence of the
youthful harlot (another conventional street sound, as she
curses in the night) is more than a source of physical infection; it is a symptom of the moral disease evident only to the
visionary poet. Except for his, there is no open rebellion in
this London, no deeply felt outrage. Each cry or sigh or curse
arises from a single individual's grief. Only the poet hears what
is *in* each cry or sees *how* it looks and acts—in short, what it
means. The gap between the suffering and the awareness is
part of the terror of the London Blake presents; it is made all
the sharper if we contrast the isolated suffering of these cries
with the echoing responsiveness on the village green of Innocence.

Only when we grant Innocence its proper value does the
full dialectical force of the two contrary states become clear.
We can see the potential suffering that surrounds the world of

Innocence and the potential triumph that Experience permits. Blake is less concerned with exposing injustice than with finding a vital response to it. The evil he presents is in each case the denial of life, whether imposed from without by society or made within by the individual. The good he espouses is the life-giving vision, whether serenely enjoyed or indignantly defended. Clearly serene transcendence of evil is seldom possible although, as we have seen, Blake rejoices in such moments. And Innocence, like Experience, has its false aspect as well as its true.

In the manuscript of *The Four Zoas* Blake made this note: "Unorganiz'd Innocence: An Impossibility. Innocence dwells with Wisdom, but never with Ignorance" (380). Wisdom need not imply self-consciousness or acquaintance with evil, any more than it does for Adam in Milton's Paradise. But in the years that intervened between the first engraving of the *Songs of Innocence* in 1789 and their yoking to the new *Songs of Experience* in 1793, Blake explored the varieties of false Innocence, which is a denial of life rather than a confident assertion of its goodness.

In *Tiriel* (1789) we encounter a seeming contrast that at last becomes an identity. Tiriel is the tyrannical father who enslaves his sons until they rebel and cast him out. Tyrant and slave are correlative terms; the slave rebels in order to become a tyrant in turn. Tiriel wanders, a bitter and blind outcast, to the Edenic vales of Har. Here we encounter the first reversal. Har and Heva are "like two children" tended by their aged nurse, Mnetha, and they prattle with childish innocence as they greet Tiriel. It is not until the third section of the poem that Har and Heva reveal their own great age, greater than Tiriel's. They vaguely recognize him from a past they only dimly retain; he conceals his identity, and they are entirely absorbed in the pleasures of the present:

> "Thou shalt not go," said Heva, "till thou hast seen our singing birds
> And heard Har sing in the great cage & slept upon our fleeces" (3:22–23).

But Tiriel is moved by "madness and deep dismay" to leave, and Har and Heva "soon forgot their tears" in the simplicity of timeless childhood.

Tiriel next meets his brother, Ijim, an embodiment of wildness and superstition. Ijim sees only a spectral fiend in Tiriel rather than the brother who has been a tyrant. Ijim brings Tiriel back to his palace under force, boasting to Tiriel's sons that he has enslaved his elusive demon in the disguise of Tiriel. When the sons claim to recognize Tiriel, Ijim goes off, unconvinced, returning to the "secret forests" where he can nurse his gloomy fears. Ijim is one of the products of Tiriel's tyranny—the Natural Man, more beast than man, full of strength but childlike in superstitious terror.

Tiriel now curses his children and brings death on all of them except Hela, his daughter, whom he forces to lead him back to the pleasures of Har and Heva. Hela hates her father's cruelty; she rebels helplessly until he curses her too and drives her mad. Finally, they reach the vales of Har and Heva, where Tiriel defies the protective Mnetha: "Lead me to Har and Heva; I am Tiriel, King of the west."

At this point comes the second reversal. For Tiriel now identifies Har as his father:

> "O weak mistaken father of a lawless race,
> Thy laws, O Har, & Tiriel's wisdom, end together in a
> curse" (8:7–8).

Tiriel further identifies Har as the source of all the evil his own life has exemplified. Har, dawdling in his earthly paradise, an ancient infant, is the source of rigid law, the teacher of the ways of the Natural Man and of subtle hypocrisy: "And now," Tiriel concludes, "my paradise is fall'n & a drear sandy plain / Returns my thirsty hissings in a curse on thee, O Har." Tiriel dies with his curse. This is the third reversal: the arrested earthly paradise of the superannuated pseudoinnocent is the source of the cycle of frustration and aggression, of slave and tyrant, that Tiriel's own life has made clear. Once he has slain his sons, Tiriel is ready to return to these peaceful vales; but he arrives only to curse his father in turn.

This poem is Blake's first dramatic presentation of a "negative" State, the mock order of spurious innocence. It is not a condemnation of Innocence itself, but rather an exposure of its use as a disguise. The reversals that run through the poem move stage by stage toward the final equation of the illusion of Innocence (which the self-righteous achieve by self-deception) with the repressive and debasing tyranny of Tiriel. The garden becomes a desert at the close, and the details of Har's great cage and the fleeces on which he lies become more obviously sinister. Tiriel complains that he has been

> Compell'd to pray repugnant & to humble the immortal
>   spirit
> Till I am subtil as a serpent in a paradise,
> Consuming all, both flowers & fruits, insects & warbling
>   birds (8:36–38).

Beyond the poem's cycles of repression and tyranny lies the memory of the "immortal spirit." Tiriel cannot revive it in himself; but he can at last come to recognize its absence from both Har's laws and his own "wisdom."

In *The Book of Thel* (1789) Blake gives us a new version of false Innocence—false here because it seeks withdrawal rather than transcendence and falls into the aimless round of passivity rather than pay the cost of living by the "immortal spirit." At the close of the poem the maiden Thel flees "back unhinder'd" to the vales of Har, where she can accept the prison of passive infancy in an earthly paradise.

Thel is troubled at the outset. She laments her mortality and transiency in images that have a telltale softness and mild charm:

> Ah! Thel is like a wat'ry bow, and like a parting cloud;
> Like a reflection in a glass; like shadows in the water;
> Like dreams of infants, like a smile upon an infant's face;
> Like the dove's voice; like transient day; like music in
>   the air (1:8–11).

There follow three dialogues, each with a creature more lowly and transient than herself; and each reveals what Thel painfully lacks—a sense of function, an ability to give oneself, and to trust in being received and rewarded with love in turn. The Lily of the Valley, small and humble, feeds the cropping Lamb and revives the cattle with its perfume—"Giving to those that cannot crave, the voiceless, the o'ertired" (33). And the Lily of the Valley in turn hears with the candid faith of true Innocence, the voice of God:

> Saying, 'Rejoice, thou humble grass, thou new-born lilly
>   flower,
> Thou gentle maid of silent valleys and of modest brooks;
> For thou shalt be clothed in light, and fed with morning
>   manna,
> Till summer's heat melts thee beside the fountains and
>   the springs
> To flourish in eternal vales . . . (1:21–25).

The Cloud, too, is transient. It vanishes into the springs from which animals drink; it weds the "fair-eyed dew"

> Till we arise link'd in a golden band and never part,
> But walk united, bearing food to all our tender flowers
> (3:15–16).

Thel's life is without service in the vales of Har; she encounters all life around her as a pleasure of the senses but not as a true confrontation ("I hear the warbling birds, / But I feed not the warbling birds; they fly and seek their food"). She speaks in self-pity of having no use unless it be at death to become "the food of worms." To this the Cloud replies in a tone that is sharp and therapeutic:

> Then if thou art the food of worms, O virgin of the skies,
> How great thy use, how great thy blessing! Every thing
> that lives
> Lives not alone nor for itself . . . (3:25–27).

But when Thel encounters the Worm, all the stereotypes of sentimental pity return:

> Is this a Worm? I see thee lay helpless & naked, weeping,
> And none to answer, none to cherish thee with mother's
> smiles (4:5–6).

At once the Clod of Clay appears, as full of protective solicitude as the mothers of the *Songs of Innocence,* and not without reproach: "O beauty of the vales of Har! we live not for ourselves."

Thel cannot learn the lesson of Innocence. The Clod of Clay is the bride of God, the mother of His children, and, like Milton's Adam in Paradise, can feel that she is happier than she knows:

> But how this is, sweet maid, I know not, and I cannot
> know;
> I ponder, and I cannot ponder; yet I live and love
> (5:5–6).

The Clod of Clay does not need to question and to seek assurances; she gives herself completely and trusts the value of what she is and does. All these creatures are taken in love, wedded to all other creatures and to God in those creatures— as the child and the lamb are one in Jesus.

When Thel at last is brought to contemplate her place in the one life that all these creatures enjoy, she can only see— in vision—"her own grave plot," and hear a "voice of sorrow

breathed from the hollow pit." What is revealed to her is what
Blake had cancelled from Tiriel's last speech—an account of
the life of formal law and inner repression. Tiriel had put it:

> Some close shut up
> In silent deceit, poisons inhaling from the morning rose,
> With daggers hid beneath their lips & poison in their
> tongue;
> Or eyed with little sparks of Hell, or with infernal brands
> Flinging flames of discontent & plagues of dark despair;
> Or those whose mouths are graves, whose teeth the gates
> of eternal death.
> Can wisdom be put in a silver rod, or love in a golden
> bowl?
> Is the son of a king warmed without wool or does he cry
> with a voice
> Of thunder? does he look upon the sun & laugh or stretch
> His little hands into the depths of the sea, to bring forth
> The deadly cunning of the scaly tribe & spread it to the
> morning? (8:12–22.)

So here, the voice of sorrow that Thel hears—the voice of her
own anxieties—reveals all the horror of malice, vindictiveness,
hypocrisy, pain. These appear as the life of the senses, and
the last of them is the repressiveness of sexual chastity:

> Why cannot the Ear be closed to its own destruction?
> Or the glist'ning Eye to the poison of a smile?
> Why are Eyelids stor'd with arrows ready drawn,
> Where a thousand fighting men in ambush lie?
> Or an Eye of gifts & graces show'ring fruits & coined
> gold?
> Why a Tongue impress'd with honey from every wind?
> Why an Ear, a whirlpool fierce to draw creations in?
> Why a Nostril wide inhaling terror, trembling, & affright?
> Why a tender curb upon the youthful burning boy?
> Why a little curtain of flesh on the bed of our desire?
> (6:11–20.)

This is the trial set in the *Songs of Experience,* the suffering
imposed from without and within by life in the world. It is
the occasion for either a lapse into Selfhood or a transcendent
return to that Innocence by which this life is judged. Thel's
faith fails her, and she flees with a shriek, back to the vales of
Har.

Thel's false Innocence defines the true Innocence of the
humbler creatures. Her self-consciousness may be the inevitable cost of being human, but her refusal to attempt to tran-

scend it in the annihilation of Selfhood and the triumph of the "immortal spirit" becomes a failure of humanity. She will have the comfort of the aged nurse, Mnetha, instead of the dignity of true existence. Blake is defending Innocence by distinguishing it from its worldly imitation, which becomes—as we have seen—a life of passive sensuousness rather than of active exertions of the spirit. We may do well to remember Bernard Shaw's Blakean vision of Hell, where the Devil is a courtly aesthete who cannot bear very much reality. To put wisdom "in a silver rod / And love in a golden bowl" is to convert the energies of the spirit to works of precious lifelessness and specious orderliness, things of merely worldly value.

The *Visions of the Daughters of Albion* (1793) carries the problem of Innocence a stage further. The three central figures are the daring virgin, Oothoon; her tortured and indecisive lover, Theotormon; and the brutal ravisher and moralist, Bromion. They appear to be characters, but, as each speaks out of a consciousness that is deep and inclusive, each becomes a "State"—a mode of vision and an appropriate world view. At the close of the poem, their relationship has become a fixed one of endless repetition:

> Thus every morning wails Oothoon; but Theotormon sits
> Upon the margin'd ocean conversing with shadows dire
> (8:11–12).

When Oothoon turns to Theotormon with frankly avowed love, defying moral conventions, Bromion rends her "with his thunders," stamps ·her with his signet as an owner does his slave, possesses her as the English tyrant does the "soft American plains," and offers her to Theotormon as his discarded and pregnant harlot. There is an anomaly in Bromion's rage; it is as much a rage of moral vindictiveness as of sexual possession. Bromion's rage is what makes Oothoon, in others' eyes—even in her own at first—a harlot; it is the open assertion of power, of a lawgiver more than a lover. As Oothoon calls down the self-punishment of bewildered remorse, her lover Theotormon "severely smiles" without turning to her. Oothoon has the strength to win through to trust in her immortal spirit; and she tries in turn to awaken Theotormon to life:

> I cry: arise, O Theotormon! for the village dog
> Barks at the breaking day; the nightingale has done lamenting;

The lark does rustle in the ripe corn, and the Eagle returns
From nightly prey and lifts his golden beak to the pure
east,
Shaking the dust from his immortal pinions to awake
The sun that sleeps too long. Arise, my Theotormon, I
am pure,
Because the night is gone that clos'd me in its deadly
black (2:23–29).

But, for Theotormon, "the night and morn / Are both alike;
a night of sighs, a morning of fresh tears."

Oothoon tries to bring Theotormon to a perception that
sees through the surfaces of the given world. All creatures act
from some power that is deeper and greater than the five
senses, whether instinct or reminiscence. Each creature has its
characteristic nature, and this cannot be altered or debased.
The annihilation of Selfhood is what Oothoon has attained,
and it must be distinguished from defilement:

Sweetest the fruit that the worm feeds on, & the soul
prey'd on by woe,
The new wash'd lamb ting'd with the village smoke, &
the bright swan
By the red earth of our immortal river (3:17–19).

Blake carries over from *The Book of Thel* the distinction between the virgin's withdrawal and the holiness of participation
in a common life and reciprocal use.

Theotormon's reply is only the lamentation of doubt. He is
terrified by the unbounded:

Where goest thou, O thought? to what remote land is
thy flight?
If thou returnest to the present moment of affliction
Wilt thou bring comforts on thy wings, and dews and
honey and balm,
Or poison from the desert wilds, from the eyes of the
envier? (4:8–11.)

Bromion, in turn, clings to the visible world. It exists for the
delight of a remote deity, "spread in the infinite microscope";
and it receives from that deity a single kind of lawful existence.
Bromion's world is one of sensuous gratification sanctioned by
religious authority, governed by a worldly but priestly code:

Ah! are there other wars beside the wars of sword and
fire?
And are there other sorrows beside the sorrows of
poverty?

And are there other joys beside the joys of riches and
ease?
And is there not one law for both the lion and the ox?
And is there not eternal fire and eternal chains
To bind the phantoms of existence from eternal life?
(4:19–24.)

Once Bromion's vision is set forth, Oothoon can recognize
its meaning. She sees Urizen, the rational lawgiver, in Bromion, and she repudiates the rigid law that rejects the facts of
individual existence: "How can one joy absorb another? Are
not different joys / Holy, eternal, infinite? and each joy is a
love" (5:5–6). Oothoon's lament opens out into a defense of
the full complexity true order must attain:

How can the giver of gifts experience the delights of the
merchant?
How the industrious citizen the pains of the husbandman?
How different far the fat fed hireling with hollow drum,
Who buys whole corn fields into wastes, and sings upon
the heath!
How different their eye and ear! how different the world
to them! (5:12–16.)

The false order surrounds man with "cold floods of abstraction" and "forests of solitude," that is, isolates him in
Selfhood; it imposes a specious structure of "castles and high
spires, where kings & priests may dwell." Love is therein
made to submit to "spells of law" which bind the wife to "one
she loaths," as Oothoon is bound to Bromion by Theotormon's
fearful doubts. The "castles and high spires" are created in
Theotormon's mind out of his cowardice; he creates mind-
forged "kings & priests." The result is the dissembling of
"subtil modesty," the "knowing, artful, secret, fearful, cautious, trembling hypocrite." If such a world were real, Oothoon would be a whore, "the crafty slave of selfish holiness";
but she is in fact "a virgin fill'd with virgin fancies, / Open
to joy and to delight where ever beauty appears" (6:21–22).

Theotormon's way is a mock order of secrecy, masturbatory
fantasies ("Where the horrible darkness is impressed with
reflections of desire"), the "self enjoyings of self denial," like
Pope's Cave of Spleen, where the repressed energies of prudes
explode in libidinous dreams or overt madness. Oothoon's
way is tolerant acceptance of "wanton play / In lovely copu-
lation," "the heaven of generous love." The conflict lies between self-love and self-surrender:

> Such is self-love that envies all, a creeping skeleton
> With lamplike eyes watching around the frozen marriage
>   bed (7:21–22).

Oothoon will catch for Theotormon "girls of mild silver, or of furious gold." This imagery of living silver and gold recalls the contrast in Milton of the spiritual treasures of Heaven to the visible splendors of Pandemonium. Blake draws a similar contrast between golden light and hoarded wealth:

> Where the cold miser spreads his gold; or does the bright
>   cloud drop
> On his stone threshold? does his eye behold the beam
>   that brings
> Expansion to the eye of pity? (8:1–3.)

His final image is one of energy transcending material bounds or making of matter its mere outward adornment:

> The sea fowl takes the wintry blast for a cov'ring to her
>   limbs,
> And the wild snake the pestilence to adorn him with
>   gems & gold;
> And trees & birds & beasts & men behold their eternal
>   joy (8:6–8).

Oothoon asserts an order of charity ("Arise, and drink your bliss, for every thing that lives is holy!") which is wedded to the energies of the flesh—only to their energies, it must be repeated, not to a life bounded by the senses or "the wheel of false desire." Here the improvement of sensual enjoyment becomes the means of achieving spiritual freedom in the body; the freedom of love makes the body its instrument without any outward limit set to its spontaneous joy. The order of mind which, for Bromion, has rationalized the order of the flesh and made it systematic is the enemy to be subdued, for it is the denial of the spirit and of charity. Theotormon's fear of his unvoiced desires makes him suppress them; he has neither the "insolent confidence" of a systematic thinker, nor the freedom from others' moral systems that Oothoon attains. The poem is a splendid attack upon the repressive nature of moral legalism, and on all those false orders that become a denial of spirit—that is, of the order of charity.

II. States and Characters

> The characters of Chaucer's Pilgrims are the characters which compose all ages and nations: as one age falls, another rises, different to mortal sight, but to immortals only the same; for we see the same characters repeated again and again, in animals, vegetables, minerals, and in men; nothing new occurs in identical existence; Accident ever varies, Substance can never suffer change nor decay (527).

> Thus the reader will observe, that Chaucer makes everyone of his characters perfect in his kind; every one is an Antique Statue; the image of a class, and not of an imperfect individual (570–71).

Blake is saying, in effect, that Chaucer's characters are properly "States." In his *Vision of the Last Judgment* (1810), "States" become the Eternal Forms, "the Permanent Realities of Every Thing which we see reflected in this Vegetable Glass of Nature." When he mentions Abel and Abraham, Blake adds, "these States exist now. Man passes on, but States remain for ever." Individuals, then, are "representatives or visions of those States as they were revealed to mortal man in the series of divine revelations as they are written in the Bible." (But in the account of Chaucer's pilgrims, Blake drew these archetypes from classical myth as well: "Chaucer has divided the ancient character of Hercules between his Miller and his Plowman. . . . The Plowman of Chaucer is Hercules in his supreme eternal state, divested of his spectrous shadow." So the Franklin becomes Bacchus; the Doctor of Physic, Esculapius; the Host, Silenus; the Squire, Apollo; and so on. "Chaucer's characters are a description of the eternal Principles that exist in all ages.")

Blake's terms are loose: characters become embodiments of eternal forms or archetypes, which are the States into which man can move in any age. These States, as Swedenborg had claimed, are also modes of vision; each State confers a peculiar way of imagining. Men will, according to their State, project their attitudes into images of reality, populating a hell or heaven in accordance with their own affections. Space and time, for Swedenborg, are projections of the States of men's souls: "A spiritual idea doth not derive any thing from Space, but it derives every thing appertaining to it from State." Blake annotates this sentence with "Poetic idea." Blake has no interest in character as we use the term or as Pope uses it (in a largely Aristotelian sense of organized moral habits). He is interested in States, and his nominal characters are in a constant movement through States, or are locked in those heroic conflicts that are really dialectical oppositions of States.

The States, in Blake's view, are created by divine mercy so that man will not be fixed in error or in a single character. The identity of each man is unique and permanent; the States are eternal conditions through which individual men travel in the course of their existence. States "when distant . . . appear as One Man, but as you approach they appear Multitudes of Nations," Blake wrote in the account of his painting of the Last Judgment. "I have seen, when at a distance, Multitudes of Men in Harmony appear like a single Infant, sometimes in the Arms of a Female; this represented the Church" (607). Only States, therefore, are condemned; and they can be thrown off and put behind one. Such damnable States are those of Caiaphas and Pilate, "where all those reside who Calumniate & Murder under Pretence of Holiness & Justice" (608).

This emphasis on States gives Blake's poetry an increasingly dense pattern, wherein action is transformed into dialectical opposition, and each term of the opposition expands into a system or an order. This is an elaboration of what is already present in Milton's *Paradise Lost,* whose literal action is simple, but whose characters and setting acquire more and more resonance of suggestion and implication as the poem goes on. By the close we have a pageant of human history in which the great figures of the poem are given new embodiments— Satan in Nimrod, Abdiel in Noah—and the great events are re-enacted again and again, as indeed they must be in all life as Milton conceives it. Blake's conception of States and contraries grows steadily more complex in the course of his career, and it demands increasingly dense mythical statement. In the early works the myths are relatively simple, and in *The Marriage of Heaven and Hell* Blake deals directly with the way in which the mind creates those rival orders that constitute contrary versions of reality.

The Marriage of Heaven and Hell (1793) belongs, as Northrop Frye has said, "in the tradition of great satires" (*Fearful Symmetry,* Princeton, 1947, p. 200). The Argument presents the moment of rebellion that is the occasion of the work. The "just man" has ventured into danger and created order, bringing fertile life out of desert and wild. But the very creation of order provides the occasion for a fall or usurpation. The order invites the "villain" to leave his own "paths of ease" and assume the guise of "mild humility" as he drives the just man out of his new realm. Are the just man and the villain two men or two aspects of man? It hardly matters. Once the villain has usurped the realm of order, the only role that remains for the just man is the prophetic rage of the dispossessed or repressed. The villain has assumed, like Fielding's Blifil, all the outward forms of virtue; he has, in fact, created the Seven Deadly Virtues. This is the dramatic occasion of the *Marriage*. The time has come for Hell to have its turn. Even Swedenborg's new heaven, which was to succeed the era of sects and churches, has dwindled to a New Church. The dull round of seeming reform that turns into new dogma must be broken by truly energetic rebellion, by open wrath rather than pious instruction.

The *Marriage*, therefore, is a work of dialectic, an attempt to awaken the respectable to the fact that, by claiming to be Angels, they are destroying life rather than furthering it. The spokesman of Energy, like Shaw's Devil's Disciple, accepts the title the "religious" give him, if only to make the religious see how much they have denied. In seizing upon an order and fixing it, they have devitalized the idea of order and made it the enemy of the ongoing process that is more essential than any of the forms in which it takes momentary rest. The true order lies in the constant reciprocal action of reason and energy, which must remain "contraries" in dialectical opposition. "Without Contraries is no Progression." The parallel of Pope's *Essay* deserves mention. Neither poem, Pope's or Blake's *Marriage*, sets out to present a full case, from the ground up, for its conclusions. Each assumes as a starting point the fashionable half-thinking it must overturn. Each takes for granted that there is need for order (including moral order) and that no existing order can be taken as the ultimate one. The Devil tries to put the idea of order on a new basis—to see it in constant process, as the outward face of energy rather than its container.

The initial teaching of the Devil is that mind and body are one, that the body "is a portion of Soul discern'd by the five Senses, the chief inlets of Soul in this age." The body is energy perceived as mass. The Devil, who represents one dialectical view, sees energy as "the only life" and "from the body": "Reason is the bound or outward circumference of Energy."

This is energy seen from within; and it takes the form of thrust or expansion, which relaxes at its periphery into a limit, as the leaf may be said to find its form when it comes into fullness of being. The laws of Reason, at their best, are codifications of what has been created by another power. As Pope puts it in the *Essay on Criticism:*

> Nature, like liberty, is but restrain'd
> By the same laws which first herself ordain'd (90–91).

Reason methodizes energy, but it must not impose a preconceived form upon it. Blake's Devil, then, is insisting upon the priority of Energy, not the denial of Reason. "Energy," as he concludes, "is Eternal Delight," rather than sin.

Blake's doctrine of energy survives the shifts of emphasis that may divide his work into stages or periods. The emphasis on the concrete and bodily form of its manifestations—upon the Eternal Human Body—may at one point become an attack upon an abstract idealism. But it may as readily become an attack upon a naturalism that discounts the Eternal for what it regards as the Human. Man, as Blake sees him, is properly Human only in so far as he remains faithful to the Eternal in himself (that is, to the energy of imagination that transcends each limited "natural" form), and man perverts the Eternal so long as he denies the Human (seeking to create a fixed order that is inhumanly regular or rigid). The Body, concrete and physical, is itself a metaphor; its vital form rather than its physicality is what Blake defends. When Blake calls for the improvement of sensual enjoyment, it is as a means of freeing the individual from the merely vegetative or natural. The intensity of consummation becomes an annihilation of Selfhood and an entry into the realm that transcends the temporal, the Eternal.

We can see a pattern much like this in John Donne. His lovers ascend by the self-abandonment of passion to a realm in which they laugh to scorn the temporal world they have left behind. In "A Lecture upon the Shadow" the lovers must cast shadows to elude the vigilance of others. So they do through the morning, until they reach the moment of noon. There time has a stop:

> But now the sun is just above our head
>   We do those shadows tread;
>   And to brave clearness all things are reduc'd,
> So whilst our infant loves did grow,

Disguises did, and shadows, flow,
From us, and ours cares; but, now 'tis not so.
That love hath not attain'd the highest degree,
Which is still diligent lest others see.

The lovers at noon replace the natural sun with the eternal
sun; they rise out of time, indifferent to its passage, indifferent
to the claims or even the existence of others, raised by love to
a splendid simplicity that has the appearance of arrogance
and boldness ("brave clearness"), but is really the transcendence of all that is not themselves. Donne's *Songs and Sonnets*
repeat this theme often: the natural man transcending nature
through the abandonment of self, treading upon all the social
or moral laws that seem to define self in the world. Donne,
like Blake, is eminently aware of a possible fall:

Except our loves at this noon stay.
We shall new shadows make the other way.

And he describes the loss of intensity, the return of self, and
the growth of mutual distrust as the lovers become locked in
disguises to shield themselves from each other. This full meaning of noon as transcendence is the heart of Donne's poem:

Love is a growing, or full constant light;
And his first minute, after noon, is night.

We can see a similar conception of a fall in Romantic poetry: the descent into passivity or a natural, law-bound world.
It may be felt in the loss of joy, in the failure of the child's
trust that it creates its own world and rules it, in the surrender
of "first and passionate love" to the deceptions and sterility
of loveless marriage. It hardly matters whether one regards
the moment of visionary splendor as intoxication (as Byron
does) to be followed by the punishing hangover; or whether
one sees it (as Donne perhaps does) as a lesser mystery analogous to the greater ones of religion. What does matter is the
way in which the idea of energy as the power of transcendence
cuts through any dualism of mind and body and serves as a
standard. By it can be judged the mere "ecstasy" of spirit that
leaves the body too far behind or the mere sensuality of "dull
sublunary lovers" content with "country pleasures, childishly."
Byron, for example, mocks the self-defeating Platonism of
Donna Julia in *Don Juan;* it is a futile attempt to find a compromise between the surrender of love and the severity of law.
But he also mocks the court that Juan and Haidée create on
Lambro's island, a kind of ritualized Cythera. Their court is

the freezing into forms of the energetic pursuit of freedom and fulfillment that their coming together first meant, or that old Lambro, Haidée's father, once stood for before he too fell, from rebellious patriot to acquisitive pirate. Blake's "villain" in the Argument of the *Marriage* might be compared to the entrepreneurial pirate replacing, within the same man, the frustrated patriot.

The false order of the *Marriage* is a usurpation. "Those who restrain desire, do so because theirs is weak enough to be restrained; and the restrainer or reason usurps its place & governs the unwilling" (149). What is created is an order that exists for the sake of ordering alone, means displacing the end. One of Blake's modern disciples, Shaw, gives us (in *Man and Superman*) such a purposeless ordering in his version of Hell—a place of eternal enjoyment of respectability, of complex organization without direction or end, a heaven of Selfhood. Shaw's true Heaven is a place of creativity and invention, without ritual and without the need for moral judgment. It is a place where the worldly could only be bored, for its life is, like that of Blake's Eden, the active exercise of spirit and imagination, and its activity imposes effort man cannot sustain too long. Shaw's men can move between Heaven or Hell at will, as Blake's men descend for repose from Eden to the softness of Beulah. Blake's Beulah is a married state, and its comforts can produce the fatal temptation of passivity. So in Shaw the Mother Woman, like Blake's Female Will, lies in wait to claim the Superman and entrap him in the domestic life of paternity; she wants him to father her children, but he needs the freedom to father ideas.

Blake's Devil offers, in place of the usurpation of reason and restraint, the sublime exertions of genius. Imagination looks through the natural object, as Wordsworth looks through the natural scene, to behold the Presences that lie behind it (or deep within it). The bird, seen with the imagination, becomes "an immense world of delight" which, for the natural man, has been "clos'd by . . . senses five." The Proverbs of Hell become the destruction of surfaces, the bursting of those categories that impose sameness on things beheld as mere objects. "A fool sees not the same tree that a wise man sees" (151). They celebrate what an energetic vision discerns:

> The pride of the peacock is the glory of God.
> The lust of the goat is the bounty of God.
> The wrath of the lion is the wisdom of God.
> The nakedness of woman is the work of God.

They decry the repressive restraint that neither satisfies nor overcomes desire: "He who desires but acts not, breeds pestilence." "Sooner murder an infant in its cradle than nurse unacted desires." They celebrate, in defiance of moral convention, the splendor of energy in all its forms: "The tygers of wrath are wiser than the horses of instruction." "The cistern contains: the fountain overflows." "Exuberance is beauty." The vital is constantly opposed to the measurable, the sublime to the regular; in each case the energetic process and vision are exalted over the outward forms in which they are expressed. But "Eternity is in love with the productions of time," and it is the disclosure of the divine energy immanent within the temporal world that gives the Proverbs their direction— they are counsels of transcendence, of movement through the surface to the living energy, of acceptance of that energy as a force to be driven forward in turn through each bound and outward circumference so that it may create another.

The dialectic of energy and reason is applied, in turn, to the institutions of religion. Like Wordsworth later in *The Excursion,* Blake celebrates the imaginative force which "animated all sensible objects with Gods or Geniuses" in the inventions of poetic myth. But from the myth come the abstractions of dogma. So, in Pope's *Essay on Man,* Tyranny and Superstition together undo the humanized world of the imaginative man

Who own'd a Father when he own'd a God (III, 234).

Superstition teaches

. . . the weak to bend, the proud to pray,
To Pow'r unseen, and mightier far than they
(III, 251–52).

She creates a Hell in the earth, a Heaven in the skies:

Here fix'd the dreadful, there the blest abodes;
Fear made her Devils, and weak hope her Gods;
Gods partial, changeful, passionate, unjust,
Whose attributes were rage, revenge, or lust;
Such as the souls of cowards might conceive,
And, form'd like tyrants, tyrants would believe
(III, 255–60).

In Blake's *Marriage,* the criticism is more radical. Priesthood has "enslav'd the vulgar by attempting to realize or abstract the mental deities from their objects." When the priests "pronounc'd that the Gods had order'd" the forms of worship that are now instituted, "men forgot that all deities reside in the human breast" (153).

In contrast to the fixed forms of orthodoxy is the energy of Poetic Genius embodied in the prophets Isaiah and Ezekiel, who find God in their own capacity to discover "the infinite in every thing" and in their "honest indignation." They, too, have seen the liberating power of a "firm perswasion" turned by others into a system of belief, and they behave with all the outrageousness of Diogenes the Cynic out of "the desire of raising other men into a perception of the infinite" (154). This destruction of conventions and needless restraints is the return of Esau to dominion, of Adam to Paradise. It is not simply the elevation to sublimity that the young Thomas Warton feels as worlds die about him; it is destruction that will release a new order. Its means are the affronts to "good sense" by Prophet or Cynic, the corrosive engraving of Blake's satirical plates, and the "improvement of sensual enjoyment." As the destruction is achieved, "the whole creation will be consumed and appear infinite and holy, where as it now appears finite & corrupt." Such an apocalypse is created by cleansing the "doors of perception":

> For man has closed himself up, till he sees all things thro' narrow chinks of his cavern (154).

Finally, Blake begins the brilliant dramatization that marks all his works of the conflict of modes of vision. Angel and Devil cannot see the same reality. Each sees, rather, what his system of belief prepares him to see. The Angel's vision of Hell is a terrifying immensity, but the Devil (it is, in fact, the poet speaking in his own person) accepts it without fear: "if you please, we will commit ourselves to this void, and see whether providence is here also: if you will not, I will" (155). The climax of this vision is the terrible appearance of a monstrous serpent, the Biblical Leviathan:

> his forehead was divided into streaks of green & purple like those on a tyger's forehead: soon we saw his mouth & red gills hang just above the raging foam, tinging the black deep with beams of blood, advancing towards us with all the fury of a spiritual existence.

The Angel flees; the poet is left alone:

> & then the appearance was no more, but I found myself sitting on a pleasant bank beside a river by moonlight,

hearing a harper, who sung to the harp; and this theme was: "The man who never alters his opinion is like standing water, & breeds reptiles of the mind" (156).

"All," the poet tells the Angel, "was owing to your metaphysics." And he offers in turn a vision of the Angel's lot: beneath the Bible on the altar lies a deep pit, where they find tethered monkeys and baboons preying on each other, like Hobbes's man a wolf to man (*homo lupus homini*). They have the nastiness of the wolf without its energy:

> the weak were caught by the strong, and with a grinning aspect, first coupled with, & then devour'd, by plucking off first one limb and then another, till the body was left a helpless trunk; this, after grinning and kissing it with seeming fondness, they devour'd too; and here & there I saw one savourily picking the flesh off his own tail (157).

Angel and poet return to the mill (to which the Angel fled from the sight of Leviathan) with a skeleton which is revealed as Aristotle's Analytics. The Angel is outraged: "Thy phantasy has imposed upon me." The poet's reply is the key to much of Blake:

> I answer'd: "We impose on one another, & it is but lost time to converse with you whose works are only Analytics" (157).

Far from wishing to reconcile contraries, Blake uses the term "marriage" to define their fruitful opposition. "Jesus Christ did not wish to unite, but to separate" contraries, and Blake's image of Christ is that of the lawbreaker (or the "freethinker" that Deists like Anthony Collins saw in Him, to Swift's scorn). Since, in the Devil's view, no virtue can exist without breaking the Ten Commandments, Jesus, who was "all virtue," acted "from impulse, not from rules." In *The Everlasting Gospel* (1818), Blake makes the problem sharper:

> The Vision of Christ that thou dost see
> Is my Vision's Greatest Enemy . . .
> Thine loves the same world that mine hates,
> Thy Heaven doors are my Hell Gates (p. 748, 1–2, 7–8).

God's admonition to Christ in that poem is much like the Voice of the Devil in the *Marriage:*

> "If thou humblest thyself, thou humblest me;
> Thou also dwell'st in Eternity.
> Thou art a Man, God is no more,

Thy own humanity learn to adore,
For that is my Spirit of Life" (pp. 752–53, 73–77).

So the Devil declares in the *Marriage:* "The worship of God is: Honouring his gifts in other men, each according to his genius, and loving the greatest men best: those who envy or calumniate great men hate God; for there is no other God" (158). And at last the Angel is persuaded. He embraces the flames of seeming hell-fire which are actually divine energy, and "he was consumed and arose as Elijah." The primly self-righteous becomes the wrathful prophet as he assumes true virtue.

Blake has created an interesting conflation of ideas and images of order. He shares the anti-clericalism of the Deists, although he repudiates their rationalism and natural religion. One can see Blake's position more clearly by comparing it with the positions of Shaftesbury and Mandeville, whose secularism fed into much of later Deism. Like Shaftesbury, Blake insists upon the primacy of Eternal Forms and of the faculty within man that conceives or imagines them. In his remarks on the third of Sir Joshua Reynolds' *Discourses on Art,* he insists, as Shaftesbury does, upon innate or connatural ideas:

> Knowledge of Ideal Beauty is Not to be Acquired. It is Born with us. Innate Ideas are in Every Man, Born with him; they are truly Himself. The Man who says that we have No Innate Ideas must be a Fool & Knave, Having No Conscience or Innate Science (459).

Blake's rejection of Reynolds' empiricism is very much in the spirit of Shaftesbury's repudiation of Locke, and his belief in innate ideas grows out of an intransigent belief in the disjunction of the orders of existence. Twenty years earlier, when Blake read in Swedenborg of the "three degrees of Altitude . . . named Natural, Spiritual, and Celestial," he was outraged by the apparent suggestion that man grew from lower to higher degrees and moved "by Continuity according to the Sciences . . . to the Summit of Understanding which is called Rational." Blake's exasperated comment is extremely important:

> Study Sciences till you are blind, Study intellectuals till you are cold, Yet science cannot teach intellect. Much less can intellect teach Affection. How foolish then is it to assert that Man is born in only one degree, when that one degree is reception of the 3 degrees, two of which he must destroy or close up or they will descend; if he

closes up the two superior, then he is not truly in the
3rd, but descends out of it into meer Nature or Hell. . . .
Is it not also evident that one degree will not open the
other, & that science will not open intellect, but that they
are discrete & not continuous so as to explain each other
except by correspondence, which has nothing to do with
demonstration; for you cannot demonstrate one degree
by the other; for how can science be brought to demonstrate intellect without making them continuous & not discrete? (93.)

There is no metaphysical point so persistent throughout
Blake's works as the discreteness and discontinuity of orders.
The higher powers—whether called Intellect, Imagination, or
Poetic Genius—cannot be explained by the lower; there is no
natural history of genius:

> From a perception of only 3 senses or 3 elements none
> could deduce a fourth or fifth.
> None could have other than natural or organic
> thoughts if he had none but organic perceptions (*There
> Is No Natural Religion,* First Series, 1788, III and IV).
> Man's perceptions are not bounded by organs of per-
> ception; he perceives more than sense (tho' ever so acute)
> can discover (Second Series, I).
> Reynolds thinks that Man Learns all that he knows.
> I say on the Contrary that Man Brings All that he has
> or can have Into the World with him. Man is Born like
> a Garden ready Planted & Sown. This World is too poor
> to produce one Seed (471).

When Reynolds intends the term "nature" to include the internal fabric of the human mind and imagination, Blake exposes
the ultimate result of a belief in continuity:

> Here is a Plain Confession that he Thinks Mind & Imag-
> ination not to be above the Mortal & Perishing Nature.
> Such is the End of Epicurean or Newtonian philosophy;
> it is Atheism (475).

The Epicureans, Blake feels, deride all opinions not "derived
from earth": their account of natural origins becomes a reduction of all higher orders to an order of flesh—or, in Blake's
terms, vegetative nature.

All of this has much in common with Shaftesbury—in its
contrast of external Selfhood and the visionary power that
comes of attending to what Shaftesbury calls "inward numbers." But the word "numbers" points up the emphasis
Shaftesbury places upon order; for all his praise of the au-

thenticity of the wild as opposed to the "mockery of princely gardens," for all his defense of the dignity of human nature and the godlike in man, his vision of order is one of moral law. Blake, significantly, rejects Platonic philosophy because it "blinds the eye of imagination, the Real Man." The Platonists "considered God as abstracted or distinct from the Imaginative World, but Jesus, as also Abraham & David, considered God as a Man in the Spiritual or Imaginative Vision." Jesus addressed himself "to the Man, not to his Reason" (774–75).

Both Shaftesbury and Blake are concerned with the discovery—or recovery—of the true self as opposed to the passive sensuous gratifications of mere Selfhood, and both stress the forming or ordering power as the divine in man. But the ordering power in Blake is conceived on the analogy of the artist's imagination: it creates original and distinctive works, with the sharp particularity that comes of a reverence for each form of authentic life ("Every thing that lives is holy"). Shaftesbury's ideal work of art—for all the interesting stress on the "characteristic"—is much closer to the grandeur of general forms. And for Shaftesbury a work of art is conceived in moral terms, as a form of implicit moral instruction through its significant ordering of experience.

The lines are difficult to draw; yet the difference is clear. Shaftesbury is open to many tendencies that appear in Blake —notably the celebration of the dignity of the human image as opposed to subordination of the human to a remote and inhuman God. But Shaftesbury wishes to stress the inherent divinity of the human, whereas Blake stresses the divine as it bursts out of the human and through the natural. This is clearest in the difference between Shaftesbury's ascent to rational enthusiasm and Blake's dramatic sense of the transcendent moment of redemption.

The case of Mandeville and Blake is somewhat clearer. Blake would have had nothing but scorn for most of the values Mandeville assumes, but, as I have suggested (see p. 123), Mandeville's celebration of the energy of the lion is the kind of denial of a rigid moral scheme that Blake shares. Mandeville's spokesman confronts the defender of traditional order with "The lion was not meant to be always in Paradise," and the remark opens up the whole question of where divinity resides, just as does Blake's dialogue of Angel and Devil. Mandeville's implication that pure virtue is impossible to attain in the world anticipates Blake's repudiation of the moral law, and in fact the Calvinism that Mandeville turns to secular ends insists upon the distinction between grace and morality.

In Blake's own day, the brilliant attack by Robert Sandeman[2] on a religion of natural morality resembles Mandeville in its rejection of a princelike image of Christ—"Something very grand, far outshining the character of the perfect prince drawn by the author of *Telemachus*." Instead, Sandeman insists upon the affront of a Jesus who was "of low condition, meanly born, of no education, choosing his friends and companions from among the basest of the people, and having no taste for the company of men of character and distinction" (84). This Jesus has much in common with Diogenes, or indeed with his Blakean counterpart, Quid the Cynic, in the *Island in the Moon*.

Sandeman, like Blake, insists on the rejection of mere morality:

> The whole New Testament speaks aloud, that, as to the matter of *acceptance* with God, there is no difference betwixt one man and another:—no difference betwixt the best accomplished gentleman, and the most infamous scroundrel:—no difference betwixt the most virtuous lady and the vilest prostitute:—no difference betwixt the most revered judge, and the most odious criminal . . . in a word, no difference betwixt the most reverent devotee, and the greatest ringleader in profaneness and excess (I, 87–91).

Accordingly, Sandeman sees the crucifixion as a work of resentment by "every human excellency. For what is it that man glories in, that did not find itself piqued and affronted by the doctrine, joined with the extraordinary circumstances of the life of Jesus?" (I, 94). Sandeman, as one might expect, scorns Shaftesbury (Socrates' "eminent modern disciple in our own country"), and has an admiration for much in Mandeville ("this author clearly demonstrates what holiness *is not,* but could not show what *it is,* as being ignorant of the true principle or spring from whence it flows").

The final conversion of Angel to Devil is symptomatic of the difficulties of Blake's dialectic in the *Marriage*. Blake is so intent upon overcoming traditional forms of dualism that he has difficulty in preserving genuine contraries. Body is nothing but soul, and the eternal delight of the soul is most easily seen in the body's energy, most readily attained through intensifying sensual enjoyment until the body is all activity (all love, all soul, in the phrases of Dryden's heroes). So, too, so-called good is the outward aspect of so-called evil; it is the resting place, the temporary self-ordering, of energy, like the churches that religion creates or the works that a man's genius produces in the course of unceasing movement.

It is difficult for Blake to make order seem more than negative. He writes of the opposition of contraries: "Attraction and Repulsion, Reason and Energy, Love and Hate, are necessary to Human existence." Yet as soon as the idea of rational order appears, it is reduced to "the cunning of weak and tame minds which have the power to resist energy." As pruning fosters the living plant, so order devours "as a sea" the excesses of the Prolific; but it is hardly a contrary with its own purpose. Only occasionally is any positive meaning suggested, as when the Messiah "prays to the Father to send the comforter, or Desire, that Reason may have ideas to build on." The obvious contrary to the prolific force of Energy is the constructive power of Order, just as the contrary to the confident vision of Innocence is the rebellious defense of it in Experience. Clearly there may be two forms of Order as there are of Experience: that which "builds on" Energy as well as that which tries to imprison or repress it. Blake's vitalism in the *Marriage* is so intense—so vehemently opposed to orthodox dualism—that he can hardly grant Order its due. When, in his later work, Blake finds his hero in Los, the imaginative spirit seen as prophet-poet-sculptor, he can deal more adequately with the idea of order:

> And every Generated Body in its inward form
> Is a garden of delight & a building of magnificence
> Built by the Sons of Los (*Milton* 26:31–33).

III. The Standard of Energy

In *The Book of Urizen* (1794) we find the beginnings of the myth that was to occupy Blake in his later poetry. This is the account of a fall. Like Milton, Blake sees all human existence as shot through with moments of fall and moments of redemption, and one fall provides an archetype for all others. This is the story of the emergence of "the primeval Priest's assum'd power," and Urizen (whose name seems to derive, as does our word "horizon," from the Greek form of "to limit") is the archetypal State of false Priesthood. We first see Urizen separating off from the rest of existence, creating a void, a "soul-shudd'ring vacuum" that keeps out the spirit and secedes, as it were, from Eternity: it is pictured as a landscape of turbulence—vast forests, mountains of ice, thunderous voices—which embodies the "tormenting passions" of a "self-contemplating shadow."

Urizen explains his divorce from life as the desire for fixity:

> I have sought for a joy without pain,
> For a solid without fluctuation.
> Why will you die, O Eternals?
> Why live in unquenchable burnings? (II, 4:10–13.)

Urizen cannot tolerate the openness of eternal movement, that is, the vital energy of imagination. He fights its irregular and unpredictable freedom until he produces a "wide world of solid obstruction." He has wrested from the moral conflict with the "Seven deadly Sins of the soul" (his way of conceiving the freedom of energy) a book of "eternal brass," and he has reduced all seeming disorder to law and to simple regularity:

> One command, one joy, one desire,
> One curse, one weight, one measure,
> One King, one God, one Law (II, 4:38–40).

The effrontery of Urizen's speech is much like that of the Dunces or of Dulness' addresses. Urizen is less a character than a State revealing itself in its fullness.

The Eternals seem, at least to Urizen, to rage furiously about him after this speech, separating themselves from him, although he has, of course, broken away from them. And now, in fear, he seeks a hiding-place, piling up mountains until he builds a "roof vast, petrific around / On all sides . . . like a womb" (III, 5:28–29). The Eternals send Los to watch over Urizen, and we encounter one of those poetic condensations that run through all of Blake's later poetry. Blake breaks down conventional narrative continuities by embodying relationships in constantly shifting images. As characters enter into new States, or as States enter into new relationships, the characters' natures alter, and they undergo the transformations that we recognize in the "condensation" of dream-processes. Here Los is sent to watch over Urizen, but Urizen is described as being rent from Los's side. If we take Los as the redeeming power of imagination, we can see Blake's desire to dramatize once more the separation of Urizen from all those other powers in man with which he should be in harmony. Urizen, wrenched apart from Los, is even more clearly a figure of pure rationality, a version of lifeless order. Tellingly, Urizen cannot generate a meaningful order even at the level he has reached. His "one law" needs some form of embodiment, and creates the senses through which he can receive awareness; for example, his eyes—"two little orbs . . . fixed in two little caves." As he takes on bodily form, Urizen's "eternal life" is "obliterated," and Los himself is dazed and paralyzed by this act. What horrifies Los is not the turbulence of life but the vacuity of "Space, undivided by existence" that now surrounds them.

When Los feels pity for Urizen's world, Pity itself grows into Enitharmon, the "first female now separate." As Urizen has fallen into a life bounded by the senses, so Los, out of more generous motives, falls into a State where he may be overcome by passivity. Enitharmon becomes a separate dominating will. The Eternals cover over the world with a great curtain they call Science; this may in turn be taken as Los's remoter view of eternal life now that he accepts a separate female partner. Los's marriage (which is, of course, like Adam's need for the Eve who will later seduce him) is an archetype of man's acceptance of a natural world about him as real as his own mind; a resignation of imaginative power. Enitharmon's first action is "perverse and cruel" coyness as she flees from his embrace. When she bears a male child, who issues howling with fierce flames, the Eternals close the tenting curtain: "No more Los beheld Eternity" (VI, 20:2). The descent has gone further: the prophet-poet is now committed to the world of his fallen self. He is absorbed into that world as a jealous father, and he becomes like Urizen.

Two actions follow, each the counterpart of the other. Los and Enitharmon chain to a rock their son, Orc, who embodies the rebellious principle of renewed and independent life. Los keeps Enitharmon protected and enclosed while she bears "an enormous race." At the same time Urizen awakes from sleep, "Stung with the odours of Nature," and explores his world. To his horror he finds his order is unworkable:

> he curs'd
> Both sons & daughters; too he saw
> That no flesh nor spirit could keep
> His iron laws one moment
> For he saw that life liv'd upon death (VIII, 23:23–26).

Urizen wanders, pitying his creations; and his tears become a web, the Net of Religion. At this point we have Blake's savage parody of the creation of man in Genesis, as Urizen's creatures contract into earthbound humans:

> 3. Six days they shrunk up from existence,
> And on the seventh day they rested,
> And they bless'd the seventh day, in sick hope,
> And forgot their eternal life.
>
> 4. And their thirty cities divided
> In form of a human heart.
> No more could they rise at will
> In the infinite void, but bound down
> To earth by their narrowing perceptions
> They lived a period of years;
> Then left a noisom body
> To the jaws of devouring darkness.
>
> 5. And their children wept, & built
> Tombs in the desolate places,
> And form'd laws of prudence, and call'd them
> The eternal laws of God (IX, 27:39–28:7).

At the close, Urizen's oldest son—a counterpart of the bound Orc—calls together the children of Urizen and leads them from "the pendulous earth": "They called it Egypt, & left it." We are at the point of an exodus of the spirit from the domination of the merely natural. The consolidation of error has brought the spirit to the point of rebellion.

The irony of Blake's poem is strongest when he describes the fall in the language of the Biblical creation. But this parody is simply the most transparent instance of the inverted order that the poem discloses. Blake's great satiric theme is the displacement of a true order by a grotesque mock order:

> Such is that false
> And Generating Love, a pretence of love to destroy love
> (*Jerusalem* I, 17:25–36).
>
> A pretence of Art to destroy Art; a pretence of Liberty
> To destroy Liberty; a pretence of Religion to destroy
> Religion (*Jerusalem* II, 43:35–36).

This verbal pattern is Blake's most compressed statement of the inversion that insensibly creeps over man and his world, offering itself in the guise of what it seeks to usurp. Only the prophetic awareness of Los discerns what is taking place; others may sustain this awareness for a time and feel the wearying eclipse—as Dulness' sons lapse into sleep—but soon

all is night. Like Pope, Blake presents the grandeur and terror
of the usurpation:

> Loud Satan thunder'd . . .
> Coming in a Cloud with Trumpets & with Fiery Flame,
> An awful Form eastward from midst a bright Paved-work
> Of precious stones by Cherubim surrounded, so permitted
> (Lest he should fall apart in his Eternal Death) to imitate
> The Eternal Great Humanity Divine surrounded by
> His Cherubim & Seraphim in ever happy Eternity
>   (*Milton* II, 39:22–28).

In the same way, Blake's Urizen absorbs much of the traditional image of God the Father, making clearer the kind of
God man must worship once he has resigned the energies that
demand free movement and has contracted into the security of
a closed system.

Blake's interweaving of mental states and outward structures, of political programs and philosophic doctrines, gives
any moment in the later poems a formidable complexity.
Characters voice the world view that underlies the moral and
social errors they embody. Their frankness, like the shame-
lessness of Pope's dunces, shows how completely they are enclosed in their limited order; they are complacently untroubled
by the claims of a rival order, or at most blusteringly defiant.
When the Saviour appeals to Albion, the primal man who is
now fallen mankind, he offers the vision of charity: "Lo! we
are one, forgiving all Evil." But Albion's denial opens out into
an opposed vision of reality:

> But the perturbed Man away turns down the valleys dark:
> Saying we are not One, we are Many, thou most simula-
>   tive
> Phantom of the over heated brain! shadow of im-
>   mortality!
> Seeking to keep my soul a victim to thy Love! which
>   binds
> Man, the enemy of man, into deceitful friendship . . .
> By demonstration man alone can live, and not by faith.
> My mountains are my own, and I will keep them to my-
>   self:
> The Malvern and the Cheviot, the Wold, Plinlimmon &
>   Snowden
> Are mine: here will I build my Laws of Moral Virtue.
> Humanity shall be no more, but war & princedom &
>   victory! (*Jerusalem* I, 1:22–32.)

The fullness with which Albion reveals his error moves the

passage toward ironic satire. Like the great speeches by Aristarchus or Silenus in the fourth book of *The Dunciad* it exposes itself in every assertion. The denial of Jesus becomes rabid empiricism ("most simulative Phantom"), Hobbesian politics ("Man, the enemy of man"), dogmatic rationalism ("By demonstration . . . alone"), and acquisitive materialism ("My mountains are my own"). Pascal's disjunction of orders was never more complete than this.

It is in such passages that we can best see Blake's resemblance to the Augustans. Like them he is acutely aware of how deeply all attitudes are rooted in systems of belief. A madman inhabits a mad world, where values are turned inside out, and each sane pattern of order has its reverse image. This takes us back to the problem of orders, to the view that each discrete order of experience tends to become self-subsistent in a world of its own making. The most insistent irony in Blake is the irony of the "mind-forg'd manacles," the enclosure and stultification of man's vision and the loss of the power even to discern the change.

Blake's constant effort is to give unmistakable form to error and thus rob it of vague and mysterious authority. To do this, he must become a master of satiric symbols and ironic confrontations. "Every honest man is a Prophet; he utters his opinion both of private & public matters. Thus: If you go on So, the result is So. He never says, such a thing shall happen let you do what you will. A Prophet is a Seer, not an Arbitrary Dictator. It is man's fault if God is not able to do him good, for he gives to the just & to the unjust, but the unjust reject his gift" (392). This is precisely the satirist's task: to appeal to men's responsibility by projecting the consequences of their action into the actions themselves, as Swift dramatizes our failure of charity in the cannibalism of *A Modest Proposal*. Such satiric prophecy is uncomfortable; it is designed to disturb. "What do these Knaves mean by Virtue? Do they mean War & its horrors & its Heroic Villains?" (400.)

It is important to make certain distinctions. Blake hates the "Accusers of Sin," the moralists who make impossible demands, rob the self of spontaneity and confidence, then punish its inevitable transgressions with a righteous show of pity. Everything that lives is holy; each man lives in the imagination. Each individual is unique, a law to itself so long as it remains truly alive and does not harden into the negation of life, the hindering of energy in itself and others. Judgments of good and evil deny this uniqueness and demand characterless

passivity. For Blake, therefore, the prophet does not defend
a moral code; he keeps the divine vision, and he seeks to restore life where men have chosen death. As a satirist he attacks not individuals but States. "Man Passes on, but States
remain for Ever; he passes thro' them like a traveller who
may as well suppose that the places he has pass'd thro' Exist
no more. Every thing is Eternal" (606). States must be identified, so that man may recognize them and pass beyond those
that are conditions of death. Man must be made to see:

> . . . What seems to Be, Is, To those to whom
> It seems to Be, & is productive of the most dreadful
> Consequences to those to whom it seems to Be, even of
> Torments, Despair, Eternal Death
> (*Jerusalem* II, 36:51–54).

The satirist exposes the nature and thereby dissolves the
solidity of those structures men build as resting places from
thought. The most splendid structures may be the denial of
life, either through externalization or through simple inversion
of values.

> The Walls of Babylon are Souls of Men, her Gates the
>   Groans
> Of Nations, her Towers are the Miseries of once happy
>   Families,
> Her Streets are paved with Destruction, her Houses built
>   with Death,
> Her Palaces with Hell & the Grave, her Synagogues with
>   Torments
> Of ever-hardening Despair, squar'd & polish'd with cruel
>   skill (*Jerusalem* I, 24:31–35).

Blake insists upon the world man inhabits as a world of his
making. Every thing is an imaginative act, and every demon
is born of terror. Satan springs into monstrous proliferation,

> Producing many Heads, three or seven or ten, & hands
>   & feet
> Innumerable at will of the unfortunate contemplator
> Who becomes his food: such is the way of the Devouring
>   Power (*Jerusalem* II, 33:22–24).

In such a situation, the prophet must become a liberator who
destroys the Babylons men build around themselves and dis-
pels the Satan they feed with their doubt or despair. To the
extent that man accepts error through a failure of insight,
through dishonesty or willful rejection of what he knows to be

true, he may be treated with that therapeutic scorn we have seen in Pope. Blake's prophet-poet Los exclaims:

> "I care not whether a Man is Good or Evil; all that I care
> Is whether he is a Wise Man or a Fool. Go, put off Holiness
> And put on Intellect, or my thund'rous Hammer shall drive thee
> To wrath which thou condemnest, till thou obey my voice" (*Jerusalem* IV, 91:55–58).

The prophet like the satirist must reject the saving lie, and he must commit himself with "triumphant honest pride" to the vision that strips away illusion. The power to penetrate the wishful blindness and the plausible pretext is the prophetic gift that leads to the satiric image. The prophet in his vision shares the detachment of the God he interprets, sees earthly power in its imminent frailty: "Though they dig into hell, thence shall mine hand take them; though they climb up to heaven, thence will I bring them down." It is this detachment, both in range of vision and in elevation of spirit above the fears of worldly power, that Blake portrayed in his version of Gray's Bard: "King Edward and his Queen Elenor are prostrated, with their horses, at the foot of the rock on which the Bard stands; prostrated by the terrors of his harp on the margin of the river Conway. . . ." As Blake says (576–77), "Weaving the winding sheet of Edward's race by means of sounds of spiritual music and its accompanying expressions of articulate speech is a bold, and daring, and masterly conception. . . ." If the Bard's spiritual music is bitter denunciation, we can turn to Chaucer, who "was very devout, and paid respect to true enthusiastic superstition. He has laughed at his knaves and fools. . . . But he has respected his True Pilgrims . . ." (575). The spiritual music of the Bard, the laughter of Chaucer, the "triumphant honest pride" of Jesus (750)—these go to compose the satirist's scorn and outrage at the pretensions of the corrupt.

What primarily distinguishes Blake as satirist from the Augustans is the shift from moral judgment to a standard of energy. It is not the evil man so much as the soulless and dead man that Blake disdains. In fact, of course, any standard of vitality tends to transform itself into one of morality, as death-in-life becomes a state of bondage to false gods. But the prophetic stance fits well, in its sense of inspiration and commanding power, with the scorn for the materialized, the rigid, the timorous and self-protective. The exposed grandeur of Gray's Bard, as well as his sacrifice of himself to the cause of liberty, becomes a dramatization of titanic energies confronting legal tyrants. So long as these titanic forces remain tied to a system or dogma, they seem oppressive. When they shake off all commitment to the limited and regular, they become symbols of infinity. They overleap doctrines and stand for the spirit that gives life and demands life of others. The pride of such a force is essential to its nature; itself infinite and divine, it can only mock any limited conceptions of its will or any simulation of its energy. And out of such pride scorn must naturally follow: the infinite can only shatter with its breath those mechanical representations of life that men devoutly compose. The spiritual music is nothing less than the whirlwind, the destruction of worldly order in the name of energy that cannot be ordered unless it orders itself.

The myths of Blake's later poetry are designed to show life under the aspect of energy. They show the primal unity of man sundered into the warring elements of the Four Zoas. Reason has been divided from feeling, Urizen from Luvah; the instinctual unity of the body from its imaginative direction, Tharmas from Urthona. Each of the Zoas is at war with the others, except for momentary conspiracies, and the conflict drives each to the impoverished extreme of its nature.

Again, Blake creates the cyclic myth of the four realms of man, which are also four conditions of spirit. Eden is a place of mastery, of active engagement in intellectual warfare and hunting, or what Shaw calls the creation of new mind. The condition of Eden is a limit of life as we customarily know it; it fixes in myth those moments of heightened intensity, confident achievement, and harmonious self-realization that confer a sense of transcendence. The principle of active mastery is crucial, for the pleasant state of repose that Blake calls Beulah carries the threat of inducing passivity. To move from Eden to Beulah is to descend from the battlefield or hunt to the domestic ease of simple accord, from vital conflict of contraries to unresisting acceptance by a benign world, like the arms of the delighted bride or the cradle of the mother's embrace. Like every descent from difficulty to shelter, it can become a movement toward dependence.

The next phase of passivity is the most important, for in the descent from Beulah to Ulro, man forgets that his imagination creates his world and accepts as solid reality what he has unconsciously imposed upon himself. Once he submits to this reality, he sets out giving it form and making it a self-subsistent order. He is under the domination of Urizen, and in *The Book of Urizen* we see the primal pattern of this self-enclosure. Just as Urizen fails to impose his law upon all of existence, so man remains aware of more than he can rationalize. The affective life he fails to acknowledge erupts into institutional warfare and sacrificial religion, the perversions of the feelings that have been repressed. (We may recall the emperor in Swift's *A Tale of a Tub,* whose blocked semen shoots up into his brain and fosters dreams of conquest.) The life man creates for himself in Ulro becomes unendurable; he is, like Pope's fallen men in the *Essay on Man,* forced into virtue. For Blake the pattern of recovery is the painful struggle of rebellion that marks the condition of Generation, the condition of the *Songs of Experience* or the *Visions of the Daughters of Albion.*

Finally, a third myth Blake uses is that of Spectre and Emanation. The Emanation that embodies man's aspirations and his vision of self-realization is driven away by doubt and jealous suspicion. The Emanation may be replaced, as Jerusalem is, by the temptress, at first in the benign image of pastoral nature, later as the whore of mystery and abominations. This is another way of seeing the descent into Ulro and the tyranny of a partial vision. The Spectre is Selfhood that encrusts man's spirit with opacity, diverts him from transcendent vision to rationalism. "Thou art my Pride & Self righteousness," Los declares to his Spectre. Opposed to the Spectre is the vision of selflessness and forgiveness:

> And if God dieth not for Man & giveth not himself
> Eternally for Man, Man could not exist; for Man is Love
> As God is Love (*Jerusalem* IV, 96:25–27).

The complex interaction of these myths and others creates the pattern of Blake's later poetry. At any moment the forward narrative movement may give way to the sense of depth, or the opening out of levels of meanings that have been compressed into massive symbols. Blake encourages this process by stressing the simultaneity of actions on various levels and by moving abruptly from one level to another. The myths, as we see, can easily merge into each other and produce dreamlike fluidity of epic movement. One is reminded of Spenser's world in *The Faerie Queene,* where the extravagances of chivalric romance are only the outward surface of a spiritual movement within the heroes. Spenser's scene is a landscape of soul, embodied in sinister palaces or castles, deserts of despair, fountains of renewal; his dragons and witches are the temptations that live within the soul. Blake carries this further. The myths he superimposes upon history in the earlier works, such as *America* or *The French Revolution,* are at last wholly internalized, and the cosmic drama is played out within the mind and soul of fallen man, the sleeping Albion. Instead of characters as distinct as Milton's angels or Spenser's Archimago or Orgoglio, Blake creates States through which man passes, and the movement from one State to another may be apparent transformation of identity. There is always the need to identify in Blake's poems. Oothoon recognizes Urizen in Bromion's voice; Los and Enitharmon (in *Milton* 10:1) see "that Satan is Urizen."

This process of naming and identifying is a process of satiric reduction. The Augustan satirists dramatize the plausible power of error in elaborate ironic structures: the systems of belief in Swift's *Tale of a Tub,* the worship of Dulness in *The Dunciad,* the queenly hauteur of Dryden's Panther. Perhaps the finest brief instance is Pope's vision, in the *Epilogue to the Satires,* I, of the triumphal procession of Vice. But all of this ironic appreciation that seems to give in to pretension and to admire appearance prepares for the act of naming, as the satirist reveals the order within which this grandeur is contained. Swift's Peter and Jack prove to be two aspects of the same selfhood; Pope's Dulness is a phantom by which man enslaves himself; and Dryden's Panther, the more dangerous for a deceptively mild manner. Significantly, all of the great Augustan satires are works whose narrative structure seems to bend or halt under their weight of symbolic meaning. Narrative gives way to dialectic.

Blake's Urizen—reason grown to a deity and despot—is a counterpart to Pope's Dulness, the usurping deity who has undone true order and blinded her adherents to their former existence. Urizen is the impoverishing tyranny of reason, Dulness the paralyzing tyranny of pure matter; but these different tyrants achieve their power in similar ways. The uncreating word of Dulness grows in the human brain as surely as Urizen's tree of mystery. Pope's skill is to make of his ridiculous pedants, poetasters, grubs, and charlatans a formidable army of the Enemy. So in Blake, the tyranny or malice of each man creates the more formidable and frightful system, the world view in which man imprisons himself. Like Dulness, Urizen is a part of the human soul usurping the rule of other parts. Dulness represents the atavistic unconscious of self-gratification and self-absorption that may include overt pride, less obvious laziness, more fundamental selfhood. Blake's Urizen is selfhood in another guise: the selfhood of prostration before one's guilt and anxiety, of assertion through vindictive law and frustration before repressive fear, a cycle—in familiar modern terms—of frustration and aggression, the aggression turned against oneself as well as others and projected into an institution that gives it impersonal authority. Dulness surrounds her sons and herself with fogs, Urizen encloses man's mind in a mundane shell.

In a larger sense, one might compare Pope's conception of Dulness with Freud's conception of the Unconscious, as Philip Rieff presents it:

> The unconscious is fertile "nature," the womb of darkness, the identity in which every distinction fades and all things reunite. . . . Freud's notion of the unconscious stresses the lack of differentiation in feeling: all unconscious desires are impersonal, as all persons are creatures of a vaguely instinctual demiurge. . . .
>
> Freud thought of the unconscious as somewhat like a hidden god—indifferent, impersonal, unconcerned about the life of its creation. It is inferred always in negative terms. . . . Consciousness is discriminating and selective. The unconscious never says *No*. . . . Consciousness is alterable. Unconscious forces are "indestructible." Instincts fill the unconscious with energy, "but it has no organization, no unified will . . . the laws of logic—above all the laws of contradiction" do not apply to it; it knows "no values, no good and evil, no morality" (*Freud, The Mind of the Moralist,* New York, 1961, pp. 36–37).

One may, as Rieff points out, see form and order as prior to the "fundamental substrate" that it shapes, or one may see the substrate as the source from which order is derived. Mandeville takes the second position, as does Freud; but Pope takes the first. Dulness seeks "to blot out Order, and extinguish Light"; their primacy is essential to Pope's conception. He recognizes the energies of self-love and the ruling passion (in the *Essay on Man*), or of wit (in the *Essay on Criticism*). But in each case there is a forming power to which the energy must be wedded, and its presence is what distinguishes creativity from destructiveness or art from madness. Pope can treat the emergence of society from chaotic selfishness, but the emergence is, for him, a restoration of primal order.

Therefore Pope suggests that the failure of mind is the failure of an energy different from, but no less important than, that of Dulness' unconscious and instinctive force. Much of the treatment of Dulness dramatizes the loss of this energy of mind. She is the mistress of the great yawn, the creator of moral inanition, the dissolver of critical effort and vigilance, the coddler of a boozy son. She may be busy and bold, but she is also heavy and blind. Her characteristic motion is the self-enclosing vortex, her characteristic form is sluggish and formless viscosity. Her followers are a "vast involuntary throng," led along by the mechanics of magnetism like steel filings or ball bearings, by "strong impulsive gravity of head." Here again heaviness represents a dehumanized lethargy of mind.

Blake, in his conception of Urizen, stresses the ongoing process of energy, which Urizen tries to block and freeze with rational structures. Yet Blake recognizes that Urizen's tyranny is not true reason. Like Wordsworth, Blake prizes "reason in her most exalted mood," when reason acts in unity with imagination and feeling. Urizen exemplifies A. O. Lovejoy's point that "rationality, when conceived as complete, as excluding all arbitrariness, becomes itself a kind of irrationality" (*The Great Chain of Being,* p. 331). As the promulgator of laws that can never be fully obeyed and the creator of excessive self-demands that can yield only neurasthenic paralysis, Urizen inevitably collapses into superstition and mystery. His rationalism produces a world more and more abstract and inhuman, ruled by a God that is a mere phantom lawgiver. What has been denied returns in a corrupt form. Urizen's temples are the scene of an erotic mystery cult, like that of the Magna Mater to whom Pope likens Dulness, and his religion is allied with war, that is, with "energy enslav'd." Just as Dulness' own energy is matched with mental languor, so Urizen's rationalism is matched with the debased emotions that Blake embodies in Rahab, the whore of Babylon: "Religion hid in War, a Dragon red & hidden Harlot" (*Jerusalem* III, 75:20).

Pope and Blake deal with the failure of both order and energy. Pope, whose concern is for order, shows Dulness foisting a mock order with the irresistible power that is freed by the mind's abdication. Blake, whose concern is for the energy that makes its own constantly renewed forms of order, shows

Urizen checking all movement and renewal or forcing energy into perverse and wasteful forms. Pope shows Dulness ruling the world by corrupting institutions and inverting their original nature. Blake shows Urizen's power in the false authority of all institutions, which by their nature seek to preserve and extend the power surrendered to them. Both poets work, by means of dialectical encounters, toward the ultimate exposure and consolidation of error so that it may be thrown off. Once the orders are distinguished, the self-enclosure of each has been broken, and a choice can be made. Pope dramatizes the choice in the satires as a moral intensity that leads man beyond selfhood and makes his will one with God's. Blake, who regards moral judgment, based as it is upon universal law, as the worst form of institutional tyranny, sees Urizen finally absorbed into the restored unity of all the Zoas, as the primal man, Albion, at last accepts Jesus and His doctrine of forgiveness.

> They walked
> To & fro in Eternity as One Man, reflecting each in each
>   & clearly seen
> And seeing, according to fitness & order
>   (*Jerusalem* IV, 98:38–40).

Blake can use the mathematical symbolism of Revelation, once it is purged of the taint of Pythagorean rationalism. Elsewhere he fuses the artifice of order with the vitality of organic life, and, like Milton, he does this through the metaphor of the dance:

> Thou seest the gorgeous clothed Flies that dance & sport
>   in summer
> Upon the sunny brooks & meadows: every one the dance
> Knows in its intricate mazes of delight artful to weave:
> Each one to sound his instruments of music in the dance,
> To touch each other & recede, to cross & change & return (*Milton* I, 26:2–6).

> every Flower,
> The Pink, the Jessamine, the Wall-flower, the Carnation,
> The Jonquil, the mild Lilly, opes her heavens; every Tree
> And Flower & Herb soon fill the air with an innumerable
>   Dance,
> Yet all in order Sweet & lovely (*Milton* II, 31:58–62).

IV. Doubt and the Determinate: Blake on Art

Blake regards the authority of the imagination as absolute, and his critical remarks are a fierce attack upon any doctrine that seems in any way to undermine that authority. In this respect, he differs greatly from writers of more skeptical temper or tentative attitudes. Perhaps the greatest threat to the visionary is the sense of self-division and doubt. Where so much depends upon the strong assertion of a vision, any flickering of its brightness or blurring of its clarity may become utterly destructive, and any attempt to see the emergence of the vision from the natural man may seem betrayal or blasphemy. Among the fragments of Blake's *The Everlasting Gospel* (c. 1818) we have one "Spoke by My Spectre to Voltaire, Bacon, &c.":

> Did Jesus teach doubt? or did he
> Give any lessons of Philosophy,
> Charge Visionaries with deceiving,
> Or call Men wise for not Believing? (756).

Doubt, as Blake puts it, "is Self-Contradiction" (753), the self divided into the visionary and the questioner. He writes to Thomas Butts (25 April 1803) of his planned departure from Hayley's patronage at Felpham. In London, Blake hopes, he

> may converse with my friends in Eternity, See Visions, Dream Dreams & prophecy and speak Parables unobserv'd & at liberty from the Doubts of other Mortals; perhaps Doubts proceeding from Kindness, but Doubts are always pernicious, Especially when we Doubt our Friends.

Blake, far more than the earlier enthusiastic poets of the sublime, is aware of the internal struggle that is necessary to achieve and to maintain visionary power. The threat from within is as great as that from without, and one's doubts of one's friends or one's friends' doubts have the power of internalizing what might otherwise be more easily fought outside oneself. Blake makes the division of self, between Los and his Spectre, as well as between Albion and his Emanation, Jerusalem, the central theme of his last major work. One passage will make this clear. In this speech Los recognizes the "consolidation of error" as the point where redemption can begin. To recognize error is to be free of it. "It is Burnt up the Moment Men cease to behold it" (617):

> Deny a Conscience in Man & the Communion of Saints
> & Angels,
> Contemning the Divine Vision & Fruition, Worshiping
> the Deus
> Of the Heathen, The God of This World, & the Goddess
> Nature,
> Mystery, Babylon the Great, The Druid Dragon & hidden
> Harlot,
> Is it not that Signal of the Morning which was told us in
> the Beginning? (*Jerusalem* IV, 93:21-26.)

Here apparent disorder begins to reveal its inherent order. The function of error has become clear, and the total design of man's redemption is made manifest. The Spectre, as Los says, "is become One with me." This pattern of reintegration is essential to Blake's dialectical conception of contraries, and it is also at work in his own struggles within himself. In his most famous letter, he writes to William Hayley (23 October 1804):

> For now! O Glory! and O Delight! I have entirely re-
> duced that spectrous Fiend to his station, whose annoy-
> ance has been the ruin of my labours for the last passed
> twenty years of my life. . . . he is become my servant
> who domineered over me, he is even as a brother who
> was my enemy. . . . thank God that I courageously pur-
> sued my course through darkness.

And we have a fragment of another letter to Hayley (4 December 1804) in a similar vein:

> I have indeed fought thro' a Hell of terrors and horrors
> . . . in a divided existence; now no longer divided nor
> at war with myself, I shall travel on in the strength of the
> Lord God, as Poor Pilgrim says.

This horror of doubt underlies much of Blake's writing on art. It does not, of course, affect the validity of Blake's argu-ments, but it helps to explain the violence and indiscriminate arrogance he shows toward such painters as Titian, Rubens, and Rembrandt. Blake rejects any attempt to derive the imag-ination from man's natural impulses. The purpose of the sev-enth of Reynolds' *Discourses on Art,* he writes on his copy, "is to Prove that Taste and Genius are not of Heavenly Origin" (437). As we have seen, Blake insists upon the innate or connatural, upon the descent of the divine rather than emergence from below. But, apart from this question of the grounds of imaginative vision, there remains the problem of its form. Here Blake insists, against the mockery and doubts of others, that vision is not mere phantasy; it is more determinate than the imitation of empirical reality. "He who does not imagine in stronger and better light than his perishing and mortal eye can see, does not image at all" (576).

The assertion of the determinate is, for Blake, the defense of the linear against the colorist method. "The more distinct, sharp, and wiry the bounding line, the more perfect the work of art" (585). The "want of this determinate and bounding form" is evidence of slackness and plagiarism. Each individual is marked off by its distinctive form. "How do we distinguish the oak from the beech, the horse from the ox, but by the bounding outline?" The bounding line becomes the test of authentic vision and, even more, of moral sincerity. "What is it that distinguishes honesty from knavery, but the hard and wiry line of rectitude and certainty in the actions and intentions? Leave out this line, and you leave out life itself; all is chaos again, and the line of the almighty must be drawn out upon it before man or beast can exist" (585). The visionary holds to the "certainty" of line even though he be "molested continually by blotting or blurring demons" (581). The certainty of line is given only to those who are Copiers of Imagination. Those who are Copiers of Nature prove only "that Nature becomes to its Victim nothing but Blots & Blurs" (595).

The colorists are Copiers of Nature, passive before empirical appearances, which they try to unify by imposing a harmony of color at the expense of sharp outlines. Blake favors clear fresco or water colors "unmuddied by oil, and firm and determinate lineaments unbroken by shadows" (504). The colorists "put the original Artist in fear and doubt of his original conception." The spirit of Titian "was particularly active in raising doubts concerning the possibility of executing without a model, and when once he had raised the doubt, it became easy for him to snatch away the vision time after time" (582). Mere memory of nature comes to possess the mind of the painter whose power of imagination is weakened. This is a surrender of the artist's individual character, a state of possession by "Venetian and Flemish demons." True painting, for Blake, is "drawing on Canvas" (594), just as true art is firm and confident invention, not imitation. The vision is "organized and minutely articulated beyond all that the mortal and perishing nature can produce" (576).

Related to Blake's defense of invention is his rejection of the charges that his own invention was far more impressive than his execution, or as Blake quotes them, "he can conceive but he cannot execute" (602). Blake acknowledges that his execution "is not like Any Body Else." But he does not intend that it should be; and he refuses to separate invention from execution. "The Man's Execution is as his Conception & No Better" (461)—the two must, in fact, be "Just Equal" (602) because they are the indivisible parts of the same act. "Ideas cannot be Given but in their minutely Appropriate Words, nor Can a Design be made without its minutely Appropriate Execution" (596). This becomes an eloquent attack upon the slavery of the official artist to the preconceived form. Blake defends the uniqueness of the individual vision against the tyranny of "one law." What he cannot conceive is that the heroic couplet is the proper and necessary vehicle of Dryden and Pope or that the colorist method of Rubens and Rembrandt has its own authenticity as execution.

The confrontation of Blake and Reynolds is perhaps the clearest indication of Blake's difference from the prevailing attitudes of his age. We do not, unfortunately, have his annotations on the later *Discourses*, where the dialectic of Reynolds' doctrines moves out most boldly to absorb the sublime and the picturesque. But even in those discourses, Reynolds hesitates to accept with Blake's tenacity and whole-heartedness the gospel of imagination. At the close of the great thirteenth discourse, Reynolds defends the dominion of Art over History. In language reminiscent of Sidney and Bacon, Reynolds describes the "object and intention of all the Arts" as

> to supply the natural imperfection of things, and often to gratify the mind by realizing and embodying what never existed but in the imagination. . . . Because these Arts, in their highest province, are not addressed to the gross senses, but to the desires of the mind, to that spark of divinity which we have within, impatient of being circumscribed by the world which is about us.

But Reynolds goes on, with a qualification that Blake would have abhorred: "Just so much as our Art has of this, just so much of dignity, *I had almost said of divinity*, it exhibits" (italics added). So again, when Reynolds speaks in the following discourse of Gainsborough, he insists upon "the slow progress of advancement" which is "in general imperceptible to the man himself who makes it; it is the consequence of the accumulation of various ideas which his mind received, he does not perhaps know how or when." Sometimes, an artist may recognize the hint that stirs him, when "he has received, as it were, some new and guiding light, *something like inspiration,* by which his mind has been expanded" (italics added). We can assume that Blake would object to the "almost" and the "something like" with the same ferocity he showed toward the earlier *Discourses;* he would have condemned Reynolds' stress upon slow growth, unconscious assimilation, and the determination of a man's art by "accidental circumstance." This, to Blake, would be the old Epicureanism that undermined the validity of imagination.

Reynolds opposes to the imitation of external nature the appeal to the disposition of the internal fabric of mind or imagination. But, in his constant reference to artistic illusion, he makes clear that this fabric of mind has at most a limited authority as truth. He distinguishes between the imitation that is narrowly conceived as deception and the ideal imitation (of a "higher order of beings") that depends upon legitimate artistic illusion. His most striking instance of this is the appeal to our "reverence for antiquity" of Gothic architecture and its "Towers and battlements . . . Bosom'd high in tufted trees." And he points out that the Gothic, "though not so ancient as the Grecian, is more so to our imagination, with which the Artist is more concerned than with absolute truth." (So, too, Shaftesbury wrote "historically true, poetically false"; see above, p. 100.) Blake does not make such distinctions; if art is conceived as invention or vision, its use of deception or illusion does not even enter into consideration.

Reynolds also shows a nice appreciation of the picturesque. Interestingly, when Blake had earlier used Reynolds in his own defense (22 November 1802), he had quoted the letter to Gilpin in which Reynolds likened the picturesque to colorist painting as "excellence of an inferior order." In the thirteenth discourse, however, Reynolds praises the architect's "use of accidents; to follow when they lead, and to improve them rather than always to trust to a regular plan." Buildings to which additions have been made for convenience often "acquire something of scenery by this accident." And the streets of London or other old towns are more pleasant in their "forms and turnings . . . produced by accident" than Wren's regular design for the rebuilt City might have been. Reynolds, like Uvedale Price, appeals from a more formal or limited art (here architecture; in Price landscape design) to the principles of painting. Vanbrugh, "who was a poet as well as an Architect understood light and shadow, and had great skill in composition." In Discourse XIV Reynolds recounts Gainsborough's frequent use of accident and arbitrary hints ("broken stones, dried herbs, and pieces of looking glass, which he magnified into rocks, trees, and water"). Reynolds mentions the danger of mere trifling, but he pays tribute to Gainsborough's desire to "keep his faculties in exercise."

Finally, in his fifteenth discourse, Reynolds moves back to the grand style, but with an emphasis now more upon its expressiveness than its ideal imitation: Michelangelo carried painting to its "highest point of possible perfection" by "the divine energy of his own mind," and in doing so he "discovered to the world the hidden powers" that painting possessed. But Reynolds also emphasizes Michelangelo's labors, and cites Michelangelo's statement about Raphael, "that he did not possess his art from nature, but by long study." And when Reynolds acknowledges the individualism of students, he is cautious: "something must be conceded to great and irresistible impulses: perhaps every Student must not be strictly bound to general methods, if they strongly thwart the peculiar turn of his own mind."

This brings us to the best known of Blake's marginal comments: "To Generalize is to be an Idiot. To Particularize is the Alone distinction of Merit. General Knowledges are those Knowledges that Idiots possess" (451). These observations are a response to Edmund Burke's praise of Reynolds' intellectual powers of abstraction as a critic, rather than to Reynolds' remarks on painting; but we find their counterpart later when Blake is annotating the *Discourses* themselves. In the earlier discourses Reynolds defends the grandeur of generality against that art, whether Gothic or Dutch, which "attends to the minute accidental discriminations of particular and individual objects." And Blake's immediate response is, "Minute Discrimination is Not Accidental. All Sublimity is founded on Minute Discrimination" (453).

What Blake is doing in this passage (as in many others) is to equate generality with abstraction, vagueness, or indeterminacy. He defends the "characteristic." Yet, as we have seen, the characteristic may signify the qualities of a class of objects as well as an individual. "We see the same character,"

Blake writes, "repeated again and again, in animals, vege-
tables, minerals, and in men" (567). When he writes on
Chaucer's pilgrims, Blake insists upon their generality or universality; and elsewhere it is clear that he wants to preserve
this generality of high art through those archetypes that are
both concrete and universal—the representations of "states"
in figures that embody them with memorable clarity. Like
Reynolds (and Shaftesbury) Blake rejects the mean particularity of those who "represent Christ uniformly like a Dray-
man" (596). But, unlike Reynolds, he does not seek his archetypes in the classical figures that are common to all modern
European culture and therefore a shared imagery, concrete
in itself but free of the fashionable and limiting particulars of
a given place or time. He rejects Reynolds' "invariable" standard of beauty, and he rejects Reynolds' description of the
attainment of generality as the stripping away of limiting particulars. But it is clear enough that Reynolds did not forsake
concreteness and that Blake did not reject generality so much
as indeterminacy.

Blake's attack upon generality gains its edge by a trans-
ference of terms, through analogy, from a moral to an artistic realm. We can see this happening in a passage of *Jerusalem*
(91:19–22, 30–31):

> He who would see the Divinity must see him in his Chil-
>   dren,
> One first, in friendship & love, then a Divine Family, &
>   in the midst
> Jesus will appear; so he who wishes to see a Vision, a
>   perfect Whole,
> Must see it in its Minute Particulars, Organized. . . .
> . . . General Forms have their vitality in Particulars, &
>   every
> Particular is a Man, a Divine Member of the Divine
>   Jesus.

The product of such analogical use of terms is a coherent
system that excludes accidents. Blake refuses to contemplate
the natural history of mind, and he derives all acts from the
imagination. Just as he cuts through the dualism of mind and
body, so he does with the dualism of God and man. God is
nothing if He is not human. "No man hath seen God at any
time. If we love one another, God dwelleth in us, and his
love is perfected in us" (I John 4:12). Blake can hardly be
identified as theist or humanist; the distinction becomes meaningless for him. God can only exist within man, but man must

be raised to a perception of the infinite. Blake rejects both transcendental deity and natural man: "God becomes as we are, that we may be as he is" (98).

The mind, in Blake's system, absorbs into itself all those limiting forces that might—in a writer like Sterne—exist outside its power. All resistances become dialectical, all necessity internal. "There is no Such Thing as a Second Cause nor as a Natural Cause for any Thing in any Way" (403). Blake gives us a world conceived as the manifestation of imaginative energy, hardened into opacity as energy fails, raised through intense and confident assertion to the image of One Man, containing all powers within himself and exercising them in the creation of works of art.

Notes

CHAPTER I. IDEAS OF ORDER: INTRODUCTION

1. "The History of the Theory of Human Proportions as a Reflection of the History of Styles," *Meaning in the Visual Arts,* Anchor Edition, 1953, p. 93.

2. The passages from Freud are taken from Philip Rieff, *Freud: The Mind of the Moralist,* Anchor Edition, p. 4. Those from Einstein are given by Cecil J. Schneer, *The Search for Order,* New York, 1960, pp. 364, 368.

3. A. O. Lovejoy, *The Great Chain of Being,* Cambridge, Massachusetts, 1936; E. M. W. Tillyard, *The Elizabethan World Picture,* London, 1943; Hiram Haydn, *The Counter-Renaissance,* New York, 1950; C. S. Lewis, *Studies in Words,* Oxford, 1960.

4. All the quotations from the *Pensées* are given in the translation of W. F. Trotter (available in both Everyman and Modern Library editions). They are cited by number of fragment, and the numbers are given according to the arrangement of Léon Brunschvicg.

5. I draw upon three discussions of satire: Maynard Mack, "The Muse of Satire," *Yale Review* 41 (1951) 80–92; Northrop Frye, *Anatomy of Criticism,* Princeton, 1957, pp. 223–39; and Alvin B. Kernan, *The Cankered Muse,* New Haven, 1959, pp. 1–36.

6. On Pascal and Hobbes, see Erich Auerbach, "On the Political Theory of Pascal," cited below, Chapter IV, note 2.

7. Stephen Salkweit, "Political Thought," in *The Ascendancy of France 1648–88,* ed. F. L. Carsten (*The New Cambridge Modern History,* V), Cambridge, 1961, p. 98.

8. Lucien Goldmann, *Le Dieu Caché,* Paris, 1944, p. 219 (my translation).

9. Clement C. J. Webb, *Pascal's Philosophy of Religion,* Oxford, 1929, p. 43.

Chapter II. Dryden and Dialectic

1. I am indebted to D. W. Jefferson, "The Significance of Dryden's Heroic Plays," *Proceedings of the Leeds Philosophical and Literary Society, Literary and Historical Section,* V, IV (1940) 125–39; to Thomas H. Fujimura, "The Appeal of Dryden's Heroic Plays," *PMLA* 75 (1960) 37–45; and most of all to discussions with Dale S. Underwood, as well as to his book, *Etherege and the Seventeenth-Century Comedy of Manners,* New Haven, 1957. Dryden's orthodoxy, which I have slighted for the sake of emphasis, is given its due in the articles by John A. Winterbottom: "The Place of Hobbesian Ideas in Dryden's Tragedies," *Journal of English and Germanic Philology* 57 (1958) 665–83 and "The Development of the Hero in Dryden's Tragedies," *JEGP* 52 (1953) 161–73; as well as in Arthur C. Kirsch, "Dryden, Corneille, and the Heroic Play," *Modern Philology* 59 (1962) 248–64. The best discussion of these plays as drama is the final chapter of Eugene M. Waith's *The Herculean Hero,* London and New York, 1962.

2. Eugène Ionesco, "Discovering the Theatre," trans. Leonard C. Pronko, *Tulane Drama Review* 4 (1959) 6, 10.

3. The most compendious discussion of the meaning of this poem is Bernard N. Schilling, *Dryden and the Conservative Myth,* New Haven, 1961. I am indebted to Dale S. Underwood in my approach to the opening lines.

4. Peter Laslett, ed., *Patriarcha, and Other Political Works of Sir Robert Filmer,* Oxford, 1949, pp. 13, 31. Sir Lewis Namier has pointed out (*England in the Age of the American Revolution,* London, 1930, p. 31) that Locke himself came round "to admitting the paternal origin, and implicitly the paternal character, of government" in *First Treatise,* 75, 76.

5. My view is close to that of Thomas H. Fujimura, "Dryden's *Religio Laici:* An Anglican Poem," *PMLA* 75 (1961) 205–17 and Elias J. Chiasson, "Dryden's Apparent Scepticism in Religio Laici," *Harvard Theological Review* 34 (1961) 207–21. These articles question the interpretation of Louis I. Bredvold, *The Intellectual Milieu of John Dryden,* Ann Arbor, 1934.

6. See Wolfgang Stechow, "The Myth of Philemon and Baucis in Art," *Journal of the Warburg and Courtauld Institutes* 4 (1940) 103–13.

CHAPTER III. SHAFTESBURY: ORDER AND LIBERTY

1. The chief texts for Shaftesbury are: *Characteristics of Men, Manners, Opinions, Times, etc.*, 1711, which I cite from the edition by John M. Robertson, London, 1900 (hereafter Ch); the collected notebooks and letters in *The Life, Unpublished Letters, and Philosophical Regimen of Anthony, Earl of Shaftesbury*, ed. Benjamin Rand, London and New York, 1900 (hereafter Rand); and the incomplete *Second Characters* first edited and published by Benjamin Rand, Cambridge, 1914 (hereafter SC). The account of Locke's teaching is given by Shaftesbury in a letter to Jean Le Clerc (8 February 1705), Rand 332.

2. John Henry Newman, *The Idea of a University*, ed. C. F. Harrold, New York, 1947, p. 178.

3. Robert E. Cushman, *Therapeia: Plato's Conception of Philosophy*, Chapel Hill, 1958, p. 143. On Shaftesbury and the Platonic dialogue, see also Robert Marsh, "Shaftesbury's Theory of Poetry: The Importance of the 'Inward Colloquy,'" *ELH* 28 (1961) 54–69.

4. R. L. Brett, *The Third Earl of Shaftesbury*, London, 1951, ch. viii.

CHAPTER IV. MANDEVILLE: ORDER AS ART

1. Preface, *Free Thoughts on Religion, the Church, and National Happiness*, 1720 (hereafter *Free Thoughts*). *The Fable of the Bees*, ed. F. B. Kaye, Oxford, 1924, is cited simply by volume and page numbers. *An Enquiry into the Origin of Honour, and the Usefulness of Christianity in War*, 1732, is cited as *Honour*. I am indebted throughout to Kaye's introduction and to J. C. Maxwell, "Ethics and Politics in Mandeville," *Philosophy* 26 (1951).

2. "On the Political Theory of Pascal," trans. Ralph Manheim, in *Scenes from the Drama of European Literature*, New York, 1959, pp. 122, 124–25, 129.

3. See below, Chapter IX, note 5. Watt is inclined to discount the irony of the passage cited in the preceding paragraph (see *The Rise of the Novel*, Berkeley and Los Angeles, 1959, pp. 119–20).

4. See Edwin B. Benjamin, "Symbolic Elements in *Robinson Crusoe*," *Philological Quarterly* (1951) 206–11 and E. M. W. Tillyard, *The Epic Strain in the English Novel*, London, 1958, pp. 31–50.

Chapter V. Pope: Art and Morality

1. The Twickenham Edition is frequently cited in the chapter by volume number, as is *The Correspondence of Alexander Pope,* ed. George Sherburn, Oxford, 1956.

2. See the discussion by Maynard Mack, Twickenham III i, Introduction, especially p. lxxix.

3. See E. Audra and Aubrey Williams, Twickenham I, 48–55.

4. For discussion of *Windsor Forest,* see Twickenham I, 125–44; Maynard Mack, "On Reading Pope," *College English* 7 (1946) 263–73; Earl Wasserman, *The Subtler Language,* Baltimore, 1959, ch. IV. Wasserman treats with great detail and subtlety the relationship of Denham's "Cooper's Hill" to *Windsor Forest.*

5. By Maynard Mack, in his introduction to the Pope selections in *The Major British Writers,* New York, 1954, I.

6. See Kenneth Clark, *Landscape into Art,* London, 1949, ch. I.

7. On *The Rape of the Lock,* see Geoffrey Tillotson's Introduction in Twickenham II; Cleanth Brooks, "The Case of Mrs. Arabella Fermor," in *The Well Wrought Urn,* New York, 1947; and the article by Aubrey Williams cited in the next note. Particularly interesting on the *Rape,* if questionable on the *Essay on Man,* is Murray Krieger, "The 'Frail China Jar' and the Rude Hand of Chaos," *Centennial Review of the Arts and Sciences* 5 (1961) 176–94.

8. Aubrey Williams, "The 'Fall' of China and *The Rape of the Lock,*" *Philological Quarterly* 41 (1962) 422–23.

9. Mack, Twickenham III i, Introduction, p. lx.

10. On this matter I follow Fiske Kimball, "Burlington Architectus," *Journal of the Royal Institute of British Architects* 34 (15 October 1927). For other views of Burlington, see Rudolf Wittkower, "Pseudo-Palladian Elements in English Neo-Classical Architecture" in *England and the Mediterranean Tradition,* ed. The Warburg and Courtauld Institutes, Oxford, 1954, pp. 143–53, and Emil Kaufmann, *Architecture in the Age of Reason,* Cambridge, Massachusetts, 1955.

11. This paragraph draws upon H. F. Clark, "Lord Burlington's Bijou," *Architectural Review* 95 (1944) 125–29.

12. *Articulate Energy,* London and New York, 1957, pp. 24–25.

13. *Italian Painters of the Renaissance*, Phaidon Edition, London, 1953, p. 130.

14. See F. W. Bateson, Twickenham III ii, Introduction, and Jean H. Hagstrum, *The Sister Arts*, Chicago, 1958. On *To Burlington*, see also Reuben A. Brower, *The Fields of Light*, New York, 1951.

15. Mack, Twickenham III i, Introduction, xxxvi.

16. Thomas R. Edwards, Jr., "Heroic Folly: Pope's Satiric Identity," in *In Defense of Reading*, ed. Reuben A. Brower and Richard Poirier, New York, 1962, p. 195. On Pope's use of Horace, see John Butt, Twickenham IV, Introduction, and Reuben A. Brower, *Alexander Pope: The Poetry of Allusion*, Oxford, 1959.

CHAPTER VI. SWIFT: ORDER AND OBLIGATION

1. I have chosen these terms with reference to W. D. Ross's famous discussion, *The Right and the Good*, Oxford, 1930. HD refers to Herbert Davis's edition of *The Prose Works of Jonathan Swift*, Oxford and Princeton, 1939–   , although I have modernized the text throughout. The *Correspondence* is cited in the edition of F. Elrington Ball, London, 1910–14. I have dealt more extensively with many of these matters in *Swift's Rhetorical Art*, New Haven, 1953, and in my introduction to a new edition of *Gulliver's Travels*, 1963.

2. Norman O. Brown, *Life Against Death*, Middletown, Connecticut, 1959. The chapter on Swift is reprinted in John Traugott, ed., *Discussions of Jonathan Swift*, Boston, 1962, as is the essay by Orwell cited below.

3. George Orwell, "Politics vs. Literature: An Examination of *Gulliver's Travels*," in *Shooting an Elephant and Other Essays*, New York, 1950.

CHAPTER VII. THE TRAGEDY OF MIND

1. I borrow the phrase from the interesting article by Thomas R. Edwards, Jr., "Light and Nature: A Reading of the *Dunciad*," *Philological Quarterly* 39 (1960) 447–63.

2. Phillip Harth, *Swift and Anglican Rationalism*, Chicago, 1961. See also Elias J. Chiasson, "Swift's Clothes Philosophy in the *Tale* and Hooker's Concept of Law," *Studies in Philology* 59 (1962) 64–82, and for more general treatment of the *Tale*, Miriam K. Starkman, *Swift's Satire on Learning in A Tale of a Tub*, Princeton, 1950

and Ronald Paulson, *Theme and Structure in Swift's Tale of a Tub,* New Haven, 1960.

3. For the Scriblerian background, see Charles Kerby-Miller's excellent introduction and notes to his edition of the *Memoirs of Martinus Scriblerus,* New Haven, 1950. For *The Art of Sinking in Poetry* see Edna Leake Steeves's edition, New York, 1952.

4. Helen H. Bacon, "Socrates Crowned," *Virginia Quarterly Review* 35 (1959) 416. All of the article (pp. 415–30) is relevant to my theme.

Chapter VIII. Orders and Forms

1. In *Some Versions of Pastoral,* London, 1935. See also Bertrand H. Bronson's essay in *Studies in the Comic,* Berkeley and Los Angeles, 1941.

2. The best treatments of the mock form are in Austin Warren, "The Mask of Pope," *Sewanee Review* 54 (1946) 19–33, reprinted in *Rage for Order,* Chicago, 1948; Maynard Mack, " 'Wit and Poetry and Pope': Some Observations on His Imagery," in *Pope and His Contemporaries,* ed. J. L. Clifford and L. A. Landa, Oxford, 1949; and William K. Wimsatt, Jr., "The Augustan Mode in English Poetry," *ELH* 20 (1953) 1–14.

3. Bruno Snell, *The Discovery of the Mind: The Greek Origins of European Thought,* trans. T. G. Rosenmeyer, Cambridge, Massachusetts, 1953, p. 286.

4. Iris Murdoch, "The Sublime and the Beautiful Revisited," *Yale Review* 49 (1959) 260.

Chapter IX. The Divided Heart

1. For the text of Defoe, I have given volume and page references to *Romances and Narratives of Daniel Defoe,* ed. George A. Aitken, London, 1895.

2. Perry Miller, *The New England Mind,* New York, 1939, p. 53.

3. William Haller, *The Rise of Puritanism,* New York, 1938, pp. 99–100.

4. Hans H. Anderson, "The Paradox of Trade and Morality in Defoe," *Modern Philology* 39 (1941) 35. The whole article is important (pp. 23–46).

5. In *"Robinson Crusoe* as a Myth," *Essays in Criticism* 1 (1951) 95–119; as reprinted in *Eighteenth-Century English Literature: Modern Essays in Criticism,* ed. James L. Clifford, New York, 1959, p. 170.

6. For the text of *Clarissa,* I cite the Everyman edition, London and New York, 1932.

7. *The Early Masters of English Fiction,* Lawrence, Kansas, 1956, p. 68.

8. Alan D. McKillop, *Samuel Richardson: Printer and Novelist,* Chapel Hill, 1936, pp. 148, 149. The passages from Dryden are identified by McKillop, pp. 149–52.

Chapter X. Fielding: The Comedy of Forms

1. Cited from Sermon 228 by Martin C. Battestin in *The Moral Basis of Fielding's Art,* Middletown, Connecticut, 1959, p. 22. The background of Fielding's ethical thought is presented in this book and in Henry Knight Miller's *Essays on Fielding's "Miscellanies,"* Princeton, 1961. Extremely valuable and different in emphasis is William B. Coley, "The Background of Fielding's Laughter," *ELH* 26 (1959) 229–52. I am indebted to the works of McKillop, Watt, and Van Ghent cited in the previous chapter, to William Empson, "Tom Jones," *Kenyon Review* 20 (1958) 217–49, and to J. Middleton Murry, "In Defence of Fielding," *Unprofessional Essays,* London and New York, 1956. Much of this material is to be found in Ronald Paulson, ed., *Fielding: A Collection of Critical Essays,* Englewood Cliffs, New Jersey, 1962.

2. *Pretexts,* trans. Justin O'Brien, New York, 1959, p. 346. See also William B. Coley, "Gide and Fielding," *Comparative Literature* 11 (1959) 1–15.

3. *Works* refers to the so-called W. E. Henley edition (New York, 1902). The novels are cited, where necessary, by abbreviations.

4. This draws on George Sherburn, "Fielding's Social Outlook," *Philological Quarterly* 35 (1956) 1–23.

5. For these quotations, see F. T. Blanchard, *Fielding the Novelist,* New Haven, 1926, pp. 96, 101, 358.

6. *New York Times Book Review,* 7 July 1957, pp. 1, 13.

7. Wayne C. Booth, *The Rhetoric of Fiction,* Chicago, 1962, p. 216.

Chapter XI. Sterne: Art and Nature

1. For *Candide* I have used the translation by John Butt, Penguin Classics, 1947, and cite it by chapter number. I use the same method of citation for *Rasselas,* from

the edition of George Birbeck Hill, Oxford, 1887. On Voltaire, two fine books should be cited: Ira O. Wade, *Voltaire and Candide,* Princeton, 1959, and Peter Gay, *Voltaire's Politics,* Princeton, 1959.

2. For Sterne, James Work's edition of *Tristram Shandy,* New York, 1940, is the starting point; A. D. McKillop's *Early Masters of English Fiction* has the best general discussion; John Traugott's *Tristram Shandy's World,* Berkeley and Los Angeles, 1954, is inspired but one-sided; D. W. Jefferson, *"Tristram Shandy* and the Tradition of Learned Wit," *Essays in Criticism* I (1951) 225–48, is important. Of interest in different ways are Kenneth E. Harper, "A Russian Critic and *Tristram Shandy," Modern Philology* 52 (1954) 92–99, a summary of Victor Shklovsky's formalist work of 1921; A. A. Mendilow, *Time and the Novel,* London, 1952; B. H. Lehman, "Of Time, Personality, and the Author," in *Studies in the Comic,* Berkeley and Los Angeles, 1941; and the chapter in Van Ghent.

3. For Diderot, I have cited J. Robert Loy's translation of *Jacques the Fatalist and His Master,* New York, 1959, and the translations of Jacques Barzun and Ralph H. Bowen in *Rameau's Nephew and Other Works,* Anchor Edition, 1956. These are cited by page numbers. The *Salons* are given in the translation of Beatrix L. Tollemache.

4. Rudolf Wittkower, *Art and Architecture in Italy, 1600 to 1750,* London and Baltimore, 1958, p. 92.

CHAPTER XII. THE THEATRE OF MIND

1. 15 September 1764, *Boswell on the Grand Tour: Germany and Switzerland, 1764,* ed. Frederick A. Pottle, New York, 1953. The entries which follow are from *Boswell's London Journal, 1762–1763,* ed. Frederick A. Pottle, New York, 1950.

2. 9 April 1772, *Boswell for the Defence, 1769–1774,* ed. William K. Wimsatt, Jr., and Frederick A. Pottle, New York, 1959. Boswell omits all but the first sentence in the *Life,* but these views are later discussed by Johnson as William Leechman's (20 August 1773; *Boswell's Life of Johnson,* ed. G. B. Hill and L. F. Powell, Oxford, 1934–1950, V, 68–69, which also supplies Hume's views).

3. For George Eliot's essay, I have cited by page number *Essays and Leaves from a Note-book,* ed. C. L. Lewes, London, 1884. For Boswell's response, see *Life,* IV, 61.

4. Marjorie H. Nicolson, *Mountain Gloom and Mountain Glory,* Ithaca, New York, 1959, p. 362.

5. On Thomson, see Alan D. McKillop, *The Background of Thomson's Seasons,* Minneapolis, 1942; Patricia M. Spacks, *The Varied God,* Berkeley and Los Angeles, 1959; and the very interesting article by Ralph Cohen, "Literary Appreciation and Artistic Interpretation: Eighteenth-Century English Illustrations of *The Seasons,*" in *Reason and the Imagination,* ed. J. A. Mazzeo, New York and London, 1962.

6. All the quotations from Constable are taken from C. R. Leslie, *Memoirs of the Life of John Constable,* ed. Jonathan Mayne, Phaidon Edition, London, 1951. This extract is from Constable's last lecture at Hampstead (25 July 1836), Leslie, p. 328.

7. This is a most inadequate allusion to the argument of the final chapter of Hoxie Neale Fairchild, *Religious Trends in English Poetry,* I, *1700–1740, Protestantism and the Cult of Sentiment,* New York, 1939, pp. 535–76.

8. Jerome Stolnitz, "On the Origins of 'Aesthetic Disinterestedness,'" *Journal of Aesthetics and Art Criticism* 20 (1961) 140. See also, by the same author, "On the Significance of Lord Shaftesbury in Modern Aesthetic Theory," *The Philosophical Quarterly* 11 (1961) 97–113; and "'Beauty': Some Stages in the History of an Idea," *Journal of the History of Ideas* 22 (1961) 185–204. In the last article he remarks that "the impact of 'sublimity' upon aesthetic thought is the single most potent factor in dislodging 'beauty' from its formerly unchallenged primacy among the value-categories" (p. 191).

9. See the discussion of Warton and others by M. H. Abrams, *The Mirror and the Lamp,* New York, 1953, pp. 38–41, 316–17.

10. Cited by Chester F. Chapin, *Personification in Eighteenth-Century English Poetry,* New York, 1955, p. 84. I am indebted throughout this chapter to Ralph Cohen, "Association of Ideas and Poetic Unity," *Philological Quarterly* 36 (1957) 465–74; S. H. Monk, *The Sublime,* New York, 1935; Christopher Hussey, *The Picturesque,* London, 1927; Walter J. Hipple, Jr., *The Beautiful, The Sublime, & The Picturesque in Eighteenth-Century British Aesthetic Theory,* Carbondale, Illinois, 1957; and to the treatment of the Picturesque in *The Architectural Review,* London, over the last twenty years by Nikolaus Pevsner and others.

I have tried to deal with problems met in somewhat different ways by Northrop Frye, "Towards Defining an Age of Sensibility," *ELH* 23 (1956) 144–52; Earl Wasser-

man, "Metaphors for Poetry," *The Subtler Language,*
Baltimore, 1959, ch. V; and Walter Jackson Bate, *From
Classic to Romantic,* Cambridge, Massachusetts, 1946,
chs. IV–V.

11. Robert Lowth, *Lectures on the Sacred Poetry of
the Hebrews, XIV* (Latin text, 1753; trans. G. Gregory,
1787). This is, for good reason, a frequently cited passage. I take it from Norman Maclean, "From Action to
Image: Theories of the Lyric in the Eighteenth Century," *Critics and Criticism,* ed. Ronald S. Crane, Chicago, 1952, pp. 408–60. I have depended on this valuable
article in my discussion of odes in the next section.

12. William K. Wimsatt, Jr., "The Structure of Romantic Nature Imagery," in *The Age of Johnson,* New
Haven, 1949. See also the treatment of Collins and
Blake's *Poetical Sketches* in Harold Bloom, *The Visionary Company,* New York, 1961.

13. The argument of this paragraph takes its departure
from Christopher Hussey, *The Picturesque,* particularly
the governing argument that is set forth in his opening
pages. I have turned it in a somewhat different direction.

14. H. F. Clark, "Eighteenth Century Elysiums: The
Rôle of 'Association' in the Landscape Movement," in
England and the Mediterranean Tradition, ed. The War-
burg and Courtauld Institutes, Oxford, 1945, pp. 154–
78. This quotation appears on p. 159; and I have drawn
upon this admirable article throughout this section. On
Shenstone see also A. R. Humphreys, *William Shenstone,*
Cambridge, 1938.

15. *Observations, Relative Chiefly to Picturesque
Beauty, Made in the Year 1772, on Several Parts of En-
gland; Particularly the Mountains, and Lakes of Cum-
berland, and Westmoreland,* 1786 (here *Lake Tour*);
Observations on the River Wye, etc., 1782 (here *Wye
Tour*).

16. There is an interesting, if limited, treatment in
Paul Zucker, "Ruins—An Aesthetic Hybrid," *Journal of
Aesthetics and Art Criticism* 20 (1961) 119–30.

CHAPTER XIII. BLAKE: VISION AND SATIRE

1. Quotations are cited from Geoffrey Keynes' edition
of the *Complete Writings of William Blake,* London,
1957. They are identified by line number; by plate and
line number for longer engraved poems; by page number
for prose; by date for letters. Of the works on Blake, I
am indebted chiefly to M. O. Percival, *William Blake's*

Circle of Destiny, New York, 1938; Northrop Frye, *Fearful Symmetry,* Princeton, 1947; Stanley Gardner, *Infinity on the Anvil,* Oxford, 1954; Robert F. Gleckner, *The Piper & the Bard,* Detroit, 1959; Peter Fisher, *The Valley of Vision,* Toronto, 1961; and to Harold Bloom, for discussion and criticism, and for his writing on Blake, now summed up in *Blake's Apocalypse,* New York, 1963, which he allowed me to read in manuscript.

2. *Letters on Theron and Aspasio,* London, 1757; cited from fourth edition, London, 1768. This was a reply to the work of James Hervey that Steelyard is found reading in Blake's *Island in the Moon.* For the influence of Sandemanianism on the elder Henry James (who brought out the first American edition of these *Letters* in 1838), see Frederic Harold Young, *The Philosophy of Henry James, Sr.,* New York, 1951, ch. III.

Index